NOTHING, NOBODY

The Voices of the Mexico City Earthquake

In the series **Voices of Latin American Life**
edited by Arthur Schmidt

Nothing, Nobody

THE VOICES OF THE MEXICO CITY EARTHQUAKE

Elena Poniatowska

Translated, with a Foreword,
by Aurora Camacho de Schmidt and Arthur Schmidt

Temple University Press

Philadelphia

Originally published as *Nada, Nadie: Las voces del temblor*,
© 1988 by Elena Poniatowska

Temple University Press, Philadelphia 19122
© 1995 by Temple University
All rights reserved

Published 1995

⊗ The paper used in this publication meets the requirements of the American National Standard for Information Sciences—Permanence of Paper for Printed Library Materials, ANSI Z39.48–1984

Printed in the United States of America

Text design by Erin New

Library of Congress Cataloging-in-Publication Data

Poniatowska, Elena.
    [Nada, nadie. English]
    Nothing, nobody : the voices of the Mexico City earthquake / Elena Poniatowska ;
      translated, with a Foreword, by Aurora Camacho de Schmidt and Arthur Schmidt.
        p. cm. — (Voices of Latin American life)
      Includes index.
        ISBN 1-56639-344-2 (cloth). — ISBN 1-56639-345-0 (pbk.)
        1. Mexico City (Mexico)—History. 2. Earthquakes—Mexico—Mexico
City—History. 3. Mexico City (Mexico)—Social conditions.
    I. Schmidt, Aurora Camacho de. II. Schmidt, Arthur, 1943–
    III. Title. IV. Series.
    F1386.3.P6513   1995
    972'.5308334—dc20   95–13130

CONTENTS

INTRODUCTION TO THE SERIES, *VOICES OF LATIN AMERICAN LIFE*

ARTHUR SCHMIDT

With the publication of Elena Poniatowska's *Nothing, Nobody: The Voices of the Mexico City Earthquake,* Temple University Press inaugurates the series Voices of Latin American Life. Over the last generation, Latin Americans have lived through formidable historical experiences—revolutionary and counterrevolutionary wars, the rise and fall of national security dictatorships, controversial forms of religious revival, the precarious reemergence of elected civilian regimes, fundamental economic restructuring, and a flowering of grassroots organization. As the century draws to a close, the American hemisphere rushes toward unprecedented levels of economic integration. Although often less recognized, social and cultural integration is taking place in an equally rapid fashion. Contemporary conditions oblige the United States to recognize what has long been true—that the character of its domestic population makes it the fifth- or sixth-largest Latin American society.

This series aims to bring the texture and humanity of Latin American experiences to English-language readers through translations of works that impart direct voices. Through testimonial literature, through interviews, and through essays reflecting on basic issues, the series will bring important Latin American views from both the famous and the anonymous. Just as Latin American fiction has found a worldwide audience because of its ability to respond in its own voices to universal questions, so the sounds of Latin American nonfiction can transmit vital news to people everywhere. The messages conveyed through the series Voices of Latin American Life will be less concerned with being representative than with being authentic. As the globe lurches into a new century, the series hopes to undertake the task laid out for the written word by

Chilean author Ariel Dorfman—to serve as "a vehicle by which different persons can create a community together."[1]

We are grateful for the opportunity to begin the series on the tenth anniversary of the Mexico City earthquake with the impressive testimonial work of Elena Poniatowska.

1. Cristina Pacheco, "Respetar al hombre como se respeta un texto: Conversación con Ariel Dorfman," *La Jornada Semanal,* Nov. 13, 1994, p. 22

FOREWORD: THE SHAKING OF A NATION

AURORA CAMACHO DE SCHMIDT AND ARTHUR SCHMIDT

On September 19 and 20, 1985, two powerful seismic movements devastated Mexico City.[1] Ten years later, the words of those who suffered
in this tragedy still speak with force and dignity. In *Nada, nadie: Las
voces del temblor,* Elena Poniatowska has offered a testimony to the
resiliency of the human spirit, reaffirming the claim made by Gabriel
García Márquez on behalf of all Latin Americans in his 1982 Nobel
Prize address: "to oppression, plundering, and abandonment, we respond with life."[2] Suffering and injustice abound in *Nothing, Nobody:
The Voices of the Mexico City Earthquake,* but they are never disconnected from compassion, indignation, and hope.

MEXICO CITY, GIANT AND HOME

In recording the voices from the earthquake, Elena Poniatowska has
reasserted the inherent value and latent power of the working people of
Mexico City. All too often over the last half century, both Mexican and
foreign observers have regarded Mexico City with a sense of horror,
viewing it as a malignant organism whose gigantic dimensions and profound social rifts could portend only human disaster. In his 1950 classic
Los olvidados (The Young and the Damned), Spanish film director Luis
Buñuel used the Mexican capital to portray a vision of urban poverty
and lawlessness whose cruelty extinguished all the tender and hopeful
aspects of human nature Others agreed with Buñuel that catastrophic
danger lurked beneath the dazzling image of the metropolis. According
to former U.S. Undersecretary of Commerce Philip Alexander Ray, "the
sights and smells of incredible human misery" and the menace of Com-
munism lay hidden behind "the fashionable Paseo de la Reforma."
When Mexico hosted the United Nations–sponsored International Con-

ference on Population in 1984, *Time* magazine warned against the "prospect of urban apocalypse," quoting the well-known Mexican writer Carlos Fuentes in labeling the city "the capital of underdevelopment." Headlined *Time:* "Overcrowded, polluted, corrupted, Mexico City offers the world a grim lesson."[3]

Most social science scholarship has long since repudiated such one-dimensional views, stressing instead the underlying economic and political reasons that have converted Mexico City into an "urban giant." Analysts have emphasized not just the city's innumerable problems and the highly worrisome conditions facing its future. They have also depicted the opportunities for social advance that its growth has offered both residents and migrants fleeing from poverty elsewhere in the country.[4] In *Nothing, Nobody,* Poniatowska looks at Mexico City with eyes of wonder, gazing upon the vast metropolis as it awakens on September 19, when its inhabitants commence their daily routines, turning over in bed, facing the early morning cold, and venturing out to work or school. As the voices of the earthquake so forcefully make clear, Mexico City is not a horror—it is home. Horror is the earthquake and its brutal shattering of human life. Horror is the arrogance, indifference, and impotence of a government unable and unwilling to protect its people or to trust in their spontaneous solidarity.

Mexico City is not an impersonal urban agglomeration, but a mosaic of *colonias,* or neighborhoods, assembled in *delegaciones,* or districts with distinct socioeconomic profiles, ambiance, and history.[5] An estimated ten thousand people died in the 1985 catastrophe, yet most of the metropolitan region experienced only a scare. The heaviest damage and loss of life took place in the central delegations of Miguel Hidalgo, Benito Juárez, Cuauhtémoc, and Venustiano Carranza.[6] This area constituted the old urban core of the metropolis that had witnessed the city's foundation by the Aztecs in 1325, its destruction and rebuilding as a colonial capital by the Spanish in the early 1500s, and its extension westward in the nineteenth and early twentieth centuries. The nucleus still held almost 90 percent of the metropolitan zone's population as late as 1940, before dropping to less than 20 percent in 1980 and under 13 percent in 1990.[7]

Profound historical roots endowed the quake-damaged areas with a strong sense of place. The voices of *Nothing, Nobody* do not lament an abstract catastrophe. Instead, they speak of the disruption of individual, family, and neighborhood lives. They speak of the destruction of a human landscape: of homes, workplaces, and particular institutions, of Tehuantepec 12, of the Nuevo León Building, of Tepito, of Colonia Roma, of Super Leche, of Televisa, of Hospital Juárez, of the city as lived and loved, of the city as remembered.

From the collective loss of the personal came the strength for many residents to act together after the earthquake. Thousands of earthquake victims refused "to go back to normality" or just to "pretend we are nobody." Their survival had endowed them with a new will to live, as it did for the informants of Poniatowska, like Pedro Ferriz de Con, Héctor Sen Flores, or Elia Palacios Cano. They shared the sentiments of journalist Hermann Bellinghausen: "I didn't want eyes to see what I saw, but if the things that my eyes saw happened in the city of my life, then I wouldn't change myself for anyone; I am happy to be here, among everyone." But like earthquake survivors Capt. Gustavo Barrera, Marco Antonio Sánchez, Consuelo Romo Campos, or Gisang Fung, what their eyes had seen happen in the city of their lives caused them to demand, with Alonso Mixteco, "decent treatment for all Mexicans."

BACKGROUND TO THE EARTHQUAKE

From the vantage point of ten years later, the 1985 earthquake can be seen as one of a series of powerful shocks that have jarred the foundations of Mexico in the last three decades: the 1968 student movement and the massacre at Tlatelolco just before the opening of the Olympic games; the collapse of world petroleum prices and the declaration of the debt crisis in 1982; the "lost decade" of economic austerity and deteriorating living conditions; the highly controversial presidential elections of 1988; the subsequent structural reorientation of economic and foreign policy under President Carlos Salinas de Gortari that culminated in the signing of the North American Free Trade Agreement (NAFTA) in December 1993; and closer to the present time, the remarkable indigenous rebellion in Chiapas in January 1994, the August national elections, the two stunning political assassinations of Luis Donaldo Colosio in March and Francisco Ruiz Massieu in September, and the collapse of the Mexican peso in December.[8] Mexico is now experiencing a deep need for renewal. In comparison to the stability that prevailed for a generation after 1940, each of the last five presidential terms in Mexico has ended in a significant crisis.[9]

These recent times of uncertainty now contrast with the experience of 1940 to 1970, when Mexico City presided over a process of rapid industrialization combined with political stability. Over those thirty years, the country's economy grew at an average annual rate above 6 percent, a phenomenon dubbed "the Mexican miracle" by many commentators despite its flagrant social inequalities. Formerly "an underdeveloped nation with a troubled and revolution-ridden history," wrote Columbia University scholar Frank Tannenbaum in 1964, Mexico had now "moved into the modern world."[10] As the concentrated embodiment of that progress, Mexico City reaped a substantial share of its fruits. By 1970, its metropolitan area accounted for about 38 percent of Mexico's GDP, 47 percent of its manufacturing output, half of the value of its services, more than one-third of federal government employees, over 40 percent of the nation's demand for durable consumer goods, and almost 70 percent of its bank assets. Migration from the provinces and high internal demographic growth rates quintupled the capital's population as the size of its urban area kept pace, spilling over beyond the boundaries of the Federal District into the neighboring State of Mexico.[11]

Aspects of this strong centralization might appear highly irrational. After the earthquake, when all telephone lines were dead for more than a day, Poniatowska asked, "How is it possible that 55,000 branches that connect the south with the north of the country and the whole country with the world were all concentrated in one single old building on Victoria Street?" Nevertheless, Mexico City's preeminence followed the logic of the country's economic development after 1940. For a whole generation, Mexico City seemed the most worthwhile site for extensive private and public investment. It offered producers the country's largest market, its most experienced labor force, its most comprehensive services, its most cosmopolitan milieu, and, as the national capital, its most powerful decision-making levers. In the view of Associated Civil Engineers (ICA), an influential construction firm, the growth of the capital city symbolized the modernization of the nation as a whole. Mexico's former "purely folkloric" image of "sun-drenched siestas" had been transformed into "a vision of dynamism, enterprise, and expansion."[12]

For the middle and working classes and for the poor, the rapidly growing metropolis provided their best chance for an improved future during this period. The voices of *Nothing, Nobody* faithfully reflect these opportunities: engineer Francisco de la Torre, who ascended into the professional classes by attending the National Autonomous University of Mexico (UNAM); seamstress Evangelina Corona, who found exploitative but steady work that valued her skilled hands; or Salomón Reyes, watchman at the Tlatelolco housing complex, who also "took care of 104 automobiles," making "a little money washing cars and waxing them," with his seven children, "all of them in school . . . and doing well in all their subjects."

As Mexico industrialized, a highly unequal social system evolved, sustained in all its contradictions by the institutions and practices of the national government. Metropolitan Mexico City reproduced this social inequality, the industrial zones and the poorer neighborhoods expanding north and east; the wealthier areas, like Las Lomas and El Pedregal, and middle-class zones developing west and south. Federal government housing and land-use policies encouraged those trends, while the ever more complex service and infrastructural needs of the capital yielded lucrative government construction contracts for firms such as ICA.

The Federal District, an administrative unit which made up most of the Mexico City metropolitan area, was ruled directly by the national government. Its mayor or *regente,* one of the President's most important cabinet appointees, attempted to oversee the complex and often contradictory insertion of the national government into the city's physical and social fabric. A politically well-connected social elite lived in opulence. (*Nothing, Nobody* gives us a taste of this life when former First Lady Carmen Romano puts a vast number of precious presidential gifts on sale.) Meanwhile, a huge web of government organizations and policies provided housing, security, employment, and services to a broad clientele amid the lower and middle classes, exemplified in *Nothing, Nobody* by the Tlatelolco housing complex and the Multifamiliar Juárez; by the State Workers' Social Security Institute (ISSSTE), the Hospital Juárez, and the Hospital General; and by the artificially controlled low rents throughout areas like Tepito or the Colonia Guerrero.[13]

Neither the private nor the public sector, however, ever met the needs of the majority of the city's residents. Even before the earthquake, for example, only about one-third of the families in Mexico City could buy or rent affordable housing in either the formal real estate market or government-subsidized housing.[14] As the metropolitan area expanded, increasing numbers of people were forced to rely on informally organized housing and work strategies to survive a precarious existence. By the early 1970s, authorities became overwhelmed by the difficulties of managing the city's growth and the politics and economics of the country at the same time. As the costs of Mexico City's social and infrastructural needs rose, serious structural conflicts developed between the policies of the national government and the demands of the residents of the capital.

The administration of Luis Echeverría Alvarez (1970–1976) tried in vain to promote a more socially and geographically balanced national development. Crucial to this effort was the attempt to limit government investment in Mexico City and to distance urban policy from the influence of the powerful vested interests associated with the city's growth. Echeverría failed. His successor, José López Portillo, sought to satisfy Mexico City's requirements for better transportation, housing, and services by lavishing federal resources upon the central metropolis. His policies left both the country and its capital city in a "fiscal quagmire."[15]

In 1968, the student movement for greater official openness and accountability had ended in the government's wanton killing of more than three hundred students at the Plaza of the Three Cultures at Tlatelolco.[16] Succeeding years witnessed a steady decline in political support in Mexico City for the government's Institutional Revolutionary Party (PRI), especially as independent movements of urban residents multiplied, demanding better housing, transportation, and services. "By the late 1970s, Mexico City had become a city of highly mobilized and well-organized urban residents who were ready to seriously challenge the PRI's urban policies and priorities; and among their principal concerns were the scarcity and high cost of urban services."[17] Some 180,000 residents were said to be active in urban social movements in Mexico City by 1982; many organizations worked not only at the neighborhood level, but also began to coordinate their efforts together through the National Coalition of Urban Popular Movements (CONAMUP). Moreover, the arm of the PRI that had traditionally been effective in linking the national government to the residents of the capital, the National Confederation of Popular Organizations (CNOP), found itself debilitated by these rival, independent organizations and by the futile efforts of officials under Echeverría and López Portillo to implement limited political reforms intended to pacify the growing urban discontent.[18]

The onset of the debt crisis in 1982 accelerated the alienation between the residents of Mexico City and the national government under President Miguel de la Madrid (1982–1988). New austerity measures left authorities bereft of resources to devote to Mexico City. Tax revenues for the capital plummeted, and living standards fell drastically; real wages for most workers in Mexico's domestic economy dropped by 40–50 percent between 1983 and 1988.[19] Public services declined in both volume and quality. In response both to the debt crisis and to economic globalization, de la Madrid promoted an administrative and economic rationalization that would hurt the nationally privileged position of Mexico City. Efforts to decentralize some of the concentrated power of the capital were not popular among its residents, especially at a time of widespread suffering. Demands for self-government grew steadily louder in the Federal District. For a time, de la Madrid hoped to regain popular support for the PRI in Mexico City through reforms that would allow for direct popular elections of officials in the Federal District. Important members of the government and the PRI, not the least of whom was Mayor Ramón Aguirre, opposed these changes, however, and they never materialized.[20] By 1985, many residents of Mexico City looked upon de la Madrid as a remote, technocratic figure responsible for economic austerity and deteriorating urban services. For them, pre-earthquake "normality" had already acquired the traits of a vast disaster.

THE EARTHQUAKE AND ITS AFTERMATH

Mexico City is situated in a highly dangerous seismic zone. More than 340 earthquakes have been recorded in the area of the capital since Aztec times in the mid-fifteenth century.[21] Several smaller quakes take place each week in various parts of the country. Yet the 1985 quake caught government unprepared despite the adoption of building codes that met advanced international standards and other research and regulatory measures that were taken after the tremor of 1957. Planners did not anticipate earthquakes of such a combined magnitude, duration, and intensity.

While the medical service network was relatively well equipped to deal with a mass public catastrophe, the city lacked a sufficient number of firemen and the other elements of an emergency infrastructure. Moreover, the historic core sections of Mexico City rested on the soft soil of a former lake bed and were subject to stronger vibratory patterns than surrounding areas. The particular trepidatory and oscillatory patterns arising from the lake bed especially afflicted high-rise buildings between six and fifteen stories, with the result that many newer constructions fared much worse than older buildings. No certain figures exist for casualties and physical damage, but the residents of Mexico City witnessed enormous and highly concentrated destruction. Central communications, finances, and government were totally disrupted.[22]

Distrust defined the mutual relations of government officials and urban society in their responses to the earthquake. Not quite a year earlier, on November 19, 1984, a liquefied natural gas processing plant belonging to the state oil monopoly Pemex had exploded in San Juan Ixhuatepec, a low-income section of northern Mexico City known as San Juanico. Hundreds of thousands were affected in this highly populated area.[23] For many, the events of San Juanico became the framework for interpreting the government's reaction to the earthquake—years of futile complaints about the dangers of official negligence, an inept and authoritarian reaction to the catastrophe, suppression of the widespread public urge to aid the victims, and a failure to hold officials accountable for their conduct. For the first few days after September 19, 1985, this pattern reappeared. Officials at the highest level acted in a confused and uncoordinated manner. President de la Madrid and other civilians evidently feared putting a national emergency plan known as "DN-III-E" into operation, lest the military gain undue control and perhaps even political support over an area as crucial as Mexico City. Moreover, it was not clear whether this plan was ever intended to apply to Mexico City.[24]

Elements of the public immediately rushed in to fill the void, even though the official schemes had left no room for either spontaneous or autonomously organized participation in relief efforts. "Let us not forget the days following the earthquake of September 19, 1985," insists Francisco Pérez Arce of the Instituto Nacional de Antropología e Historia, "when, weighed down by the tragedy, the people of Mexico City yet showed themselves ready to organize and run their own lives in the face of the complete failure of government to find an effective response."[25] Some of the most severe damage took place in areas where popular movements were already strong in the years before the earthquake. Organized popular efforts were joined by the spontaneous participation of hundreds of thousands. Over half of the brigadistas came from outside the damaged parts of the city. Most were young, between the ages of eighteen and twenty-nine.[26] Disaster analyst José da Cruz argues that September 1985 proved that spontaneity and decentralized mobilization could work rapidly and effectively: "The official response should have supported spontaneity instead of attempting to gain control over it in the name of order, efficiency, or specialized skills."[27]

Earthquake victims were not the helpless suffering lot that government thinking had expected. Spurred on by the newly formed Coordinadora Unica de Damnificados (CUD) (Overall Coordinating Committee of Disaster Victims), tens of thousands marched over the next few months, denouncing plans for relocation of downtown residents and demanding that new housing be built in the heavily damaged neighborhoods. The earthquake revealed the presence of a socially conscious "civil society" that would no longer permit the state to be unchallenged in setting the terms of Mexican life. As noted journalist and intellectual Carlos Monsiváis said:

> Not even the power of the state . . . managed to wipe out the cultural, political, and psychic consequences of the four or five days in which the brigades and aid workers, in the midst of rubble and desolation, felt themselves in charge of their own behavior and responsible for the other city that rose into view. If it is true that in a strict sense people organized a specific movement on behalf of earthquake victims in the weeks that followed the tremor, the will to take action in a broader arena was strengthened among hundreds of thousands.[28]

Postearthquake organizations like the CUD and the Asamblea de Barrios (Neighborhood Assembly) joined with CONAMUP to constitute a vocal urban movement of middle-class, working-class, and informally employed people. One of the most visible elements of the urban popular movement was Super Barrio, a masked male dressed as a professional wrestler in red and gold full-body tights who symbolized the struggle of the urban downtrodden.

The urban popular movement pressured the government on behalf of earthquake victims and also promoted broad popular housing and service needs. Its demands linked the fulfillment of social needs to other issues, such as the repudiation of the foreign debt and democratization of Mexico's political life. On September 19, 1987, it marked the second anniversary of the earthquake with a march of nearly 90,000 people to the Zócalo.[29]

Women were particularly important in the functioning of the urban popular movement, indicating "one more time that women are the social group that responds with the greatest agility to the needs and emergencies in the realm of housing and community life."[30] One of the most impressive cases of women's organizing power was the Nineteenth of September Garment Workers' Union, whose voices speak so strongly from the rubble in *Nothing, Nobody*. Some four hundred production centers were destroyed or damaged by the earthquake; eight hundred garment workers were killed, and another forty thousand left without work. Just a few weeks after the catastrophe, the union gained legal recognition and set about attempting independent labor organization in an industry previously characterized by either a total absence of unionism or by "sweetheart" and *charro* unions, the former created by the employers themselves, the latter by PRI, government-affiliated unions. Organization in a context of high unemployment and official harassment proved a very difficult challenge for the Nineteenth of September, but the union learned to make effective use of its ties with the women's and urban popular movements in maintaining its autonomy and gaining a toehold in the garment industry.[31]

The years immediately following the earthquake were an important high point in popular organization in Mexico.[32] Yet ultimately the high hopes of a powerful future for grassroots solidarity remained frustrated. "The experience of the earthquake gave the term *civil society* an unexpected credibility," noted Monsiváis, but the immense obstacles to continued popular self-expression surfaced almost immediately. "There is no such thing as absolute independence," he warned. "The resources of the state and the business class are great enough to be able to frustrate independent projects. It is not simply a question of consolidating autonomous spaces. Historical barriers of collective psychology and of power structures have to be broken down."[33] After their initial moment of confusion, authorities did develop a more coordinated response to the earthquake. They admitted their need for foreign assistance, and in the end, Mexico received help from sixty sovereign states as well as from nongovernmental and multilateral organizations. As time went by, the volunteer teams obtained the equipment necessary to do their difficult tasks. Official information networks and shelter and relief programs for victims were put into place. Within two weeks of the initial tremor, the period of acute initial emergency had ended, and a longer time of reconstruction and political readjustment had commenced.[34]

Regaining its political skills, the government soon abandoned its initial commitment to decentralized reconstruction. On October 11, following the first meeting of the National Reconstruction Commission (described in *Nothing, Nobody*), the government expropriated thousands of properties damaged by the earthquake by extraordinary decree, yielding to popular pressures for the restoration of downtown housing. With the help of major financial assistance from the World Bank, the de la Madrid administration provided close to 50,000 new and rehabilitated housing units over the next two years through the Popular Housing Renovation program. Former renters in these central neighborhoods were able to buy these units at substantially subsidized prices. In all, roughly 100,000 families benefitted from a variety of postearthquake housing programs by 1988. More than 10,000 of these were residents of the Tlatelolco housing complex. Despite the government's agreement to an official investigation, no one was ever punished for negligence in the case of the Nuevo León Building. Nevertheless, Sedue head Guillermo Carrillo Arena lost his job. His replacement, the more politically skilled and cooperative Manuel Camacho Solís, managed to conduct more successful negotiations with the angry residents' associations.[35]

While many inhabitants of the capital shared the sentiments expressed by Cuauhtémoc Abarca to Poniatowska that it was "about time we get rid of all these Neanderthals in politics," events would not prove so easy. All the government would offer to *citadinos* anxious for self-rule was an advisory assembly, elected but virtually powerless.[36] Popular organization, public distrust, and economic suffering produced an electoral revolt in 1988 that almost denied the government its ability to manage the presidential succession. Nevertheless, after a week of "fallen" electoral computers, the official candidate Carlos Salinas de Gortari was proclaimed the winner with a fraction over 50 percent of the votes. As cartoonist Alberto Beltrán told Poniatowska in *Nothing, Nobody,* "Humans do not change only because an earthquake has shaken the earth. . . . Solidarity cannot be stretched, just like that. . . . Mexican society moves slowly, little by little, not in leaps." Civil society in a country with so many social, cultural, and geographical divisions could not bring about systemic change overnight. Organizations established as a result of the earthquake to express local needs and aspirations were not, as Beltrán warned, "the harbinger of a social transformation."

In the wake of the earthquake and the election of 1988, the governing system realized that it had to restore economic growth and to improve the provision of services to potentially vocal grassroots elements if it were to survive. A reform from the top after 1988 brought a renewed emphasis on market forces along with the North American Free Trade Agreement with the United States and Canada. New political strategies like the National Solidarity Program indicated that the government's postearthquake experience of making deals with the numerous components of the urban popular movement had been instructive. It now knew how to rebuild local bases of support for existing politics without yielding to a widespread democratization of the ruling system.[37]

ELENA PONIATOWSKA AND POPULAR TESTIMONY

> I like to sit under the
> sun among the people, those
> of my city, in my city, in
> the center of my country, in the
> navel of the world.
>   Elena Poniatowska, La "Flor de lis"

Born in Paris in 1932, the daughter of a Frenchman of Polish origin and a Mexican mother, Elena Poniatowska first arrived in Mexico City in 1942 in a journey of escape from World War II. Her somewhat auto-biographical novel La "Flor de lis" (1988) shows the child and young woman discovering Mexico in its capital city, dazzled not by its magnificence, but by its people: by her own aristocratic Mexican mother, first of all, but also the by servants of Indian origin from whom she learns a Spanish full of domestic warmth and popular texture; and by the proletarians who take the buses that become her "secret life." She becomes fascinated by the large square by the cathedral, where the Aztec Temple of the Sun once stood in majesty, "my great intense *plaza,* the Zócalo, electric, charged with currents and resistance."[38]

After an education that included boarding school in the Philadelphia area, Elena Poniatowska began conducting interviews for the Mexico City newspaper *Excélsior* in 1954, transferring to the daily *Novedades* the following year. She is fondly remembered by television audiences of the late 1950s as the young woman who interviewed major Mexican cultural icons of the size of Diego Rivera, in a program titled, like her newspaper column, "Crosswords." In time, she established herself as a major fiction writer, chronicler, critic, and journalist. She has also written texts for several photographic essays dealing with Mexico City, Mexican architecture, and the women of Juchitán, Oaxaca, site of confrontations between political opposition and government forces.

Many of Elena Poniatowska's books remain to be translated into English, but she is well known to scholars in the United States, who consider her one of the major Latin American writers of the present hour. She is a master of testimonial literature whose work defines and defies the boundaries of this new genre. Her writing is characterized by a disarming but carefully crafted simplicity of language, the language of kitchens, of telephone calls between old friends, the language of the street and the proletarian bar, of an urban bus that goes too fast, of a group of students in a stadium. The written text holds the textures of spoken Mexican Spanish in a variety of registers that capture nuances of gender, social class, political affiliation, age, place of residence in the city, occupation, and even moral intention. The French-speaking refugee girl who had to listen so hard to learn her mother's tongue in this new world preserved a love for speech as music to be savored in every note and in every cadence and silence.

Elena Poniatowska writes about women. She is a practical feminist who believes in women's power of authorship, and who has influenced a generation of young women writers in Latin America. She loves to find and recreate female characters from history and present-day life who allow her to tell intensely feminine stories. Often these are foreign women who look at Mexico City as outsiders and are seduced by its powers. She believes in the power of ordinary women, especially poor women, to have intelligent notions about life, politics, and art.

The testimonial novel *Hasta no verte, Jesús mío* (1969; Here's Looking at You, Jesus) fictionalizes the life of Jesusa Palancares (Josefina Bórquez), who migrated to Mexico City from Oaxaca after being married to a revolutionary.[39] The vicissitudes that she confronts every day of her life make her a survivor whose only constant companion is the city, at times merciful and motherly, at times a debasing, hostile actor. In this novel, as in her two other major testimonial works, Elena Poniatowska writes intensely about the city of Mexico as a live and formidable force.

The city is not background in Poniatowska's narrative; it is not a stage where the drama of the student movement unfolds or the earthquake shatters lives; it is not the unifying space where the tough life of a woman gets tougher. It is itself, as critic Cynthia Steele has established, a "literary and political protagonist."[40] Poniatowska textualizes the historical geography that at once integrates and disintegrates, devours and consoles.

In *Massacre in Mexico,* readers hear the voices of eyewitnesses of the events of October 2, 1968, when the army brutally repressed the student movement by firing on a demonstration at the Plaza of the Three Cultures at Tlatelolco in the heart of the city. *Nothing, Nobody* depicts the earthquakes of September 19 and 20, 1985, which destroyed downtown Mexico City, caused thousands of deaths and mutilations, and left hundreds of thousands of poor people bereaved, homeless, and jobless overnight. There is a dialogue and a semantic contagion between these two texts. In fact, a scene in *Nothing, Nobody* establishes that parallel as it reveals the senseless series of objects that, taken out of the collapsed apartments, form piles of personal belongings in a baseball field in an absurd juxtaposition: sofas, mattresses, photos, a black velvet jacket, shoes, and more shoes, "just as on October 2, when the Plaza de las Tres Culturas of Tlatelolco awoke covered with odd shoes like crushed flowers!"

But the parallel goes further. Both the action of the army and the earthquake are acts of betrayal. In 1968 the citizens of Mexico learned that there was a deep fissure between them and their government, a sort of telluric fault. The army exists not to defend them but to control them. In 1985, after the ground of the city gives way, the government of Mexico fails to respond. The destruction of the facades of many buildings unveils sordid poverty and obscene working conditions, at the same time as it unmasks the hypocrisy and incompetence of the nation's costly state institutions.

The city then, is not unity, but fragmentation, especially after the devastation of the Mexican army's action and the tremor. But it is precisely this fragmentation that Elena Poniatowska relies on to build a whole chronicle, to reintegrate the dismembered city into a body and a text. In this sense the structure of Poniatowska's testimonial works reflects their content, as critic Ronald Christ underscores:

> *Massacre* consists of quoted graffiti, placards, speeches, journalistic reports, firsthand accounts, interviews, hindsight interpretations, official declarations, and private comments. Like a movie, then, the book is conceived and presented in fragments, in staccato "shots" and more developed "sequences."[41]

Nothing, Nobody is similarly made up of fragments At times those fragments are jarring, and may sound as foreign in English as they do in their original Spanish. The informants of Elena Poniatowska are angry, or full of sorrow and grief. Some of them are also prejudiced: anti-Semitic, sexist, homophobic, or outright arrogant in the security of their own social class as they look down on poor people to whom they are offering help. But most of the voices in the book are there to do Elena Poniatowska's job, a job that critic Beth Jörgensen identifies with the business of testimonial literature: "to offer an alternative view of official, hegemonic history."[42] This view is presented by a not-so-innocent bystander who injects her testimony with humor, tenderness, and the contagious ability to be amazed by the quotidian characters and realities of the city. Poniatowska's writing is celebration at its core.

Throughout the text, the writer gives form to the voices of her informants and helps them to impart their collective testimony. In this intense editorial role, the borders between fiction and oral history blur. We find a master narrator who is all eyes and ears most of the time, only to become self-conscious and give herself a voice at key moments, when she is one more character invented by a mischievous author. What emerges is a truth bigger than the truth of a tape recorder.

Nothing, Nobody began as a series of articles in the Mexico City daily *La Jornada* after *Novedades* refused their publication.[43] Poniatowska compiled her chronicle from newspapers, official speeches, and the voices of countless interviews. Some readers may find this format somewhat unusual and even confusing at times. A few simple points about the text may make it clearer.

Eighteen writers helped Elena Poniatowska assemble her testimonies. Their names appear in the text as subheadings of the sections for which they were responsible. Most parts of *Nothing, Nobody* have a single major narrator with whom a journalist like Poniatowska or one of her helpers is engaged in dialogue at any one given time. Usually that person's voice does not appear within quotation marks unless he or she is recounting a previous conversation. Quotation marks thus indicate the voice of the interviewer or of other persons in that part of the story. While the text does not always announce a switch from one major narrator to another, it introduces personages in such a way that the reader will be able to determine who is speaking to Poniatowska or to one of the writers who assisted her.

One Mexican critic of Poniatowska's work wrote, "Impelled by a sense of both obligation and commitment, Elena Poniatowska . . . continues to help the people of Mexico elucidate who we are and what we want."[44] With her friends and colleagues Carlos Monsiváis and José Emilio Pacheco, Elena Poniatowska is a voice of moral force in Mexico. Only someone who loves her country as deeply as she does can dare to tell its intimate stories.

TEN YEARS LATER

A decade after the earthquake, the urban needs that gave rise to the popular movement remain in massive housing shortages, a serious lack of basic services, and growing environmental problems.[45] The Nineteenth of September Garment Workers' Union still exists, but barely, buffeted by low-cost imported clothing and problems among the seamstresses themselves. Ironically, the difficulties and dangers of the city itself drive more residents to enclose themselves within the confines of a privatized world of "cultura a domicilio" as the television and video cassette recorder replace the old public culture of the park and the cinema.[46]

Nevertheless, popular movements still insert themselves into the changing fabric of Mexican life. Hundreds of thousands of people have participated in organizations and campaigns associated with human rights, labor, environmental, and political education issues in the context of the free trade pact, the Chiapas conflict, and the elections of 1994. Mexico continues to be a society that is organizing and constantly reinventing itself.[47] New testimonies follow in the tradition of *Massacre in Mexico* and *Nothing, Nobody* to illustrate "the remarkable flexibility, clear-headed thinking, ingenuity, and courage of people who take great risks to meet challenges they might wish had never come their way."[48]

Elena Poniatowska recorded some ancient Aztec words, repeated by Miguel León-Portilla before the National Reconstruction Commission: "For as long as the world is world, the glory and fame of Mexico-Tenochtitlán will endure." In assembling the voices from the earthquake, Poniatowska shows that this glory and fame derive from the very members of Mexican society, at once ordinary and extraordinary. Their testimony projects a collective message of importance to the wider human community. As the twentieth century draws to a close, the economic and technological forces underlying contemporary globalization have privileged the position of social elites and economic bureaucracies, giving them an almost unchallenged power to determine the fate of peoples around the world. In the midst of the disruptions, uncertainties, and estrangements attendant to these changes, the voices of the earthquake lay claim to the right of ordinary people to exercise influence over the forces that shape their daily lives. They attest to the creative power of solidarity to triumph over human tragedy, if only for a moment. In a fast-paced world order in which "a huge and increasing proportion of human beings are not needed and will never be needed to make goods or to provide services," the voices from the earthquake reassert the primacy of human dignity over the production of wealth, affirming the capacity of ordinary people to make history.[49]

Their voices must never be forgotten.

NOTES

1. Following the practice employed by many writers, this introduction will use the word *earthquake* in the singular to refer to the two tremors of September 19 and 20, 1985.

2. Elena Poniatowska, *Nada, nadie: Las voces del temblor* (Mexico City: Ediciones Era, 1988); Gabriel García Márquez, "Nobel Speech," *Americas: An Anthology*, ed. Mark B. Rosenberg, A. Douglas Kincaid, and Kathleen Logan (New York: Oxford University Press, 1992), p. 269.

3. John King, *Magical Reels: A History of Cinema in Latin America* (London and New York: Verso, 1990), pp. 130–131; Philip Alexander Ray, *South Wind Red: Our Hemispheric Crisis* (Chicago: Henry Regnery, 1962), pp. 3, 13–14; "A Proud Capital's Distress," *Time*, Aug. 6, 1984, pp. 26–27.

4. For responsible, balanced treatments of Mexico City, see Martha Schteingart, "Mexico City," *The Metropolis Era*, vol 2., *Mega-Cities*, ed. Mattei Dogan and John D. Kasarda (Newbury Park, CA: Sage, 1988), pp. 268–293; Peter Ward, *Mexico City: The Production and Reproduction of an Urban Environment* (Boston: G. K. Hall, 1990); and Bernardo Quintana Arrioja, "The City of Mexico, Its Future," *México-Tenochtitlán, 1325–1975: Pasado, presente y futuro de una gran ciudad* (Mexico City: Fomento Cultural Banamex, A.C., 1976), pp. 77–84.

5. Following the 1980 census and the figures originally accepted by most experts, Poniatowska refers to the population of metropolitan Mexico City as about 18 million. The 1990 census brought a downward rectification of earlier figures with the result that the Mexico City metropolitan zone was estimated to have slightly more than 15 million inhabitants then and a growth rate that would leave it with between 15 and 16 million today. See María Teresa Esquivel Hernández, René Flores Arenales, and María Eugenia Medina, "La Zona

Metropolitana de la Ciudad de México: Dinámica demográfica y estructura poblacional, 1970–1990," *El Cotidiano* 54 (May 1993): 11, 13.

6. Alan Gilbert, *The Latin American City* (London: Latin America Bureau, 1994), p. 137. Estimates of the number of dead range from slightly under five thousand to twenty thousand, with ten thousand serving as the mostly widely accepted conventional figure. See José da Cruz, *Disaster and Society: The 1985 Mexican Earthquakes* (Lund, Sweden: Lund University Press, 1993), pp. 118–122.

7. Ward, *Mexico City*, p. 35; Esquivel Hernández et al., "La Zona Metropolitana," p. 14.

8. For short accounts of Mexico's post-1968 history, see Peter H. Smith, "Mexico Since 1946: Dynamics of an Authoritarian Regime," *Mexico Since Independence*, ed. Leslie Bethell (New York: Cambridge University Press, 1991), pp. 356–396; and Héctor Aguilar Camín and Lorenzo Meyer, *In the Shadow of the Mexican Revolution: Contemporary Mexican History, 1910–1989*, trans. Luis Alberto Fierro (Austin: University of Texas Press, 1993), pp. 199–267.

9. Miguel Basáñez, "Is Mexico Heading Toward Its Fifth Crisis?" *Political and Economic Liberalization in Mexico: At a Critical Juncture?* ed. Riordan Roett (Boulder, CO: Lynne Rienner, 1993), pp. 95–115.

10. Frank Brandenburg, *The Making of Modern Mexico*, intro. Frank Tannenbaum (Englewood Cliffs, NJ: Prentice-Hall, 1964), p. vii.

11. Ward, *Mexico City*, pp. 19–21; Schteingart, "Mexico City," p. 272.

12. Special edition "El México de Hoy," *Auge Internacional de México*, April 1973, p. 26.

13. See Ward, *Mexico City*, chapters 2, 4, 5–6.

14. Keith Pezzoli, "The Urban Land Problem and Popular Sector Housing Development in Mexico City," *Environment and Behavior* 19.3 (May 1987): 378.

15. Diane E. Davis, *Urban Leviathan: Mexico City in the Twentieth Century* (Philadelphia: Temple University Press, 1994), p. 238.

16. Poniatowska recounted the events of the student movement and the horrifying brutality at Tlatelolco in her testimonial work *La noche de Tlatelolco: Testimonios de historia oral* (Mexico City: Ediciones Era, 1971), translated by Helen R. Lane as *Massacre in Mexico* (New York: Viking Press, 1975; later paperback edition, University of Missouri Press).

17. Davis, *Urban Leviathan*, p. 237 and, more broadly, pp. 219–253.

18. Ibid., pp. 237, 272.

19. Nora Lustig, *Mexico: The Remaking of an Economy* (Washington, DC: Brookings Institution, 1992), pp. 66–69.

20. Davis, *Urban Leviathan*, pp. 264–270.

21. Linda Manzanilla, "Relación de los sismos ocurridos en la ciudad de

México y sus efectos," *Revista Mexicana de Sociología* 48.2 (April-June 1986): 265–282.

22. da Cruz, *Disaster and Society,* pp. 99–102, 112, 115–116, 120, 122–125, 132–135. See also J. Flores, O. Novaro, and T. H. Seligman, "Possible Resonance Effect in the Distribution of Earthquake Damage in Mexico City," *Nature,* April 23, 1987, pp. 783–788. According to sources cited by da Cruz, the September 19 and September 20 quakes, respectively, had durations of four minutes and one minute, magnitudes of 8.1 and 7.3 on the Richter scale, and intensity levels of VIII–IX and VI on the Modified Mercalli scale. Ultimately, the official figures of the Department of the Federal District declared 12,747 buildings damaged, yet researchers from the University of Delaware Disaster Research Center considered such estimates well below the total of structures that experienced some form of damage or loss of services because of the earthquake. Official estimates of the number of injured survivors range from 35,000 to 45,000 people, while the homeless may have exceeded half a million. University of Delaware analysts claimed that as many as 2 million may have left their homes at least temporarily.

23. Carlos Monsiváis, *Entrada libre: Crónicas de la sociedad que se organiza* (Mexico City: Ediciones Era, 1987), pp. 123–150. Ultimately, some 10,000 residents suffered damages, while 375 were killed and over 26,000 injured. Less than a thousand collected some form of indemnization. See "A diez años de la explosión, San Juanico continúa en riesgo," *Siglo 21* (Guadalajara), Nov. 30, 1994, p. 16. PEMEX was also responsible for a gasoline leak and explosion that devastated low-income neighborhoods of Guadalajara in April 1992.

24. Luis Pazos, "El ejército y los desastres," *El Financiero,* May 18, 1992, p. 56; da Cruz, *Disaster and Society,* pp. 178–185.

25. Francisco Pérez Arce, "The Enduring Union Struggle for Legality and Democracy," *Popular Movements and Political Change in Mexico,* ed. Joe Foweraker and Ann L. Craig (Boulder, CO: Lynne Rienner, 1990), p. 120.

26. Results of the University of Delaware surveys as reported in da Cruz, *Disaster and Society,* p. 156.

27. Ibid., p. 229.

28. Monsiváis, *Entrada libre,* p. 13.

29. Daniel Rodríguez Velázquez, "Mexico from Neighborhood to Nation," *NACLA Report on the Americas* 23.4 (December 1989): 22–28; Tom Barry, ed., *Mexico, a Country Guide* (Albuquerque, NM: Inter-Hemispheric Education Resource Center), pp. 196–203.

30. Alejandra Massolo and Martha Schteingart, comps., *Participación social, reconstrucción y mujer: El sismo de 1985* (Mexico City: El Colegio de México, 1987), p. 23; see also two other publications of the Programa Interdisciplinario de Estudios de la Mujer at the Colegio de México: Alejandra Massolo, *Por amor y coraje: Mujeres en movimientos urbanos de la ciudad de México* (Mex-

ico City: El Colegio de México, *1992*), and Alejandra Massolo, comp., *Los medios y los modos: Participación política y acción colectiva de las mujeres* (Mexico City: El Colegio de México, 1994).

31. Teresa Carrillo, "Women and Independent Unionism in the Garment Industry," *Popular Movements and Political Change in Mexico,* ed. Foweraker and Craig, pp. 213–233. According to Carrillo, the union won seventeen contracts and had a membership of less than 1 percent of the workers in the industry.

32. Vivienne Bennett, "The Evolution of Urban Popular Movements in Mexico Between 1968 and 1988," *The Making of Social Movements in Latin America: Identity, Strategy, and Democracy,* ed. Arturo Escobar and Sonia E. Alvarez (Boulder, CO: Westview Press, 1992), pp. 253–257.

33. Monsiváis, *Entrada libre,* p. 13.

34. da Cruz, *Disaster and Society,* pp. 154–160.

35. Ibid., pp. 210–225. Analysts vary in their interpretation of the results of these efforts, particularly the Popular Housing Renovation program. Ward sees the land expropriation as a populist-style gesture that paid landowners inflated prices for deteriorated properties. The replacement housing, while of high quality in his view, represented the government buying off internal popular organizations with the aid of international subsidies, giving the former renters a windfall benefit that created an irrational downtown land use for small residential property ownership. On the other hand, Eckstein along with Gamboa de Buen and Revah Locouture see the measure as a practical, economical reinvestment in the downtown that enabled the former renters to preserve their neighborhoods and jobs, and the PRI to regain voters from among the beneficiaries. See Ward, *Mexico City,* pp. 194–195; Jorge Gamboa de Buen and José Antonio Revah Locouture, "Reconstrucción y política urbana en la Ciudad de México," *Foro Internacional* 30.4 (April-June 1990): 689–690; and Susan Eckstein, "Poor People Versus the State and Capital: Anatomy of a Successful Community Mobilization for Housing in Mexico City," *International Journal of Urban and Regional Research* 14.2 (1990): 274–296. Camacho Solís later became mayor of the Federal District during 1988–1994.

36. Davis, *Urban Leviathan,* pp. 286–287.

37. See Susan Eckstein, "Formal Versus Substantive Democracy: Poor People's Politics in Mexico City," *Mexican Studies/Estudios Mexicanos* 6.2 (Summer 1990): 213–239, as well as the essays in Wayne A. Cornelius, Ann L. Craig, and Jonathan Fox, eds., *Transforming State-Society Relations in Mexico: The National Solidarity Strategy* (La Jolla: Center for U.S.-Mexican Studies, University of California, San Diego, 1994).

38. Elena Poniatowska, *La "flor de lis"* (Mexico City: Ediciones Era, 1990; primera edición, 1988), p. 261.

39. Elena Poniatowska, *Hasta no verte, Jesús mío* (Mexico City: Ediciones Era, 1969).

40. Cynthia Steele, *Politics, Gender, and the Mexican Novel, 1968–1988* (Austin: University of Texas Press, 1992), p. 29.

41. Ronald Christ, "The Author as Editor," *Review* 75 (Fall 1975): 78, cited by Elizabeth Starcevic, "Elena Poniatowska: Witness for the People," *Contemporary Women Authors of Latin America: Introductory Essays*, ed. Doris Meyer and Margarite Fernández Olmos (Brooklyn: Brooklyn College Press, 1983), p. 73.

42. Beth E. Jörgensen, *The Writing of Elena Poniatowska: Engaging Dialogues* (Austin: University of Texas Press, 1994), p. 68.

43. Jörgensen, *Ibid.*, p. 71.

44. Eugenia Meyer, "Elena Poniatowska, Task and Commitment," *Oral History Review* 16.1 (Spring 1988): 5.

45. See the articles on the problems of housing and environment in Mexico City by Victor Ballinas, *La Jornada*, May 3–4, 1993, and Angélica Enciso, *La Jornada*, May 5–6, 1993.

46. Remarks of Eduardo Nivón of the Universidad Autónoma Metropolitana at the Conference on Globalization and Resistance, Bryn Mawr College, Bryn Mawr, Pennsylvania, November 12, 1994.

47. The phrase "society that organizes itself" derives from Monsiváis, while the idea of Mexico reinventing itself comes from Héctor Aguilar Camín, "La invención de México: Notas sobre nacionalismo e identidad nacional," *Nexos*, July 1993, pp. 49–61.

48. Judith Adler Hellman, *Mexican Lives* (New York: New Press, 1994), p. 13.

49. Richard J. Barnet and John Cavanagh, *Global Dreams: Imperial Corporations and the New World Order* (New York: Simon and Schuster, 1994), p. 17.

NOTHING, NOBODY

The Voices of the Mexico City Earthquake

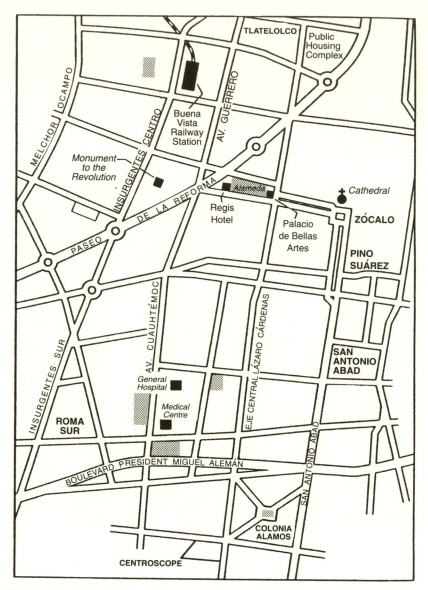

The earthquake in Mexico City: The main area affected. From Alan Gilbert, *The Latin American City* (London: Latin America Bureau, 1994). Used by permission.

THURSDAY, SEPTEMBER 19, 1985

7:18

The sun and the Mexican people have been up for a long time. My window, outfitted with a screen, is open; the morning is still cool. Because of the time difference between Europe and Mexico, I have been awake for a few minutes (a strange thing for anyone who knows me!).

For two days I have lived in a charming little hotel right in the middle of this monstrous megalopolis of 18 million inhabitants and 232 square miles. It is just a step away from the Paseo de la Reforma. The Zona Rosa is located on the other side of the Paseo de la Reforma.

Walking toward the golden Angel of Independence that presides over the traffic circle (which the earthquake of 1957 knocked off its pedestal), one finds the historical heart of Mexico: a huge square—the Zócalo, the National Palace, the cathedral, the ministries, the big stores, and the hotels, some of them newer than mine.

7:18.30

I do not know yet whether I made a good choice staying in this pleasant pink three-story building, constructed in the Spanish style, with its courtyard, its wide stone stairway leading to each floor, and its lobby furnished with leather armchairs and sofas and a television set in one corner. Without luxuries, but comfortable. My room is on the second floor. The noise of the city climbs toward me. Students have been in class for nineteen minutes, but employees are still on their way to work.

Traffic is heavy as always. Mexico is one of the most polluted cities in the world. Not only by the factory smoke and gases that escape, but also by noise. Here car horns are not prohibited, and they are played to a Latin beat.

7:19

A sudden muffled rumble. I am in bed, and I feel something like a momentary dizziness. As the roar of the earth grows, I have the slight impression that my bed is in motion. The bathroom door, which had remained open, bangs its frame without closing, then hits against the wall. For a moment, not fully awake yet, I ask myself who has entered the room. Is it perhaps the chambermaid thinking that I have already left? I hear the noise of clinking glasses, and the light I had left on above the basin goes out.

7:19.30

My God! Of course, this is an earthquake. They are frequent in Mexico. I immediately recall the feeling of the earthquake I experienced in Martinique at Christmastime in 1969. Not only my bed, but everything now moves: the door bangs as if an invisible hand were trying to close it; the hand keeps pushing, strongly, obsessively, it pushes the table, the armchair. My radio falls off the nightstand. The sound of breaking glass comes from the bathroom.

7:20

All right, let's wait. This has to come to an end. But then a stifled blow of startling violence shakes the wall behind me.

The distant sound of broken glass enters through my window. Later, out on the street, I will discover that it came from the glass of surrounding buildings.

Frequent blows jolt my wall, acquiring the rhythm of a metronome, approximately every five seconds.

This time I am in the cabin of a yacht in the open seas in bad weather, rocking bow to stern and port to starboard.

The rhythm of titanic shocks accelerates. I try to get up. It's impossible to stand without holding on to the wall or the bed.

7:20.30

From that moment on I lose all sense of time. Only later, after the earthquake is over, will I know that it lasted almost two minutes, with an intensity of 8 points on the Richter scale (9 points being the top!).

Through the window the spectacle is terrifying. Parked cars move forward, backward, collide with each other. Electric wires stretch, contract, and thrash about, spitting sparks.

But the worst are the buildings of twelve to fourteen stories that surround us, moving several yards from left to right in front of me.

I understand at that point that the shocks that jar the hotel come from the oscillations of the building next door. I seem to remember that it is four times as tall (later verified to have about fourteen stories).

My hotel and the neighboring tower are out of sync.

When the hotel leans to the right, the tower bows to the left, and they bump each other as the movement is repeated, each time with a greater intensity.

The people who are on the street huddle together in the middle. They cannot remain standing. I can't either. Two policemen cling to each other by their belts. Others hold hands or lean on someone's shoulders, possessed by the strange frenzy of Saint Vitus' dance.

7:21

Frightened, I lie down.

I am inside a cocktail shaker, agitated by the masterful hand of a bartender whose energy grows by leaps and bounds.

On the wall, the pictures gyrate like the hands of clocks. Nothing remains on my nightstand, dresser, or table. My room has been turned into a heap of books, newspapers, and personal gear. Trepidations, deafening blows, undulation of the floor. The door to my room unlatches and creeps open. To tell the truth I am beginning to feel anguished.

7:21.30

Stretched out across the bed, I stare at the ceiling. It cracks. Small chunks of plaster fall from the ceiling and the walls. A smell of dust invades my room.

It has been an eternity since the tremor began.

I do not think of anything.

I stare at the ceiling.

Little by little I have the certainty that it's going to collapse under the weight of the adjacent building, that is, pushed by the walls of the hotel.

7:22

At this point I become aware of the fact that the building is no longer hitting the wall behind me. I also realize that the headboard of my bed is swinging. The hotel and the tower now rock in unison.

This may seem strange, but I still don't think about anything. I'm not an actor, not even a spectator. I'm outside time and the space of this room. Unconsciousness? Surely lack of courage!

Unexpectedly it occurs to me that I should be unrolling the film of my life, thinking of the people I love.

None of that. Only a profound, selfish anxiety. As if anesthetized by the intensity of the cataclysm.

7:22.30

Now I think of myself.

Hesitating, I get up and walk, bent over, toward the door frame, recalling that one is somewhat protected there, that the structure may resist the weight of a collapse.

Little by little, I gain the impression—but this is my wish, is it real?—that the movement is diminishing. In a few more seconds this becomes true.

I am still out of sorts but solidly protected under the door frame.

Calm returns. I still wait a good while, thinking that it might come back any time. How long? I don't know.

7:23

It's over: all is still.

No outside noise.

I walk to the window.

Survivors embrace in the middle of the street.

I have no one to embrace.

I dress quickly and go out. I want to see. In the stairway, I run into other guests from the hotel. Some are half naked. They look ashen. I must look the same . . .

At the end of the street, the Paseo de la Reforma teems with people and stilled automobiles. The scene resembles a horrific hallucination. The silence is strange.

But I am still far from the load of horror that awaits me in the coming days and nights.

———————

4

I am overtaken by an immense sense of relief. An extraordinary will to live, as if to exorcise those four minutes.

Not until that moment was I truly possessed by fear. The neighboring tower is still standing, the wounds from its blows evident at the level of the terrace of my hotel. And I discover a few yards away, three hotels reduced to pastry sheets of concrete and iron under which, I am certain, hundreds of tourists are trapped. I have two feelings: one, it was not my turn, and two, after I look back, I did not imagine even once that something awful could happen to me. It was not a presumption, but a profound intuition.

From this experience, two realizations enter my head: the discovery of vanity and the awareness of the ephemeral.

In the final analysis, nothing is useless.

Forgive me, but when I was in the street, I smiled. I had left a sign on the doorknob: "Do Not Disturb."

An hour later, it would have been the holocaust.

The version that Jean Miot, a stringer for *Le Figaro*, gives to Concha Creel is less immediate than that of the reporters of *Unomásuno:*

At 7:21, the driver of patrol car 5214 reports nervously over the police radio:

"Control, it's an earthquake!"

Anonymous voice of another agent:

"Wake up, pal!"

At 7:22, the now anguished voice of the driver of patrol car 5214:

"The SCOP has caved in. Send me all the rescue units and ambulances from the Red Cross!"

7:36

Across the street from the paralyzed clock of H. Steele, the Hotel Regis collapses with a roar and dies in a cloud of dust. The limpid morning sky of the city is already a huge gray mass—because buildings are caving in one after another. And the tragedy goes from north to south.

And the city is divided between people who know and people who do not know . . . people who, at top speed, evacuate classrooms because the schools are collapsing . . . people who finish their morning exercise and get ready to take a shower. Parks and gardens are emptied out. And there are people who face the tragedy, who begin to remove the debris, who recover lifeless bodies, who save lives, who, waving rags and red flannel, redirect traffic away from the damaged areas. People who struggle in the flames.

Every morning before four o'clock the grid of the city is covered by a tide of trucks, buses, and passenger vans that thicken the metropolitan area; from Milpa Alta to El Peñón, from Los Reyes to Nezahualcóyotl, from Ciudad Azteca to Texcoco, Barrientos, Ecatepec, Ciudad Labor, Moctezuma, Iztapalapa, Contreras, Cuajimalpa, Cuautitlán Izcalli, Molinito, Nadim, Chimalhuacán, beyond Neza toward Tlalpan, Santa Fe, La Estrella, Tlanepantla, Tultitlán, Zona Industrial de Toluca, taking the Super, via Tapo, Calzada Vallejo, Camarones, Central, 965 square miles are traversed from edge to edge by collective taxis, vans, minibuses, suburban railways, long-distance or urban buses, subways, motorcycles or bikes, by hitchhiking or any other way, by men and women on their way to their jobs, boys and girls on their way to school; the traffic grid swallows them all.

The crisscrossing of the city is the x in Mexico, a cross, the one traced again and again on the gigantic crossword puzzle of 18 million people (560,000 are born in the capital every year), cross, cross, cross, the same that Christ carried on his way to the Crucifixion, the one seen at the seven o'clock mass at the Temple of the Sacred Family at the intersection of Puebla and Orizaba or at the Coronation at Parque España or at St. John the Baptist in Tacubaya or at Our Lady of Fátima in Colonia Roma, in the name of the holy cross, deliver us from our enemies, Lord Our God.

The long sleepy litany of those who cross themselves invades the Centro Médico, and nurse Natalia Cruz gets ready for a shift change, in five minutes it will be somebody else's job. The patients love to see them come in: their fresh faces replace those of the night; the affectionate chitchat begins: "How are you this morning? Did you sleep well last night? Today you're having Jell-O." One new day, one more, toward recovery.

In Tlanepantla, the Pérez Cruz family is cross: "At four in the morning, I heat up a little bit of coffee or herbal tea so as not to go out with an empty stomach," says Martina Pérez Cruz. "We live in the dark. If we don't set up our stand that early, we miss out on the night workers and party goers."

Every day they set up their taco stand near the bullring at Ciudad de los Deportes. "We serve *mole de olla,* oxtail soup, beans with pork rind, stuffed rolls, and tacos, and I don't want to sound vain, but it's all delicious." Each day the distances are greater, and the trip is slower: "It takes two and a half hours, and two when I am lucky," says Jorge Múgica, a lathe operator who lives in Colonia Pólvora, "and I switch buses three times. Sometimes I just hang on the outside of the bus, and then I am happy because I save the three-peso fare. I walk a bit over half a mile to the workshop, and I like it because at that hour I think about home and about my children, who are still sleeping."

Jesús Zavala, who comes from Cuchilla del Tesoro, West Eighth Street, block 12, lot II, says: "I get up at five in the morning, and if there is time, my wife gives me breakfast, and if not, I leave just like that with my stomach lonely as a lamppost until I get to work. I wait for the bus for about fifteen or twenty minutes on Texcoco Avenue, but if it comes too full, I have to climb onto the next one, and so I get to Francisco del Paso Avenue, where I wait for another bus to take me to Nativitas. Then it's just a question of walking eight blocks to get over here. That's why I have to rise with the roosters, because the buses are so jammed full, and when you are inside, it's all push and shove, but what are you going to do, right?"

The lovely morning light, who would remember it? The sun is not even up when already the overwhelming number of engines is adding to the layer of scum in the air from yesterday, from many days ago. It's like a cap of grime that our city wears.

Silvia and José Luis Vital wake up at four. "You can't sleep?" José Luis asks his wife.

"No, I can't."

They chat until six in the morning when he asks, "Aren't you going to get up and take a shower?"

"No, I don't even feel like going to work."

At quarter of seven, José Luis insists, "Let's go, woman."

"No, I'm not going."

Silvia works in Gynecology-Obstetrics at the Hospital General. "You played hookey on the sixteenth." José Luis works at Secofi. "If you stay, we both stay. Neither of us goes to work." Silvia starts work before José Luis; she dresses very quickly and locks the door. José Luis, as always, takes the children to the day-care center. What an ugly day, maybe it'll get better!

At her apartment at 12 Tehuantepec Street in Colonia Roma, Judith García says to her second son, "Rodrigo, hurry, it's time to get up; it's unbelievable that América, who is younger than you, is already in the kitchen eating her fruit." Rodrigo is a heavy sleeper. In the same building, his neighbor, the engineer Raúl Pérez Pereyra, offers to his wife, "I'll take the kid to school, Elvira, don't worry." In the Nuevo León Building of the Tlatelolco complex, Gloria Guerrero gets the clothes ready for Gabriela; her twin sister Alondra is still asleep.

As he has done every day, Lucas Gutiérrez arrives early to open the restaurant with thirty-three tables plus booths along the wall, the famous Super Leche cafe that her father founded in 1949, says Elena Alonso. The staff (thirty waiters, cooks, and helpers) begin to work; at seven o'clock on the dot, the doors of this establishment at 41 San Juan de Letrán Avenue, now called Eje Central Lázaro Cárdenas, at the corner with Victoria Street, open for the regular customers.

At ten minutes past seven, Lucas varies his routine and announces, "I'm going to the drug store to get a shot." He has the flu. On his way out, he hears a girl with her hair carefully braided say, "Chocolate and biscuits for me, please."

At 7:18, a strange deep noise followed by a powerful jolt scares everyone, and someone shouts, "Calm down! It's an earthquake, but there's no problem." As the movement intensifies, one of the waiters lets go of a coffeepot and runs outside along with a terrified Argentine tourist. From across the street, they see how a hole opens in the ground and swallows the restaurant and the adjacent apartment building where more than three hundred people reside, as if a giant vacuum cleaner had sucked them down. Disbelieving, petrified, they hear the explosion of gas tanks and see intensely black smoke rise to cover the sun, the sky, the earth.

Three blocks closer to downtown, the large building that houses the Offices of the Attorney General collapses. And on Victoria Street, the same thing happens to the central telephone exchange. On Juárez Avenue, the Hotel Regis, Conalep on Humboldt near Balderas, the Hotel Romano on Artículo 123 (a gigantic layer cake), Televisa, its super antenna and its master transmission tower, the Centro Médico, the Hospital Juárez, the Hospital General, the Nuevo León Building of Tlatelolco, the Ministry of Labor on Río de la Loza, the Ministry of Communications, the Juárez Housing Project, the Ministry of Commerce, the Ministry of the Navy, the buildings at Tehuantepec 12 and Bruselas 8, the Versalles, the Hotel de Carlo, the adjacent Hotel Principado on José María Iglesias Street, Secofi, Colonia Roma, Colonia de los Doctores, the tenements of Tepito, Guerrero, and Morelos, five substations of the Federal Electrical Commission, all lie wrecked on the ground.

The city is bathed in dust that grates the throat, coming from hundreds of buildings; dust suffocates and covers everything. Terrified, early risers try to find their way through this brown and sandy fog. Suddenly, a voice: "The Regis is on fire." Someone has turned on a transistor radio at top volume in a parked car. The announcer says, "Part of the Pino Suárez complex has just caved in, and Super Leche is a pile of rubble."

I'm nobody anymore.

Silvia Reyna

I was on my way to work, says José Luis Vital, when someone who lives on our street said to Gloria Pallares, our neighbor, in a very, very soft voice, "Listen, Gynecology collapsed."

Gloria turned toward me. "Run, man, Gyne's caved in . . ."

And I darted out. As I hit Cuauhtémoc Avenue, I stopped: "Hey, I don't have to run or be desperate, Silvia just left, she could not have arrived yet." And sure enough, further ahead, I found her. She was running like mad, unbelievable, bathed in her own tears. She didn't know where she was; among all the people I saw, she was the most desperate. I don't know whether she started shouting because she saw me:

"Everything's fallen down, everything's fallen down, everything! Come and help us!" I embraced her. "Run and see if you can help get them out!" The girls, her friends. I tried to calm her down.

At the site of the Hospital General, I turned to the place where the gynecology wing had been; it was as if it had never been there. I saw a heap of concrete. Excuse me, but I exclaimed, "Motherfucker!" That day I was wearing my new boots for the first time. Since I'm not rich or anything, I thought, "Oh, my poor boots," and then I said, "Viva México," what the heck! If I manage to save a life, that's worth the boots. And we started scratching away at the rubble with our own paws. I don't know, I don't know. When we hauled out dead bodies, we didn't say anything. When we brought out someone alive or even someone badly hurt, man, it was a party: "Here's another one!"

"Alive?"

"Yes."

"Yeaaaaaaaa!!!!!"

The scouts arrived, and one of them, noticing an opening under a concrete slab in the middle of the pile of debris, said, "I'm going in."

We could hear someone crying. The little guy went in and came out with a child. Then he said, "There's another one."

He went in, and the slab fell on him.

A man, older, came to the residents' tower:

"I came to look for my son."

He climbed over the rubble and said, "Here's my son, right here in this place is my son, I'm going to get some people to help me get my son out."

He came back with six or seven, and with the rest of us that were there, we got together and started digging where the man had said, "Here's my son, he's alive, and I'm getting him out."

He got his son out, very, very badly injured, I don't know whether he died later, but he got him out, out of that place, down below where he'd pointed when he said, "Here's my son."

The headlines of the afternoon papers are screams of horror:

OH, GOD! says *Ovaciones*.
TRAGEDY, *Ultimas Noticias*, first edition.
CATASTROPHIC, *El Sol de México*.
QUAKE, *El Gráfico*.
IT WAS AWFUL, *Novedades*.
THOUSANDS DEAD, *Ultimas Noticias*, second edition.

On the 20th, the screams become fragmented information. *Excélsior, La Jornada, El Día, Unomásuno, El Universal, Novedades, La Prensa, El Sol de México, El Financiero, Ovaciones, El Nacional* talk initially about four thousand dead, seven thousand missing, ten thousand injured, although the exact number may never be known. The damage cannot be calculated, the losses are in the billions. The newspapers stress the fact that one hundred physicians, two hundred women patients, and many newborn babies are trapped in the Hospital General. Two thousand three hundred patients are transferred from Centro Médico to other hospitals or abruptly discharged. *El Día* praises the popular heroism and the solidarity of the auxiliary brigades, and *Unomásuno* describes the crazed atmosphere in which the screams of people and the ambulance and police sirens are mixed.

The Nuevo León Building (sections E and F) lies on the ground, bent over upon itself like a poorly baked cake; its rubble alone is four stories high. On this amorphous mass, the improvised rescuers start an antlike operation.

As it was seventeen years before, the Plaza de las Tres Culturas is a battlefield; camping tents have been rigged up where incomplete families share their misfortune with their neighbors. Broken television sets, sewing machines, typewriters, canned goods, tablecloths, sheets, and mattresses form small pyramids.

The cadavers are lined up in the laundry room, more than thirty in the first few minutes. The woman in charge relates, "People ran in panic in their underwear. The Veracruz Building was vacated in a flash, so great was the fear of dying buried in the wreckage. Mothers with children in their arms were hurled to the ground. Within minutes, the laundry area was insufficient for so many bodies."

There is no more space anywhere for dead bodies. "Where shall we take them?" The offices of the Ministerio Público are saturated with corpses. There is not a coffin left in the funeral homes. The injured ones must be taken to the hospitals of the State of Mexico.

Around the ruins, enormous chains of people of all ages begin to form. The debris and broken concrete are passed from hand to hand in buckets, pots and pans, all sorts of kitchenware, any container at all. The spectacle of a single arm stretching for air among the masonry and iron rods seems intolerable.

The atrocious knowledge that living people breathe, trapped in the rubble, motivates the survivors. Hardware stores are emptied of picks, shovels, and flashlights, and the ones who don't have tools remove dirt with their hands. The threat of fire, gas explosions, cave-ins, and other accidents is constant; yet no one thinks of going home.

With each new minute, the tremor gains more victims. Bad news is transmitted by word of mouth. The Conalep Building (the National College of Professional Education on Humboldt Street, almost at the corner of Juárez Avenue) has buried within it hundreds of young students. Four hundred attend each shift in a variety of classrooms. At night, in spite of having to work with the aid of flashlights, the firemen manage to make contact with a group of survivors. They say that there are eighteen of them, and that they are still breathing because air reaches them through a fissure. "Don't worry about us," they add, those courageous kids, according to Jorge Escobosa Licona. "Just do us a favor, bring water and food, please, we're thirsty and hungry, don't worry about anything else."

Marcos Efrén Zariñana, "The Flea," is just a hair over five feet tall and can enter tunnels that are impossible for others. He arrives from Cuautla, where he is a rescue worker, and saves many lives, among them the life of little Abel, three days later, after eighteen hours of excavation.

"Precious nothing. That's what was left."

A crowd thrusts itself into the streets, a frightened mob stops in front of the buildings. Many volunteers come from that human mass. They join the chain of hands, they climb over the debris, they ask for a pick, a shovel. "I'm going home to get some food and boil water," says Doña Carmen, "and I'll be back in a flash."

"What's the matter, compadre?"

"No, man, it's just that every morning Conchita fetches the milk, and she walks by this corner of the Yucatán Building, and look at it now."

"We'll start digging right now, and we'll get my compadre out, right away; yes we'll do it, man."

Many were trapped in the stairways and elevators, only a few untaken steps away from life. The dwellers abandoned their apartments; they took only what they are wearing. They kneel to pray in gardens and in parking lots.

We didn't know yet how many Mexicans had died when the Organizing Committee for the World Cup "Mexico 86" sent a telegram to the the International Soccer Federation (FIFA) that very Thursday, the 19th of September, informing it that despite the tragic events of the tremor, the installations designated for the events had not suffered any damage. Neither the Estadio Azteca nor Mexico 68 of the Ciudad Universitaria suffered in the quake, and neither did the offices of the organizing committee or its press and information centers.

The cable spoke of the "best disposition of the Organizing Committee of Mexico to continue with its work with the accustomed normality."

Sevilla, Spain, September 19 (*Efe*). The World Cup will not be canceled because of the earthquake: Guillermo Cañedo.

Rio de Janeiro, September 19 (*Efe*). The FIFA convened an urgent meeting today in Rio de Janeiro with its president in attendance, and at the end of the meeting Abilio Almeida (of the organizing committee for "Mexico 86") declared that the location for the event could not be changed nine months before the opening because everything was prepared to welcome the teams and the tourists.

The areas of Tepito, La Merced, the Lagunilla, and Morelos are very badly damaged. The pavement of Avenida Circunvalación buckled upward, forming mountains of rubble. The estimate is of some fifteen hundred dead.

The second floor of La Merced market collapsed on top of its main wing, flattening cars. To avoid personal tragedies, authorities have ordered the closing of other markets—Mixcoac, Ampudia, and Flores—plus the annex and small and large wings of La Merced.

At six in the morning, many humble seamstresses start working in clandestine sweatshops in old downtown buildings that have not been maintained and strain under the weight of heavy machinery and bolts of fabric. The Avenue of San Antonio Abad seems to have suffered a blitz. A man with the arrogance of one who is used to calling the shots attempts to break through the police circle in order to recover invoices, while physicians improvise stretchers with the fabric found in the ruins.

"It's nothing, my son, it's nothing."

"We need glucose, syringes, bandages, equipment for intravenous feeding, disinfectants, suture materials, antibiotics, Merthiolate," say the students of the School of Medicine of the UNAM and the Instituto Politécnico Nacional (IPN) in charge of a relief station in Colonia Roma.

At the corner of Fray Servando Teresa de Mier and Doctor Vértiz, the five-story building of the Ministry of Labor and Social Protection was flattened. At least fifteen people are trapped and are able to answer the calls of their colleagues. Yet they cannot be rescued because there is no machinery available to lift the tons of concrete that are above them.

One of the towers of the Pino Suárez compound turned three-quarters of a circle on its vertical axis and then fell over on its side, dumping its fourteen stories on the ground. Other towers in the same compound show evidence that they too had started to turn.

Many buildings are useless: the Office of the Attorney General of the Federal District, the Offices of the Arbitration and Conciliation Boards, located in Colonia de los Doctores, and the two towers of the Civil Courts on Niños Héroes. On the Eje Central de Lázaro Cárdenas, many rescue workers struggle to save the lives of the employees of the Ministry of Communication and Transport; the four top floors of that building crumpled. At eight o'clock a fire broke out in the central tower of Telecommunications, interrupting all telex, local, and long-distance services, national and international.

Five people were found on the destroyed floors. Other injured employees were rescued by firemen who had to climb up on ladders.

The Ministry of Protection and Traffic Safety—oh, irony!—has practically collapsed, so its services have moved to a warehouse in Tlascoaque. The Ministry of the Treasury and Public Credit and the Mexican Bank Association announced that seventy-one out of its 902 buildings are seriously damaged. And the Ministry of Commerce and Industrial Development (Secofi) is like a crumbled cookie.

Not quite a week ago the Hotel Regis was celebrating the seventy-first anniversary of its foundation with a special Day of the Guest. It was 90 percent full. Sixty people are still trapped.

The Hotel Romano, in the corner of Humboldt and Artículo 123 streets, had twenty of its rooms occupied, most of them by fellows of the Ministry of Foreign Relations. The hotel is totally destroyed, and none of its occupants made the list of survivors.

The Hotel Versalles, on Versalles Street, fell down completely.

The Hotel Principado, on José María Iglesias Street, near the Monument of the Revolution, was more than 60 percent occupied. A fire broke out and is still burning. Until now, no rescue operation has been possible. The Hotel de Carlo, a neighbor of the Principado, also went down, and it was half full. No rescue work has started.

One hotel in the south, the Finisterre, on Calzada de Tlalpan close to Taxqueña Avenue, lost two of its stories. It threatens to come down entirely, and in the process, to destroy the pedestrian bridge crossing the Calzada near the Metro Taxqueña.

Among hotels that did not crumple but require evacuation are the Hotel Ambassador on Humboldt Street, the Hotel del Prado on Juárez Avenue, and the Presidente and Chapultepec hotels in the Zona Rosa.

As the day goes by, the disasters accumulate. It is impossible to imagine the consequences.

MEXICO REJECTS FOREIGN ASSISTANCE

Based on his first tour, President Miguel de la Madrid Hurtado announces, "We are prepared to respond to this situation, and we do not need to request foreign assistance. Mexico has enough resources, and together people and government will overcome. We are grateful for the good will extended to us, but we are self-sufficient."

The Mexican ambassador in Washington, Espinosa de los Monteros, declares, "We'll get out of this by ourselves. Mexico is greater than its problems."

NO MORE, DEAR GOD, NO MORE

On the 20th of September at 7:39 at night, a new earthquake registering 5.6 on the Richter scale jars Mexico City. People kneel on the street. "No more, dear God, no more," Marta Anaya hears someone say on Cuauhtémoc Avenue. Volunteers and rescue operators dart out in terror from the ruins in which they were at work. A crowd advances in despair in a haunted walk, not knowing either the how or the why of things.

At 9:20 people are looking for a place to sleep; benches, parks, median strips.

After this second tremor, President de la Madrid addresses a message to the Mexican people on television:

The tragedy that hit us yesterday has been one of the most severe that Mexico has suffered in its history. There are hundreds of dead and injured. We still do not have precise or complete numbers.

There are still many people under crumpled buildings, whom we have not been able to rescue yet.

In the face of this calamity, there have been numerous acts not only of extraordinary solidarity on the part of many sectors of our people but also acts that deserve the name of heroic, acts that honor the people of Mexico.

Moreover, an hour or an hour and a half ago, we had another tremor of less intensity and shorter duration than the one yesterday, but it still caused great uncertainty, fear, and anxiety.

The government of the republic and the governments of the states have reacted to the maximum extent of their efforts and capacities. Unfortunately—I must admit it—the tragedy is of such magnitude that it has overtaken us in many cases. We cannot do what we would like to with the speed that we also desire, especially in the task of saving lives.

Before this picture of tragedy and sadness, we take heart in the attitude of the citizenry expressed personally and through its institutions . . .

According to *El Universal,* injured people who were counted at relief stations reached 7,160, and more than 800,000 people who were forced to abandon their homes are out in the open air. Meanwhile, the subsecretary of government, Fernando Pérez Correa, acknowledges only 2,000 dead, but Locatel registers 28,000 missing persons.

Thirty thousand victims are in more than thirty gyms and other sites turned into shelters.

According to Carlos Alvarez H., the walls of Colegio Juan Bosco, held together with wires, killed the teacher of chemistry and her twenty-five students. The parents of the students and some of the girls had denounced the poor conditions in which the facility operated. Out of fifty students, half managed to get out, and the other half died as they sought protection with their teacher.

The Centenary of the National Anthem School crumpled, reports *Unomásuno.* Trapped were a woman teacher and many children. The teacher was taken out on a board.

At Hospital General, in the gynecology unit, thirty-five young physicians were killed and buried as they were having breakfast; more than one hundred patients died too, *Novedades* states. A nurse who declined to give her name had finished her shift in pediatrics moments before the quake. Stupefied in the street, she saw several cribs with babies in them being hurled out through windows that burst open.

In front of Centro Médico, a long line of ashen faces waits for a turn to ask about relatives.

One hundred sixteen severely injured people were admitted to the Green Cross Hospital in Xoco. The Balbuena Hospital requests that no more victims be sent there.

This morning, forty people were rescued who had been buried for more than twenty-four hours.

Unofficial estimates indicate that nearly three thousand persons could still be trapped in 90 percent of the approximately three hundred buildings that collapsed in the center of the Federal District and in the Roma, Guerrero, Morelos, and Doctores colonias, among others.

More than two thousand cadavers have been unearthed from the rubble, according to *La Jornada*. State television announced today that in Colonia Roma alone there are fifteen hundred dead. Funeral homes declare they can't handle any more bodies.

Most of the dwellings in San Camilito, where the mariachis sleep, were occupied; all the musicians had just gone to bed.

The coffins form a long row in the corridor of the funeral rooms of ISSSTE and in the Gardens of Remembrance, San Lorenzo Tezonco, Memorial Park, and the Civil Cemetery of Dolores.

The General Ministry of Protection and Traffic Safety announced that 6,299 cadavers had been recovered, and that they had seven hundred in the Forensic Medical Services. Thirty-five bodies were disinterred from the building that had been at 14 Ahorro Postal Street.

Out of the Ministry of Labor, they rescued twenty-two people who were alive and eight dead; fifty are missing.

Bodies are in the offices of the following delegations: Cuauhtémoc, Venustiano Carranza, Benito Juárez, and Iztacalco. That's where relatives must come to identify and claim them; thirty-six hours later they will be buried in a common grave.

A HURRICANE WAS PULLING US AND TAKING US OUT INTO THE OPEN AIR

Representative Jesús Martínez Alvarez from the State of Oaxaca left his room at the Hotel del Prado early in the morning to go jogging. He went by to meet his fellow Oaxacan representative Erciel Gómez Nucamendi, who was staying at the Hotel Regis, and while they trotted along the Alameda Central, they saw the Regis collapse and the Del Prado wobble. Another representative of the trade union sector from Nuevo León had left the Principado minutes earlier to run around the Monument to the Revolution.

Héctor Sen Flores, the representative from Veracruz, was listed for three days among the seven missing members of the lower house of Congress after the earthquake: "One day before," he relates, "I asked the hotel to switch me from room 506, overlooking Balderas Street, to 602, overlooking Juárez Avenue. This was a vital change, since the former was located in the new section, the first part to collapse." When Héctor Sen Flores was about to meet his colleagues from the navy committee of the Chamber of Deputies, the Regis started to move; everything vibrated; he and a friend, Matías García Cobos, ran to the door frames: "At that moment, I observed through the window how the building of the Ministry of the Navy crumpled with a deafening noise. That was when I felt the greatest fear. We felt that something like a hurricane was pulling us and taking us out into the open air.

"Everything got dark, and the air, filled with dust and intense heat, became unbreathable; then the hotel tumbled down. There was an eerie sound. Matías García Cobos and I ran in search of the stairs, where sixty or seventy people were afraid to climb down. There was a horrible smell of gas, and one could hardly see through the dust. It was impossible to breathe inside the cloud of powder. We were just above the hotel lobby. We began the descent in an orderly way. These were moments of profound terror in which only a survival instinct goads you into looking for an exit. When we saw that the stairway of the second floor was gone, and that at the end of the hallway the light of day was visible, we skipped over the wreckage as best we could in that direction," said Sen Flores to Manuel Ponce. "A wall fell down in front of me, and I took advantage of the moment to run toward the light and get out with the others onto Juárez Avenue."

"I heard chilling cries of terror and despair; hysteria and panic had gotten hold of most of the people.

"A few minutes later, an explosion took care of the other part of the hotel, destroying my room.

"I didn't stop to think twice; I took off for the airport, boarded an airplane for Coatzacoalcos, and arrived home at five o'clock in the afternoon, as my family was watching the burning of the Hotel Regis on television.

"They thought that I was dead, and they were crying—my wife, Lidia Carmen, and my children, Lidia, seventeen years old, Héctor, fourteen, and Octavio, only five.

"It was by pure miracle that I was saved."

"There are people alive in the hotel, please, come and get them out," desperate police kept yelling.

Ramón Uribe Urzúa, former federal representative in the Forty-Eighth Legislature, was living permanently in a room on the seventh floor of the Regis. The hotel was 90 percent occupied. "When the earthquake began, I left the room with my briefcase and walked toward the stairs. Only four of us were able to leave."

The journalist from Acapulco, Mario García Rodríguez, reporter for *El Día,* who was on the fifth floor, looked out the window as soon as he felt the first oscillatory movement of the tremor: "Now I will see how well these damned people from the capital take a real earthquake, those whiners." No sooner said than done. But as he leaned out the window the tremor intensified, and Mario García Rodríguez grabbed hold of the heavy drapes, which buffered his fall as he was thrown headlong onto a mountain of broken concrete, and that's the way he was rescued, wrapped in the drapes, with some bruises, but alive and well and wagging his reporter's tail.

"It was a ghastly scene, a hell, and we are living extra hours, no?" Manuel Bustillos Valdez and Joel Lazaga Macías tell Sergio Galindo. "We were about three hundred guests in the Regis, although I only saw fifty coming out. Some people attempted to jump out the window.

"First-aid workers, sailors, soldiers, firemen, and volunteers were working; with the help of heavy machinery, they lifted rubble, sprayed water, used blowtorches to break through iron rods: they wanted to stop the fire, they did not believe that there were any survivors. In the end, at dawn today, the facade of the Regis succumbed to the flames. It had burned for fifty hours. Officers of the judicial police waited impassively; they wanted to recover the hotel's safe.

"We took a taxi cab to the airport, which took three hours, paying with a watch and a name bracelet. There were many people; all wanted a ticket to leave town."

In the opposite direction, Miguel Capistrán, coming from Veracruz, took a taxi to get to the home of his two sisters and nephews on Chilpancingo Street. Near the site the taxi driver said, "That's it, man. I can't go any further."

Capistrán walked in a cloud of dust to the building where his relatives had lived. It was on the ground.

The last corpses to come out were those of his sisters and little nephews.

Tally of the First Day
- 250 buildings destroyed
- 50 at risk of collapsing
- 1,000 useless structures
- 5,000 injured
- 1,000 or more under the debris

- Water should be boiled.
- The center of town is blacked out, as are many areas of the city. Damaged are eight power substations of the Federal Electrical Commission, four transmitter lines of 230 kilowatts plus two of 85, and an enormous number of cables.
- There is no telephone service.
- In 60 percent of the residential areas of the Federal District, there is no drinking water.
- The supply of food and fuel is normal.
- Movies, theaters, nightclubs, and stadiums are all closed.
- It is guaranteed that in the city, strictly watched by police and the army, any act of looting or pilferage will be severely punished; the Federal District is under control.
- Some 250,000 Mexicans are homeless.

- The Department of the Federal District (DDF) is sending one hundred stores on wheels to disaster areas.
- After the second tremor, 500,000 Mexicans sleep on median strips, the street, or anywhere else outside their home. "We don't want to lose the little we still have."
- The Hospital de la Raza, which had been receiving patients from other collapsed hospitals, is also evacuated.
- The Hotel del Prado is seriously damaged. Diego Rivera's mural is in danger.

Joerg Hafkemeyer
It has been the most devastating and extreme experience that I have ever had in my life. In four blocks I counted thirty-six dead. People were removing corpses from the ravaged houses. From the street one could see the insides of apartments and offices. I saw dead people sitting at their desks.■

I SAW THEM PLANTED IN THE DIRT LIKE LITTLE PINE TREES
Rodolfo Mora Rodríguez belongs to the executive committee of Section 15 of Hospital Juárez; he is a small man, thin and rather shy:

I'd like to give a quick explanation, so as not to bore you, of what happened on the 19th. The earthquake got me on my way around the Monument of the Revolution. I immediately thought of Hospital Juárez, which was already damaged. I managed to get there at ten. The sight was pure chaos. On the way in, I ran into the director, Jesús Aguilar, and at that moment I felt like striking him.

The compañeros went in through the small openings in the rubble without minding the danger of steel and concrete falling on them. We saw an opening of about eight inches, and we heard voices calling, help us, help us, so we started scratching with whatever we had, trying to move the chunks of masonry with crowbars, with shovels, with bare hands. One of the guys ended up with the bloodiest hands I've ever seen.

A rescue worker said, "We need tiny people—a skinny person that can manage to go in."

At that moment, I—who, according to the guys, am very hyper and daring—felt my legs wobble, and I tried to hide. I saw them looking at each other and not saying anything, so I said, "I'll go in."

"Here's a flashlight. Go in and see," they ordered, "or, are you afraid?"

The slabs were almost all vertical. I went in as best I could.

"How many are you in there?" I asked once I was inside.

"There are eight of us."

"How are you doing?"

"Bring us oxygen."

Our medical compañeros gave me glucose and oxygen and with the crowbars and other instruments I tried to make the opening a little bit bigger, just a little. I barely could go in.

"Calm down," I said. "We'll get you out."

One of them recognized me; in the hospital they know me as Niño Mora, my name being Rodolfo Mora Rodríguez.

"Niño Mora, Niño Mora, get us out."

We sent away for a blowtorch to break the rods and enlarge the hole, and that way I could go in a little better, with the guys pulling me by the feet. Then I asked them for a bucket to get the dirt out, but when I saw the picture, I was afraid that I was going to be trapped inside because all of them were standing, buried, with the rubble covering the better part of their bodies—only one of them had his hands more or less free—they were all stiff, lined up, planted like little pine trees in the dirt. A profound despair overcame me. I shouted to the ones above, "Pull me out, pull me out." They pulled me out, and I told them what the situation was like. We propped up the ceiling of the hole with lumber to prevent it from falling in; we started about twelve noon and finished at eight at night. At the end I was so ill that they told me not to go in anymore: "Better have yourself put to bed."

"No, these are my compañeros, and I can't leave them down there. If I cannot get them out, I'll stay here."

The crowbars helped us make the entrance bigger. They were calling me, so I went in again. There inside, a physician, the only one who could move his hands, grabbed me by the shoulders: "Mora, Morita, I'll give you anything, but get us out." I thought of lifeguards in swimming pools, the ones who drown trying to rescue someone: "Wait, otherwise we'll both die here."

Together with the outside compañeros we went to ask the other physicans for help. I would show my face through the opening once in a while: "Hang on a little bit more, we're getting you out." We got three out, I don't know how. Then the physicians told me that I needed to conduct a test with a surgical knife on the ones that remained, to see if they were still alive. They said I should cut them, anywhere, any little bit, just to make sure. After seeing a very young woman doctor, really young, I felt . . . well . . . I was afraid. Any movement would be dangerous. Then I told the truth to the ones waiting outside, that there was no life left in them.

VALUABLE DAYS WERE LOST WHEN LIVE COMPAÑEROS COULD HAVE BEEN RESCUED

Afterward a physician came—nobody wanted to get in there—also a skinny one. He managed to get in. We had to recover the dead ones— right?—but the most urgent thing was to rescue the ones that were more or less alive, so we kept up with our ant's job until around three in the morning. At that hour the army came, and all of us civilians were kicked out; we were told that they had trained people. We couldn't go on with the job. Friday they pushed us further away, they cordoned off the entire disaster area, and they didn't let us do a blessed thing, but they didn't do a blessed thing either. They milled around trying to find out where they could get in, and Saturday it was the same. On the other side of the hospital fence, relatives stood night and day, asking, asking. They wanted to help.

It was already Sunday when the French and Israeli teams arrived and started to work. We wanted to shoulder the burden too, as a crew. When we saw that they were already leaving, we stopped the French with the help of a kid that knew some French. They answered they were withdrawing because the soldiers had kicked them out. And that they were near some compañeros that were buried alive, and that what they needed was time, and to be left alone to do their work, and pow! just like that, the soldiers arbitrarily threw them out. Time? No, man, the army was in charge and that was that.

Since we were members of the executive committee, we wondered what to do. We went to talk to the director, Jesús Aguilar, but he wouldn't give us the time of day. In a flash, we got a little rally together. We started to say that the authorities were to blame because our compañeros were still underground, and we weren't allowed to go to their aid. After that, the soldier in command of that whole area came and laid on a heavy rap, that no, he was there to take care of our physical safety. We told him that instead of machine guns all his people should be carrying shovels, no? So in the end they allowed us to go in as crews, and I was put in command of one of them, and a compañera warned me, "You know what? Be careful, don't you go in, because they'll stick you in a hole, and they'll fix you."

"No, I don't think so. There are several of us going in together."

Anyway, Sunday night and even more on Monday, they started to push people back. And very valuable days were wasted when we could have saved the lives of many compañeros.

At this point what we demand is that the bodies be recovered, and that the relatives that are camping outside Hospital Juárez be informed. These poor devils spend all night out there, and there isn't even a friendly soul to give them a cup of coffee. What they want is to see their people and bury them.

We are angry, fucking mad. Our anger will make us rebuild Hospital Juárez, because at this point, what with the government's austerity plan, with the World Cup coming up, they'll plant a few trees, design a recreation center, whatever, but no hospital. We want the Juárez to be what it used to be: a hospital for the neediest people in this country. They want to prevent an organized group from pressuring the authorities at any cost. That's what makes us so mad, the deafness of the authorities.

We couldn't even remain there as a committee. At night they sneak the corpses out another way, fast, as if they want to erase everything and finish off the job.

Elena Alonso

Lucas Gutiérrez had to be treated for a deep depression. He asked constantly, "Why did I have to go out to get that shot?"

In another part of the city, Víctor Manuel Fernández, a partner of Super Leche, safe with his family, heard about the disaster. His mother, sister, nephews and nieces, and brother-in-law lived in the apartments above Super Leche. He thought of his uncle Lucas, of the employees and customers that he knew—his entire world destroyed in barely two and a half minutes.

When he arrived, crazed, he joined the group of desperate people removing masonry with their bare hands in the vain hope of saving lives. Two days later, not having left the site, he identified the body of his mother. He went to have it cremated, took care of the ashes, and came back. His sister, nephews, nieces, brother-in-law, and many employees were still missing. He learned that an old friend and neighbor of his mother's had been saved.

He had some hope and kept searching. Then he saw the heavy machinery move in to bulldoze the rubble of the building. The bodies of his people were never found.

Ten days after the disaster his search has not ended: he walks through hospital wards, through shelters, he places ads on TV and in newspapers, and every day he expects someone to call him. ■

"Nothing, man, I want nothing."

The buckets of rubble pass from hand to hand along chains of fifty to a hundred men and women. Volunteers sweep away debris. Desperate voices try to orient the disaster brigades.

Someone shouts, "A flashlight, a flashlight!" And the demand, according to Ricardo Gómez Moreno, reverberates from the heap of rubble all the way down to the parking lot.

"A flashlight!" continues the anguished petition, and suddenly another cry from the same rescue worker: "Silence, silence!" Everyone is stilled. "Nobody move, nobody move. Silence!"

Silence falls, and the worker calls out, "Guadalupe Molina, Guadalupe Molina is here!"

Guadalupe Molina can barely be heard under enormous concrete slabs.

The flashlight arrives at the end of the long chain, and the worker shines it under the slab, but Guadalupe Molina cannot be seen. A chain of hands and buckets works in that direction, and small fistfuls of debris are taken out. The sudden hope of saving a life gives new strength; the emotion is high, and the empty buckets fall without reaching the trembling hands that should pass them to the next compañero.

Efforts like this one are multiplied at entrances C, D, E, and F of the Nuevo León Building. Hundreds of persons collaborate there, and many of them started at the very moment when the cracking sounds and lamentations announced the tragedy at 7:19 in the morning.

"There are ten of us here, get water for ten people," says a firefighter.

From down below, reporter Ricardo Gómez Moreno asks for the speaker's name.

"I'm a fireman," he replies.

"But what is your name? Tell me."

"I'm a fireman" is the only answer.

Another firefighter says, "His name is Jesús Vásquez, but here we are simply firefighters."

"What time did you start work?"

"We arrived at ten in the morning."

Among the volunteers a young man, tall, bearded, with dust-covered spectacles, stands out. He looks exhausted.

"What is your name?"

"What for? I am simply here helping out."

"Why not give your name when you are doing something worthy?"

"My name is Alberto, that's all."

"What is your line of work, Alberto?"

The man, about twenty-seven years old, drops his arms, shakes sand off his beard:

"I teach philosophy at the ENEP, Zaragoza. My name is Alberto Herr."

He arrived at ten in the morning, and at 5:30 in the afternoon he has not eaten yet. But he has drunk a lot of water.

There are others like Alberto Herr. Eligio Avalos, gaunt, five feet tall, about thirty years old, is there, "I don't know why," but "I had to do something, I could not simply watch with my arms folded."

Night begins to fall, and a woman, Doctor Martha Solís, is seated on a bench with a tiny dog that barks softly and whiningly. It doesn't belong to her; someone found him in the rubble and put him in her arms. She has wrapped him in her housecoat.

It's beginning to get cold.

"Where is Jorge?"

"Have you seen Patricia and Roberto?"

There is no answer.

"Do you want some coffee?"

"No."

"Do you need anything?"

"No, nothing."

Alonso Mixteco

MIXTEC ON THE FATHER'S SIDE, NAHUATL ON THE MOTHER'S SIDE

When Alonso Solano González first came from Guerrero to work in the General Administration of Indigenous Education, he never imagined that one morning he would find himself looking for a ray of light among the wreckage of building number 39 of Manuel Doblado Street. A translator of the Mixteco language, he came to the city seconded to the Department of Educational Resources. Alonso Solano González is a good-looking man, not because he is handsome, but because his words are whole, rotund, resonant; they are bells. He is small and strong, "*xocoyotito*—as Jesusa Palancares would say—a little compact thing like this," his head round and solid as his words, his cheekbones high, his body movements convincing. Oh, how good it would have been to listen to him at the gathering of the Reconstruction Commission in the National Museum of Anthropology! How beautiful his old-fashioned voice would have sounded in place of the tiresome repetition of political raps!

I FOUND WHAT HAD BEEN MY BODY, AND WITH MY ARMS
I STARTED TO FIGHT

I am Mixtec on my father's side, that's why I write my name as Alonso Mixteco; I am Nahuatl on my mother's side. I come from two indigenous cultures. I came to work all the way from Guerrero. I came with some affection for the capital city, but now I'm sad to relate all that has happened here. On September 19, at seven in the morning, I left the place where I live and ten minutes after seven I arrived at the building that housed the National Commission on Seniority at Manuel Doblado 39. Compañeros, I have always made it a point to start work a little earlier. Ever since I was in the countryside, where I started school at seven, and the same in my city. At 7:10 my office, Educational Resources, was still padlocked, so I sat on the stairs. At 7:15 a compañera arrived, may she rest in peace. She had the key, she opened the door at 7:16, and at 7:17 we signed our attendance sheet, we chatted for a moment, and I was going into my cubicle when the compañera said, "Professor, it's an earthquake."

I saw a baby crib that one of the secretaries had hanging as an ornament, and I saw it swinging like this. The compañera ran to lean against a wall, and I couldn't run after her. I was standing by the door, and the building was a sea wave. I shouted to her, "Come over here, Virginia."

The building roared, falling into pieces. Suddenly, the wall the compañera was standing by fell on her, and still another wall tumbled on top. I then covered my head with my briefcase. Something fell on my head, and I fell in a sitting position, I don't know how far, I fell way down, I fell, I fell hemmed in on all sides and then I said these words, forgive me, forgive me, I don't usually speak this way, but I said, "Motherfucker, why am I going to die? I don't owe anything."

When the building crumpled, just imagine that someone pushed it toward the north. If you pay attention, you'll see that all of the buildings fell toward the north except for a few that fell on this side. Then I managed to say only, "My children, goodbye to my children, I'll never see them again."

Everything turned dark, and I was wholly covered, wholly buried on the floor where I remained seated, well, not completely seated, almost in a standing position, I had no space to move, but I found a little can, and I began to hit the floor with it, over and over again, because I could move my arm, and I shouted for more than fifteen minutes, "Help, come and get me out of here, please. Help."

I continued shouting alone, alone, banging the can over and over. A little later—you must remember that it was foggy that morning—a ray of sun came in, but at a distance of a hundred feet. I said to myself, "Here's my salvation."

Crawling, holding my head like this, with all the strength of my whole body, I went toward that opening. My hand hardly fit into the little hole, this tiny. I turned this way and that way to see if I was well. I found what was my body. I recognized it, and then I started to struggle with my shoulders, with my arms, with my head, like someone who hits his head against the wall.

My head is good and hard, my bones are hard as iron, and even if I went bald I was going to open that hole, and I opened it so much that I was able to pull the rest of my body, and with my body I excavated about a hundred feet of tunnel by creeping, holding my head like this until I arrived at the place where there was light. I didn't even put a scratch on my noggin. Only then did I speak again, and please forgive the offense, I'm not used to speaking like this: "Motherfucker, this was tough."

I saw my eight-story building compressed into one. I ran shouting, "Virginia, Virginia." I shouted "Virginia" a lot, but Virginia never answered.

"She's dead."

Then I ran in a different direction. I remembered compañero Javier Garnica, a draftsman, who also started work early, and I started to call out his name on the heap of rubble.

"Javier," I shouted, "Javier."

"What?"

Then I said, "You're alive."

Later I thought, "How stupid I am! Why do I ask him if he is alive. He's answering, right?"

Then I said to him, "Don't worry brother. I'm coming back to get you, I'm just going to get some help."

I turned east. Natural gas was leaking into the street. I said to myself, "I have to shut this off," but the cap, who knows where that was? That was the moment when I realized—excuse me for being so natural, when I say natural I mean that I am an Indian—but I thought that gas was hot, and no, it was freezing cold, and I couldn't shut it off.

"Help! Help!" It was then that I realized that there were many people trying to get their loved ones out. I took off my sweater—look at it, this sweater is my witness, I wish that it could talk—and I started to wave it up in the air like this: "Help! Help!" Nobody came. Then I went down, because I had just been going around the building of Manuel Doblado 39, until I found a man who was the watchman.

"Professor, professor, you saved yourself."

"Yes, sir, I'm alive."

I ran to the other side. There was nobody. I only met a policeman who was scared stiff. Then I saw a fellow teacher who was just arriving, and he said to me, "Maestro, you were born again."

"I think I was born again, but let's go look for help to get out Javier Garnica and the other compañeros who are still up there."

Curious onlookers started to arrive, and then I realized that many other buildings had collapsed. I kept repeating, "Garnica, Garnica." All the time I said the name of Garnica. I ran on Argentina Street; on Venezuela Street I ran into our general director for indigenous education, Professor Cándido Cueto Martínez.

"I'm so glad to run into you, the building at Manuel Doblado 39 fell down, and Garnica is trapped along with others."

"Well, since you always arrive early."

"Yes, Maestro, we always arrive early."

"I didn't know about the building."

"Yes, Maestro, but now we have to get Garnica and the other ones out."

What I wanted was a volunteer compañero who could help me get Garnica out, along with the other compañero and the compañera Virginia.

There was a young guy; nobody remembers his name, nor which department he works in; he was the one who didn't treat me as if I were crazy. He helped me. I said to him, "They are around here." We didn't have any tools. We got a sledgehammer here, a hacksaw there, and a pickax.

"Hey, you, stop it," the others shouted contemptuously. "Stop it, you, you are not from the rescue brigades."

That's why I hate those people.

"Javier," I shouted, "Javier."

I insisted, and I would point to them, the place where the compañero Javier and the compañera Virginia were buried.

"Get out, you; we are the ones who know how; you don't know how, you can't do this."

How couldn't I do it when I was the only one that knew where they were. But in their eyes I couldn't get my hands in because I was not from Rescue. They were the sole authorities. That is why I, as an Indian, do not like those rescue people because they don't do things as they should. All they want is to be heroes.

"Get him out of here," they shouted. "Get him out of here." What right did they have to treat me like this? Had they ever been under the wreckage, or could they share my despair? No, they were the technicians. I insisted, I said where, excavate here, here is where the compañera Virginia is. "Yes, but you get away from here; we'll get her out; you don't know how to."

They got me away, and as you know one person can hardly do anything against so many people . . . one simply can't. But from down below I kept shouting, "This way, in this direction is my compañero; on this other side is my other compañero. Compañera Virginia . . ."

The journalists arrived, and they spotted me there on the same Manuel Doblado Street. One guy from the press approached me because the men there had told him, "This is the man that got himself out."

I did not want to be interviewed because what I wanted was to see those trapped bodies come out. The reporter asked, "What is your name?"

And I answered, "I'll see you later."

NO MORE DUST OR SALTPETER FOR ME; NOW I REBEL

I heard them hit with the pickax for a while, and I didn't want to wait any longer. I climbed up again because they didn't find where my compañera was. Nobody would give me the opportunity to work; everyone thought I was crazy. They didn't believe that I had really gotten myself out because I didn't have a scratch on me, nothing, only this grungy sweater.

I thought, "I won't pay any attention to them, arrogant people," and I went at it hard with the pickax, and we got compañero Javier Garnica out. When I got out the compañera Virginia, already dead, that was when they believed me. I calmed down, because at least, alive or dead, the bodies were out in the open air. I couldn't stand the thought that they were in there asphyxiating, with dust in their eyes.

No, I am not brave, when I saved myself, my first thought was to go home, to see my family. I looked for a telephone in the street, but where in hell, everything was out of order, nothing worked in Mexico City, and I was eager to be with my people. I thought of abandoning my compañeros, and I said to myself, "I am a great coward if I don't rescue these people."

It's a good thing I stayed behind because the rescue workers had no idea where to start working with the pickax on the eighth floor. It was not until 9:30 in the evening that we recovered them. I felt much pain for my compañera Virginia, because she was the one who had warned me, "Professor, it's an earthquake."

"What are we going to do with the compañera?" said the other colleagues that had arrived. We took her to the Gayosso funeral home on Sullivan Street, and as we traveled along Reforma we took in the full extent of the disaster. On my transistor radio I had heard that the states that had suffered most were Michoacán, Guerrero, Jalisco, and Nayarit. At that moment I wept thinking of my children. They didn't say what part of Guerrero, and I thought of my children all by themselves. What might have become of my house made of adobe, river stones, and clay shingles? Uh, it must be crumbs. If Mexico City, built with great technology, has collapsed, how could my little house be spared?

The next day, I returned to Manuel Doblado, looking for my sweater because it's the only one I've got. There it was, like trash, the sweater that you see me wearing, and it does me fine. I went back to Sullivan for the burial, and the father of the dead woman said to me, "Professor, Professor, what are we going to do? They don't want to take care of my daughter here because we don't have enough money, we're missing the number of the death certificate, but we're mostly missing money."

Consider how low humanity can sink.

The President visited many buildings, the Regis, Tlatelolco, Colonia Roma. So many places, but they never said that Manuel Doblado had fallen, this never came out. I feel that all the people like myself could be called third-class people, and this is why the President never visits them. And the ones who had it the hardest on Thursday the 19th and Friday the 20th were the poorest people. And I, as an Indian—you realize— call those who live poorly third-class *marginados*. The man did not even have the kindness to visit all the damaged areas—only the important ones, not the kennels.

On the other hand, the elders in Guerrero told me that the water of the land of Tenochtitlán, as Mexico City was named, should not have been extracted. That is what the old ones know, and they say it. But modern technology, why doesn't it know that that was a fatal blow to the city?

Oh, compañeros, one more thing I want to tell you: here one can go mad from so much paper, so many documents, so many bureaucratic certificates to be written. Paper and more paper. Look at it now: all the paper has flown in the air! The earthquake tossed it all up.

If you remember, in 1980 there was an earthquake, and the building was heavily damaged. But the government chiefs soon forgot! The government does not hear warnings; this is why we could not be in peace because with that mistreatment they can lead us to damnation.

And so, compañeros, I was tired of chewing dust as I was leaving the hollow and approaching the opening. As a worm I crawled, as a worm. Now I rebel. No more dust nor saltpeter nor a home torn apart. I demand decent treatment for all Mexicans.

MEXICO CUT OFF FROM THE WORLD

With the telephone center on Victoria Street destroyed, Mexico remained disconnected. (How is it possible that 55,000 thousand branches that connect the south with the north of the country and the whole country with the world were all concentrated in one single old building on Victoria Street?) Only transistor radios worked, and many listened to them incredulously. Our administrative facilities, our archives, and, worse still, our great housing complex were lying turned into a bundle of twisted iron rods, unplugged cables, and mountains of trash.

Telephone operators: ten dead, eleven injured, twenty-nine missing.

As the telecommunications system collapsed (radio, telex, and television), the country was cut off from the world. Ham radio operators, travelers, and reporters turned into messengers to connect Mexico with the world and also the capital city with the states of the republic.

"Through a ham radio operator we learned of the tragedy that happened in Mexico," says Cecilia Alvear Treviño, chief producer for Latin America for NBC, one of the three most important U.S. television networks. The news was known in the United States at nine in the morning by means of a ham radio. At four in the afternoon, eight planes arrived in Mexico with ultramodern equipment produced by Japanese and North American technology—equipment that links directly to satellites. Only then was the world able to observe the extent of the disaster.

Marshall Gourley, friend of our Miguel Concha and a priest like him, received the news of Mexico's cataclysm over cable TV. He turned his parish in Denver, Our Lady of Guadalupe, into a collection center, and in a matter of hours the place, rather than a church, looked more like the Aztec Stadium on a soccer day. Mexicans, documented and undocumented, donated 35,000 pounds of food and medicine, and $21,000 in cash was gathered little by little in contributions of one, two, and five dollars per person.

The mobilization was so great that Anglos joined them with the offer of packing boxes, three trailer trucks, and an airline that committed itself to transporting everything to Mexico. Donors wrote on the boxes, "Mexico, we love you; Mexico, we are with you."

The world found out what had happened to Mexico thanks to the 1,820 licensed amateur radio operators. The signals sent through the high and thin air spread urgent notices. Frank J. Meckel, from Lago de Guadalupe, leaped into a fantastic marathon of communications with the United States, sending Red Cross messages: medications, surgical instruments, and first-aid materials. The day before he was unknown, but today he had the gratitude of Mexico, this North American whose father came from Illinois in 1902, and whose children are Mexican.

"As if nothing had happened, young lady, nothing at all."

Francisco Durán
LETTING PEOPLE KNOW WAS URGENT
There were no telephones. People from the provinces feared for their relatives in the capital city. In the city, many wanted to say they were

well; others would never say anything anymore. The radio started transmitting messages to relatives:

"The López family informs Sr. Heriberto López in the city of Puebla that they are well."

"Aurora and Amparo Zúñiga want to let their parents in the city of Jalapa know that they are well."

One after another the messages came through. The telephones of the local radio stations were constantly busy.

"Tell my mother we are well."

"In what city, Miss?" they would ask on the radio.

"Tell her we are well, please, not to get scared, that we are well."

"In what city, Miss? In what city?"

"That we are well, for God's sake, that we are well."

Anguish prevented people from speaking. People did not reason; they wanted to say that they were alive.

"Sir, my father hasn't been found, his name is Eduardo Rodríguez, he has not arrived at the place where he works. I think that place no longer exists, in Azcapotzalco. Ask if anyone has seen him."

The crisis of the citizenry poured into the only means of communication that was accessible: radio. There was no other voice. For two hours, depending on the area, radio stations transmitted from their emergency plants, giving information on the disaster. We were all listening to the radio, we measured the magnitude of the disaster through the voice of announcers who, moved by the powerful messages, gave us data not yet approved by the government.

With the authority of radio voices the first rescue brigades were organized; through those voices the full extent of what had happened was revealed to us. The history of the calamity was being woven. Radio stations were engaged in social work. Sra. Elsa Jaramillo announced by radio that she was able to transmit messages to people in Veracruz. Her telephone numbers: 523–8333 and 687–2966.

José Luis Armida, twenty-two years of age, rescued from a building that collapsed on Querétaro Street, wanted to let his brother in Veracruz know that he was at the Red Cross. The brother had no phone. He lived in the Ruiz Cortines Housing Unit, at the corner of Bugambilia and Pensamiento streets, number 216. Sra. Jaramillo transmitted the message; three days later José Luis's brother arrived at the Red Cross to see him.

Unfortunately, José Luis Armida died a week later, as a consequence of respiratory failure. But at least he didn't die alone, he was not another unidentified cadaver. Even in death company is good.

There were hundreds and hundreds of radio messages. Hernán Figueroa, rescued from a building on Monterrey Street, had serious injuries: a dislocated shoulder, a collapsed lung. He was taken to the Rubén Leñero Hospital, bed number 2504; but his parents in Villahermosa, Tabasco, needed to be notified. A driver traveling between Puebla and Veracruz heard the message. He stopped to write down the number and as soon as he got to Veracruz he called Villahermosa. He informed the family. A day later the Figueroas had joined their son at the Rubén Leñero.

Radio Universidad started giving information after 7:30 on the day of the earthquake. Manuel Alvarez of the programming department said he had not kept a tally of the calls they received and transmitted, but they were in the thousands. Radio Universidad, like other stations, had to rely on its emergency plant. Two hours later, they were able to broadcast with normal strength in spite of the blackouts. Three weeks later, Radio UNAM was still giving information on the needs of the rescue brigades and shelters, and on the social consequences of the cataclysm, as well as transmitting more personal messages.

Radio Fórmula was one of the stations where the earthquake claimed some victims. While the program "Robes, Pajamas, and Slippers" was being broadcast, Sergio Rod, Marcelino Bravo, Gustavo Armando Calderón, Francisco Garamendi, Francisco Margarito, Alejandro Sánchez, and Miguel Morales perished.

The Radio Mil Network provided the services of more than fifteen reporters who transmitted vivid and as yet unofficial information from the damaged areas. They made others feel the catastrophe under the impact of the moment; many, choked up and with trembling voices, described the bodies, the rescue work, and the attitude of a people who threw themselves into the operation without regard for their own lives.

Radio Mil also transmitted messages to relatives in the provinces during these calamitous days.

Radio Barrilito, the Charrita del Cuadrante—the Country Girl of the Dial—and Radio A-I fulfilled an invaluable social function: they informed, they served, they were an authentic link to connect people; their messages brought peace to listeners.

Radio Educación, at the initiative of its own workers, organized the Broadcasting Brigade, sending messages in English, French, Italian, and

German, retransmitted later by ham radio operators. This station became the center for the collection of medicine. The work that Radio Educación carried out came from its profound social conscience, which naturally flourished as the crisis broke out.

More than thirty AM and FM stations in the capital city linked up with radio stations in the provinces and foreign countries through short wave, giving information on the most urgent needs for the victims and reciting the names of people who had not been found.

Car and transistor radios became the most efficient means of communication, acquiring a true social dimension. In spite of the collapse of Radio Fórmula and the toppling of FM Globo's antenna during the second earthquake, their microphones were open for public service, and anonymous but helpful voices collaborated in broadcasting in all possible frequencies, including FM.

XE–1–RCR (Ratón con Ruedas, or Mouse on Wheels), from its base in Mixcoac, never missed a beat. Sra. Mónica Miguel needed to tell her mother, in Nayarit, that she and her sister were all right. All attempts of Ratón con Ruedas to communicate with Nayarit were in vain; finally the station contacted an amateur radio operator in Sonora: "Pass on this message to Sra. Miguel. There are no phones open in Mexico." Emma Ortega informed Silvia Sandoval, from Alfonso in Maracay, State of Aragua, in Venezuela, that everyone was alive.

Sigfrid Lind told his parents in Germany that he was doing well. Eftalía Chopa received messages from aficionados; from as far as Greece and Australia they wanted to know.

The activity of amateur radio operators, a hobby until then, acquired a definite importance. Everyone felt a fraternal duty in the task of relaying vital information.

After the transmitting tower of Televisa Chapultepec tumbled over, radio took its place until the electric power plants could be reorganized and broadcasting signals were restored.

Ernesto Villanueva, copy chief of the "Hoy Mismo" newscast, died as he carried out his duties. After September 19, the hope that Félix Sordo would become another Paco Malgesto was abandoned. What had once been Radiópolis in 1943, founded by Emilio Azcárraga Vidaurreta, came back to life, assuming control of public information.■

"Fucking government, good for nothing."

PLACE OF DISAPPEARANCE, NAME, AGE, AND IDENTIFYING CHARACTERISTICS

Telephone 550–5824 at the Technical Council for Scientific Research rings. Volunteer Claudia Ovando answers. A female voice inquires about a missing person. "What are the two surnames?" Franco Arellano, María de Jesús, age thirty years, place of disappearance, the Attorney General's office. "Your name?" María Concepción Arellano de Franco.

Since September 23, six calls per minute have come to the Institute of Astronomy, the Division of Sciences, the Engineering Department, the General Office for Computing Service, the Research Institute for Applied Mathematics and Systems, the Institute of Physics, and others. Claudia Ovando always repeats the same words: "At the moment we cannot give you any information. We've included your name in the list, and as soon as we have some news we'll reach you by phone." The calls continue, searching for the whereabouts of Peña Peláez Gabriel and Sanabria Hugo Martín, both from Conalep. Claudia Ovando asks for descriptions: "He combed his hair back and had acne"; "He is tall, about five foot three"; "She was pregnant"; "That day she was wearing a white dress with little blue flowers; I remember very clearly." The mother of a Conalep child cannot give her telephone number: "5–82–5 . . ." "We're missing a digit, lady, we're missing a digit."

"Two days before," says Claudia, "I went with a brigade that left from the Medical Center of the CU to the Social Security baseball park to fumigate corpses and live people who were coming in to identify them. The bodies were waiting on the ground in plastic bags, covered with ice. What a terrible thought, the possibility that these bodies corresponded to the names that I was asked about with such anxiety during my hours as a volunteer."

WALLS COVERED WITH THE NAMES OF MISSING PEOPLE AT CHANNEL 11

Not until five days after the tragedy was a data bank of missing people assembled at the UNAM. The information of the first few days was lost. On Friday, on Channel 11, lists and more lists of the names of the missing covered the walls of the assistant director's office like wallpaper.

Diana Sánchez Mújica, coordinator for press and public relations, was totally dedicated to the search for relatives of people who came to the station to inquire with anguish and bafflement. "Where does he work?" "Downtown." "But where?" People were beside themselves. "He was wearing his working clothes, but I don't know where his job was."

In the midst of the confusion, Diana Sánchez Mújica cleared things up and calmed people down. People searched at Locatel, at Channel 13, at Televisa, at Channel 7; they made an atrocious pilgrimage from one shelter in Colonia Morelos to another at Crea in the Villa Olímpica, from the Red Cross to Xoco, walking exhausted in a city drowned by sirens. "Hugo Martín is in Xoco." No, mistaken information.

Only three times in four days could Claudia Ovando and Maurico Derbez say, "He's hospitalized." The two usual responses were "He's reported as missing" and "He's now been reported, we'll put him on the list." Channel 11 served as the connection between thousands of afflicted persons and transformed itself into a service center for society.

"The UNAM has three Burroughs 7800 models, three large computer systems," says Mauricio Derbez. "Various government offices have similar equipment, but the UNAM facilities are the most sophisticated. However, they were not put at the service of the population until five days after the quake, although their contribution would have been indispensable from day one.

"From September 23, some 12,449 calls were reported. If the UNAM had proposed transmitting messages about the circumstances of families in the Federal District via the Morelos satellite to the interior of the republic, television and radio could have avoided repeating for hours, 'The Pérez family advises its relatives in Tabasco that they are well,' and the time and projection facilities of Televisa, Imevisión, and Channel 11 would have served to link together the offers of aid and priority needs."

What fed the computer? In a partial and disorganized way, it was learned in which hospital or shelter the victims were located. The telephone made demands, but the Burroughs computer did not have answers. The volunteers on duty felt desperate because they could give no answer. Volunteers skipped lunch so as not to miss any calls, but the disorganization of the operation broke the enthusiasm of people.

No direct inventory was ever taken in hospitals, shelters, and disaster zones. Today, Locatel continues informing, but it was never prepared for such a vast volume of data. The number of telephones and telephone lines is sufficient, but the computing system lacked an adequate program. The dimensions of the problem had never been imagined by the creators of the most advanced techniques. It becomes terrifying to think of the failures that cause loss of human life. How much suffering could have been avoided!

Meanwhile, in some subway cars, riders have pinned up ID-size photos: round faces, severe, sometimes smiley, information requested, in case someone has seen, just in case someone knows. The missing person "left home on September 19 and has not come back. Please communicate any information to telephones . . ."

"How many and who were in the wrecked buildings? We will never know." Miguel Angel Granados Chapa.

Ovaciones, September 21
Locatel receives twenty-five calls per minute from people looking for missing relatives. By yesterday, 25,000 calls had been received. Locatel reported that 4,000 injured people had been treated as of yesterday.

Excélsior, September 21
Crea disclosed that there are 20,000 missing persons in its lists, out of which only 2,500 have been located.

The bodies are in the Cuauhtémoc, Venustiano Carranza, Benito Juárez, and Iztacalco delegations. Relatives should proceed there for their identification; in thirty-six hours they will be buried.

Unomásuno, September 23
In coordination with the Ministry of Tourism, information modules have been installed in the city's airport in order to provide addresses, telephone numbers, and a partial listing of foreigners who were in Mexico City at the time of the earthquake.

La Jornada, September 23
Hundreds of unidentified corpses that had been deposited in the Social Security park were sent to a common grave. Relatives are concerned about the "inhumane treatment" of the remains, transported in sanitation trucks to the common grave. They were told that public health dictated these measures.

Ovaciones, September 23
According to the Department of the Federal District's computer, 40,300 phone calls have been received from relatives of living and dead victims, and information was released to 4,150 of them.

Official number of dead in the September 19 earthquake: 6,000.

Number of calls received by the Technical Council for Scientific Research of the UNAM, one of the centers of information on the missing: 12,449.

On the walls of hospitals lists of missing people are displayed with facts provided by relatives.

- Since September 19, we have been looking for René Antonio Loo Almaguer. He is wearing denim pants, white windbreaker, white socks, "Charly" navy blue sneakers. He is eleven years old, five foot six, has brown skin, straight hair. He attended Universidad Chapultepec located at 156 Chihuahua Street, Colonia Roma. This school collapsed as a result of the earthquake. Information: 597–4621 and 392–1978.
- Flor Angélica García Morteo. Twenty-one years of age, five foot one, heavyset, long black wavy hair. Pregnant. On September 18, she gave notice that she was being admitted to the gynecology department. She was about to give birth. It is not known what hospital she was admitted to, and she has not been located as of this moment. Please call 687–7476 and 687–5090 with information.
- Will be grateful for any information on the whereabouts of Dr. González Sierra Francisco José, who was in Hospital Juárez on September 19. He was wearing a white uniform. 557–8087.
- Elisa or Erika Kuntze Navarro, Nuevo León Building, fifth floor. Light-skinned, sixty years old. Five foot four in height. Thin, blond, with long wrinkled face. Missing since Thursday the 19th. A neighbor saw her alive, out of her wits. We fear she might have lost her memory and doesn't know her own name.

"Who goes there?"
"Nobody, it's me."
"I have nothing left."

Fidela Cabrera
THE BUILDING WAS ROCKING WITH A FORCE I CAN'T DESCRIBE
It's a real miracle that there are any survivors, says Pedro Ferriz de Con, because the way things happened, we should all be dead.

It all began at 7:18 in the morning. We felt the typical subtle quake. I was broadcasting a news item about the confirmation of Mario Moya Palencia as Mexico's ambassador to the UN. We continued feeling that oscillatory quake.

The corner of Cuauhtémoc Avenue and Río de la Loza is the area where the muddy underground of Mexico City begins. I thought that the earthquake was going to be of an oscillatory nature all the time and that, as so often happens, it would steadily diminish. I asked the sound engineer in the booth, separated from me by only a glass partition, to interrupt the recording so that we could talk about the earthquake. It is my professional bias to start talking about things instead of running. Then I saw his eyes bulge out of their sockets; he was truly scared. I saw him half seated in the air, about to leap. Margarito, calm down, stay where you are, and let's tell the people what is going on.

"Ladies and Gentlemen: In Mexico City, an oscillatory earthquake is being felt. We are going to get in touch with the Tacubaya Observatory to learn its magnitude." I thought that it would last about a minute and nothing! What minute? It continued oscillating more and more each time. I started feeling a little fear, and I thought of my loved ones: my wife, my children.

The building was rocking with a force I can't describe. I saw through the glass of my booth how the lockers toppled onto the people in front of me—the executive producer of the program and my engineer—then the columns cracked and so did the concrete slabs, and that was when I realized that we were in the midst of a cataclysmic tremor.

I saw the engineer's eyes, his expression of panic. The muscles of his face no longer obeyed him, and he was frozen in an expression of terror. I saw him jumping like a gazelle to the door of his booth, and at that point everything went dark, we lost the floor under our feet, and I fell in the void with tables, chairs, carpets, all the things that to my mind are the symbols of solidity.

Ours was a staggered downfall; I think that from the seventh floor we fell to the fifth. The building consisted of a ground floor and six more stories. Then we tumbled to the first floor on a big slab along with an avalanche of rubble, chunks of concrete, iron rods, phonograph records, glass, wood, noise. Noise, most of all. What I most vividly remember is the noise.

I thought of Alice in Wonderland, when she is falling forever into a tunnel in the midst of the most total darkness. And then, buried under so much stuff, I remembered Joaquín Pardavé. As a child, my father or my mother told me that when they exhumed his remains he was found face down with the silk that lined the coffin all scratched up. Supposedly he had been buried alive. I told myself that precisely that horrible death, the one I had feared the most, had come to be my lot. I prayed to God that I would die quickly so that I wouldn't asphyxiate.

I wasn't terrified, but I felt a profound resignation and sadness about my wife and my young children. I started saying the Our Father, and lying face up without being able to move, I knew that God was there with me and told me, "Now look for the means to survive." It took an enormous effort to remove a piece of concrete from my face, and I realized that over me a window frame was still standing that had prevented the rubble from flattening me. I twisted my face a little bit and looked behind me, where I perceived a small circle of light. I imagined that a little bit of oxygen had to come through the opening, and that I wouldn't suffocate. I tried to spit as hard as I could, and I produced a great snort with all the ground-up concrete that I had in my mouth, in my nose, and in my eyes. I couldn't open them well because everything was all a cloud of dust.

Suddenly I saw Alfonso Chang, whom we call El Chino, the producer of our program "Robes, Pajamas, and Slippers," coming out from under the debris with a bleeding head. He asked: "Pedro, can you walk?"

"I don't think I can because my back is broken."

"You know what? If you don't get up and try to get out, all this is going to fall on us."

I turned my face and saw a very tall, tall wall, with parts of floors still stuck to it and leaning toward us. I could smell the adrenalin secreted by my body. El Chino pulled me, and I felt my body breaking in several chunks, but I got up and leaned on him, and we walked along with a young guy named Ricardo who appeared suddenly out of nowhere.

We climbed a mountain of wreckage. From there the street could be seen. As we were going out we could hear the screams of despair. On Cuauhtémoc Avenue, instead of cars, people circulated, people running from here to there like a disoriented anthill. I saw everything in black and white as if color had vanished in the dust of so many crumbling buildings.

As we climbed over the wreckage, I could hear the muffled cries and lamentations of my compañeros, and I could even make out what they said: "Get me out of here"; "Don't you see I'm down here"; and I couldn't do a thing, as if I were in shock.

They helped me down to the sidewalk, and I remember seeing a fellow reporter named Rosa Haydée Castillo who broke out in tears when she saw me. "I must be in a deplorable state if you cry as you see me." and I asked, "Give me a kiss, Rosa Haydée, so that you'll see that I'm well and that we're all well and we're going to be saved." It was Rosa Haydée's own father, Sr. Castillo, who volunteered to drive my station wagon, the keys of which I still carried in the back pocket of my pants, and he took me to the hospital.

As they were about to start the station wagon where they had carried me, I asked them if they thought I was so selfish as to take a solo ride to the hospital, and I said they should load up with as many as would fit, especially my compañeros of Radio Formula. "No, you go; the others will ride in other vehicles." They said that because they didn't want to say that all of the others were dead.

My father arrived.

"How did you get here so soon?"

"On a motorcycle."

"And how is everyone doing?"

"Very poorly, son. It's a disaster."

I started to ask about my compañeros. About Gustavo Armando Calderón, so dear to me, with whom I used to take the elevator every day, getting off at the fifth floor. There we would meet the skinny guy who did the cleaning: "Good morning." "Hi there, how are you?" They told me that Maestro Gorbachov was dead along with the people of the program "Robes, Pajamas, and Slippers," and that Gustavo Calderón, Senior, was also dead, and I remembered how he would greet me with a hug every day; and Sergio Rod, with whom I was always joking, and he would share a tamale with me in his booth, and in the midst of the tamale and its leaves and our cups of coffee, we would tell jokes to each other. And shivering I dared to ask, "And what about Margarito?" I felt remorseful because I had prevented Margarito my engineer from leaving, perhaps just in time. "He's dead."

It was all a frightful nightmare that I hope we will bank away as a learning experience. We must learn a certain form of behavior that will prevent things from getting out of hand on such an enormous scale. Professor Zeevaert, an expert in structural mechanics, used to say that there is no human-made structure that is guaranteed to withstand a major earthquake; nor is there any structure of human feelings capable of withstanding a disaster like this.■

"I have nobody."
"I am nobody any longer."
"I am no longer myself."
"Here no one has stolen nothing."
The policeman: "I saw him stealing."
"If we never had anything, as dirt poor as you see us, we are not going to take advantage of others now, the other poor people who were left with less than nothing."

SEVENTY-SEVEN DEAD IN TELEVISA

We knew where the body of Félix Sordo was, but it was impossible to recover it, it wasn't until October 1 at 3:45 in the afternoon that we got it out, says Miguel Alemán Velasco, vice president of the consortium and one of the owners of Televisa. Ernesto Villanueva Bustamante ducked under his desk and ended up crushed, not by the slab from the roof, but by the one from below. Probably the side of the elevator shaft stuck in the foundation of the building on the north side and pressed upward. It smashed his chest. One yard further on, where the cadaver of Félix Sordo Medina lay, the slab came tumbling down, and Florencio Martínez Domínguez, Antonio González Alemán, Cérvulo Ramón Casarín, Ernesto Villanueva Bustamante, and Luis Alberto Delgado Anaya all died instantly. We recovered the name tag from Ernesto's body, and we could give his ring, his watch, and other personal things to his widow, but the slab made it impossible for us to see the body of Félix Sordo.

Miguel, an elevator operator, stayed inside the frame of the elevator, the door closed, and the building collapsed in front of him, but nothing happened to him. Nothing. He walked away, just like the two policeman; others, however, had bad luck. They ran, or else they did not move from the spot where they were.

Unfortunately the building fell onto the corner of Río de la Loza and Niños Héroes. The building at Chapultepec 18 fell onto Chapultepec Avenue. Its support pillars were probably loosened during the construction of the subway, because first the whole front part of the building fell over while the part in back was suspended for a moment before falling. The other building that was located in the extension of Río de la Loza,

Pino Suárez Street, where the Radiópolis system functioned, was a rented building. It sandwiched downward, floor upon floor, all eleven stories.

The duration of the seismic movement, and most of all its change in oscillation, caused the plunge. I don't discard the possibility that the buildings were poorly constructed, or that there was poor quality in the materials or outright theft.

A LOSS OF TEN BILLION

The loss has been great. Seventy-seven lives of Televisa employees. Approximately fifteen more people among the newspaper and juice vendors, shoe shiners on the sidewalk at Niños Héroes 27, or messengers who had come to deliver a package or a letter. Their bodies were taken to morgues for relatives to identify. We have not followed the fate of those fifteen bodies. During the first few days, we recovered the bodies of Guillermo Gutiérrez Colmenares, Sotero Mejía Haro, Alejandro Fuentes, Erick R. Yáñez, and Pablo Téllez, who died in the hospital. Félix Sordo was twenty-five; Ernesto Villanueva was sixty-one. Do you want the complete list of the dead? I have it here, but it makes it very sad to enumerate so many deaths.

We compensated each one of our dead. Ten million to Ernesto Villanueva and Félix Sordo—both because of the responsibility that they carried and because of their seniority. Sordo was very young, but he started in XEW—a part of Televisa—and all the others, all kids, technicians with sensational capabilities, have received 4 million pesos and 1 million from the union's insurance, the STIRT. They received 5 million altogether. The old gray-haired shoeshine man, a very pleasant old man, the lady who used to sell newspapers by the door of the Niños Héroes building, and the people from the juice stand and the magazine stand have received economic aid, even those who were not Televisa workers.

Many people died under a door frame; we found them pressed together along with cables and cement slabs.

We lost 18,000 square yards of building and all the newscast equipment, cameras, film, videotapes, sets. What used to be the News Department was wiped out. Half of our video library had been previously duplicated; that part was saved, thanks to our wish to decentralize.

The one thing left standing was the "Paco Malgesto" Studio A, which had to be demolished because it was in danger of collapsing. At the beginning we had to rent equipment, and afterward we petitioned the

Ministries of Commerce and Finance for permission to import equipment. Because the World Cup was coming they made an exception and allowed us to bring in newscasting technology.

For our live programs it is indispensable to have a centrally located site; that's why we will not go south. Teletheaters? Those did not belong to us, we rented them. People thought they belonged to Televisa because of their name, but that wasn't so; we rented them.

The cost of our loss has reached 10 billion pesos, but the insurance will pay only about 2.9 billion, so we need to recover more than 7 billion.

Will we recover with the World Cup? The only thing that Televisa can do is to project the image of the games. It doesn't intervene in their preparation. The whole world thinks that it's our business, but that's far from the reality.

WHO IS IN CHARGE HERE, ANYWAY?

Four hours and forty minutes later we were back on the airwaves, but we had lost our capacity to send filming units out. As soon as we could get hold of a helicopter we filmed the full consequences of the earthquake. Afterward, I went personally to the crumpled buildings; for example, we supported Plácido Domingo at the Nuevo León in Tlatelolco; we helped Yuri, Susana Alexander, and another group of actors who would not give their names; we helped the seamstresses. We formed brigades of actors—Chabelo, Ana Martín.

In Gynecology-Obstetrics at the Hospital General we heard the French and the North Americans ask, "Who is in charge here, anyway?" And they were right; the lack of responsibility and organization in the government caused the brigades to waste a great deal of time. I think that for forty-eight hours this city was an open city. Do you remember the movie *Rome, Open City?* The people could have taken up arms, and they didn't do it. This fact demonstrates clearly the human quality of the Mexican people.

No organization that I know of to date did more than the people themselves. There were volunteers who would work one hour or eighteen with the same good disposition, without eating, without getting paid, without a drink of water; the popular organization was unbelievable. There were children and scouts who directed traffic during those days. But the second tremor caused panic; as organized as people could have been, the situation overpowered us all.

WORSE THAN A WAR

The Israeli rescue workers commented that this was worse than a war. In a war there is more order, there are air-raid shelters, one knows where to run to, where to find a haven, and how long a bombardment will last, more or less. There was nothing like that in Mexico.

In Mexico, a fearful vacuum was all there was. There was no one in authority, until bit by bit the authorities were resurrected. When the President spoke, a certain calm came back, but meanwhile it was the people who occupied that void. When de la Madrid spoke about unity, many people thought he was talking about uniformity, about absence of criticism and obedience to the commands of the authorities. I think that unity is what we expressed immediately after the earthquake when we all helped each other without stopping to think about it.

Miguel Alemán, Jr., mentions the loss of the El Cisne restaurant, but he forgets the people who were inside, the people that *La Prensa* of September 21 talks about: approximately sixty people missing and fifteen recovered bodies.

MORBID CURIOSITY AND YELLOW JOURNALISM

Televisa engaged in yellow journalism involving the missing, as the case of Elia Palacios Cano shows. She suffered the amputation of one arm and a fracture of the jaw, after being stuck for more than sixty hours under the ruins of her apartment with her youngest son, Quique.

In the hospital, Sra. Palacios learned that her husband and her daughter Leslie had died, but the woman in the hospital bed next to hers said that the Televisa news show "Hoy Mismo" had reported, "Sra. Elia Palacios is advised that her daughter Leslie is alive in the Children's Hospital." Elia told Beatriz Graf, "I got all excited, it was something extremely beautiful. I spoke with the doctors of the Red Cross and asked them to consider transferring my baby next to me because I was desperate thinking of her alone all by herself in another hospital. My family also saw the news on television and went out to search for her. Two reporters from Ochoa's program even returned to assure me categorically that the kid was alive.

"My nephew César Piña got in touch with my family: 'Tell Elia that this is all a lie, I retrieved Leslie, I am at the crematorium of the UNAM with the bodies of my uncle and the child. Why is it that people are so heartless?' I lost my daughter for a second time; that caused immense grief, I suffered very much."

César Piña suffered too from this news item. "From the crematorium I called Elia by telephone. I told her that I had the bodies; unfortunately, the reporters made up this horrible lie."

I'LL KEEP ON WALKING IN HOPE OF FINDING MY LITTLE RICARDO

With his black puffy cap with the English word *captain* written across the visor, his arms snug against his chest as if to hold back the emotion, Salomón Reyes begins his tale:

From parking space Z–650 at the corner of the Nuevo León Building, I saw the tremor unleashed, and the first thought I had was of my children, my wife Jose, because I thought she was up there, but she had gone to fetch the milk at Conasupo. I saw as clear as day how the building fell over, but what can you do? Turn into Superman and stop it? My children were waiting for breakfast to go to school: the oldest, Gloria Leticia, seventeen; Miguel Angel, fifteen; Guadalupe Adriana, eleven; Mayito, Mario, whom I found dead in the Cuauhtémoc Delegation, ten; Danny, seven; Ricardo, five; Alma Celia, three. The first thing I thought was, "My children, my children, God of mine!" And the building came down, nothing but a screech, and when it hit the ground as if yanked out from the roots, it raised black smoke, really black smoke that spread all over Reforma. I sprinted like everyone, going to look for their family, their loved ones, their relatives, their acquaintances. Absolutely everyone running this way or that way or let's see where, all doing the same, to see what they'd find.

They'd get someone out here, they had gotten two or three over there; from the fallen walls they were taking them out. I ran, I climbed up, and nothing, that hard stuff, solid, and they underneath, and how are you going to break it. With my hands I broke, I stayed many days digging away, hard, hard, hard; then when they brought instruments, well then with a shovel, or a pickax. My family and I had a room on the rooftop all the way up, in the part of the Nuevo León that fell over, so I thought that they would be on top of the rubble, right? But the building, who knows how, got all twisted like a cruller or a snail shell. After many days, when I saw they didn't turn up, why, I had to look for them. I've been to many places, many hospitals, day-care centers, shelters, and I'll keep on looking.

Some treat you like despots, only because they see who you are; I also understand that people are nervous and hurried, so in the hospitals they give you nasty answers, and you feel something ugly. What with the grief you can hardly stand it. You are ignored, left to talk to yourself, there's nobody here, there are many bad reasons. At number 27 in Tlatelolco they told me, "Look, man, all the folk that were badly beaten up were taken to the First of October Clinic."

I arrive at First of October, and no, they were taken to Lomas Verdes, not really, rather to Hospital Militar; they have you going from here to there like a madman, I feel my head turning on its own, I have no idea what I will have to do, but I walk, I ask questions, I walk from one place to another place and I ask questions.

When I arrived at First of October, they told me that all the children had been evacuated; that they only keep them for three days in the hospitals, and then they send them elsewhere. In some cases the people in charge yell at you all the way from the doorway, "Who? That one? We sent him home." What home? Who has a home anymore?

I walked through so many hospitals, forget it, the ISSSTE, units 17, 24, 18, Rubén Leñero, Xoco, La Raza, Español, Twentieth of November, Bernardino Sahagún, and many more that I no longer remember. Also in Naucalpan, units 76 and 68. I asked a congressman for a letter so that they would let me in, and Sr. Verdugo gave it to me, and with that letter I have been everywhere.

Mario—Mayito—died but, well, what about the others, I don't know where they are, and I live with the uncertainty: are they alive or dead? I went all the way up to the place where you identify all the corpses that they put in the common grave; I went to the Benito Juárez Delegation in front of the Parque de los Venados, and there I just looked through photographs, and no, nothing, nothing, nothing, until I went to the Magdalena Salinas Hospital of the Social Security and there on the second floor, bed 209, I found Néstor Quiñones, a five-year old boy who'd been admitted there and who lived in the same building as my children. He saw me searching, and he asked: "What happened, Sr. Salomón? What are you doing?"

"Looking for the kids."

"Ricardito was here."

"Are you sure, son?"

"Yes," he said. "Look, I'm messed up in my cheek, my hand, and this foot. Ricardito only had scratches on his arms. I'm really sure that he was here."

HE DOESN'T SHOW UP ON ANY OF THE LISTS ANYWHERE

Then I summoned up some strength, and I requested a list of all names, but no, he's not anyplace, he doesn't show up on any of the lists anywhere; he is not on the long typed lists of people who were transferred from one place to another, or among the ones who were taken to the rehab centers after hospitalization.

The lady leafed through a pile of papers searching for my boy, and I said, "Hand them over," and I kept on looking through the lists, just in case they might have messed up the order among the mountains of names, because it happens that they misplace things; on the radio you hear a stream of names, and you go there with a great hope and then it turns out that, no, it was all a mistake.

I have walked from San Pablo La Merced to Emergency Number 68 in la Villa; my shoes are gone, and I no longer feel my feet, they are so swollen. I have cut through streets and more streets, I have flattened their sidewalks with my steps and I don't care about eating or sleeping, I don't care about nothing, I will keep on walking in hope of finding my little Ricardo, because that is the hope that I hold on to, I'll see what God wills, I resign myself to seeing one of them, my God, only one of them, Ricardito. I have gone back to look for Néstor Quiñones in bed 209, but they say that he's not there, maybe because they only keep them for a while, and they let them go, no matter how they feel, only half recovered, they kick them out because they need the bed.

Well, wouldn't you know, my wife got very sick; twice she tried to kill herself. Didn't she go and try to hang herself in the bathroom? And then she jumped into the pool of the Morelos sports club where we were sheltered. That night I found her strapped to the bed; they had to tie her up, and the people in charge told me that I had to talk to her, that they couldn't keep her there that way, that I needed to see what I could do. Her nerves were all screwed up, she trembled, she shook from head to toe; of course it is very difficult to take all this, very, very tough. Her name is Josefina Salgado Sánchez, but I am cross with her, disappointed because she's not helping out. I realize that she's in a bad way, but I am too, and she's only thinking of herself, of her own sorrows. She is bereaved, and what if I also crack up. Think about it: no children, no home, no job.

In addition to being a watchman, I made a little money washing cars and waxing them; I took care of 104 automobiles, and I had all my children, all of them in school, and they were doing well in all their subjects. We had their diplomas on the wall, but it all came down. I don't even have a photo, nor the papers of high school number 9 of the university, nor those of junior high school 106, not even a certificate from any of the schools.

I have seen others finding a picture among the ashes, a report card, but I don't have even that, not a souvenir, nothing. I would be washing cars and telling them, go on, kids, for as long as I can I'll keep you in school. And I was pleased because they would come and say, "Look Dad, here are my grades, here are my grades, Dad, look at this, Dad, here's my notebook." Jeez, it was nice, it was nice. "Look at what the teacher wrote here." But look at it all now, look at what's become of me. From having a big family of seven children to having not a one, and all of them in school, every one of them was being educated.

And now what? What awaits me? Nothing.

> Hour: 7:19 A.M.
> Day: Thursday, September 19, 1985
> Magnitude: 8.1 degrees on the Richter scale; 8 degrees on the Mercalli scale
> Energy: The equivalent of 1,114 atomic bombs of 20 kilotons each.

TO EACH HIS OWN EARTHQUAKE
September 20
Excélsior
Mercalli 8 degrees, Richter 7.8 degrees.

The worst tremor of the century. There were nineteen secondary quakes between 7:20 A.M. and 4 P.M. The epicenter is located 50 kilometers away from the shore of Michoacán.

The earthquake registered 8 degrees on the Mercalli scale.

Dr. Ismael Herrera, director of geophysics of the UNAM, explained that because the sensitivity of seismological instruments is very fine and the readings are highly precise, much more than people's own sensitivity, it is impossible to determine the exact duration of the earthquake, generally considered to have been oscillatory in nature.

La Jornada

Mercalli 8 degrees, Richter 7.3 degrees.

The telluric movement registered 7.3 degrees on the Richter scale and 8 on the Mercalli scale. It was an oscillatory quake, considered a cataclysm because of its magnitude. Its epicenter was located 50 kilometers off the coast around the mouth of the Balsas River, between the states of Guerrero and Michoacán. The oscillatory movement was perceived over an area of 800 square kilometers.

In Paris, TV transmissions were interrupted to report about the 7.3-Richter-scale quake.

Novedades

Mercalli 8 degrees, Richter 7.8 degrees.

The most intense, long, and lethal in history. It reached 7.8 degrees in the Richter scale, the equivalent of 8 on the Mercalli scale, which measures telluric movements on the planet's crust.

It quaked for 3 minutes and 2 seconds starting at 7:19 A.M.

Ovaciones

The worst earthquake in memory. The virtual cataclysm had its epicenter at 350 kilometers off the coasts of Guerrero and Michoacán, according to the seismological service in Tacubaya. It lasted for 7 minutes and reached an intensity of 8 degrees on the Mercalli scale.

La Prensa

7.5 degrees on the Richter scale. Epicenter located in Guerrero and Michoacán.

The seismological instruments of Tacubaya indicated a duration of 1.30 minutes.

Dr. Herrera and physicist Zenón Jiménez explained that after the earthquake more than ten tremors of lesser intensity were registered by the Tacubaya seismographs.

A seismological expert declared that the earthquake registered in Mexico was the equivalent of an 8-megaton bomb.

El Heraldo

Duration, 2 minutes.

El Día

The epicenter of the seismic movement was located at 7.6° N latitude and 102.5° W longitude, off the coasts of Guerrero and Michoacán. The cataclysms originated in the seabed 50 kilometers from shore, and their range of influence covered 800,000 square kilometers. It affected the states of Jalisco, Michoacán, Guerrero, México, Puebla, Veracruz, Oaxaca, and Chiapas, plus the Federal District. The region that was affected the most by the earthquake was the area of highest population density in the republic, Mexico City.

Unomásuno

Since the earthquake of September 19, there have been thirty-eight seismic movements; their intensity has ranged from 3.5 to 5.5 degrees on the Richter scale according to the National Seismological Service (SSN).

Ecological groups and professionals in the fields of engineering and architecture attribute the brutal effects of the earthquake to the overexploitation of the aquifer under the city. Forty years ago, Nabor Carrillo, an engineer in soil mechanics, raised a voice of alarm over the sinking of the subsoil, but the city government not only continued extracting water, but in addition, wells that had been capped were reopened, as well as new ones put into use.

The intensity of the quake reached 8 degrees on the Mercalli scale and 7.8 on the Richter scale, after 7:19 A.M.

The tremor was trepidatory in nature and reverberated in Mexico City as an oscillatory movement. The needles of the seismograph in the National Seismological Service of the UNAM stopped at 7:19. Data on the earthquake could only be obtained from stations located far from the Pacific coast, given the loss of power in the Federal District.

The first information of the SSN captured by the stations and experimental networks supported by the Institutes of Engineering and Geophysics was turned in at 8:30 A.M. Later, there were some corrections. The quake's epicenter was located at 7.6° N latitude and 102.5° W longitude, off the coasts of Guerrero and Michoacán. It originated 50 kilometers from shore, and its region of influence covered 800,000 square kilometers, affecting the states of Jalisco, Michoacán, Guerrero, Puebla, Veracruz, Oaxaca, and Chiapas.

Mexico City is situated on the Ring of Fire that surrounds the Pacific Ocean, a seismic zone extending from Australia, Japan (the most intensely seismic area), Alaska, and the west of the United States all the way to Central America and the southwestern coast of South America.

According to the SSN, our seismic history began to be recorded around 1400; later religious figures like Sahagún and Clavijero made reference to telluric movements.

Antonio Lazcano

"February 20. The day has been memorable in the annals of Valdivia," Charles Darwin wrote in his diary, "for the most severe earthquake experienced by the oldest inhabitants. I happened to be on shore, and was lying down in the wood to rest myself. It came on suddenly, and lasted two minutes; but the time appeared much longer. The rocking of the ground was most sensible. . . . There was no difficulty in standing upright, but the motion made me almost giddy. It was something like the movement of a vessel in a little cross ripple, or still more like that felt by a person skating over thin ice, which bends under the weight of his body.

"A bad earthquake at once destroys the oldest associations: the world, the very emblem of all that is solid, has moved beneath our feet like a crust over a fluid."

Darwin was not mistaken. Contrary to other bodies of the solar system such as the moon, Mercury, and Mars, whose small size allowed them to cool off rapidly and acquire a crust of considerable thickness in a few million years, the surface of our planet is formed by a dozen large plates that float as an enormous fragmented skin on the terrestrial mantle.

Pushed by the heat that escapes from the interior of the earth, these plates, on which both the land as we know it and the ocean bed rest, have been displacing for millions of years, forming and breaking continents, opening and closing seas, and altering the face of the planet constantly. Without these movements, which we know as plate tectonics, some 100 million years would be enough to smooth the surface of the earth, to make it flat without either mountains or valleys, covered in good measure by shallow seas barely stirred by wind.

Rain, the sun's heat, the flow of rivers, and biological activity all tend to level off mountains and fill up the valleys, flattening the terrain, but the constant displacement of plates generates new ranges, ignites volcanoes, and builds islands up from the bottom of the sea in a process of geological recycling of enormous proportions, renewing the ocean crust every 200 million years.

The topography of our planet changes and is enriched constantly because of plate tectonics. These modifications in the configuration of continents and oceans have in turn altered the marine currents and climate, also changing the distribution of nutrients and generating environmental conditions that have accounted for the disappearance of innumerable species and the appearance of many others.

Earthquakes have always accompanied the displacement of these great plates. The earth quaked before humans populated it, and it will continue quaking for many millions of years after our species has been extinguished. We cannot avoid tremors. Except for very few exceptions, as happened in China in 1975, we cannot predict earthquakes with a margin of days or even months.■

Helga Herrera

"I don't believe that the dimensions or length of this kind of earthquake could have surprised a seismologist," says Doctor Cinna Lomnitz. In fact, it was known that a segment of the cracking of the plate that started breaking away in the year 1911 still had to separate. The rupture in effect took place in a region and after a lapse of time that had been foreseen; it was calculated that it would happen between 1985 and 1991. On the 19th, it didn't break off completely; a small segment remained attached (off Zihuatanejo and Petatlán) which tore away 36 hours later. This earthquake is one of the best measured in the history of seismology because of instruments to register acceleration that were set up in the State of Michoacán in 1984.

We know that the great tremors on the coast always provoke disasters in the Federal District. In other cities located in regions of high seismic movements, such as Los Angeles or Tokyo, epicenters are located not far away and thus produce movements that are long and slow.

In the case of the Federal District, the location of the epicenter on the coast has disastrous results. We knew that, but what we didn't know was just how disastrous it could be.

What was new about this earthquake was its high energy content. The question is still in the air. What went wrong? Of course, no building should have failed. Lack of respect for the construction regulations became lethal.■

They were two buildings, nine stories each; you see the illusions of the middle class crumbling down.

The earthquake of 1957 was a revelation for the engineering profession, says Felipe Ochoa, who holds a doctorate in planning and systems. It caused the Engineering Institute of the UNAM to open a new field of research on urban emergencies. Esteva Maraboto and Emilio Rosenblueth incorporated seismic technology into Construction Regulations of the Federal District in 1976. This field of investigation has been recognized internationally.

All construction rules must take into account seismic degrees. When the natural phenomenon of an earthquake presents itself, it affects the totality of the urban complex; the infrastructure (potable water, sewage, traffic network, electricity) is highly vulnerable.

In 1977, under the influence of many groups that were aware of the danger that our city faces, a program for urban emergencies was created. The SAHOP was in charge of administering it. But on the 19th, we faced an utterly different phenomenon . . .

Robert Burns declared in 1973 that the cause of seismic movements on the Pacific Coast from Central America to Chile is the displacement of volcanic magma that emerges from the interior of a widespread submarine range. The magma rises from a depth of 180–250 miles, and the pressure of the widening of the mountain range produces fractures, followed by the terrestrial movement.

Burns heads a team of scientists aboard the ship *Oceanographer* that studies the movements of the terrestrial crust. Although in 1970 a group of U.S. scientists asserted that tremors could be predicted a few hours before the fact, until now only the Chinese have managed to do so with precision, foretelling the earthquake that destroyed the city of Haichen in February 1975. They evacuated a million persons, avoiding a great catastrophe.

DAMN, ALL THAT DIRT ONCE AGAIN

In the Fourth Delegation located at Chimalpopoca 100, Colonia Obrera, the official of the Ministerio Público demanded various sums of money from the bereaved relatives of the victims in order to "speed up the release of corpses." Before the very eyes of the zone head of the Cuauhtémoc Delegation, whom we knew only as "Zorro 1," members of the Ministry of Protection and Traffic Safety devoted themselves to looting the apartments that remained standing in the Nuevo León Building of Tlatelolco, according to *La Prensa*.

The "overly helpful" policemen appeared to be recovering "cadavers" wrapped in sheets, but in their immorality they were taking to their patrol cars clothes, appliances, and other objects stolen from the apartments. Bank police did the same, and they were discovered by neighbors. First Commander L. Hernández was responsible for the disappearance of a jewel case that his men had put away in one of the cars.

Norma Ramos, a reporter for *La Prensa,* was threatened, detained, and finally expelled from the area.

Some were charging fees for allowing relatives into the dangerous cordoned-off zones. At the intersection of Mosqueta and Guerrero streets, policemen in patrol car number 15114 and patrol wagon 19901 only allowed entry to those who "identified" themselves with a bill. Raúl Hernández, a photographer, was beaten up when he attempted to take pictures of these officers.

"No, come on, it's nothing."

I HAVE LOST MY SISTER, MY DAUGHTER, MY THREE GRANDCHILDREN

Each day we are impressed more by the fortitude, I should say the greatness, of our women. Rosario, Chonita, Doña Lupe, Cata, Romelia Navarro of Dimensión Weld, Elena Rosales who, protected only by her red sweater, faces the boss Elías Serur—"No, Sr. Elías"—Evangelina Corona of Jeans S.A., Margarita Flores, Luz Suárez, the workers who wait on San Antonio Abad Avenue and remain in the middle of the street in this battlefield that San Antonio Abad has become, covered with heavy machinery, tents, desks under an awning where the rhythm of a typewriter is heard, cars parked at a prudent distance, on the corners of José T. Cuéllar and Manuel José Othón streets, six hundred seamstresses who lie under rubble, compañeras who wait for them, literally out on the street, in spite of their twenty, seventeen, or twelve years senority. There are no bosses here, only this affected population.

From the top of the building at Tehuantepec 12, Antonio Lazcano saw "the broads" install a kitchen. They arrived in a van and took out their big aprons, the type that you have to put your head through, their shopping bags, their pots and pans. "They brought these superpots with delicious cooked pork rind, and the rice that smelled wonderful. Here's dinner, they would shout proudly, dark, big, wide as the women Zúñiga paints. Because of them, we in the rescue brigades ate."

No one had to tell them what they had to do. They called their own shots and decided to feed victims and volunteers, and not only that, they had a bucket with water and soap so that rescue workers could wash their hands: "Scrub them good!" Afterward, they installed their kitchen a few steps away and tended shop for days and days.

In an improvised tent, across from Topeka, Consuelo Romo Campos, a burly woman, strong, fat, dark, with the portly carriage of a Tehuana, with arms that were so generous and gallant that one would expect her to be able to hold all by herself the building at San Antonio Abad 150, tells the story of how she came from Mazatlán in a monotonous, muffled voice:

I HAVE PUT SO MUCH LOVE IN THIS, EVERYONE LOVES ME BY NOW

When I first saw in the news that the Nuevo León Building had collapsed, I came as best I could because I didn't have no money for nothing. When I saw that side C of the Nuevo León Building in Tlatelolco had fallen in—where my sister lived and my daughter and three grandchildren were visiting—I felt real despair. I went through an entire week without wanting to eat or sleep, clinging to a tree, waiting for my family to be unearthed. I have a witness here.

I took a look around me and saw other desperate mothers. Then, instead of eating my heart out, I said to myself, "Shouldn't I try to be helpful?" And I started taking water to the soldiers, to the workers, and to the relatives who were waiting just like me. Later they asked me to distribute food. I am strong. I still had hope, just like anyone, of finding my family; I still had the dream that they would find them all alive in a little hollow.

I would be giving out water and feeling hope, but the days passed, and no, it would no longer be possible, not anymore. I lost a sister whose name was Estela Romo, I lost my daughter and three grandchildren, my own, I lost my only family, all I had, the only thing I had, I had them, I have nothing and nobody else. I was left completely alone. I wept alone. But I said, "I have to help, I am not the only one, I must try, and I kept giving out water, crying, but, taking water around!" Somebody had to do it, right? And then the food, to give it out too.

They noticed me, and Sr. Plácido, in charge of rescue operations in Tlatelolco, named me volunteer coordinator, and he even gave me an

ID that says "coordinator," I have it folded up in the pocket of my other apron, together with the letters they have written me. I have put so much love in this, all I have inside me to be able to help. I knew what people were feeling, I felt it in my own flesh, because it was happening to me; they were as torn apart as I was. So I gave more and more of my love as a volunteer; I lost myself in volunteerism, I came and went, I did, I carried, I took, I distributed, I prepared food, I heated up water, I served coffee, I opened sodas, I did it all. I swept, I cleaned up, I took out rubble. I carried masonry.

THEY CALL ME MAMA, THEY CALL ME AUNTIE

My family was never found, they only found my little granddaughter in the very last days; she was the one that was found, the littlest of the three. (Her voice breaks.) Well . . . the way it is, I have put so much love in this, everyone loves me by now, some call me the star volunteer, they call me pretty things, they call me boss, they call me mama, they call me auntie. I have even received anonymous letters—go get them, sweetheart, they're over there, yeah, right there—they're anonymous, I'll read you one, how about this one?

"Señora Chelo, thanks for all that you have been doing for our brothers and sisters in this disgrace, I wish there were many people like you, I know how you are feeling, very sad now, but God is great and God will reward you. My family and I were not affected, thank God, I feel a great pain and grief in my heart, but—you know?—I have a husband with a bigger heart than mine with the courage to overcome our problems and help out in whatever is needed without expecting anything in return."

"Chelito," says this other letter, "I offer you my sisterly hand, you're not alone, you have countless friends and brothers and sisters. Your sister, Marta."

And how about this one, to make me laugh? One of the volunteers gave it to me. It says, "This card is for you; if you throw it away, that means you love me; if you tear it up, you adore me; if you save it, you really mean to marry me; if you give it to someone, that means that you like me; if you give it back to me, you are asking for a kiss; if you fold it up, you're deeply in love with me. Hey, honey, how will you get out of this one?" He's a young kid who was trying to cheer me up, the sweetie.

The noise of the machines, the voices of the people coming in and out of the tent, sometimes drown the voice of Consuelo Romo. Outside on the sidewalk, a line of coffins await the corpses of the seamstresses (six hundred under the wreckage); the relatives lean against the wall. It's only five days before the 19th of October, and each day the recovery of corpses becomes more painful, as they are mostly ravaged, if not decomposed.

Since there is no longer the expectation of finding anyone alive, the job is slow and the air is unbreathable. Doña Consuelo is in charge of taking the volunteers to the top of the heap:

"I show them, I speak to them lovingly, I tell them what it means to be a volunteer, and why if they find a corpse, they mustn't touch it. If they are thirsty, I offer water, and if they are hungry, I give them a big roll sandwich. They have to wash their hands very well. If they get nauseated, they take a rest in the tent so that they won't get sick. The ones who are waiting in crews of six and eight, and even up to ten and twelve, have to be patient. We get a group in to work and after six or seven hours, I see that they are tired, so I tell them to come down, and then I take the other group up. That's how they get coordinated.

I'M WITH YOU UNTIL THE BITTER END

Sr. Plácido liked the way I treated my volunteers, so he promoted me to chief of volunteers. I'm nothing but a housewife, a fat lady—they even draw cartoons of me—that's me. When the work in Tlatelolco was over, I said to Sr. Plácido, "I'm with you until the bitter end." I could do no other; I had to keep on going.

Go back to Mazatlán? If I go home, the memories . . . I'll sit and wait until my family comes back, and when they don't, I won't know how to take it. I have nowhere to go, this tent is my home, my new relatives are here. From all these people I have received lots of love, from Don Plácido and everyone else in Tlatelolco: they have helped me in my grief, they tried to save my family. They are witnesses to my catastrophe, that's why I cannot go back to Mazatlán.

"Chinito," Doña Consuelo orders, "let the señoras with the pots come in. Go with them please." Doña Consuelo extends a hand. She has nothing to lose and extends a hand, she has lost it all and opens her hand. In the most complete selflessness, the uprooted extend a hand to each other. They protect each other. They don't intend for history to remember them. They don't pretend to be heroes. They live their grief, it consumes them, and together they support each other. Leaning on one another, none of them chooses to be in the shelter. "No matter, Doña Chelo is very good at pitching tents."

In the middle of San Antonio Abad, arms akimbo, Doña Consuelo gives instructions: "Put the plastic this-a-way, the roof that-a-way, tie it with rope good and tight like this, nice and taut, make it sturdy, pull down the rope like you mean it! These tents are guaranteed against downpours."

Doña Consuelo calls a brigade worker who is dragging her shovel: "Come wash your hands and have your sandwich. Take off the helmet, cool off, kiddo."

Like the meaning of her name, her voice alone is enormous consolation, as is the chipped enamel basin where brigade workers wash their hands. While the clean hands of clean men are being washed, Doña Consuelo stands in front of them with a would-be towel, and she says, for the first time showing infinite fatigue, "Go ahead, son, back to work."

"Nothing, nothing, I ask for nothing."

We're all part of a great response of compatriots. I think that there was practically no one who didn't do something.

> Diego, I am alone.
>   Frida Kahlo in her diary, 1955.
> Diego, I am no longer alone.
>   Frida Kahlo, three days later.

> World, I am alone.
>   Mexico, September 19, 1985.
> World, I am no longer alone.
>   Mexico, September 21, 1985.

The NBC, CBS, and ABC networks gave news of the death of the Federal District. Earth had swallowed it. "A hellish panting that wiped it all out," said George Natanson, of CBS. The newscasts in Europe said that the Latin American Tower had toppled over. "The worst tragedy in five hundred years of Mexican history," said the Latin American newsreels. In Havana, in the Press Forum on the Regional External Debt, Fidel Castro informed the assembly, "It is not a national disaster;

it is a world disaster." He donated $2 million and offered all possible Cuban aid. The Nicaraguans sent a plane with blood plasma.

Barricada, a Nicaraguan newspaper, noted that nobody could forget that Mexico was one of the first countries to respond with aid during the 1972 Nicaraguan earthquake and the first to break diplomatic relations with Somoza, as well as an active participant in the Contadora Group, bent on avoiding war in Central America.

Practically all countries made their presence felt. A brigade of young rescue workers in a shabby car came from El Salvador. In Chiapas, Guatemalan refugees collected 300,000 pesos. Aid began to flow in from Colombia, Argentina, and the Dominican Republic.

In the United States, entire cities stood on their heads to provide emergency aid: Los Angeles, San Diego, San Antonio, Houston. The one plane that made the most trips between San Antonio and Mexico was a Boeing 707 called *Queen of the World.* On boxes, anonymous hands had written, "Mexico, we love you"; "Mexico, we are with you." Argentine President Raúl Alfonsín sent the $15,000 he had received from Spain as part of the Prince of Asturias award.

Canada, the United States, and several European countries sent experts and emergency rescue equipment. Thirteen foreign brigades participated in rescue work using highly sophisticated tools and bloodhounds: Algeria, Belgium, Belize, Canada, the Federal Republic of Germany, France, Holland, Israel, Italy, Spain, Sweden, Switzerland, and the United States all sent specialists in seismic phenomena. On September 21, the Swiss and their dogs initiated the search for survivors in Conalep, the Regis, and the Romano.

Amazingly, de la Madrid had declared, "We are self-sufficient." We read with astonishment, "Mexico rejects foreign aid." Two days later, the second earthquake overwhelmed us. Meanwhile, at the Benito Juárez Airport, airplanes with provisions were stopped; the authorities couldn't escape their autism.

The *Washington Post* wrote on September 22, "As the pictures and stories flow in conveying the horror of the earthquake in Mexico, a kind of earthquake of feeling for Mexico is being registered in the United States. The Mexicans are proud, and they do not come running for other people's help when disaster strikes, and if they did, they might not come running immediately to the United States. If they did, however, they would find a large reservoir of compassion for a friend and neighbor in distress."

Workers in the socialist countries offered a day of salary. The Polish Football Commission donated the earnings from the game between Poland and Italy on September 23. The Soviet Union donated $6 million. The UN made $2 million available to Mexico for the most urgent tasks, and Mohamed Essaafi, coordinator of UN disaster aid, came representing Secretary General Pérez de Cuéllar. (President de la Madrid had canceled his visit to the UN scheduled for September 24–26.)

The pope sent half a million dollars to the homeless, and on September 22, in the Sports Palace of Geneva, he lamented not being in Mexico:

"I should not be here, I should rather be with the Mexicans who suffer in the sanctuary of Our Lady of Guadalupe."

International solidarity toward Mexico is evident: an air bridge has been kept up for three consecutive days with the help of fourteen nations. The president of the International Red Cross says that what Mexico needs now is money, because it has received lots of clothing, food, medications, et cetera.

A list of the official planes: eleven from the United States, two from the USSR, two from France, two from Argentina, one from Guatemala, one from the Dominican Republic, four from Algeria, one from Switzerland, one from Colombia, one from Canada, one from Peru, one from Italy, one from Cuba, one from Panama, two from Spain.

According to *La Jornada*, President Reagan spoke by phone with Miguel de la Madrid. Ambassador John Gavin toured the affected areas. Mrs. Reagan is arriving today. John Paul II expressed his support and invited all peoples of the world to stand in solidarity with Mexico.

Airports and Auxiliary Services (ASA) declared that thirty-two airplanes with 1,300 tons of cargo have arrived, and indicated that this aid has been immediately channeled to the areas that require it, in accordance with directives from the Ministry of Government, the Department of the Federal District, the Ministry of National Defense, and the Red Cross.

At the UN, they will try to provide aid over the medium term. In Puerto Rico, a committee for economic aid has been formed. Many organizations and countries have sent money: the German Red Cross donated $130,000, Japan sent $250,000, Austria sent $500,000, Cuba asserts that our foreign debt should not be collected.

The *Washington Post* asserted that government, financial, and corporate institutions should change their attitude toward Mexico.

THE WORLD TUCKS US IN

The director of ASA, Humberto Lugo Gil, reported that from the moment the extent of Mexico City's tragedy was known abroad until now, 1,100 tons of cargo have been received: provisions, medication, hospital equipment, helicopters, and rescue vehicles from thirteen countries. Twenty-eight special flights have been received. Yesterday, two military transport planes, a C-141 and a C-5A of the U.S. Air Force, arrived with three Bell helicopters and four trucks. Also, three armored cars and a 1985 limousine with several security agents from the White House arrived in Mexico City. There was no explanation, but it is evident that the visit of Nancy Reagan, wife of the U.S. president, was being prepared.

Mexico didn't know how much they loved it.

"I have nobody left."

Beatriz Graf

"IT'S AN EARTHQUAKE," I SHOUTED

The day began normally, says Elia Palacios Cano. My husband was the first one to wake up. He had a breakfast appointment at eight. Then I got up and went to our little girl's room.

I took out her uniform and put it on the bed, then went to the kitchen to prepare her fruit. "Let's get a move on, baby, your friend is outside already."

We lived at Bruselas 8 at the corner of Liverpool, apartment 5, second floor. The neighbors at number 3 had already left.

"Yes, Mom, I'm just getting my shoes on."

I was going to rinse a glass and I got dizzy. "It's an earthquake," I said in a loud voice, and then I thought, what do I say this for, and then I saw the light bulb swinging. "It's a quake," I repeated. I called out to my daughter, "It's an earthquake."

"Yes, Mommy," and she came and stood next to me.

My son was still asleep, I picked him up and walked toward the door. My husband Enrique came out of the bathroom and held Leslie by the hand. He tried to open the upper lock, then the lower. He dropped the keys, he picked them up and finally opened the front door.

The door started to swing wildly from one end to the other in such an awful way that I said, "Go out in this? No way. This is going to toss us down the stairway." I turned toward the street: the building in front of me was moving in a way I had never seen anything that big move before. It was slamming into the building next door.

A great crack opened in the wall of our living room. "This is not an earthquake, this is a cataclysm." I thought of my mother, who lives in Colonia Obrera in a very old and dilapidated house. Then I felt that I was falling and I shouted, "Enrique, the girl."

OH, MOMMY, YOU'RE CRUSHING ME, YOU'RE HURTING ME

It happend in a flash. I fell on my left arm and chin because with my right arm I was carrying Quique; I didn't want to fall on him, so I stuck out my chin. When we stopped, he said to me, "Oh, Mommy, you're crushing me, you're hurting me."

"Get out, quick!" I answered, and I got him out from under me.

I tried to get up but I realized that my left arm was trapped. I touched my son; I asked him if anything hurt. "It's so dark," he said.

"Yes, sweetie, it's a blackout. Stay still."

I tried to look for my husband in the dark, and I found his head: "Enrique, talk to me." He didn't answer. I took his pulse, nothing, I tried to move him, nothing. He was dead.

When I realized that I could neither sit nor stand, I remained lying face down. I took in the situation. I had to stay calm and collected. I tried to imagine which roof or wall had fallen, but it was too dark for me to figure that out. I looked for my little girl, calling out, "Leslie, Leslie," and took consolation from the thought that if I could not hear her, she probably had died instantly, without having suffered. I touched my husband. His head was bleeding. I took his pulse again, but no, no, no . . .

I could not be the only one in this situation. I had to be alert in case someone was trying to rescue us. Then I said to myself again, "I must stay calm" so as not to consume the oxygen in the nook where I was trapped.

How did my mother's house fare? At this moment, people would be trying to find out how their relatives were. When my family noticed I wasn't calling on the phone, they would come and look for us and rescue me. I thought, "May it be that way."

After ten or fifteen minutes, I heard a person who was asking for help: "Help me! Help me!" I also started to shout, "Help me! Help me!" It was surely someone who lived in the same building and was trapped, but it was useless. I could not help him, and he could not help me, so I shouted, "Calm down, they'll come to get us out, don't use up your oxygen."

After a while, I heard voices, a man and a woman were asking, "Is someone in there?" I answered that I was there with my son, but they couldn't hear me. With my jaw broken, my voice was not very clear.

We were in a small cranny no more than two yards long; maybe two feet wide and another two high. I was face down, but with my feet I could hold the slab that we had over us. It was a very confining space.

When my nephew César rescued me, he had to stand on top of me trying to free my arm because there was no other room for him to work; that's why I believe it was only two feet wide. I told him I wished we had been lucky enough to be all trapped in the same nook, my husband and my daughter, so we would all be alive, but he answered that four people in that reduced space would surely have suffocated. Later, a great anguish took hold of me: "If I only had held my daughter, too."

It smelled of gas. Maybe the stove pilots had gone out, or maybe the living room wall had fallen, but the kitchen was still standing there, so I asked my little boy to crawl and see if he could get to the kitchen and grab some juice from the refrigerator or a soda or a piece of fruit, I told him to look out the balcony very carefully and to shout to the people that we were still there, but Quique would have none of that, and now I'm very glad—he would never have made it. The odor of gas disappeared after a while, or maybe I just got used to it.

I made an attempt to free my arm. There were some boards near me, and I hit myself hard with one of them, trying to break my arm. I thought, "If I pull it I'll break it, I then can cut it, and then I'll tie it up with my nightgown so I won't bleed to death." I hit myself with the heel of the slipper and with a stone, but nothing happened. I reflected, "If God wanted me to be trapped like this, maybe there's a reason. Maybe if I try to get out on my own, I will really die."

Quique didn't even have a scratch, and I kept saying to myself, "Oh, my God, please let me get out alive, please let me feel well, because if I die my son will stay here alone, trapped, and his death will be awful; I must endure." I remained still next to my son. I felt that there were some towels around my feet. I pulled them a little bit, but I could not reach them. Quique could sit up, so I said to him, "Sweetie, can you feel my legs? Feel around my feet and you'll find some towels."

He gave me the towels. I used one to cover the body of my husband so that my son would not touch it. I placed another one under Quique so that he could lie down. And the other one I tried to put under my own legs, because something was hurting me, something like jagged blocks of concrete. I couldn't manage to do it, so I covered Quique when he said he was cold. I don't think he was, he was just nervous. He didn't ask for food, for water, or for anything, he only asked what had happened, and I told him that it had been an earthquake: "But they are coming to get us out, be still, we'll be here together." And then he fell asleep. He slept a lot.

I SHOUTED, "HERE WE ARE"

Hours later I heard machines nearby, I heard voices, drills. This gave me some serenity, but it also made me afraid that maybe without realizing it, they might knock down the protection that we had. I heard them, but they never listened to me. I shouted, "Here we are, help us." It was one of the things that kept me awake almost constantly, the preoccupation that they could get too close and drill the slab that was our roof. In the darkness, I had no idea whether it was day or night. I imagined it was nighttime whenever I heard less activity above my head. "It must be night. They are not working in the same way."

After a day and a half, I felt very thirsty. My face was terribly inflamed. I was not hungry, but I was thirsty and worried that in the process of trying to rescue us they could hurt us. I also felt a desire to live, to be alive outside that hole. I felt they were closer all the time. I could smell them; I could feel them. I would shout, "Be careful; we are alive but I can't break loose; be very careful please."

I thought that they were going to remove the slab from over us, to take my husband out, to take Leslie and then Quique and me out. When I felt that they were very near, I touched my husband's arm, I touched his hand, and I told him, "Here they're coming for us but you'll be gone." I caressed his face, I embraced him, "We'll be separated physically, but we'll always be together." I said goodbye. That's when the second earthquake came.

I heard the people outside saying, "It's quaking, guys, calm down, don't panic." I put my son face down, covered his face, and raised my feet so as to hold the slab in place. I asked God to spare the little hole that we were in. They no longer tried to find us. I must have fallen asleep, because later on I could not tell whether there had been an earthquake or I had dreamt it. I didn't know whether they had been close or I had just imagined it. I wondered if they were afraid and left. In truth, as I found out later, only my nephew kept on digging.

On Saturday, the day we were rescued, I was losing my mind. I saw my mother and my sisters in perfect condition. They told me not to worry, and that gave me some peace, but I began to hallucinate. I dreamed that they had taken me to my apartment and I told Quique, "You're going to sleep in your own bedroom."

"But which bedroom are you talking about, Mommy?"

"In your bedroom, the television is on."

But he still saw things as they were.

"No, Mama, that's not true," he would say.

I dreamed that I had a lot of money, and I was buying a house with a swimming pool. I even had a servant. Around the swimming pool there were many stones that hurt me: "See here, see these stones here, wax them, polish them, paint them, see what you can do with them because I can't stand them anymore."

I kept asking my little boy what he wanted to eat.

"But there's no food, Mama."

"Yes, my sweetheart, here's the maid and she'll prepare you whatever you want."

"Well, let me have spaghetti with a little cheese and cream."

"Is that all? Go on, sweetheart, you can get up. There is your food on the table, go get it."

"No, Mama, I think you're dreaming because I don't see anything; I better not eat any more. I'm not hungry."

That was one of my hallucinations, and that is why, when Quique came out, the first thing he asked for was spaghetti.

There was a moment when he said, "You know what, Mama? I have a better idea for us to be able to eat. Why don't you go out and look for food." He didn't know that I could not move.

At another time, I saw a light; I felt the presence of a person even if I could not see him. I said, "Please help me, I do not ask for much, just to free my arm; see, I won't report you to anyone; I won't tell anybody that you didn't want to help me." But instead of freeing my arm, he went on drilling, so I turned my child's face down again and raised my feet, and in this position I kept telling this person, "Look, I'm not crazy and I'm not drunk, I'm trapped. If you help me get out I won't tell anyone that instead of rescuing me you let the roof fall on me; I won't tell anyone, but help me. Don't you have a heart? Don't you have sisters? Why don't you take pity on me?"

I realized that I was doing poorly, I was very weak. What was to become of Quique?

"Son, tell me, what is your name?"

"Oh, Mama, my name is Quique, of course."

"Let's see, son, repeat, my name is Enrique Cano Palacios."

"My name is Enrique Cano Palacios."

"I'm three years old."

"I'm three years old."

"My sister's name is Leslie, and she's six."

I drilled him over and over.

"My name is Enrique Cano Palacios. I'm three years old. My sister's name is Leslie. She's six years old. My father's name is . . ."

When he knew it by heart, I felt better.

The first thing that they saw were my feet. Someone said, "Quiet, stop the machines, there are live people here." I recognized the voice in spite of the fact that I was hallucinating only moments before. It was César, my nephew. He said, "Little mother, be calm, we're going to get you out right away, what's your name?"

"It's me, son, your aunt Elia."

His voice changed, he was profoundly moved, and at that point, I became myself again. "Are you okay, Aunt Elia? Do you need air?"

"I'm truly very well, the boy is fine, stay calm, and you'll be able to get us out better."

César kept cutting the rods, sprinkling the broken masonry with water to keep the dust down: "Almost there, we're almost getting you out."

My boy saw his cousin: "You're César, the one who told me he was going to give me some puppies, right? You're going to get me out of here." Only then he started to cry. Through the hole that my nephew had made, my son went out. Then César climbed down and tried to loosen my arm.

I saw my husband's body. Three days had gone by and it was decomposed. It stank and was all black. I thought that it was a puppet, so I asked, "César, are we in a theater?"

"I don't know where we are, but you've got to help me. Relax so that I can pull your arm out."

They lowered some gauze with water. "Don't drink the water, rinse out your mouth, and spit out the blood." Once I stopped spitting out blood, they gave me glucose, and I drank a whole liter. Afterward, I learned that it had taken three hours for César to unpin me.

While we talked I asked him how it had all happened and what day it was. The hollow was too small, he had to lie down on top of me as he worked, and from above they gave him tools. I asked him if I still had fingers, if he thought he would have to cut my arm. He said no, he didn't think so, even if he knew he would have to and didn't have the courage to do it just then.

They laid me on a stretcher, and they pulled it out. "I'm going to cover your face because there's a good deal of dust."

It was raining. They covered me with an umbrella. There were many bystanders, and my family surrounded me. They took me to an ambulance. My little boy had been taken to a first-aid station, and he was perfectly well. They bathed me, they called the doctors, they realized my jaw was broken, they injected me with glucose.

Another doctor came and said to me, "Señora, you are incredibly collected, and I have to be frank with you, your arm is in bad shape. We're going to try to save it. You spent close to sixty hours with your arm being crushed, so we're going to see how much of it can be saved."

"Doctor, how I'd love for you to save my arm, but if you believe that it's beyond help and you can save me by cutting it, then cut it."

They took me to the operating room, and I slept until until 2 A.M. Sunday. I then felt cramps and moved my arm upward until I could see the stump. I'd given it up for lost. When I was trapped I realized that my arm was near the decomposing body of my husband, and for them to cut my arm was simply a lifesaving measure.

Many people, relatives and friends, came to see me at the Red Cross, but I didn't want to see them cry and drain me of my strength.■

THE HOLLOWS WERE LIKE OPENINGS FOR HOPE
I didn't know the building at Bruselas 8. Elia had moved a short while before, says César Piña, and when I saw it, I couldn't believe that had been her apartment building. In the heap of rubble, the hollows were like openings for hope. I saw one and threw myself in. I wanted to hear a little noise: "Elia, are you here? Answer me. Answer me. Is there

anybody here?" All I could hear was noise. "Silence, for God's sake, silence." The first cadaver was that of a man totally covered with mud, the second one was of a very young blond man, with wavy hair. I'd be telling people, "Help me, I can't lift him alone." But nobody would come, they did not want to touch him, his lungs were crushed.

Again I entered the cavity and crawled in with the hope of finding Elia and my family. By this time the crane had arrived, and I went down to talk to the operator.

"The slab has to be raised a little bit higher for me to climb in."

"No, the crane might turn over."

"Listen to me, you bastard, I have relatives down there. If your family were there, you'd do it, wouldn't you?"

He finally looked convinced. When I pointed with a flashlight under the slab, I saw another blond man, and I was hopeful, thinking that it could be my uncle. I got nearer. It was not one body, there were two. They were stiff, naked, embraced, their faces together, their legs entangled. It was necessary to get them out joined together. I would wipe my tears and sweat: "Don't be desperate, hang in there." When I lifted them up, I saw that the girl was also a blond. Outside, people mummured, "See how the earthquake caught them, see this, see that."

They were laughing, the bunch of creeps, laughing instead of helping.

I went into the hole again and lost all sense of time.

They called me from the other side of the building to say that there was a woman there, and that I should come see her. She was lifeless, on her knees. I took out that hardened body and I turned it in.

THIS IS NOT THE RIGHT CORNER

I started to throw whatever I found out to the street. I shouted to the crane operator that he should lift a slab first, and then another slab. I ran like crazy; I demanded that he lift all the rubble. And soon enough I found the walls of the children's room: "Here it is, here it is."

I went in the bedroom, but nothing . . . I found a package of dollars and threw it out. My own family was yelling at me not to throw things out, that they belonged to Elia. But I cleaned out the space perfectly, and I went into the space that I thought was the children's room— nothing. Nothing in the living room either.

I found pictures of the family all scattered, and my heart was breaking. I found clothing and thought for a moment that I had found them. But no, nothing . . . I recognized pieces of furniture and records.

There was a man who is an engineer who was there with me, and he kept asking, "César, and what do we do now?"

"Make more holes so that the crane can come in and lift up slabs."

It must have been four in the afternoon when someone shouted, "Something's moving, something's moving." We saw a foot that was moving.

"Just a moment, please, there are people here, don't make noise."

"Lady, are you all right? Don't worry, I'll take you out, are you all right? What is your name?"

"It's me, son, your aunt Elia."

I shouted, "Sun of a gun! I'll get you out right now. I swear to you, Auntie, I swear that I'll get you out."

She answered, "Calm down, son, calm down. That way you'll be able to get me out better."

I asked one of my cousins to let everyone know that Elia was alive, and that I was trying to save her.

We made a bigger hole, and I went in as soon as I could. Quique recognized me. It surprised me that they were so collected. I threw light on them. I thought I would die. The slab had stopped two feet above them. It smelled terrible, like gas or a dead body. I cursed. This couldn't have happened to them. My uncle's head was next to Elia, and it was black.

Elia asked me to get the child out first. I searched for Leslie, but I couldn't find her. I wet their lips with water and explained to Quique how he was going to come out all scrunched down. He did just as I told him. When we took him out in the afternoon light, we felt that he had been born again, that this child was the most precious thing on earth.

Then I went back to Elia, and I went to work to free her arm trapped by a beam. My uncle was next to her, so I asked her not to turn her face. There was no room for both of us. The arm was far from me. I was sweating, weeping, cursing. The truth of the matter was I could hardly take it anymore.

They sent us an oxygen tank and glucose. Elia drank very slowly through the little hose from the solution, barely wetting her lips. I had no idea that her jaw was fractured, and she certainly didn't say.

It was very difficult to work in that position: "Elia, please forgive me, but I'm going to climb all over you." I pinched her arm with a knife: "Do you feel this?"

"No."

"Do you feel here?"

"No."

I could only see half an arm. All I needed came in through the opening as if it were a variety store. I asked for a screwdriver and they gave
it to me. I worked with chisel and hammer. At one point, the doctor
said, "César, if you wish, I'll go down." He must have realized I was in
rough shape.

GIVE ME STRENGTH, GOD OF MINE

Elia started to speak incoherently. She said that someone had taken her
out of there earlier, that she used to have many servants. We kept working for three hours. People outside were asking what the matter was,
and Elia said, "Please get me out, any way you can, but get me out." I
just didn't have the courage to cut her arm. "Cut it," she repeated, and
I felt terrible.

She was losing her mind. She thought that the body of her husband
was a doll, a puppet that belonged to Frederick Van Malle, the theater
director who lived in the same building, together with "Rockdrigo."

In the midst of her delirium, Elia tried to encourage me: "Calm
down, I'm all right, you're the one who is in bad shape, be calm so that
you can get me out of here."

I asked for baby oil, and in less than two minutes they gave it to me. I
hollowed out the rubble around the arm with a screwdriver, covered
Elia's arm with oil, and pulled with all my might. She turned her face
and the arm came out. But it came out undone: the hand was crushed,
like a pancake, without a drop of blood, like cardboard. She couldn't be
still until she touched it. I dragged her all the way to the opening. She
still asked me who was out there, and I told her that many people were
waiting to see her alive. She had the chutzpah to say to me, "Then cover
me up well; I don't want to give autographs."

NOW WE KNOW WHOM WE CAN COUNT ON

"There were no blueprints for the buildings, let alone for the streets
closed to traffic. Not a single delegate came up with a map of his delegation to facilitate location of the disaster sites. There was never an
announcement of which zone should be covered, or where this and that
rescue brigade was at work. Because of this chaos, because of this lack

of information—which can be understood when it happens during the first three days after the earthquake, but is unforgivable afterward—many people who could have been rescued were buried in the rubble."

That's how several representatives of Emergency International Action (AUI) spoke, those who are trained to converge upon places where a catastrophe has hit. They are extraordinarily capable in facing disasters: cataclysms, hurricanes, floods. These men and women are always in readiness to go where they are needed at the drop of a hat. They have been in Italy, Yugoslavia, Tunisia, Honduras, Guatemala, the Dominican Republic, and Haiti working with the victims.

"Time was wasted. It was a shame."

The hours, days, and weeks after September 19 were marked by a struggle for survival, a need to save lives. Nevertheless, these experts in emergency aid found countless obstacles, a scattering of efforts, lack of organization, and squandering of time, when each minute that goes by can be fatal. In many cases, they ran into open rejection on the part of authorities, who claimed that they could take care of things by themselves. Our leaders' proud ineptitude and fear of foreign intervention were stronger than the lives of thousands of Mexicans whose pulse went on beating in some corner of a wrecked building.

Plan DN-III? What is that?

Secretary for National Defense Juan Arévalo Gardoqui explained that this very plan was launched at the Plaza de la Constitución on September 20 with six generals, 84 high-ranking officers, 257 other officers, 3,500 troops, 25 ambulances, and 600 motorcycles. He said that 600 Dina buses were ready to transport the population. More than 50,000 men had been deployed to the disaster zones: members of the army with automatic weapons made sure that nobody would loot the shops.

Secretary of Government Manuel Bartlet underscores that the administration is in control all over the republic. Aguirre Velásquez exhorts the inhabitants not to go out at night except in cases of emergency, and argues that everything is being looked at, "even if not with the speed we all desire." De la Madrid assures the people that the government has the material and human resources to face this tragedy. Since the 20th he has been broadcasting his assertion, "We are prepared to return to normality."

"Here I am, with nothing and with nobody, my dear lady."

The "gigantic crossword puzzle" of the Mexico City metropolitan area. (Photo: Paul and Mary McKay. Used with permission of the American Friends Service Committee.)

What remained after the earthquake was "like a crumbled cookie." (© Marco Antonio Cruz. Photo in possession of Elena Poniatowska.)

The earthquake area "turned into a bundle of twisted rods, unplugged cables, and mountains of trash." (© Marco Antonio Cruz. Photo in possession of Elena Poniatowska.)

"*Excélsior*: 'Mercalli eight degrees, Richter 7.8 degrees. The worst tremor of the century.'" (Photo: Richard Erstad. Used with permission of the American Friends Service Committee.)

"It sandwiched downward, floor upon floor." (© Marco Antonio Cruz. Photo in possession of Elena Poniatowska.)

"The city lived days of devastation, days of heroism and misery." (© Marco Antonio Cruz. Photo in possession of Elena Poniatowska.)

"The improvised rescuers start an ant-like operation." (© Marco Antonio Cruz. Photo in possession of Elena Poniatowska.)

"The debris and broken concrete are passed from hand to hand in buckets." (© Marco Antonio Cruz. Photo in possession of Elena Poniatowska.)

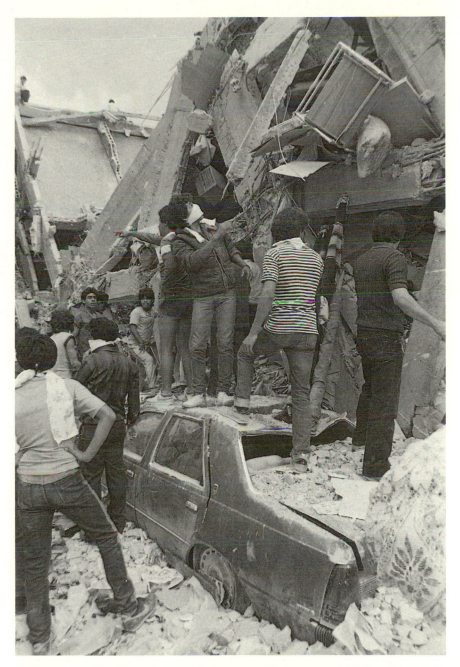

"We started scratching away at the rubble with our paws." (© Marco Antonio Cruz. Photo in possession of Elena Poniatowska.)

"The only thing that existed was an organizing of civil society, small groups, each doing the best they could." (Photo: Richard Erstad. Used with permission of the American Friends Service Committee.)

"In the crumbled buildings some people are still searching for bodies." (© Marco Antonio Cruz. Photo in possession of Elena Poniatowska.)

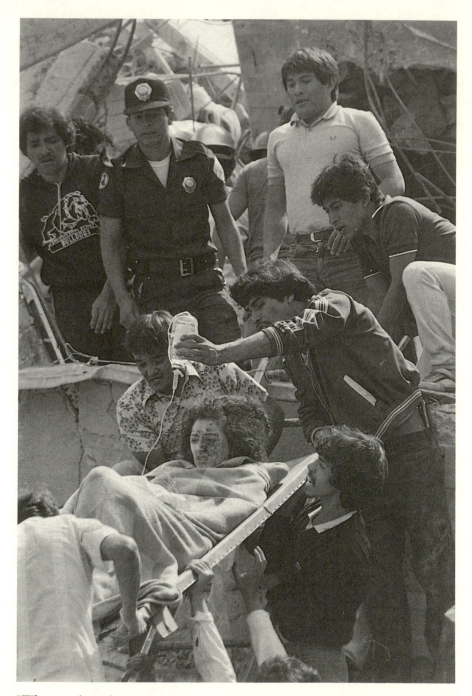

"When we brought out someone alive or even someone badly hurt, man, it was a party." (© Marco Antonio Cruz. Photo in possession of Elena Poniatowska.)

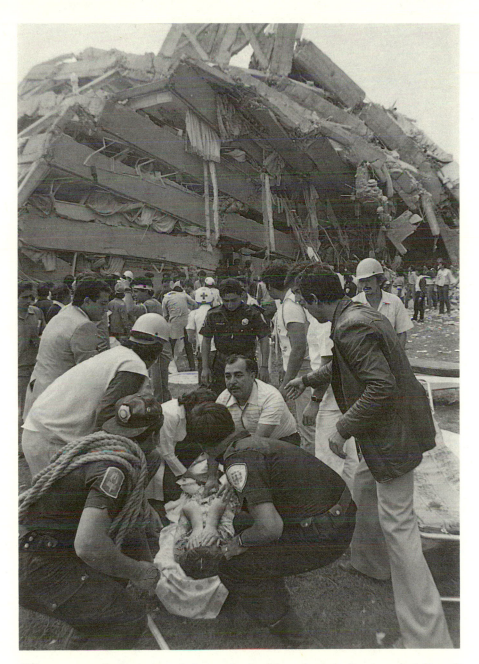

"The process of adaptation of those who had been buried alive is very delicate."
(© Marco Antonio Cruz. Photo in possession of Elena Poniatowska.)

"The hope that kept us all going was the possibility of finding a person still breathing." (© Marco Antonio Cruz. Photo in possession of Elena Poniatowska.)

WHAT ELSE IS GOING TO BE CORDONED OFF?

When the army started to take the lead, nobody knew what to do because no one had any experience. The lack of experience is easy to explain. What is not easy to explain is the arrogance: the Spanish, for example, had their equipment held up in customs at the airport.

Roberto Zamarripa wrote in *La Jornada* that the firefighters from Marseilles were taken to sleep, have breakfast, and bathe at the Fiesta Palace when what they wanted was to go into action, and said so constantly.

María Stoopen, who offered to interpret for the French, said that they had no escort, no map of the city, no support as they traveled, and no guide to the damaged zones, and she added that a criminal delay made every movement difficult and clumsy. "The French rescue brigade that I was working with that day in Tepito coincided with two other groups, one French and one Mexican, and when we were about to leave, another one came, from Algeria, and it had to be told that there was nothing else to do. The French dog trainer commented with great irritation that they were being called much too late to the proletarian sections, when there was no longer any hope of finding anyone alive under the debris. Many buildings among the hundreds that were destroyed received little or no help. It is very important to stress the vacuum of authority and administration that plagues the government of the Federal District, made manifest in this catastrophe."

The government went so far as to prevent citizen action. Many desperate people were forbidden to dig into the rubble that buried their relatives, as in the atrocious case of the Gironella family, in the building at Liverpool 24. According to journalist Manú Dornbierer, General Mota, Chief of Police, arrived at 4 A.M. on September 20 and ordered a rescue brigade to come to the site. The brigade never came, but meanwhile the soldiers prevented volunteers from entering. Later that morning, they saw the bodies of a father and young daughter lying on the highest heap of rubble. The relatives had to get ahold of a crane so that the bodies could be lowered. Not even then did they get any help.

TO CORDON OFF IS TO IMPEDE, TO OPPRESS, TO INTIMIDATE

To cordon off is to separate. Many soldiers did not even know what street they were on.

"Me, they just sent me here."

"I'm not from here, I'm not familiar with it, I just obey orders."

It was the relatives who could report about the building, where the garage was, where the bathrooms were, where the stairway was, where the central courtyard was, the back door, the kitchens. These were the people who were kept at a distance. "Move back, move back."

Popular instinct found itself restricted; the willingness to aid halted. Powerlessness makes people feel sick. Citizens were coerced to stay at home. "Don't come, don't get in the way, don't leave home. Don't move, freeze. He who doesn't get in the way helps a lot."

Instead of making an appeal to the populace, authorities cloistered people in their homes, with the result that in a city of 150 square miles a thick absence fell over its length and breadth, and entire neighborhoods remained ignorant of the tragedy and only at night began to visualize its magnitude.

Thousands of human lives lost, thousands of beings beaten and cracked forever. Nevertheless, the order was "abstain," "go away," "beat it," "don't be in the way."

If not for the disobedient, those who ignored orders and just went as they were to the disaster zones, if not for those who spontaneously organized themselves together in Colonia Roma, in Tlatelolco, if not for those who scratched with their fingernails, if not for the volunteers, the kids of the gangs, more Mexicans would have died.

We all asked, "Why have the members of the army arrived with machine guns instead of turning up with picks and shovels? Must they add this aggression to their ineptitude? Or was it that they were going to shoot right on the spot anyone caught in the act of looting?"

Even the UNAM judged it necessary to close the university after Thursday, thus depriving the population of enormous human and technical resources. With the university closed, about 300,000 or more could neither get together nor organize the sort of brigades that were assembled later through sheer pressure from the students, who turned up on their own at the Medical Center of the CU. Even as it was, mutual aid proved formidable. Among neighbors, among compadres, among buddies, among fellow sufferers. Despite the political parties, the slogans, the organizations.

WE COUNT ON "EL CHANFLE" AND VASELINE HEAD, ON FATSO AND BOBBY-BRASS-TACKS

Now we know whom we can count on. On El Chanfle, the Vaseline Head, Disco Kid, the Flea, Kid Mora. Those are the saviors, the displaced and the kicked around. What normality are they going back to? What chance will they be afforded in the reconstruction? Won't they be "decentralized" forever? What else is going to be cordoned off?

Clara Arnús, Marisol Martín del Campo

I came to Mexico with a rescue group organized and coordinated by the Ministry of Foreign Relations of Israel, says Shlomo Cohen, fifty-two years old. We're a military brigade of twenty-five persons, and we've brought 17 tons of equipment. We got here Monday at six in the morning and received an extraordinary welcome. At the airport we turned over thirty field tents and five tons of medicines, after which we went directly with our equipment to the Super Leche restaurant, then to Banamex and to the Nuevo León Building at Tlatelolco.

Up to now we haven't had a chance to use our air cushion that can lift up to 50 tons of concrete. It only makes sense to use it where you have a possibility of saving lives, and until now we haven't brought out one survivor. That's why we came, to save lives. We're waiting to be coordinated. We're under the authority of Dr. Aries, but we haven't seen her. Do you know who Dr. Aries is?■

Clara Arnús

I'm a volunteer working as coordinator of foreign rescue teams, especially the Israeli brigade of thirty military people, says Marcos Béjar, sixty, director of Amber Cross of Mexico. First they were at Super Leche, then in Banamex and Tlatelolco. They were called to the Hospital Juárez, but they didn't want to stay. The area looked like a circus; it even had platforms built for the military personnel.

In spite of the Yom Kippur holiday, the Israelis worked two complete shifts. I really admire them. Because of the constant earthquakes in Israel, they have highly developed equipment, and they managed to save ten people. One piece of equipment consists of three hoses, the first with ultrasound that you insert in order to listen, the second with infrared rays that can detect signs of heat given off by bodies, and the last one, connected to a television monitor, actually to see. The Israelis brought portable compressors that made an entire brigade out of one man. You carry them on your back like a frogman, and you change it when it runs out of air. Each one has a power saw, hammer, and chisel.

Even though they brought out a baby alive yesterday, they're all let down. What counts in a rescue operation is saving lives. Nobody likes to take a risk just for dead bodies, and now it's the dead who remain in the rubble.■

"In Mexico, nobody takes responsibility for nothing."

"Who are you waiting for?"
  "Me? Nobody."

MY FAMILY WAS NOT KILLED BY THE EARTHQUAKE; WHAT KILLED THEM WAS THE FRAUD AND CORRUPTION FOSTERED BY THE GOVERNMENT

Bent over, Judith García passes by unnoticed. Her pretty face, small and fine like that of a Filipina, has a humble expression. Everything about her is modest and humble—her clothing, her low shoes, her voice that cracks. But when she speaks, she takes on the force of her tragedy:

I was the first one to get up on the morning of the 19th of September at 7:11. I picked up the telephone to verify that it was 7:11. I went into the kitchen to warm up milk for my daughter América, three years old. She was lying down with her father. I returned to get my other two children dressed, Rodrigo and Alvaro Darío, when I began to feel the movement. At that moment I called to my husband. He stood up and took the girl in his arms. "Luciano!" I called out again. He said, "Yes, I hear you!" The movement was quite light, and I said to Alvaro Darío, "Go with Dad." He took the two children in his arms and carried them while I was waking up Rodrigo, who was still fast asleep. I was afraid that he could be flung out the window—the windows ran from floor to ceiling, and the beds were right there next to them. That scared me very much. Meanwhile, I got Rodrigo.

My husband sat down with the children in an interior corridor. I grabbed Rodrigo by the shoulders, and we were hustling along toward Luciano when I heard him tell the children: "We're going to lie down here like we were playing." That was the last I ever heard from my husband.

I was going along holding Rodrigo by the shoulders when I felt a powerful jerk, and he fell. I couldn't grab him because I felt my feet sinking into the floor. I screamed. I saw my husband and my children and this child who just slipped from my grasp, face downward. At this instant it seemed like the walls were compressed, and the doors of the closet popped out. I was shot out through the air from where I was. I felt a strong rush of air that carried me, but I could still see my husband with the other two children in his arms and my son collapsed next to them.

I thought, "I'm going to die; I'm on the fifth floor, I'm going to die." I was conscious of this moment. I knew I was being ejected. It occurred to me to look for the window frame, and I thought that by falling from the fifth floor I was going to be the one killed, while they would live. I fell onto the the rooftop of the second floor of an adjacent building. I lost consciousness for who knows how long.

When I came to, I realized I could move. I had the closet door on top of me. I pushed it off and turned around to take a good look. I was horrified. I said, "My God, my God, how can this be, this can't be." The only thing that I could think—in total disbelief—was to repeat that it couldn't be, that it wasn't fair. "Why, my God? Why have you foresaken me, my God?"

After looking at the building for a few seconds, the only thing that occurred to me was to stand up. I was the first; there was absolutely nothing to be seen, nobody to be seen; there wasn't dust, there was nothing. Slab upon slab.

Right above the apartment in which we lived was a 40-ton water tank. When I saw some workers from the subway, I began shouting, "My children, my children, help me get my children out! My children are up there, my children, please help me, my husband, my children are there and this can't be! My husband, help me!" I didn't know what to do; I even saw a hole with the carpet that had been in the room, and I thought that I could lower myself through it; from the start I thought that my husband and my two children were dead because of the weight of the water tank, but since the boy had been with me, I clung to the hope that he could be alive. Even if he were injured, I was going to find him.

There was some construction going on next door. I saw the workers there, motionless, terrorized. In spite of my shouts, they did not dare come with me. I told them, "My children, my children are in there. Get them out! There's a hole there, I came out through it. I know where they are. Help me get them out! My family is there, I know where. Help me, I can't go."

They told me, "No, señora, we can do nothing." And they turned away.

I had dropped to the street totally naked, without shoes, with nothing. People began to arrive, and it was a moment of desperation. They told me that people were being rescued behind at the Renault building, and I asked a man, "Let me go up, help me, I know where my children are, help me look for them."

And he said to me, "No, ma'am, you haven't got anything on, and you can't go up like that."

I insisted.

"Señora, the gas tank is going to explode; it's very dangerous, señora, nothing can be done."

PEOPLE REMAINED IN A DAZE, STARING

By that time, there were a fair number of people in the street. They remained dumbfounded. Somebody lent me some overalls from Renault, and I climbed up on a wide board as best I could, but I saw nothing. It was impossible to get across the roof. I went back down, and by now everybody knew my children were inside. At that instant, a woman and a volunteer came running to say, "Señora, Señora, Señora, they're getting people out at the Renault building next door, and two children came out."

I ran over, but the children were dead. They'd never told me they were dead. They delivered Rodrigo to me dead at ten in the morning, completely bloodless and broken up. He had gashes in his back and a blow on the eye. His little body had a damaged eye.

I told everybody about my children and my husband, everybody, everybody. I shouted it. When I got there the only thing I could see was two broken bodies, all destroyed, laid out on the ground. A great despair came over me. It was my oldest son Rodrigo and the son of my maid Guadalupe Martínez Hernández, twenty-four. They had no idea what to do with the bodies; they were the first ones.

By this time, the police were there, and they wouldn't let me touch the bodies. It didn't make any difference to me that the police were there, and I stayed with the body of my son and the body of the son of my maid. The two together. All was confusion at this point. They didn't know whether to call the delegation, what to do with the cadavers, what was going to happen. I demanded that they leave them with me, and that they take them some place where I could be with them.

Someone brought a sheet and laid the bodies on the floor at Renault, and I stayed there about two and a half hours with the children's bodies. The ambulance from the delegation arrived. They identified themselves, and I went with the bodies because I didn't want to lose sight of them. I stayed at the delegation until eight that night, when they issued a death certificate. I went back to Tehuantepec Street to find out what had happened to my daughter América, to my son Alvaro Darío, and to my husband. Friday night, I held a wake for my son Rodrigo. The arrangements were made with the undertakers, and he was buried. Friday, Saturday, and Sunday I was involved with the rescue work.

Some of my husband's fellow workers at the Federal Electricity Commission arrived on Sunday night. They went to work excavating everywhere in the building, except right there because of the 40-ton water tank. It was a matter exclusively of friends, volunteers, and relatives with picks and shovels trying to recover bodies that were rotting day by day without help from the government or from any authority at all. But with just picks and shovels? Never, we'd never get anything accomplished! The crane couldn't lift the water tank; it was impossible, a matter of desperation. Sunday night they brought in some jackhammers and managed to put holes in the concrete. Still, we needed electric saws and a large number of people to do the work. Sunday, I thought, "My family's coming out, this time it's time," and I steeled myself. I hoped that their bodies could come out because the firemen and the families that were working had managed to perforate some of the concrete, but no, it wasn't possible. They began cutting the concrete, but a grid of rods prevented getting the bodies out. The rods had to be cut.

Around Monday noon, they were at work on the water tank and cutting the rods. I was certain that my children were coming out. A little after twelve, they located them. They told me that they'd be coming out soon, but the rescue work took four or five hours. I thought that the bodies were completely destroyed by the quantity of concrete and rods that had fallen on top of them. I simply told them that they could identify Luciano by this cross that he wore on his chest that I now have hung around my neck. By that and by the children he held in his arms. At one on Monday afternoon, they discovered a person with a chain and a cross. With a little more digging, the rescue worker saw the hand of a child that he held. It was, in fact, my family. By five o'clock they had recovered the bodies of the two children. I'd been waiting since Thursday, but when the moment came to identify them, I couldn't go. I knew it was them, but I didn't want to be there nevertheless.

People told me, "Señora, they're your children, go ahead . . ."

"I'm not going, I'm not going, I can't go."

I felt a frightful dread of seeing them all destroyed and decomposed. When they brought down the stretchers with the children, one of the workers ran to tell me that they were mine and that I should go. Right then I told him that I wasn't going, no way in the world; I wasn't going to show up there; no sir, I didn't want to.

"If you don't go to identify them, you'll never know where their remains will end up . . . I'll accompany you so you'll go."

Other people told me that if I didn't identify them they'd cremate them. I dreaded seeing their destroyed faces and their broken bodies when just on Thursday morning I had had them with me and seen them laugh.

I went finally. First they brought down the body of my son Alvaro Darío, who would have celebrated his fourth birthday on October 17. A kind of calm came over me at the moment when I identified his remains. I saw him far away, without details; I immediately recognized his clothing, his body, his face, his hands, surprised to find them whole, and I said, "Yes, yes, yes, this is my son." Right away they brought down the stretcher of my daughter América, three years old, and I also recognized her and said, "Yes, yes, yes, it's my daughter, it's my daughter."

At that moment, as they were taking the bodies away, one of the workers said, "Let the lady stay; wait, her husband is coming down . . . In ten minutes, tops. Wait, it's the body of the gentleman who is this lady's husband." I recognized Luciano.

Fortunately, the bodies were not mutilated. The space they were found in had a height of about a foot and a half; I could see that the bodies were not flattened; I said, "They're okay, they don't smell." In other words, you see what's not there, make up what's impossible, in the midst of your despair.

I got very upset, I started to fight with everyone, with the volunteers, with absolutely everybody; in the office where the bodies were being held I protested because nobody had been with me at the moment of identification, not a relative, not a soul, other than the workers, and I needed someone to say yes, that I was right, that this was my family, someone who would give me some certainty that they were my people, because I no longer knew. I longed for someone to say yes, that these were in fact their bodies. I quarreled with the soldiers. They blocked the way with their weapons. I went and pushed them away, and, after that moment, the bodies of my children and husband were placed in plastic bags and tied up.

In the five days I had spent there, I had not worried about the cemeteries. I had lost all documentation. I knew that my husband owned burial vaults in Mausoleos del Angel, but they required proof, so I couldn't do anything there. We went to the Eighth Delegation. I couldn't get any coffins, so we had to use the ones the delegation provided, and thus we arrived at the San Lorenzo Tezonco Civilian Cemetery.

One after the other, the bodies were brought in. There were hundreds and hundreds of people racing to close up the holes with shovelfuls of dirt that never ended, one after the other. We didn't even have a chance to hold a proper wake, nothing like that. They had to be buried quickly.

Three of my loved ones are together, but Rodrigo, my oldest, is separated from them because we buried him on Friday. Now I am trying to get an order to exhume his body so that at least I may have the material remains of my family together. This causes me great anguish and despair, to know that three are in one place and one in another.

There was a considerable lapse in between burials, a period of four days. Rodrigo got out Thursday morning. The others were buried Monday night at nine, because in San Lorenzo Tezonco the burials were like frenzied races. One was interred, and then another, one in one hole and another in the next hole, in an endless row.

EVERY NIGHT I SAVE THEM MENTALLY

At this point, I don't think that I have tears to cry anymore. Now, at night, I live the anguish of thinking in my solitude about the thousands of possibilities that could have existed for my family to be saved, like on a chessboard. I save them mentally all the time. Why was I spared? This is a disaster. And then there are the portraits that I carry with me to witness that at one point in my life I had a family and a home.

I want to state that the people who died didn't die because of the earthquake; that is a lie. People died because of poor construction, because of fraud, because of the criminal incapacity and the inefficiency of a corrupt government that doesn't give a damn about people living and working in buildings that can collapse. The government knows that many buildings are death traps.

The fraud is not committed only during construction, but in each and every one of the acts of government that lead to the construction of a building. After September 19, I've been talking to people, gathering with those who used to live in the condominium, my neighbors, the rescue crew who worked in my building—and there are still cadavers to bring out. I have been walking through the sites where hundreds of people died. In the building at Tehuantepec 12, eighty-five people were killed; 90 percent of the people living in Tehuantepec 12 were killed.

I have seen injustices at all levels, as in the case of my maid Guadalupe Martínez Hernández, twenty-four. She suffered a rupture of the spinal column and compression of the spinal cord. Aside from having lost her son, she is handicapped for life, paralyzed from the waist down, unable to work ever again, and now she lives with her sister. They practically kicked her out of bed 636 of the Social Security Hospital. There is no insurance for the handicapped. There is no chance for any institutional care for her. Her financial situation is obviously very bad, I have tried to help her to the extent of my resources, but there are hundreds like her. They are in their own homes, they can't come and protest, and we do not even see them. It is the greatest injustice ever.

CARRILLO ARENA, ASSASSIN
Let me make it perfectly clear that this was not a seismic problem but a problem of having assassins in power who couldn't care less about the life of children, the life of what could have been a future for this country. Thousands of dead cannot be erased overnight.

It's unbelievable that a man like Carrillo Arena should find himself in the Fund for Reconstruction, when he's responsible for our tragedy given that he signed the blueprints for the construction of buildings in which so many people died. And what about the Hospital General and the Hospital Juárez? What an enormous shame! We should not allow the government to forget and to push for a return to normality when they are to blame. Don't they see this is genocide? We have to assign blame.

It's not possible that the man responsible for the death of physicians, nurses, and children in hospitals and in Tlatelolco, the buildings of Colonia Roma, the man who is in charge of Sedue should be the one who will head the investigations and direct the process of reconstruction. The hands of assassins that got the profits should not be the hands that give back to us what we have lost; that would be an abomination. It is as if on top of it all we were begging. They now demand that the people whose houses will be rebuilt demonstrate financial ability to pay for them. We can't allow our sorrow to be the object of derision. Our dignity demands that we do not let our dead be forgotten. Society cannot remain aloof from this rottenness. The ruins that buried thousands of people are still visible. There were not four thousand; that's a lie, there were sixty thousand. This we should shout.

I INVITE ALL WHO SUFFER AS I DO TO JOIN ME IN DENOUNCING THE CRIMINALS

I invite all who suffer as I do at this moment to point to responsible parties and accuse them. We won't let things rest. Let people use the proper tribunals to denounce the fact that international aid never reached the hands of victims, that the supplies were sold in the provinces and the Federal District; that the army, far from helping us, stole people's belongings—as engineer Raúl Pérez Pereyra can attest, he who lost everything he owned and who had to go to the Campo Militar to search for the jewelry of his wife, who died at Tehuantepec 12; as his son Jorge Alejandro Pérez Lara Pardo can tell you too. Let people come before the attorney general to denounce the injurious treatment they received.

Let the people from Colonia Morelos, Tepito, Colonia Guerrero, Tlatelolco, the ones who lost homes and jobs, speak up. And let them not be content with just making accusations, but go on to create an organization with staying power because Mexico's social problem goes way beyond the earthquake.

For the victims, for those of us who lost everything, a way of being able to live with ourselves is to participate in this change and not to allow business as usual. Let no one live in a house that can crumble.

On September 19 at 7:19 my husband and my three children died because of the faulty construction of the building at Tehuantepec 12. My family was not killed by the earthquake; what killed them was the fraud and corruption fostered by the government of Mexico.

The names of my dead children were Rodrigo, Alvaro Darío, and América. The name of my dead husband was Luciano Vega Calderón.

My name was once Judith García de Vega.

We're no longer the same.

"Who came?"
"Nobody."

Novedades, September 23

In Tezonco the ditches are ready to be filled with 1,500 cadavers. Four hundred fifty have already been interred. Twenty more bodies arrive from ISSSTE. Students from a vocational school make wooden caskets.

More than a hundred bodies have been cremated in the Dolores Cemetery. The crematory has been active twenty-four hours a day, and its ten staff have had no rest. This is the report submitted by auxiliary units: from the core of the downtown, 410 living people and 160 dead bodies have been recovered. Out of nineteen people yesterday, five passed away.

As of 1:00 P.M. yesterday, the agencies of the Ministerio Público had received 1,700 cadavers, of which 225 have not yet been identified. In the ruins of the Attorney General's Office, eighteen dead bodies and eighty-four injured people were recovered, and some agents of the judicial police are still trapped under the rubble. Rescue units were able to get the two bodies, kneeling in an embrace, of Margarita Rodríguez Meza, seventy years old, and María de Jesús Ramírez, thirty-three.

Excélsior, September 23

The Ministry of Protection and Traffic Safety said that the number of victims rose last night to 2,822, the missing to 4,180, and other victims to 6,000. Hundreds of corpses were ordered buried at the cemeteries of Dolores, San Lorenzo Tezonco, and San Nicolás Tolentino.

In the morgues of delegations the situation was further complicated because of the stench of decomposed bodies: 140 victims were buried in three common graves wrapped only in sheets. Their photos and fingerprints were taken beforehand for later identification.

La Jornada, September 23

Hundreds of cadavers deposited in the Social Security Park that had not been identified were sent to a common grave. Interested parties denounced the lack of equipment that led to the death of people who had been still alive when they were rescued. Others, they said, died in spite of having received water and oxygen because rescuers could not get them out in time. In the building at the corner of Liverpool and Bruselas streets, only six people of a family of twelve could be saved. Dismembered bodies are wrapped in plastic bags.

PEOPLE CLAIM THE REMAINS OF LOVED ONES IN DELTA PARK

If you are fumigating, you need to wear boots up to here, a thick jacket like a French fireman's, and a cloth cap. At Centro Médico we got robes, gloves, and masks. You fumigate with a tank that you carry on your back, a cylinder like divers have or like people who sell coffee in the streets. When you turn the system on, it vibrates like crazy.

Look at all the levels that coexist at a time of tragedy like this. We left the university in a van, looking like astronauts with our white caps, boots, tanks of formaldehyde and pine-scented disinfectant, with the door wide open because we couldn't stand the smell, and a patrol car in front of us to open the way. At one point, at the corner of Insurgentes Avenue and Vito Alessio Robles Street, the lights stopped us. A young woman, dressed in a nice little tailored suit, with her nice little purse, approached the van thinking it was a collective and taxi and asked, "Excuse me, sir, do you go to the subway station?" and got ready to get into the van. We couldn't believe it. Three days after the earthquake, there were people for whom life was the same as ever, while a good part of the city had been razed.

We reached the baseball park of the Social Security in the corner of Cuauhtémoc and Obrero Mundial avenues, known as Delta Park, and I choked up as soon as we arrived. We unloaded our equipment, the formaldehyde, the disinfectant, the spraying hoses and tanks. Then I looked at the stadium. It was as if you were in the center of a show, but without an audience, all the seats up there were empty, but the field was illuminated and the actors were all there, on the stage, dead. Further back stood three tents, also covered with spotlights. They displayed signs: first, "Unidentified Bodies," second, "Identified Bodies," and the last one, "Remains." There were limbs and other body parts in plastic bags that I never wanted to see, and, thank God, I never had to see. These smaller plastic bags were handled with the same care and respect given to the bags that contained full bodies.

People were coming to identify their "remains."

As a defense mechanism, I think, I started to see myself as a spectator watching a movie. The smell of formaldehyde was very strong. At the entrance you could hear the click-clack of the clerks as they typed death certificates.

The vans kept arriving with more cargo—more and more bodies.

WHAT'S THE DEAL ON THE COFFINS?

The first thing we did was to establish a line beyond which nobody could go without being fumigated. This is called a sanitary carpet. By this time men, women, and children had been dead for three days, and the process of putrefaction was advanced. We created a layer of plastic and cloth on the ground to serve as a boundary and as the spot where people would stand and be sprayed. And we sprayed people going in and out: the stretcher bearers, the relatives, the people who brought in the coffins.

The doctor in charge ordered, "Start fumigating the corpses. Now."

Fortunately I was not involved in the first spray, nor even the second. At a distance of some 20 yards you could see the plastic bags, the dry ice, and the mounds, but those mounds poorly covered with plastic sheets were bodies. The power hose was so strong that it blew off the plastic sheets, so I thought, "I have to overcome my fear, because if I don't do this right I could be spraying other workers and cause them a problem. Death is part of life: I must force myself to look."

The first I saw was a tall girl, lying on the ground, very fair, her body covered with bruises, totally naked, with a shaved pubis and big breasts, full of milk. The sign said, "Number 74, Gynecology-Obstetrics, Hospital Juárez." I noticed she had a crescent-shaped gash in the lower abdomen. I realized sadly that she had just had a baby; her womb had not been barren. She was so pale, she looked like a statue, a mistreated statue. "You, why did you have to die?"

Unconsciously I started a dialogue with the dead. I kept spraying them, and in talking to them, I talked to myself. I kept asking them why. I saw a fat woman with a very cheap dress. I saw so many people. I felt shame, as if I were feeling their modesty for them. I told them so: "I have no right to be seeing you like this, with your dress up your legs, with your naked body; I have no right to see you."

I saw dark, blackened bodies, and then I said to myself, "This stuff here has nothing to do with the people; this here is no longer human." I kept saying that to protect myself. "This here is simply organic matter, these crushed arms, these swollen faces, these tongues sticking out; this is no more than organic matter; there are lots of bacteria here and I have to prevent them from spreading, and that's why I'm spraying."

When I turned my head to the left I saw a little girl with eyes wide open and the grimace of an interrupted smile, an eight-year-old: "Little girl, why on earth didn't you run? Why did the beam fall on you?" I insistently spoke to the cadavers to the point of rage, wrath, and hatred: "This isn't fair." "It is not fair that in this country hospitals, schools, government buildings, and public buildings should collapse just like that. It is not fair that this should happen to the most screwed-over people. It isn't fair."

All of us in the crew were cold in our legs because of the dry ice and the Formol. Besides, we were scared. Maybe at the beginning we were afraid of contamination, but we soon realized that those of us with the formaldehyde were the best protected. Someone told us, "If there is an immune bunch, it is you."

A small, skinny, brown guy appeared, the typical Mexican who has had to work very hard from birth, someone who probably lived in some lost tenement in some lost slum, with a sweater that was all too thin, Jesus! Really! Why are our people so unprotected? What helplessness, God! Really! It makes you mad to see people like that, with nothing. "And the coffins?" he asked, "What's the deal on the coffins?" He needed three of them. Three coffins. He wanted to know how much they were. And how would he have paid for them, the poor bastard?

"Have you identified your family?"

"Yes, they are there. But tell me, how much do those caskets run?"

"No, the coffins are free; we'll give them to you right away. Are you here by yourself?"

He was there to claim his sister and two nieces, one fourteen, the other nine years old. I was profoundly sorry; I am a coward, and at that moment I was incapable of lifting a body; I could not help him carry his people. I had no strength, and I said to him, "Forgive me, I can't pick up a body, I just can't, I don't have what it takes." A more robust volunteer worker connected with the university said, "Hell! I don't like it either. It's not that I'm disgusted: I'm afraid, but I feel sorry for this guy. Let me help him, just spray the Formol good and thick on me." And he went on with the skinny one.

Meanwhile, Claudia, Giovanna, and I prepared the caskets, a big one and two small ones, and I realized one of them had two nails sticking out, but I said "Too bad! It won't matter." Later we saw how the skinny one stepped on the nails with his sneakers, and since that didn't work, he got ahold of a big board and bent them backward. This simple act restored a human dimension to the piles of bodies in the stadium, because after four hours I thought that the only real things were the bacteria. But for the skinny guy those bodies, even all messed up, were his people, and his cadaver had a right to be in a casket where it wouldn't be hurt by the nails.

The big man helped him place the bodies in the coffins, and we had the task of sprinkling them with limestone. We always asked permission to do this: "Can we sprinkle the body with limestone?"

This big guy from the university was as afraid as we were, but he had the courage to help out. Then I asked the skinny man, "Listen, can we sprinkle limestone on your relatives?"

"Yes."

The fourteen-year-old had to be transferred to an adult casket because she was too big for the other one. As I sprinkled her I thought of Hamlet, when Ophelia, after losing her mind, drowns. Hamlet's mother places violets on her body and says in her mind, "Look, I come to put flowers on your body, the ones I should have placed on your nuptial bed." I had exactly the same sensation: "Girl, I am sprinkling limestone on you, so you'll go all whitened up, you who have not lived at all, fourteen-year-old girl. There you go, all white." You know, all those mental associations that we have about purity, dignity, an untouched body . . . but I could only sprinkle limestone on her. Not a single flower, just a lot of white dust.

That's how she went.

This is the tale of Professor Antonio Lazcano Araujo, founder of the "Origin of Life" course at UNAM.

This is what he lived through on Sunday, September 22, in the Social Security stadium, from ten at night to two in the morning, when he went back home with nine other crew members in the same van, with empty tanks of disinfectant, the door still wide open because of the intolerable smell of formaldehyde, now impregnated in robes, caps, and masks.

"Say, is it true nobody came?"

CHRONICLE OF A DISAPPOINTMENT

Invited by the President of the Republic to the installation of the National Commission on Reconstruction in the Anthropology Museum, we will attend the most gravely important gathering after the tremor, on Wednesday, October 9, at 11 A.M. The appointment is at the Museum of Anthropology and the reason couldn't be more powerful. From here each one of us—pained and frightened citizens—will leave with our marching orders under our arms. There will be a popular consultation, and together we will honor our dead, repeating what years ago Father Angel María Garibay K. wrote as a translation of the Anonymous Tlatelolco Manuscript:

Broken spears lie in the roads; we have torn our hair in our grief. The houses are roofless now, and their walls are red with blood. Worms are swarming in the streets and plazas, and the walls are splattered with gore. The water has turned red, as if it were dyed, and when we drink it, it has the taste of brine. We have pounded our hands against the adobe walls in our despair, and our inheritance is nothing but a net full of holes.

We'll hug each other. Engineers, architects, and seismologists will talk to us about their special field of work, and from the audience the hands of those who know will be raised. We will hear from the victims. The volunteer community will surely be there, they who are still active even now, and the people from the first-aid stations, the firemen, the residents of Tepito, Colonia Doctores, Colonia Morelos, and Colonia Guerrero, the survivors of Colonia Roma, those who for several days occupied the space that Carlos Monsiváis spoke about. All Paseo de la Reforma will look like a great funeral procession.

Dream on!

On October 9, I arrived there with my heart pounding, ready to shoot out of my chest, and immediately the process of intimidation was unleashed, with grinding solemnity and gloom. I still managed to pretend I was hopeful as I filled out a card that ushers were handing out: What committee did I want to participate in? Housing, health, education, job procurement, social assistance, safety, metropolitan area reconstruction? I say "social assistance" in my mind, and put a check mark next to it, name, address, telephone number.

Inside, the lectern for speakers was placed too high above the audience, the green, long platform separating the experts from the folding chairs where two thousand members of the public were already seated, waiting. Under the giant stone umbrella that Pedro Ramírez Vázquez built, Governor Cervantes Corona of the state of Zacatecas combed his hair, no speck of rubble dust on his person.

The freshly shaved bureaucrats, their suits just out of the cleaners, began to fill the seats that were waiting for them on the platform. How many interruptions on the way! A hug here and a pat on the back! Smiles. Don't they know that, at the moment of truth in the streets, the institutions they lead have proved their worthlessness to the Mexican people? No, they pat each other on the back; they sow for the future; they are all presidential material; they greet the ones who should be greeted; they trip over each other in their eagerness. Here it doesn't smell of gas.

My eyes look for Humberto Romero, director of communications for the Department of the Federal District, and once the secretary to President López Mateos, with the impeccable suit of a career politician, his hair glued to his scalp. He is the protagonist that reveals the attitude of the authorities toward the people. A reporter asked him why his new bulletin cited 2,500 dead as the official toll of the earthquake, when one day before his office had reported 3,000. "Sir, shouldn't the number be 3,500? It stands to reason." Romero agreed without further thought and said, "Why don't you say it's 3,100." Not only is life worthless, but for these officials it is also a matter of flights of fancy. Who could worry about 400 dead, more or less, if they all land in a common grave, anyway? Why should Humberto Romero be concerned about a 6-by-12-foot burial hole in the ground, when he has a fortress in Tlacopac?

The hit of the moment: five former mayors of the city sit next to Octavio Paz: Uruchurtu, Corona del Rosal, Baz, Sentíes, Hank González. Are they coming to talk about their own experience, while in the crumbled buildings some people are still searching for bodies? Outside, Operation Ant has not yet come to a halt, and each minute is precious. Bathed in dust the rescue crews stop to drink water, but under the stone umbrella, time is the older time, the time of slow politics, rhetorical politics, anachronistic politics, tricky politics, egotistic politics, the politics of avarice.

There are nine speakers. Angel Olivo Solís, president of the Labor Congress, stitches together sentences that say nothing. Engineer Claudio

González, president of the Entrepreneurial Council, warns that inflation will not be abated. Secretary General of the National Peasant Confederation (CNC) Mario Hernández Posadas shouts his unshakable faith in the most dreadful clichés. Fernando Favela Lozoya, representative of the Engineers Association, ventures that those of us who are professionals have the privilege of being the guardians of two of the expressions of nationalism—science and art—and thus our responsibilities are unrenounceable.

And nobody says what we are waiting to hear, in spite of the fact that we all turn our tense eyes toward the presiding table. Some phrases attempt to take flight: "Mexico never shows its virtues better than when it faces adversity"; "With renewed faith we salute the commission and congratulate ourselves for the opportunity to become an integral part of it"; "Now we understand the full meaning of the fatherland"; "Pain and anguish are the spur that compels us to help"; "Human emotion and exemplary attitude of the citizenry"; "We have been called to be the heroes of a major epic"; "We are not daunted in the face of adversity, and we know how to unite in a common effort"; "It is the moment to correct our mistakes"; "To produce and to distribute with social justice and economic efficacy"; "For our country nothing has ever been easy: two centuries of independence stand as a strong reminder of this"; "The imperative: to rebuild and to strengthen"; "Presidential leadership continues to be serene and firm"; "Nations and men can be truly known only in tough times"; "Opportunities are almost always ephemeral, and they never come back to us in quite the same way"; "To have the fortitude to face the task . . ."; "Let us be sorry for the evils that have befallen us, but let's turn them into points of departure, not in search of answers, but in search of the one answer that can comprehend the sum total of our problems."

Jorge Carpizo, president of UNAM, speaks: "We in the university are committed to Mexico"; "Civil society, convinced of its enormous responsibility, has responded from the first moment with agility, energy, and solidarity, as corresponds to the greatness of our people; it has caused a resurgence of humanism, which should be the basis of all our actions and which places man in the center of all things, instead of things above men."

Enrique Alvarez del Castillo, the governor of the State of Jalisco, insists on federalist solidarity. Alfredo del Mazo says that "in San Juanico, part of the State of Mexico, we Mexicans knew how to solve the question of presidential leadership and national solidarity, taking care of the severe emergency with transparency and opportunity."

San Juanico is an absolute proof of the abandonment and orphanhood that Mexicans, always far from the hand of God, live in. According to Enrique Maza, 550 persons died, there were 7,000 injured, more than 200,000 were left homeless, and hundreds of houses were destroyed. Nearly 16,000 cubic yards of gas burned, fifteen tanks of 20 tons each exploded, flying more than 110 yards, their pieces falling some 1,100 to 1,300 yards away from their point of origin.

How does del Mazo dare talk of transparency when a year after this disaster its causes still had not been elucidated, the investigation promised by the government had not been made public, and no one knew whether it was even conducted? When responsibilities had not been clarified, except for the civil charges assigned to Pemex, and instead it was known that there was criminal neglicence in the maintenance of their facilities? Even more exposed to danger than during the earthquake, because here a guilty party could be found, Mexicans in San Juan Ixhuatepec continued living without an alarm system. And who protects us? We, ourselves. Are we believers? Yes, we believe in ourselves.

Inside the assembly hall, a butterfly takes wing without finding the door; an ambulance siren is heard. When the turn comes to Cuauhtémoc, we all follow him with our eyes; he walks toward the tribune. Ah! The son of Cárdenas! The expectation is widely shared. (Probably Tata Lázaro would have installed himself in the Zócalo.) He speaks without the flair of orators, with reading glasses on, the features of his face profoundly underscored. The wrinkles at either side of his lips sink downward. He speaks dryly, succinctly, of the effects of the earthquake in his state of Michoacán, the destruction of Lázaro Cárdenas. His terseness contrasts with all other speakers; not a word of self-praise, no self-complacency, not an ode to the President either.

But it is Miguel León-Portilla who harvests the best oration: "For as long as the world is world, the glory and fame of Mexico-Tenochtitlán will endure." And I remember that last night I heard the voice of Alonso Mixteco Pastor, from the state of Guerrero, Mixtec on his father's side (that's why he writes his name Alonso Mixteco), Nahuatl on his mother's side, who works for the National Mixed Commission for Seniority at Manuel Doblado 39. Well, I mean he used to work, and he saw a ray of sun at a distance of 330 yards when his building fell and crawling, "holding my head like this, the whole of my body, until I reached that hole, a little opening this size, but hurting myself, I could come out."

There, under the words engraved in stone over the thick walls of the museum, the speech by León-Portilla coincides with the tragedy and attempts to still it: "All moons, all years, all days, all the wind walk and pass. All the blood, too, arrives to its place of stillness." The presidential cabinet in full has the opportunity to read the power written over the wall of the western wing.

I'd like to find the face of Hermann Bellinghausen, the face of Antonio Saborit, my fellow journalists, but instead I meet the face of La Quina (Joaquín Hernández Galicia), and that of Fidel Velázquez.

DO OFFICIALS HAVE THEIR OWN PRIVATE EARTHQUAKE?

Does Arsenio Farell—up there on high behind his dark glasses—know that more than seventy thousand women work in clandestine sweatshops in Mexico City, without social security, without benefits, living in infamous hovels, and that eight hundred of them remained buried because their bosses preferred to recover their machinery? Prosecutor Victoria Adato de Ibarra definitely doesn't know. What happens in the Attorney General's Office only surprises her when among the ruins appear the bodies of lawyer Saúl Abarca and the tortured Colombians, but then she denies knowing.

I sense a gesture of mourning in the navy blue suit of the President of the Republic, a tone of mourning in his words. No president in the history of Mexico has had this sort of luck; none have been obliged to see their city destroyed, their country struggling against suffocation, their people digging to find bodies. The earthquake has caught him without resources; the earthquake is "rain on soaked ground."

Enrique Maza says:

In Mexico there is misery, because of despoiling, because of injustice, because of plunder, not as part of life, but as *all of life* for many Mexicans. Misery is a condition of servitude without exceptions; it is a living death. . . . And the crisis that comes on top of this disgrace reveals to what extent we are laid bare, weary, needy. We know that our needs could have found a solution if our resources, instead of being shipped abroad, had been used here, and if attention had been given to so many of the things that should have been done.

I think that the President of the Republic probably feels very bad, overwhelmed by the tragedy, hurt to the marrow of his bones. Not in vain did he see up close the ferocious helplessness of the people that he governs. He proposes a structural change:

> The question is not to return to our point of departure, simply replacing what was destroyed, but rather one of transforming reality to benefit man and laying the foundations of our national destiny again. Reconstruction will require additional hard work, productivity, savings, investment, and foreign exchange.
>
> Paradoxically, the basic solution for the capital city lies outside its domain. The decisions lie in the hands of the entire republic, in the provinces, and there are programs now under way.
>
> The decentralization of national life must be supported by a reorganization of federal public administration in which the headquarters of the government ministries are in the capital, but their resources, offices, and especially their facilities are decentralized as part of a broader process that includes higher education, industry, services, commerce, and finance.

In his words I hear questions and appeals. The President requests. He states that the government alone cannot deal with the scope of the tragedy; that he wants to involve workers, intellectuals, professionals, and especially the young people who can keep alive what they demonstrated in the days of catastrophe: their commitment, their disinterestedness, their heroism. We are interested in listening, in dialoguing, we're still in an emergency situation; we must restore basic services. He insists upon the structural changes demanded by present-day society, he recognizes that the task requires transforming reality. While these are not his exact words, I feel that the President *is asking* for help.

Cracks have appeared within the monolithic state "apparatus" and the gray-suit uniformity of officialdom that could not be papered over by the progovernment rhetoric of the previous speeches so full of repetitious and commonplace phrases. The President inquires, posing the same question to us that he has asked himself: How are we going to improve the quality of life? How are we going to transform suffering into an active process? What will be our way of living together from now on? What fiscal remedies are we going to adjust or promote?

The President asks. To restructure is to renovate. Not even the tiniest split appeared in the oratory of the previous nine speakers, but now there are cracks. How wonderful! We the citizens can get inside through them.

The National Reconstruction Commission establishes six committees; one for the reconstruction of the metropolitan area, another for decentralization, others for financial matters, social assistance, coordination of international aid, and the preparation of civilian security. I want to think that the President is calling out from this intimidating bunker to the victims, to the poor. Will the next working sessions include the sanitation workers of the Federal District, the nurses, the street kids from the gangs?

All those invited to this gathering are proud—they greet one another, they smile, they cross and uncross their legs. Will they have lost a bit of their sense of self-importance? Will they cease being yes-men? Does it have to be like this—on one side, government officials, on the other, the people?

Raúl Trejo wrote, "The tragedy moves us all, in some way equalizing us, it evens us out." Right now, I am not so sure. Oh, my Mexico, my wounded Mexico, my Mexico that contents itself with so little! Is it possible that we can still believe in the efficacy of government when, at the crucial moment, *it was the people who did everything?* Even yesterday, people in the street appeared grateful because the Route 100 bus was free, pay phones were free, even when they had to break the hydrants open in the street because the water trucks hadn't arrived. People ask for little and are satisfied with exceedingly little. The populace, these days, takes care of itself.

In any case, those on the bottom are accustomed to the fact that nobody even throws them a line. The absolute uselessness of government is nothing new to them. They are so different from the apparatus of power, such helpless onlookers at government decisions, so elbowed to the side that one would think they do not speak the same language. What's going on outside has nothing to do with what's going on underneath this monumental umbrella of stone, nothing. The language of power is simply "other." For all the talk about "the people," they have never been granted anything but the role of extras; leaders have always been there to obstruct, to paralyze, to block the way, to work the waiting room. If this is not the case, why aren't any of the protagonists of the tragedy here? Why, instead of hearing a seamstress, a quake victim, an aid worker, do we have to listen to the same old politician, the bureaucrat, the official with car and chauffeur?

Dream on!

Are the insides of officials sufficiently shaken up? Do they have their own earthquake? At the moment, it is impossible not to notice the President's solicitousness.

A Mexican joke:

"Why did the President go to the Social Security Building?"

"To get another three years of disability."

THE EARTHQUAKE SEEN BY THE PROVINCES
Olga de Juambelz
Torreón: *El Siglo*

NEW EARTHQUAKE CAUSES PANIC IN MEXICO CITY. Since they baptize hurricanes, we should also name earthquakes: Thursday's could be "Luis Echeverría," and yesterday's "López Portillo." (9–22–85).

In Torreón, the quake was truly felt. The water in swimming pools moved, lamps swung. However, it was not these facts, imperceptible for most, that moved the city, but rather the clear resonance of the disaster that befell the Federal District. The local press captured the attention of people living in the lake region and was prodigal with news, stories, analyses, and the never-to-be-missed healthy sarcasm.

LACK OF WATER WHIPS RESIDENTS OF THE CAPITAL . . . SINCE 1910 (9–24–85)

Hours of anguish, despair, and fear were the lot of lake region residents who have relatives in the Federal District. . . . They all followed attentively the tales of radio announcers in the capital. . . . Outside the windows of the downtown furniture stores, where televisions for sale were displayed, many passersby gathered.

This was the picture: out in the streets, these "community" screens; in churches, people praying; in offices and workshops, a demand for information from anyone coming from the capital.

Many anguished people came to the telegraph offices inquiring about urgent telegrams addressed to them by their relatives, or trying to send them out with questions about the well-being of their loved ones, even when they knew that telegraphic service was badly disrupted. Some, anxiety stricken, took off for the Federal District to locate family members.

Two days later, more than seven hundred families in the lake region of the states of Coahuila and Durango had received news of their families living in Mexico City. "Only in three cases was the news negative."

MMH EXHORTS VICTIMS TO BE SERENE AND BRAVE. What we should really ask for is dollars from the gringos to see how we get out of this one. (9–24–85)

The newspaper on the 20th registered all these emotions and also the opposite attitude: it's important to go back to normal; the media surely exaggerate. They resort to tales of the earthquake that hit the City in July 1957, "when the Angel of Independence fell down." The newpaper coverage was alarming; it was said that the entire city had been destroyed, and some people, who had left that morning on an airplane, asserted that the Federal District looked like a bombed-out area. "Fortunately, all that was a mere exaggeration."

Exaggeration or not, from the very first day, solidarity has been expressed in concrete action. From the 20th on, food, medication, and cash have been collected. On the 22nd, the citizens were active in collection drives. In Lerdo, a marathon was conducted for this purpose, and all municipal employees donated a day's salary. On the 23rd, the cotton and grape fairs announced that all their income at the ticket windows would be sent to the Federal District. The students of the normal school in Torreón donated 34,709 pesos as well as clothes, food, and medicines. In addition to the 25 million pesos that small farmers in the lake region agreed to raise for the capital city, peasants have all promised to send grain from their own harvests to the victims (9–27–85).

NANCY REAGAN HANDED A CHECK FOR $1 MILLION TO MMH. Once endorsed, the check was given back to Nancy, asking her to credit it to the national debt, since during the time that it took to get the pen out and sign, the debt grew by $12 million because of interest. (9–25–85)

And along with economic support, the exhortation: let no one steal; "watch out for the way in which the product of social altruism is administered"; and later, the denunciations. Sr. Héctor Sánchez gave a donation to the office of the Municipal Committee of the PRI in Torreón. An unnumbered receipt with an illegible signature and the wrong date was handed to him. "We don't want to imagine the reaction that the wrongful use of the donated cash and goods would provoke among the people of Torreón," he said (9–27–85). Let no one steal.

In Torreón as in other parts of the country, the question arose: Why? Why a disaster of such scope? Errors in construction, corruption, and bad government were all talked about.

> It is doubtful that the responsibilities will be clarified in spite of the fact that the archives of the Department of the Federal District have information on construction projects. Even when tragedies such as the one we lament occur, we Mexicans lack the clarity of mind to protest opportunely and thus to minimize the damages or to allow for future corrective measures. The owners of these buildings are not criminals, they are simply what we who renounce the exercise of our rights allow them to be. (9–24–85)

> Corruption has exacted its tragic price: the buildings erected by official institutions crumbled with frightful ease. (9–27–85)

GOVERNMENT TO RECONSTRUCT DAMAGED PUBLIC FACILITIES. Does this include the facility we know as nation? (9–24–85)

Criticism of the government and profound distrust encompass the before, the during, and the after of the earthquake. The organization of rescue and assistance was plagued by faults that clumsy official declarations tried to whitewash. "On a U.S. TV channel, I heard the Mexican ambassador to the United States say that we had all we needed to face the tragedy. The station showed scenes from the rescue operations: a squad of men who were shouting, hauling rubble away from a building . . . in buckets! The minister of health saying, hours after the tremor, 'Everything is under control.' The minister of tourism: 'We are certain that no U.S. tourist perished.' The inconceivable fact that even when there is such a thing as an Emergency Plan for Disaster Situations, with the resounding and mysterious name of DN-III, that plan did not include picks and shovels to carry it out, a monstrous oversight that even the President was forced to admit." The awkward demagogy of those who pointed their TV cameras and declared that their agencies were working "side by side with the Sr. Presidente and his government" also infuriated people.

MEXICO WILL COME OUT STRONGER FROM THIS TRAGEDY. I don't see why. The San Juanico tragedy left us just as weak. (9–22–85).

Also evident was the official incapacity to take advantage of foreign aid. Customs officials confiscated the tools of the Spanish "suspecting it was contraband."

> The Swiss and Germans went back to Europe upset because every-one in the disaster zone gave orders, there was no coordination, and international aid was all concentrated in one single area. Mexi-can bureaucracy, as always, scored a ten. (10–16–85)

In the meantime, it was business as usual for some. Sr. João Have-lange, a director of FIFA, declared in relation to the 1986 World Cup:

> Mexicans are very sad, and they need the joy that springs from the feast of soccer. On the other hand, they will need lots of money to repair the damages caused by the earthquake, and the World Cup will help them with cash. (9–28–85)

Yeah, sure.

Mérida: *Diario de Yucatán*
Seismographs in Mérida did not register the second tremor; the inten-sity of the first one threw them off.
The first news reports, on September 21, stated:

> Canacome and Canacintra trust that the earthquake will not cause problems in the process of supplying merchandise and raw mate-rials to the state. However, representatives point to the fact that the disruption of telephone service affects their communication with the metropolis.

"The earthquake will not affect the arrival of provisions to Yucatán," another article soothingly stated, also registering preoccupation with the possible delay or cancellation of visits by federal officials, and finally it affirmed, "It is not necessary to send aid to the victims." This surprising declaration was backed up by those of Governor Cervera Pacheco, who said, "We are waiting to be able to be in touch with them to see what they require." The same edition of *Diario de Yucatán*, however, stated with certainty that the day before some phone calls had gone through, and that the telegraph office was relying on an air message service in addition to that provided by passenger buses.

The governor, corporate executives, and the press were mostly concerned about Yucatán and the inconveniences that the earthquake could produce for the state.

Besides, the Federal District is very far away. "It is difficult to imagine a macrotremor similar to the one that hit Mexico City in Yucatán, given the difference in soil consistency," reassured the press on September 22. In short, there's no danger to us. Instead, recent catastrophes are remembered, the ones that are more real, like the destruction of Chetumal by Hurricane Janet.

However, the evocation of the Hotel Regis, under the distant rubble of the capital, surfaces:

We were intimately familiar with its facilities and with the Yucatecan ambiance and conviviality that were enjoyed there. We used to admire the elegance of its wonderful chandeliers, which were reduced to tiny shards. The Regis Hotel shared a lot with the Yucatecan heart. (9–24–85)

So far, the *Diario de Yucatán* registers the needs of Yucatán, the dangers for Yucatán, and the tastes and fears of Yucatecans.

On September 24, the press quotes data on a collection for aid to the victims organized by Canacome. On the 27th, the state's contribution is set at 29 million pesos, of which 7 million have been sent to the Federal District.

Along with the first news on economic aid, denunciation of malfeasance can be found:

On Jalapa Street in Colonia Roma, there is neither power nor water. The precious liquid is sold for twenty thousand pesos a quart. (9–24–85)

In an article signed by Jorge Eugenio Ortiz, published on September 27, we can appreciate an analysis that goes beyond lamenting or telling the misfortune, but rather tries to explain it:

> The earthquake could have been less painful if the gigantic urban sprawl in the Valley of Mexico had not been allowed to flourish . . . . The Spanish were adamant about erecting a luxurious city over the wreckage of the vanquished one . . . . From a lake with islands and shore villages, the colonial town turned into a solid settlement mounted over the desiccated marshes. This lack of ecological awareness continues to our time. There is not even a chart of the subsoil to orient construction programs, and urban proliferation has been indiscriminately permitted to the point of converting the Valley of Mexico into the most populous urban center in the world.

Immediately, nostalgia sets in, and Mayor Ernesto Uruchurtu is remembered, along with the measures he took to harness urban growth: to limit the height of skyscrapers, to multiply green areas, and to forbid new housing developments, "but corruption has mocked all norms, and many poorly built facilities fell as if under a cruel bombardment on Thursday, September 19." In fact, corruption has been a bad builder.

Sonora: *El Imparcial*

El Imparcial of Sonora declared its solidarity with affected people on September 21. "Count on us Sonorans," said the newspaper, although it never specified what aid they were prepared to give.

> If we look beyond the catastrophe, we can see that in the world there are countless human problems that cannot be solved except through the effective solidarity of all people. The scandal of squandering resources becomes intolerable for any conscience when disasters like that of Mexico City strike, in which innumerable human beings die in a sudden and atrocious way, or are abruptly left without protection. (9–26–85)

As hundreds of buildings that housed government offices fell in the capital city, the question arose, Will they be rebuilt? And if so, where? The idea of changing the capital to a new place became real for some who went as far as formulating it as "a true national clamor."

It is not possible that the life of a whole nation should depend on the flimsy fact that its capital and its government are located in a highly seismic zone that will never guarantee that something like what happened on Thursday the 19th and Friday the 20th won't happen again. (9–27–85)

Article 44 of the Constitution was quoted in support of that idea, as it foresees the possibility of such a change of residence. The attempt to reconstruct the buildings where official agencies had their offices was seen as sheer temerity. Besides, the desired political and administrative decentralization could be a relief from the "avalanche of population" that Mexico City has received.

In uniting its voice to the "national clamor" for decentralization, *El Imparcial*, just like the *Diario de Yucatán*, "longs for Uruchurtu . . . the Iron Mayor." "Once he was accused of being inhumane, fascist, and what-you-will. Time has proven him right" (9–28–85). Nostalgia for the imposition of order is repeated at the opposite ends of the country: Sonora and Yucatán.

Guadalajara: *El Informador*

The earthquake affected the south of the state of Jalisco. In Ciudad Guzmán and Gómez Farías the tremor killed people; on the coast, there were lesser calamities. The city of Guadalajara, in contrast, suffered no damage. Nevertheless, *El Informador* stressed the local situation.

In Guadalajara's metropolitan area, more than 98 percent of the houses would be unable to withstand a telluric movement of such intensity, in spite of the fact that the capital of Jalisco is located in an eminently seismic zone.

A few weeks before the earthquake, the Council of Civil Engineers of Jalisco warned that the city's construction was substandard, that it lacked adequate foundations, and that walls were erected on these weak bases without the firmness of support columns, and with materials of minimal resistance. The council stressed that in Guadalajara the number of solid buildings capable of resisting an intense earthquake did not even reach 2 percent. "Even so, as is to be expected, costs are reduced, in exchange for the creation of enormous danger to the safety of all inhabitants" (9–23–85).

Guadalajara has experienced sizable tremors, like the cataclysm that was registered in the first half of the nineteenth century, in which the towers of the newly built cathedral toppled over. In the last few years of the last century and the beginning of the present one, the city was affected by a series of shocks that forced a good deal of the population to live in plazas and public gardens for weeks at a time. In 1912, between May and September alone, fifteen hundred tremors of varied intensity were registered.

The talk is about the risks to Guadalajara, the construction in Guadalajara, the misadventures experienced by Guadalajara. And then, categorically, the same criticism of the centralization of the capital:

It has been more than a week since the fateful date, and we are still far from observing normal activity in the Federal District, which, given its central importance, multiplies the noxious effects of all problems and radiates them to the rest of the nation. (9–28–85)

This comment gives the feeling that Guadalajarans have no clear idea of the scope of the disaster:

One could ask reporters for more moderation and discretion in this alarmist avalanche of words, and for more emphasis on the positive facts, on the lessons of solidarity, on the words of encouragement, and on the appreciation and ennoblement of the great values of man. (9–24–85)

Monterrey: *El Porvenir*

Press in Monterrey focused on three problems: the ecological question in the Valley of Mexico, the lack of foresight on the part of the authorities, and corruption as a backdrop to everything.

The ecological problem of the capital city transcends the matter of overpopulation. While it is said that "it's not possible for civilization to permit such complex and dense urban concentrations" (9–23–85), journalist Jorge Eugenio Ortiz Gallegos goes even further when he says:

There is no program to regulate the growth of this valley metropolis, the largest conglomeration of people in the world. Mexico City is an ecological aberration. The population of the metropolis is condemned to continue suffering not only earthquakes but many accidents typical of daily urban coexistence and, in particular, the deterioration of its atmosphere and its way of life. (9–27–85)

Anarchic, uncontrolled growth indicates a lack of governmental foresight. But improvisation reaches astonishing levels:

Administrations never formulated emergency plans to attend to the constant disasters provoked by earthquakes (in one of the most earthquake-prone countries on the planet), or those that come from catastrophes like the oil explosion in San Juan Ixhuatepec.

That strange plan called DN-III, of which soldiers and sailors are in charge, seems to have been a card that someone pulled out of his sleeve at the last moment, and which proved to be "useless, inefficient, and pompous."
Less than a week after the earthquake, President de la Madrid ordered a thorough revision of the law of construction in Congress.

We can talk about the need to revise the law and in this way avoid the dire consequences of the tremor that shook the capital of the republic, or we can simply talk about the enforcement of what is already there. The Nuevo León Building, which crushed dozens of people, was propped up with wooden poles that residents had placed in key areas. How many other buildings were in a similiar situation? . . . A large number of government facilities came down. (9–28–85)

Naturally, the picture would not be complete without someone who would attribute the disaster to the hand of God. Bishop Genaro Alamilla interpreted the tremor as divine word, uttered so that "we will behave as a mature nation and modify the laws to permit religious education." In other words, if Article 3 of the Constitution were repealed, Mexico would be exempt from earthquakes. On September 29, *El Porvenir* asks itself if maybe then

hurricanes would not hurt us, nor torrential rains, and we in general would be saved from all cosmic catastrophes. And, who knows, maybe the foreign debt, the PRI, and all our social evils would find a solution.

On September 24, DIF in Nuevo León sent eight trailer trucks with perishable food and medication to the Federal District. It also announced that 20 million pesos in cash had been collected.

On the 28th, a great marathon, combining sports with a variety show, was held for the benefit of the victims. Large corporations in the private sector announced that they would make important donations. But the mistrust of the government and concern for the fate of those resources was also expressed clearly, tersely:

> Generous and disinterested aid will line the pockets and the bank accounts of government officials, as happened with the San Juanico disaster. (9-23-85)

The lack of confidence spreads, it multiplies. Nobody knows what's happening with the money; the official numbers are not believed; promises and administrators are suspect.

> There are physicians in the Centro Médico who are certain that the deaths must reach half a million; others, more optimistic, say no, they should only be between 30,000 and 50,000. This happens in a country where we are never told the truth, as if we were children. (9-30-85)

> The Office of the Attorney General of the Federal District said: "Colombians who appeared dead in the holding cells of the judicial police belonged to a great drug trafficking ring." At the same time, it denied categorically that they had been tortured, as it has been alleged. (9-30-85)

> The government demonstrated that it is better prepared to squelch the people's popular movements than to meet national disasters. Last May 1, during the events connected with Labor Day, police used antiriot dogs against independently unionized workers, and now we realize that no dogs were ever trained to detect survivors under the wreckage left by earthquakes. (9-28-85)

> God, God, why? Why are you quaking us like this? (9-24-85)

There was plenty of speculation, as well. Maybe the earthquake would allow us to get out from under at least part of the foreign debt. On September 20, the papers announced that the IMF would cut off funds for Mexico, but later the report was discredited. Or was there a change of position because of the earthquake?

The organizers of the World Cup Mexico '86 traveled to Zurich a few hours after the earthquake to inform João Havelange on the conditions of stadiums. Great economic interests are on the line.

But Televisa stands in readiness. Nothing will stop the World Cup. Not even an earthquake of 8 degrees. Even if it was so bad it almost wiped out its facilities. (9–28–85)

The authorities did not support the collective effort, they hamstrung it. The lack of organization has been mentioned, as has the absence of emergency plans, the clumsiness of government officials, and even their incapacity to take advantage of aid sent by foreign countries. The state obstructed solidarity instead of channeling it. The criticism that the media leveled against the government and all the structures connected with the state apparatus was not solely the result of the aftermath of the earthquake: it obviously comes from way back, it is a distrust of years that has been fed by events like the San Juanico tragedy, to give but an immediate example.

The social solidarity in Mexico City, which everyone insists on pointing to, was not always supported by national solidarity. In some cases, the states did not demonstrate any willingness to collaborate with the battered metropolis.■

IN SEARCH OF MAESTRA CARMEN

I am Lourdes Calvario. I am twenty-eight years old. I work in the ENEP Acatlán with folk and modern dance groups.

I live downtown, on Ecuador Street, in a house that fortunately remained standing, but when I learned at nine in the morning that the Nuevo León Building had fallen down, on the side where my teacher Carmen Castro lived—she was the director of the modern dance group, La Rueda, where I work—I bolted out of the house. When I saw the wreckage, I started to shout, "Carmen! Jorge!" Among those who also lived there was José Sandoval—a former dancer who was now devoted to what he called "the dark side of the moon"; in other words, he was a technician, he controlled the lights of the theater at ENEP Acatlán—and Jorge Sánchez, a dancer. Carmen Castro was married to Leonardo Velázquez, and they had two children, Adrián and Gabriel. Leonardo

Velázquez is a composer. I met them all because they used to come to our recitals. I also met his sister, Guadalupe, also a dancer.

Jorge Sánchez was a great guy. He lived alone. He had a mother and two young sisters, fifteen and sixteen. We would all meet at Centro Cultural Acatlán for rehearsals. As fate would have it, that night José Sandoval stayed over at a friend's house. He was saved.

At the Nuevo León, at nine in the morning, one could hear the screams:

"There are people in there, please help."

I was crying out, walking around the rubble, "Carmen! Jorge!"

"Don't shout, lady," someone told me. "Bring tools instead."

He was right. I had spent a year in a mountaineers' club at UNAM, and I also knew how to dive, so I said to myself, "What I know is applicable here." I went back home—just six blocks away—got hold of my equipment and came back running. No one knew how to get in. It was all a big ruin. It smelled like gas. It was rumored that the underground gas lines were about to explode, but I went in through a hole.

Once inside, I called out, "Carmen! Jorge!"

They never answered.

"Carmen! Jorge! Carmennnnn!"

I shouted until I was hoarse. I shouted and shouted, "Are you all right? Please answer me . . ."

Then I heard the voice of a woman and child: "Someone get us out of here, please." I crept until I thought I heard their voices, but the cavity was too narrow, and since I am heavy, I could not go forward without excavating. I went out and asked someone else to go in. I made a hole elsewhere and kept on shouting.

There were other moles going in. I shouted some more, "Carmen! Carmen!" My despair for my teacher was so great that I cried in impotence and wrath. I saw the size of the slabs and said to myself, "This is not possible, nobody will ever be able to lift them up." At three in the afternoon, I realized that I had lost my voice.

Without machines, we would never be able to do anything. We needed cranes.

At 11 A.M., they had started getting injured people out, live people. The moment when they started getting the dead from under the debris, I had the certainty that Carmen and Jorge would be found lifeless.

I kept on helping out. I would assist the injured ones to reach the DIF on the other side of the Paseo de la Reforma. I would take their information and tell them which hospital to go to. I referred them to different places according to the seriousness of their condition. I paid attention to the corpses. "Maybe with so many people coming out, I've missed some of them."

It occurred to me to go back home and call the dance group on the phone to see if by chance Carmen had gone to teach. I thought that for some reason that night she could have slept somewhere else and gone directly from there to the school. When you are so afflicted, you fantasize all sorts of things and come up with alternative outcomes for the events at hand.

I was terrified. Someone was saying to me, "She died," but the fact was so intolerable that I kept repeating, "Maybe she was not in the Nuevo León, maybe she's teaching her dancing class right now, as she always did."

But when they told me, "No, she didn't show up," I went to the Fifth Delegation where the corpses of Tlatelolco were being deposited.

Frankly, I still don't know why I went to the delegation.

I asked, "Are there bodies from the Nuevo León Building here?"

"Are there ever! There's bodies from everywhere here. Come right in, honey. If you find what you're looking for, just let us know, and we'll write up the death certificate."

I remained outside for about ten minutes, summoning up courage.

"Well, this has to do with Carmen, my teacher, I've got to do it . . ."

I tried to concentrate, I had never in my life seen a dead body. I went in, but I rushed through, and I didn't see anything, because I was blinded by tears and petrified with fear. Once I was outside again, I wept with sorrow and frustration with myself, so I said, "Calm down, if I'm trying to help, I'm going to do it well, and if I can't, I'll get out of the way and go home."

I really felt like running away. But I got hold of myself. I went in; I saw corpse after corpse, children, women, men. I saw a señora who impressed me terribly, because she was old and her body was totally smashed up, but her face was so peaceful, she looked like she was asleep, having nice dreams. I saw everyone very carefully, and nobody was Carmen, so I went out and thanked the people there, and I went back to the Nuevo León.

At seven in the evening, the army arrived and forbade us to get close. I argued that I had my own tools, that I was a mountain climber, and they answered that the operation was well organized, and that as civilians we had to step back. I said that I was looking for my relatives; I insisted; and finally with two other friends, we were able to go in through the back, holding flashlights. We burrowed another tunnel in, and when I threw light into the cavity, I saw a hand, and frankly that was too much. I felt exhausted, I went out, I sat under a tree and waited:

"Teacher, where are you? Carmen, which of these damned holes will I get you out of?"

My friends came looking for me:

"Lulú, you know what? You're very tired, let's go home."

"No."

"It will be a miracle if we find Carmen and Jorge still alive. No one who lived on the thirteenth floor survived."

Each time they called out that they had more bodies, I would run to see if it was they. And the most horrible thing is that I had to keep going back to the delegation. There were so many bodies on the floor that you had to skip over them looking for your own.

They had no power. A gas lamp shone on the bodies. I made three trips to the delegation that night. I went back home at 6 A.M., and at nine my group of mountaineers called to say that Hospital Juárez needed volunteers, and maybe my sister Dalila, who is also a climber, and I could go.

"Are you up for this?"

"You got it. I've slept three hours, but I think I can manage."

IT WAS HAUNTING TO HEAR CHILDREN CRY

I thought that this was going to be an easier job, because I was not looking for someone I was close to, but if in the Nuevo León the shouts of people asking for help were dreadful, in Hospital Juárez it was haunting to hear children cry. Outside, standing on the wreckage, they instructed us that the first ones to receive aid should be the women who had just given birth. When I got near with a shovel to excavate and heard a baby, I was petrified. I heard the baby cry and I said, "My God, what do I do, tell me, dear Lord, or is fear getting the best of me?"

I stood there, with a shovel in my hand.

"If you are not working, beat it, don't get in the way."

As hard as I tried to be courageous and order my body, it refused to obey me. Dalila told me, "You either help or you get the hell out and sit at home to whine until you get all the frustration out of your system."

But the truth is that we were both weeping. We didn't even know that tears were running down our cheeks. I spent all day removing crushed concrete, making tunnels, propping them up, and coming as close as possible to people. I was never able to reach a person. I had been too afraid to find one, dead or alive. I told Dalila, "I'm going back to the Nuevo León to see what's going on there . . ."

I found some compañeros from the dance school who notified me, "You know that they are now sending bodies to other delegations because the Fifth is overflowing?"

I ran to the Fifth. It was incredible to see the line of people waiting to identify cadavers. It was almost seven in the evening on Friday. I went in, I started to walk, and the moment I leaned forward to see a body, I thought; "God, I'm dizzy, I'm in rough shape."

Then I heard someone shout, "It's quaking."

The second earthquake caught me inside the Cuauhtémoc Delegation, identifying cadavers. People were yelling; many stumbled over one another and trampled on the bodies. The only way out was a spiral stairway in this two-story building. Someone shouted, "This building will fall in, it's brand new." I moved toward the stairway with my back up against the wall. Some of us fell on the stairway, and others stepped on us. I got up as best I could, and a hand grabbed mine: "Help me, help me." I never knew whose hand it was that I took and helped down the stairs. Outside the tremor continued. Presently I dashed to the Eje 1 North, thinking of my family, and ran from Cuauhtémoc to my house.

The second earthquake brought down what remained standing after the first one—the Pino Suárez skyscraper, for example, which killed many rescue workers. That night, I could not go back to the Nuevo León, I needed to be with my family, to fill my eyes with the sight of my sisters, to say with them, "Isn't it great to be alive?" I needed to look at them for a good while to convince myself that, yes, it was they, I wanted to fix in my mind the face of each one of them, to engrave in my mind the details of my house, to pay attention to everything, because I was thinking, "Maybe if it keeps on quaking, it will soon be my turn."

We slept out in the street; the truth of the matter is that never in my life had I slept in the street. Our house on Ecuador Street had to be evacuated because all the walls were cracked. Frankly I don't know how we slept; I don't remember what happened; all I know is that I slept soundly.

WE CAN'T HAVE THEM GO TO THE COMMON GRAVE

I went to call the guys from La Rueda on the phone, and they told me that Carmen's husband and Jorge Sánchez's relatives were asking about me. They wanted me to meet them at Coyuya Park and help them look for the bodies, because we couldn't have them go to the common grave. They said that there were 30 people looking for Carmen Castro among the cadavers, but even so, there were too many bodies, so they needed my help.

I took the subway to Coyuya. It was impossible to circulate by car through the devastated city, so I went the best I could, asking here and there for directions, and they would tell me that Coyuya was close to Jamaica, close to this or that . . . So I arrived there, finally, and even before I went in I felt my nose and my eyes burning because of the formaldehyde injected or sprayed on the cadavers.

"Get in line, you."

We were all standing in line, packed together against one another, pushing forward. They would fumigate us at the entrance, and we would go in, twenty at a time, stumbling over each other, and then file past the bodies to see if we could find the one we considered ours. The stench was hard to take. Some bodies were so badly crushed, they were beyond recognition.

"There's nothing here, let's go, there is nothing here at all . . ."

"Are you sure?" my compañero kept asking.

"I'm positive, but if you want, you go in and check. As far as I'm concerned she is not there."

When I arrived at home I burst out in tears, and my mother said, "Go to sleep, Lulú."

Around 3:00 A.M., my sister Dalila shook me and said, "What is it, Lulú? Are you sick or something?"

I shouted, "It's quaking!" and jumped out of bed like crazy.

"Come on, it isn't quaking, Lulú. But you were asleep with your eyes open."

"But I was resting. Why did you have to wake me up like that?"

"Because your eyes were open; I thought you were dead."

From then on my sister Dalila was afraid, and it was my fault. In the early morning my mother ordered, "We are going to see the doctor right now."

The doctor said I was suffering from extreme nervous tension. He gave me medicine and told me to stay home. I did, but I felt restless, and around six in the evening I could not help it:

"Have you found Carmen?" I asked on the phone.

"No."

MY PARTICIPATION IN RESCUE WORK WAS MY HOMAGE TO MY TEACHER CARMEN

I told myself once again, "It isn't fair for Carmen Castro and Jorge Sánchez to land in a common grave," so I went to Delta Park. I had to stand in line there for about an hour, and while I waited, I ran into two teachers from ENEP Acatlán, a man and a woman. At the doorway, when we saw the cadavers, the woman teacher fainted. I told the other one, "Look here, you take care of her, while I go see, and I'll be right back."

I walked among the bodies and all of a sudden, halfway through the circuit—there were hundreds, thousands, many more than the day before—I said to myself, "I can't see one more body, not one more." I left feeling terrible, and a young man wearing glasses said to me at the exit, "What happened? Didn't you find your people?"

"No, señor, I couldn't finish checking, excuse me."

And before he could start a conversation, I left and sat on the sidewalk to have a good cry: "I can't bear it, let someone else do it, I can't stand it anymore."

They saw I was so overwrought that they took me home.

On Monday, the experts came to check our house on Ecuador Street and told us we had to leave because the walls were giving way and the roof could come down at any moment. We started to collect our belongings, and I think that was very good for me, the packing, looking for a moving van. We had spent the second night out in the street, on Friday, but now, where were we going? Some of us with relatives, and the rest with other people. At dawn on Tuesday, I called some people to see what they knew about Carmen Castro, and one of my compañeros said, "Adrián, Carmen's son, is in the DIF standing guard, right in front of the Nuevo León. Many others are there waiting for the bodies to come out so they can identify them."

"Okay, I'll stand guard, as long as I don't have to see more bodies."

"That's fine, but at least you'll keep Adrián company . . . His brother and Leonardo are at Delta Park."

I was there from seven in the morning to six in the evening, and during those hours Carmen wasn't found. I went home to my relatives' house. My mother was very worried:

"Lulú, have you been taking your medicine?"

I went straight to the phone and called one of my compañeras:

"They've found her."

"Alive?"

My heart was pounding, galloping; all my blood was beating. I thought absurdly that maybe she had been out of town or something.

"Dead."

"Where is she? I need to go . . ."

"No, Lulú. Calm down. She is buried in a common grave."

There were thirty of us looking for Carmen Castro, plus her husband and two sons, and not one of us could identify her body, not one of us had been able to say, "Yes, this is Carmen."

I asked myself, How is it possible to have done so much work for nothing?

A woman like Carmen Castro, a woman we looked for in all the delegations, in Delta, in Coyuya, had to end up in a common grave. She gave ten years of her life to form a students' group, she gave freely of her time, and she ended up in a common grave. God! How's it possible? Didn't we have eyes? Didn't we pay attention to what we were doing? Why was I crying instead of looking?

Carmen, you would stay after class, teaching us not how to dance, but how to live. That's who she was. She would sit down and listen to you, drink a glass of milk or wine with you, give you good advice. She was the friend who gave of herself, you could walk to her and say, "You know what, Carmen? I am feeling down because of this or that . . .," and she'd listen. And she, Carmen Castro, had to end up in a common grave.

She, who never failed anyone, was failed by life.

She was buried in a common grave, like an unknown person, because none of us who wandered all over the place since Thursday could identify her, or Jorge, for that matter. We only know that they were buried because Jorge's relatives were notified that many bodies had been taken out from the back of the Nuevo León immediately to the Dolores Cemetery. Jorge's family went to identify him, and they saw Carmen; they recognized her because she was wearing a bracelet with tiny hearts. Jorge was identified only by the clothes he was wearing a day before the earthquake. But we can't even say, "Yes, they are the ones." We can't; they went as anonymous corpses to their rest.

A common grave is a health measure. Well, maybe Carmen is not even there—who knows—the thing is that nobody could ever see her, nobody. How many other people are there, buried next to her?

The only solution to the grief I felt was to go back to rescue work. I went to the Pino Suárez complex, with fifty kids. If I'd stayed cooped up in the house I would have gone nuts. I went with the mountaineers. And there I felt only rage. They'd say to me, "Lulú, that hole's all yours because you're a little padded, and you can hack it."

"You got it," and I'd go in.

Everyone there was real young, I was the oldest at twenty-eight, and the youngest was a little skinny girl of fifteen. I had to stand watch in the Pino Suárez complex for forty-eight hours, and I took it because many medical school interns were going on for seventy-two hours at a time, although I saw them dozing off in fits and starts; then they would get up, and I thought, I take my hat off to these people. In the tunnels I would lose track of time, asking myself whether it was night or day when I came in.

We were working in a tunnel to reach the cafeteria, where it was thought that survivors could be found, since they had food and water, but in that hodgepodge—the building no longer had any shape—cafeteria workers did not survive either. We didn't find one single survivor. It all took too long, and the removal of broken masonry was much too slow.

I feel that what compelled me to keep trying to get bodies out—even though I never rescued anyone alive, but only found five bodies, not one of them alive—what compelled me to go back and to stay there until November 1 was the love and admiration I had for Carmen Castro. It was like saying to her, "My dear teacher, I thought of you. These are the roses you like best."

THE BUILDING AT TEHUANTEPEC 12 WITHSTOOD THE EARTHQUAKE FOR ONE MINUTE
I SAT DOWN TO THROW STONES; I FELT INCAPACITATED

Among the people who came to give testimony at the Center for Information and Analysis of the Effects of the Earthquake, in painful sessions in which we all participated, the only two witnesses in a tie and business suit were engineer Raúl Pérez Pereyra and his son Jorge Alejandro Pérez Lara Pardo. The dark blue suit of Pérez Pereyra underscored his condition of mourning, but even more revealing were his reddened face, the tears he barely contained, and the trembling of his son's lips:

My name is Raúl Pérez Pereyra. I'm a civil engineer, and I have worked for some construction and industrial design firms. Because of my profession, I feel a certain responsibility for not having detected the faults that caused the collapse of the building where we lived at Tehuantepec 12. Unfortunately, one doesn't have X-ray vision to see the inside of walls.

Ten minutes before the earthquake on the 19th, I went out with my young son to take him to school. It was a mere coincidence, because it was my wife's turn to take him. The moment when the earthquake started I was approximately two blocks away from the building. I was able to return immediately, taking my son by the hand and leaving him with our neighbors so that I could climb on what was left of the nine-story apartment building. Nothing was left. According to the observations of neighbors who watched, the building did not withstand two minutes of the earthquake, indeed, it collapsed after the first minute. According to the accounting that we have so far, seventy-eight people perished (but the number of victims could reach eighty), among them my wife Elvira, my daughter Diana, and my two grandsons, Leonardo and Orlando. They all were trapped under the weight of the wreckage.

When I climbed up to see whether I could rescue my family, I immediately saw that it would be impossible; the floors were sandwiched one over the other. It was physically impossible for a person to remain alive under those conditions. I understood this fact from the start, and yet hope takes a very long time to die.

I couldn't say how long it took, perhaps fifteen or twenty minutes, for me to react. I stood motionless, staring at the sight. I probably didn't think for an hour and a half. There I was, in a business suit. I took off my jacket and tie. I sat on the rubble and threw stones, that was all I could do. I felt totally useless. The neighbors started to come, and I sat directly on the spot where my family should have been. I didn't think of any other family; I didn't think of anything at all.

On top of my family's apartment, there were four levels, four concrete platforms, each sitting heavily on the one below it. I remained there waiting for help, perhaps from rescue workers, perhaps from people I thought existed in Mexico, people who knew how to do this kind of thing: excavators with picks and shovels, radios, and heavy equipment, the army, the Red Cross, the police, other institutions.

During the three days that the recovery of my family took, I never saw a digger, an ax, or a shovel belonging to the army or the police. All the help I received came from volunteers. The army came to cordon off the area, to obstruct the work, to steal. They blatantly stole money and jewelry before my very eyes. I can bear witness to these things at any time because I consider it my civic responsibility to do so. I have the names of people from the army who infamously and before our very eyes took jewels and other valuables from the condominiums while making it impossible for the courageous volunteers to go up.

The building at Tehuantepec 12 received more immediate attention than any other one in the city for this reason: across the street was a major construction site for the expansion of the subway and a sewage tunnel. So there were two high-capacity cranes that were put to use that afternoon. Yet I realized that all of us who participated in the recovery operations were completely incapable of doing it right. None of us had the psychological or physical training to carry out work of this sort. We were totally incapable.

Some time ago, I used to hike. I was a pentathlon participant. I learned about rescue operations and methods of survival. I had read a lot on ways to survive a disaster in the air or at sea, but when it happened to me, in my own flesh, I was helpless.

Those of us interested in saving the lives of our relatives had no clue as to how to penetrate that mass of concrete. Little by little, aid began to come in a totally disorganized fashion. People from the Associated Civil Engineers (ICA) who were active in the subway construction took a direct interest, but they didn't know where to start; nobody knew what to do. When someone thought of using torches to cut rods, we all worried about the smell of gas. A giant stationary tank could blow up the whole district. We started to work with our hands, without a jackhammer, without a chisel, without any tools. Around twelve noon, the people from ICA lent us rudimentary tools, hammers, chisels, hacksaws that broke immediately and could not be replaced. By nightfall, we saw that we had no lamps. At that hour we thought of going to buy them, but there was not even one store open.

I tried to lift hunks of rubble with my hands, but very soon I got awfully tired. I felt that I was fat, awkward. A fine drizzle scared some volunteers away. It got colder. I had taken off my jacket and tie, and now I was cold. I saw a clothesline with lots of clothes still attached, and I grabbed the first thing I found, a woman's white sweater; I still have it. I must have looked ridiculous, but that was the least of my problems. I excavated all night long until Friday the 20th, when the aid got somewhat organized. Some tunnels were burrowed with a certain success. We felt that we were seriously learning how to rescue.

At six in the afternoon, that very Friday, we had made a tunnel all the way to the living room of my apartment. My three very young nephews had come to help me, and they had gone in like moles. We could see some of the furniture smashed in a space of less than a foot and a half.

The kids were some twenty feet under the slabs in the tunnel when the second tremor started a little after seven. Fifty of us were on top of the building. They all started to slide down an inclined wall full of debris. I waited for my nephews to come out. I remained calm until that moment, but once I saw the last one out, I was possessed by a powerful panic like never before in my life. Because the earth was still quaking, I threw myself where everyone else was jumping, but I got hooked on a steel cable until someone came and freed me. The whole elevator shaft was dancing above us, threatening to fall and crush us.

At that moment, even though I'm an engineer and I've dedicated my life to design and construction, I couldn't think of anything except to get my family out and to run and protect myself. This was the first night I was taken to sleep at the house of some friends; I was exhausted, and besides, after the second earthquake, all the volunteers had fled. That night I didn't know what else had been done in the building until the next morning, very early, when my nephews and I realized that the tunnel that we had so painstakingly opened had been blocked up by other volunteers who came in the night and in the darkness filled the tunnel with debris.

Saturday at eleven, we recovered my wife Elvira Lara de Pérez and my grandson Orlando Morales Pérez. The two of them were in the bedroom hugging each other. They were in very bad shape. We took them down to a storefront that was serving as the repository for cadavers. There the army and police were fighting for control of the bodies. Some were being taken to one place, some to another. I asked some friends to stand guard by our bodies because I had to go up and find the rest of my people. But as soon as I left, they were taken to the baseball field nearby, the Delta Park, where the other corpses were concentrated.

Somebody went up to tell me that I needed to go to the Delta Park, and I had to abandon the recovery of the other two bodies: that of my daughter Diana Pérez de Morales and my grandson Leonardo. Thus I started instead a kind of way of the cross that still lasts until today. I had to face bureaucrats instead of soldiers or police. At that point a war was declared that has not ended, and whose outcome is unknown. I was in the baseball field for close to six hours to avoid having my people buried in a common grave. I had to struggle against men who acted as if they didn't have a gram of brains in their heads, but that's another story.

When I went back to what was left of Tehuantepec 12, the bodies of my daughter Diana and my grandchild had been uncovered, embracing each other. They could not be taken out because they were totally crushed. We had to get jacks to lift the slabs, and once we got them out at seven on Saturday, we took them to the baseball field, Delta Park, where we put them together with my wife and my other grandchild.

After another struggle with bureaucrats, at eleven at night we were successful in getting an ambulance to take them to the Jardines del Recuerdo Cemetery. Although I had paid all the required fees four years ago, the cemetery charged me 240,000 pesos, that is 60,000 for each one of my loved ones, because according to their arithmetic, 30,000 pesos were due to pay the government program plus 30,000 for the red tape to permit interment. I didn't pay them right away, but I had to come back with the money the next day because they would not bury them until they could see 240,000 pesos free and clear.

I was at war with bureaucrats, the Ministerio Público, the physicans who were tending the dead. The bodies of my family were wearing identification tags, but I saw the physicians removing tags from other corpses, probably with the purpose of sending them to the common grave and not having to wait for relatives.

Since we were watching closely, nobody touched the bodies of our people. They put them all together along with their bags of ice, because it had been three days since they had died. If we had not been extremely vigilant with our cadavers, they would have gotten them mixed up with others. I don't know what imbecilic objective those people had in mind—physicans, bureaucrats, the police—in attempting to mix up all the corpses.

To gain permission to transfer the bodies to the Jardines del Recuerdo Cemetery was sheer torture. We wandered from one delegation to another. Once the bodies were in the cemetery, they were trying to make us take them back to Mexico City because we didn't have a transfer certificate. Our leaders did everything within their means to obstruct our work. I never felt in them any human warmth, any disposition to help—nothing but hellish paperwork and total dehumanization on the part of government bureaucrats and the vultures of the Jardines del Recuerdo Cemetery.

Once the recovery and the anguish and grief of identifying the bodies of our loved ones were over, with the full knowledge that they had been located and given a proper burial, I began to think a little bit about my neighbors. I feel responsible and guilty because once I recovered the remains of my relatives I could not go back to help my neighbors find their own. I am profoundly sorry that I could not do it, because they, my neighbors, were immensely helpful to me. I simply could not get myself back to Tehuantepec 12 for three or four days. It all hurt too much. I think that my conscience is clear because even if I had tried, I could not have done it. These are mental pretexts, not enough to exculpate me. To my neighbors whom I failed to help, I here beg your forgiveness, I'm truly sorry.

TRIALS AND TRIBULATIONS: RETRIEVING A BOX OF JEWELS

THEY TREATED US AS IF WE WERE ACCUSED OF HIGH TREASON

Young Alejandro Pérez Lara Pardo, the son of engineer Raúl Pérez Pereyra, was in Paris when he heard of the September 19 catastrophe in which he lost his mother, his sister Diana, and his two nephews, Leonardo and Orlando:

Friday afternoon at four they gave me the news. Knowing that my family lived in a tall, modern building, at Tehuantepec 12, I wasn't afraid. Fourteen hours later I had a message from my father, in English. I speak English, but I just couldn't get it; I didn't want to understand: "Building collapsed, four are missing." Four loved ones, my family.

I imediately went to the airport with a cassette so that Aereoméxico could take it, a passenger or anyone else on board, while I gathered the money for my own airfare. My friends were enormously helpful. They collected money for me and gave it to me so that I could leave on Sunday at 11 A.M., Paris time. The ticket cost some $850, twice the normal price. My brother, who was in Lisbon, got a ticket on a different airline for $450. The only airline that wasn't helpful was the one from Mexico, not only in matters of ticket costs but also concerning the transportation of medicine.

In Miami, I asked customs officers to allow me to buy medications in the airport drugstores, with money collected in Paris for that purpose, and they made it easy for me to do so. Not the people from Aereoméxico: they warned me that I could miss the flight if I took too long, that this was my problem. Most likely, these people knew that their relatives had not suffered any damage, so they could simply wash their hands of the relief efforts, and couldn't care less about what I was trying to do.

I bought antiseptics, aspirin, penicillin, antihistamines, tablets to combat intestinal infection, the works—anything I thought could be useful. The money had been donated specifically for medicine. I was able to fill a whole suitcase. No one at the Benito Juárez Airport checked my bags.

I arrived at eleven at night at the house of some relatives, and there I found my father. I knew from the first moment I saw him that I would have to weep with him, not just help him reorganize our lives. I could never say the last farewell to my mother, to my sister Diana, to my nephews. They were all under the ground.

Trying to make myself somewhat relevant, I decided to become my father's chauffeur. Even though I have an international driver's license, cops kept stopping me to ask for my documents. I never held a shovel in my hands; I never went to the heap of rubble to see where my relatives were. My father requested that I be in charge of recouping my mother's jewels and her clothing. He himself had recovered the jewelry case from the fallen building. The only problem was that when he brought it down, a captain took it away from him and rushed away. A cousin of mine—she was a first-aid worker—saw him and ran after him, asking, "Where are you taking that case?"

"To a safe place; they can be stolen here."

"No, Señor, you cannot take those jewels because they belong to my aunt."

"You don't know whether they belong to your aunt or not."

"Well, you're not taking them until we have a signed inventory of what is inside."

"No, Señorita, I'll do nothing of the sort. My job is not to take inventories."

"But you have to, if you're taking them."

"Shut up."

He left running, and some soldiers followed him.

At this point, my niece, interjects engineer Raúl Pérez Pereyra, with all the courage in the world, a young woman of twenty-five, married, a first-aid volunteer during all those days, ran after the captain, took him by the arm, and confronted him:

"Señor, you have to give me that inventory. I'm going to follow you wherever you go until you do so."

"Hey, that's fine with me, lady."

"Wait, I'm going to get a compañero."

"No. Either you come now or not at all."

He didn't want anyone else to come, putting her in a very compromising position. They got into a jeep and took the jewels to the National Palace. There they waited six hours before the inventory could be taken. When they finally opened the case, they found twenty bullets.

"Now," they told my niece, "you have to be detained. What are these twenty bullets doing here? You must be into arms dealing."

"Señor, it's clear that someone put them there. My aunt kept her jewelry in this case, not bullets. There's a compartment where the jewelry is, take a look."

They took the inventory and made several copies, refusing to give one to my niece, but she managed to sneak one out.

"Aren't you going to give me the jewels?"

"No, not now. You ought to be satisfied now that we took the inventory. It's right here in multiple copies. We'll notify you when you can come to get them."

When engineer Raúl Pérez Pereyra recovered from his stupor, he took the copy snatched away by his niece and went to claim the jewelry case at the National Palace. There soldiers of all possible ranks from captain on sent him from one office to another without telling him anything.

Finally, continues engineer Pérez Pereyra, the man who had taken the inventory was definitively identified by my niece.

"We are not in the habit of taking inventories. Where did you get that piece of paper?"

"Look here, whether you're in the habit or not, this is the inventory."

"We can't give you the jewelry unless you show proof of ownership."

"How in the world can I show you proof of ownership when everything I have is buried under that building? My whole family is there, dead! And you want me to show proof of ownership! This is the one memento I have."

"I don't have those jewels under my control anymore. They are warehoused at Campo Militar Number 1."

At Campo Militar Number 1 they sent us to three different offices. We felt as if we had committed high treason. They looked down on us, they searched us, they questioned us, and they displayed their rifles and submachine guns for our benefit. They shoved us. They blocked our way.

Six hours later, a captain said, "The point is, we have nothing here. All valuables have been stored in La Ciudadela."

It was nine o'clock at night. In Mexico, if you don't have connections, you're lost. Through friends of friends, we managed to locate someone with ties to the army who recommended us, and with that recommendation, we went to La Ciudadela. Then to the National Palace. To make a long story short, it took us twenty-five days of red tape, comings and goings that left me totally exhausted before 50 percent of the jewelry that had belonged to my wife Elvira was given to me. The rest disappeared forever.

The delivery itself was painful. They showed me two numismatic collections in albums that must have been worth a fortune. I saw clearly that it was a trap to bring me down.

"This must belong to your wife, since this collection has always been next to your jewelry case."

"No, Señor, this is not mine."

I saw the soldiers looking at each other, laughing as if to say, "He didn't fall for it."

"All right, so we will show you the rest now: Can you identify this necklace?"

"Look here, this is a blown glass necklace; it's worthless."

"What about this?" They showed me a pair of cheap earrings.

"You can have them."

"A brooch."

"Also for you with my compliments."

It was sheer torture. They brandished trinkets before my eyes. They wanted me to reach out for them.

"This bracelet must be yours, it's a good one."

"It did not belong to my wife; I don't know who the owner is; I don't want it."

It was a dreadful scramble of valuable gems, costume jewelry, and trinkets.

"How about this ring?"

"That is worth something."

"Ah!" he'd say sarcastically, "you only want the expensive stuff."

"No, Señor, what I want is the jewelry that belonged to my wife. Whatever I can recognize. Unfortunately, I may not be able to recognize everything."

I lived with my wife Elvira for thirty-one years. Each year, for our anniversary, I gave her a gem. She had, therefore, thirty-one valuable pieces. Since she wore them, I could recognize them perfectly. But my children also gave her some lovely things for her birthday, her saint's day; those were difficult for me to tell apart. The jewels I gave her, all thirty-one, I remember perfectly, since I chose them with love, good gems.

After I retrieved half the jewels, one of our neighbors, Guadalupe Sandoval, asked me what I had done to get them back. I told her about my way of the cross, and she decided to follow it step by step personally. They had the gall to tell her at the National Palace that she should bring any claim to me, because I had kept all the jewelry that had been found in that building.

She was also made an object of mockery by members of the army. They followed the tactic of showing her junk. It must be said that Guadalupe Sandoval is a very attractive woman, young and spunky. Finally, after three days of getting nowhere, she told the army, "Señores, you are obviously needier than I; you are dying of hunger; you have resorted to petty thievery. Why don't you keep it all?"

Engineer Pérez Pereyra adds gravely: I am ready to testify before the Attorney General's Office, before Prosecutor Victoria Adato de Ibarra. I am willing to denounce this outrage before the highest authorities in the army. I have proof, names, and witnesses. There is Guadalupe Sandoval, who never recovered anything at all and who wants to testify. She agrees with me that if it were not for volunteers who worked at Tehuantepec 12, we would not have done anything; they are all a bunch of thieves, and I'm prepared to say this again, anytime, anywhere.

I want to say that the three firefighters who came to our aid did it with integrity, calm, and competence. They intervened at crucial moments. They wouldn't remove rubble in the human chain, but when it came to rescuing bodies, they participated fully and directed operations knowledgeably. I feel that the firefighters fulfilled their duty. Even though one could have hoped for a more heroic attitude, one cannot expect everyone to risk life and limb when I myself succumbed to cowardice and ran like a bullet away from the building when the second earthquake struck on September 20.

We finally ask engineer Pérez Pereyra, the specialist, about construction codes: Why are buildings so poorly put together in our country? Why do contractors cheat by using substandard materials like inferior rods? Why do they endanger the lives of hundreds of people with impunity?

I have found myself in difficult circumstances. From the time I studied engineering we were told, "An engineer is the one who can build the same building with half the money." An engineer must build economically. Engineers must save in building procedures. But the engineers that built the fallen buildings—especially Tehuantepec 12—found a way of saving exorbitant amounts to amass illicit fortunes while placing the lives of the occupants at a very high risk.

What's the dividing line between economical construction and criminal irresponsibility? What made the buildings collapse, the earthquake or poor construction?

People in highly specialized and scientific circles are saying that it was the earthquake; that the buildings fell because the tremor had a very high period of vibration, as compared to the ones we have calculated in accordance with the construction regulations of 1957, after the biggest seismic movement the city had suffered.

When the Angel of Independence fell, the construction code was modified by Doctors Emilio Rosenblueth and Esteva Maraboto. They are responsible for the new regulations for the Federal District. Buildings were classified according to their height and the characteristics of the soil where they were built. The Federal District was divided into three types of ground: soil of low compressibility, that is, soft soil; soil of high compressibility, that is, soil with a high content of tepetate, a type of flagstone; and soil that is transitional between the two.

A seismic map of the Federal District was drawn up, and buildings were assessed according to this map. At a very high academic level, in the university, they are saying that the earthquake made the buildings fall. I disagree. I believe that there is corruption, even at the level of the highest authorities.

In the United States, there is a construction code. My son Alejandro Pérez Lara Pardo attended a construction symposium at the university, and when he spoke up about the lack of adequate materials used in the buildings, as well as the lack of adequate calculations, they asked him, "Are you a student of engineering or of law?"

"I'm in law school."

"This is an engineering conference, not a legal one. Please do not intervene."

The official version is that the whole matter of the earthquake will be buried. No guilty parties will be found in this collective assassination. If an investigation were undertaken, many of the authorities who have looked the other way while allowing this kind of construction would be found to be in collusion with the biggest contractors in this country. In fact, many officials own their own construction firms and give themselves juicy government contracts. Many capitalists have invested in construction and coerced their designers and builders to keep quiet by means of moral blackmail. To find a guilty party is to get ahold of the tail of the mouse, but the head of the mouse is in the highest spheres of government. This is true of the present administration and of former ones. It's far easier to point to the small and not-so-big wrongdoers than to the real culprits.

I feel that our responsibility—the responsibility of engineers—consists in unmasking those who are to blame for the murder of September 19. We must press morally and judicially until justice is done.

I'm not fooling myself, I know that in many similar cases major problems have simply been filed away. I'll keep on struggling. I have an appointment at the Office of the Attorney General. I will continue denouncing. I wish at the very least to exercise the right to be a critic, and not to appear as a coward in the eyes of my sons and my friends. I will not allow the tragedy of Tehuantepec 12, where my loved ones died, to be filed away. I lost my wife Elvira, my daughter Diana, and my two grandchildren, Leonardo and Orlando. Their bodies were retrieved with the help of volunteers by my nephews Antonio, Octavio, and Juan Mendoza Lara, three young men who endangered their lives going into the tunnels until they reached the apartment where the shattered bodies were found.

Young people are the only thing I believe in.

Moisés Martínez

Nearly 60 percent of the inhabitants of the Federal District are young people and children, all of whom offered their aid, their lives. Maybe I'm mistaken, but our young people seemed taller, stronger, braver than those of earlier generations, more organized. There was no mobilization like this twenty-eight years ago when the Angel of Independence fell. Youngsters work together from all neighborhoods, from Santa Julia, Guerrero, and San Angel to Polanco and Las Lomas. ■

Novedades

A young couple was found and rescued alive from under the wreckage of the Nuevo León. Rebeca and Oscar, twenty-nine years old, were discovered by a minuscule television camera just minutes after the visit of Nancy Reagan and Mexican first lady Paloma Cordero. A man who described himself as an engineer was standing on his hands and cheering Oscar and Rebeca, to the astonishment of hundreds of foreign reporters.

Tlatelolco woke up with the news that the sixty-year-old woman who had been found yesterday among the sixth-floor rubble declined to leave the crevice where she was, even when nothing blocked her way to the surface. Volunteers, firemen, the police, and even soldiers were anxiously waiting for the moment when a special basket held by a crane would bring her out from under the wreckage: just like that, she said no.

With a flat, "I'm not coming out," the lady, who did not want to give her name, got hold of some stones and from the cavity where she had been for four days started pelting anyone who got near. Finally, Dr. Francisco Villanueva Medina, chief of medical services in the area, approached her shielded behind a piece of wood and asking for a truce was able to exchange a few words with the lady.

"Look, I'm not leaving until you've rebuilt all this . . . Tell the President that I'm not leaving until they have put up a new building here," the woman shouted.

In forty-three hours of work, 172 cadavers and fifty-four living persons have been recovered from the Nuevo León.

At ten minutes after midnight today, five survivors were rescued from San Camilito in Garibaldi.

At 2:58, eight additional survivors in Mitla and Luz Saviñón streets, Colonia Navarte.

The streets of San Luis Potosí, Tonalá, Tehuantepec, Alvaro Obregón, and Colima received the worst punishment. At the corner of

San Luis Potosí and Tonalá, an eight-story building became a heap of rubble. In another ruin, at dawn, two babies, three and five months old, were rescued alive.

Juan Antonio Ascencio

Saúl Abarca was alive on September 12. He is missing. His family has looked for him in many places, among others in the Attorney General's Office, the Procu. Why would he be there? Of course he is not. They clearly told the relatives that he wasn't there, that they knew nothing about him, and one would have to think that they were telling the truth. He did not appear in that day's list of missing, nor the next, nor the next. He had not been released, nor transferred to the care of any judge. He had neither been found dead nor detained in any hospital. He did not sleep in the aisles of the Procu, nor was he in charge of bringing food to his two detained clients, one of whom was a Colombian citizen, nothing like that.

The following day, September 13, Mrs. Yolanda Raya, wife of litigator Saúl Abarca, filed an affidavit, document 12–2833–85, charging the judicial agents with responsibility for anything that could happen or might have happened to her husband.

Neither the chief prosecutor, the subprosecutors, nor the other officers found out or tried to find out the whereabouts of Saúl Abarca.

When the entrails of the earth shook on the morning of September 19, Saúl Abarca was already dead. When the building of the Attorney General's Office crumbled, the wreckage covered the car (What color, brand name, model? Who was its owner? What was the plate number?) in whose trunk lay the cadaver, gagged, with feet and hands tied. When that car was found in the sea of rubble, a car that was allowed to park inside the Procu, the trunk was opened, and everyone thought that the body found there was one more victim of the earthquake.

No, no, the experts said. Nothing like that. On September 22, the cadaver was in an advanced state of decomposition, and the only evidence was a bullet (Who owned the weapon? What caliber? Where was it used?) that had entered the body many hours before the earthquake.

The agent's car (Was he a commander?) was in the parking lot at least since dawn on the 19th, when many woke up for the last time. Maybe its owner was among those who died, and the earthquake prevented his getting rid of the body. The author of this crime was surely occupied with the high designs that only the authorities can deal with, and he may have forgotten that, for hours or days before, he had been carrying a big nuisance in his trunk, something that had to be disposed of, not knowing that this would be for him the very last morning.

And nobody ever knew even the color of that car, parked inside the Attorney General's Building.■

Gisang Fung, A Singular Character
MY BEHAVIOR CHANGED AFTER I WAS IN THAT TUNNEL

Gisang Fung is Chinese; I mean, his parents are. He's already a Mexican, but his eyes are like slits, his mouth is round, his face is round, and he has thin eyebrows. His parents own a wine store at 929 Revolution Avenue. Gisang works there when he is not busy with the theater group With You, America. He is one of the most singular characters of postseismic days. Maybe his name and last name are not spelled that way, but Jin Sahn Fung. From the moment on September 19th when he was in the store and heard people say, "No, this was terrible, everything has been destroyed," he has been helping out with his friend Raúl.

We were standing there trying to see what we could do in the Hospital General, and all the people we saw were dumbfounded, with lost gazes, as if they were looking inward, when I stood beside a fireman and said, "Listen, let me give you a hand."

Roll the cameras! I got ahold of an enormous pressure hose, this big, and everything was full of smoke. And it was a matter of taking it and seeing what happened, and I started to help as an apprentice firefighter. The fire was interminable, all the furniture thrown in there, burning, smoking to death. To put out part of the fire was useless, and it was impossible to know when it was going to be over, and I started taking all that smoke in, smoke, and more smoke, and a moment came when I had cried all the tears I had, so I started to talk to a fireman:

"Hi, what's been your worst experience?"

"Brother! San Juanico of course."

There we were talking with our hoses, shooting water all the way down because the building was hollow. Everything was sunken. It was all red hot, and lost in the red you could distinguish chairs, beds, sofas, all ignited and sunken in the same big hole. There was just no way to put the fire out. There I learned what it means to wait for certain things to happen, but I was out of my wits. I was staring at the fire captain, a fat man with big shadows under his eyes, and each time he drew in the smoke from his cigarette it seemed like an eternity. He smoked intently. He would take the cigarette out of his mouth and wait until the next interminable sucking. I thought, "That's it, you have to treat the fire in the same way, just as calmly."

Firemen stood there trying to put the fire out hour after hour, smiling politely and going on with their jobs; I truly have no idea for how many hours. Later, Raúl, my pal—I don't know his last name—said to me, "Let me help with the hose." But since he wears glasses, and they were covered with smoke, he had to come back down quickly and go to another part of the hospital where they were cutting through concrete slabs.

Firemen had already removed a big piece of ceiling, and they were making holes to get to the newborn babies and their mothers in the maternity ward. We were there until five in the morning.

"Thank you, brother," a fireman said to me.

"My name is Gisang Fung."

"Nice to know you."

I joined Raúl. There were so many spotlights, it was like a movie set, and the actors were ropes, torn concrete, picks, shovels, men in groups of three or four hammering away at the rubble with all their might, with a gut wish to help the ones that were still alive. They would get a flashlight in and shout, "Anybody there?"

And if anyone answered, they would introduce a hose, would summon a doctor, and would start excavating even faster.

I started breaking slabs, too, along with a construction worker (a soldier who forgot he was a soldier and put his gun on his back and started using a crowbar to lift rubble), some laborers, and a bunch of young guys who had never learned how you hold a sledgehammer, but there they were, nonetheless, very willing. We made the hole bigger and bigger, and cleaned it up. We took out lots of bricks. We broke through the steel grid. Concrete slabs are held together by a kind of thick mesh of steel rods, and you have to break through it. Since I'm short and thin, they would say to me, "Hey, you be the one, get in there, see what you find."

The most wimpish among us got in, the real señores couldn't make it through; so they were in charge of the sledgehammers. In that first hole, I went way in and shouted, "Is anyone there?"

Nobody. Nothing. A complete vacuum. I went out to start another hole with Raúl, and under that slab we started to find the live ones, including a newborn baby. As soon as we got him out, a man held him and started to run with him toward the doctors, but people tried to stop him, "Wait, wait," and the man kept on running with the child in his arms, eager to give the baby medical attention.

We were still making the hole, propping it up inside with all the people outside waiting. They were standing in a long chain of a hundred people to carry one single body, when suddenly they took out this chick, pulling her by the feet, with gangrene on her leg. They took her alive, and that was the first time that I felt like crying along with everyone else because there she was, this girl, thin, petite, skinnier than I with very long hair, and they put a white robe on her because people appeared naked after the earthquake. As a man said to me, "You wouldn't believe it, but this chick here was found naked."

This girl was so eager to get out, just so eager, that she was pushing herself onto the stretcher with her feet, and when she did it, she turned her face to see all the people who were watching her. When she saw the sheer joy that her rescue was causing, she must have felt like she had just been born. So she wept as she looked at them. I found that very impressive, that such a small person was working so hard for her own survival, that she got on the stretcher by her own strength, and knowing that she had survived, she had a special radiance in her face.

Later on they took another newborn baby and then another little child. By this time, it was about six in the morning, and I said to Raúl, "Hey, let's go."

"Sure, man."

We left the General all covered with dirt. On the corner by a newspaper stand were three survivors waiting for their relatives to pick them up. They were lying down with their heads bandaged, covered with blankets, all downcast, when suddenly three photographers in short pants appeared with something like 50 cameras, a real ton of equipment. They began taking pictures, pum, pum, pum, pum, just like that, a bunch of photographs. We were leaving, but I said to Raúl, "Hey, Raúl, this can't be."

We went back and asked them what they thought they were up to. We said that it wasn't right, that the people were too screwed over to react, that they surely didn't appreciate being photographed like that. We really told them off.

"Listen, I'm just doing my job."

"Oh yeah? You know what, bud? You can't take any more photos, so move it."

The survivors, they didn't catch on to anything; they didn't even see them. The photos that were taken caught them bent over, a face in the dirt, a head on the ground, damn, just like if nothing mattered. It made a real bad impression. Meanwhile, the buildings were still full of smoke. Sheets were tied to the rubble here and there, possibly marking spots where some people might still be alive. The people . . . But I was asking myself, how could anybody be alive in the midst of such smoke. Just a moment before leaving, Raúl asked a little old man, "And what are you doing here, Señor?"

"I'm waiting for my daughter, to see if they found her."

But he was not crying, he didn't look desperate, he was only there, helping by watching over the firemen's tools. I said to him, "Man, I really hope they find your daughter. I really hope so."

For real, man, something was calling me. I don't know what, a special voice inside me was saying, "Go and stay there." So I called my family and my sister, for sure:

"You know what? To tell you the truth I called to say goodbye— who knows what will happen to me?—so I'll see you later."

I really meant it, I was speaking from the heart.

"Where are you going?"

"I don't know, wherever they'll take me, that's the truth."

"Go ahead, then."

"See you, then. Good-bye."

I knew that if something happened to me, I had said my good-byes.

Around the Eje Central, we went toward Conalep. A bunch of guys in a van said, "Get on, you guys," and that was our ticket into Conalep because these dudes were wearing helmets, so the soldiers and the police quickly allowed us in: "Come in, come in." For sure, they had rope, they had everything. They gave us other helmets, picks, shovels, gloves; and then some men came over:

"We're engineers and we came to explain to you how to remove the slabs because we will soon go in with the machines."

"You can't yet, they're still getting people out."

One part of Conalep remained standing, while the other was shattered on the ground.

"I need an electric drill. Who's got one?"

And before I knew it, my big mouth had said, "You bet, one electric drill coming right up."

I went and asked for one, pretending to be in charge of coordination. What I really wanted was to go all the way in to Conalep to see what was going on there. A drill appeared in my hands—who knows how?—and I went back to the one who had requested it:

"Here's the drill."

The other guy said to me, "Listen, I'm looking for my daughter; she's a student there in Conalep; I need to know where she is."

"Jeez, this is a real bitch."

"Please give me a chance to go in, she's my daughter, please," he said to the engineer.

"No, that's impossible."

"Hey, pal, you come with me."

So I said to one of the engineers, "Okay, I'll go with him."

So, when we got there, we walked over to the center of Conalep, to the little courtyard, and I stayed there listening to the engineers and rescue workers for an hour. And this poor, desperate man, who knows where he went? But I was still there with the engineers, and when they organized the rescue brigade to actually go in, I stuck to them. And that's when I started to function as a human being. That was the prelude, the beginning of something that was happening to me because never in my life had I been in a tunnel like that, at Hospital General I had merely propped up the excavation, but the Conalep tunnel, that was truly something; going in there changed me.

Everything changed: the way I am, the way I behave, the way I feel, the way I show emotion. So in I go, man, and all those lamps strewn about in the tunnel, you know? And then the stench of death, Jesus, man, you've never smelled something like that. All of a sudden, there they are, the bent body of young guy and a chick, like this, gone, dead, in a tunnel half a yard tall max, man, barely high enough for a guy like me. I said, "Jesus, is this a movie or what?"

We put stanchions in to hold the tunnel open, we asked for hydraulic jacks, and we brought in a chain of battery-operated lamps, a bunch of little lamps giving light in that god-awful tunnel, like it had some life, like a light of its own, you know? And I kept on crawling, going by the side of those two lifeless bodies. Was that ever creepy, man! Someone else and I shouted together, "Is anyone there?"

And, just imagine, we heard a voice:

"Yes, we're down here."

"Don't worry, we're getting you out."

"What are your names?"

They gave their names, seven students.

"But hurry, because there is a body above us, and it is getting putrid very fast."

"Yes, yes, we're coming."

We had made a tunnel about 50 feet long, but the students were separated from us by a girder 20 inches thick. How on earth were we going to cut through it?

The Star Brigade Worker of Conalep

ROLL THE CAMERAS! IF THE FLOOR COLLAPSES, THAT'S THE END OF MY SHOW

The stanchions and the hydraulic jacks were very helpful—says Gisang Fung—because they allowed us to lift slabs and slip through toward where the bodies were. The man who was looking for his daughter and had asked me to help out went in with me, desperate:

"Is my daughter Silvia there, with a red sweater and a white shirt?"

"No," someone answered him through the wall, "she's not here. I know who she is. I had seen her in the other building. She could be in the auditorium, under us."

They had no idea that everything was smashed together, that the floors were scrambled.

Those of us who were in had our name written on a piece of adhesive tape, while they recorded it on a piece of paper, so before you entered the tunnel, they would ask you, "Do you have your name already?"

"Yes."

"What's your name? Where do you live?"

"Gisang Fung, and I live at Van Dyck 3, Colonia Mixcoac." And that's how the brigades were being formed. That was Brigade One at Conalep: five persons and in you go. You ask for the names of engineers and other helpers, but damn, the truth of the matter is that there, in the middle of all that, you don't ask names, or what do you do, nothing. You just say, "Pass me a chisel, stay here, put this on, do that," and you see people who are giving everything, who are open to everybody and simply offer, "Here it is, what else can I do?"

"Go get some batteries for the flashlights."

And off they go, running to get them. All these people without surnames, so attentive, so ready. Nothing else matters, not even their
names. I don't know, we were too busy to ask for people's names.

The man who was looking for his daughter Silvia was saying, "Let's
go upstairs," but what stairs? They were like horizontal, you know?
The ceilings were down, everything full of bricks, the floors sandwiched
together, ceiling on top of floor, so don't talk to me about stairways.
Crawling we went into a tunnel—into the third floor? who knows?—
the slab on top pressed on our backs, so we were crawling like this
(Gisang throws himself on the floor, face down and creeps forward
with his elbows), and we went back to the seven students. The tunnel
had been cut out and shored up, which made us feel safer. They had
thrown in fire hoses and smaller hoses for oxygen, all helter-skelter on
the ground. We arrived to the spot and told the seven buried survivors,
"Here we are, very close to you. Just you wait."

The engineer of Brigade One gave an order:

"It's impossible to breathe. We need oxygen masks."

You could hear a sizzle, grgrgrgr, as if something were being deep-
fried and popped suddenly. It was the swollen bodies bursting like bal-
loons. Boys and girls, bloated, their heads, their hair, their lifeless legs,
papers and notebooks all strewn around them, little address books or
pocket schedules, the kind that a student might use to write a love note
or the names of real people, addresses, telephone numbers, all that in
the middle of a jungle of plaster dust, chunks of masonry, and steel, and
us, crawling toward the survivors.

"Please get us out, we have been here for four days, we are thirsty,
we want to go home, please."

Some were crying, some were shouting in unison, 'One, two, three:
get us out! One, two, three: get us out!"

"Yes, we really are getting you out now. Hang on just for a bit. Don't
worry."

But what are we going to do about that girder?

We're separated from them by the damn girder and a big displaced
slab; they're on the other side of the girder, and it's of pure stone, so
we've got to put holes into it somehow or to excavate below with all
our might until we see a light—one stupid tiny ray of light, that's the
only way. We need lots of tools.

We took in twenty sledgehammers, fifty picks and shovels, three
crowbars, oxygen tanks, masks to help us deal with the stench, all
scrambled together down there:

"Look, what we have to do is grab a hammer, a mallet, and a chisel and break the girder, make an opening any way we can, man, but we'll have to put some supports here and there so that the concrete plate will not fall on us."

"No, no, if we break the slab, we will get it out of the way, quick as a fart. We need a drill to start making little holes and remove the pieces bit by bit."

"No, no, what we need to do with mallet and chisel is one single hole. I know what I'm talking about. I'm getting them out alive. Get me the mallet and the chisel, you."

"No, look, I'm going to get you a tungsten saw to cut through concrete, and we will get these kids out through that hole, because otherwise the hammering is going to be very hard, and without oxygen in there, one spark and we all blow up."

"You don't know what you're talking about. Bring me the hammer and the mallet. I'm taking them out."

There was a danger that we would all get blown up with the tungsten saw because it emits sparks, and with the oxygen tanks, we could cause an explosion.

I'll never forget a Frenchman, a guy whose name I don't even know, but a person of tremendous human quality. Jesus, he was awesome. He wasn't only excavating constantly, but he was also worried about us, and when I was excavating without gloves, he said to me, "Gisang, please put your gloves on, or you'll cut yourself."

With the anxiety and nervousness I would just keep on going.

"Gisang, I won't let you work unless you put gloves on."

Anyhow, I started to make the little hole, very small. But at least we could pass a flashlight through for the seven survivors, and through the hole we were able to chat with them:

"What's your name?"

They turned on the flashlight.

"Can you see me?"

"Yes."

"I'm Gisang."

They sounded glad.

"Well, then, we are working on this hole, but for now, we are going to give you oxygen."

We passed a thin hose, like this, pushing it through with a crowbar, and we gave them water through it. The hose was tiny, really; it was a plastic pipe used for oxygen; and the students were very thirsty.

Through the hole we couldn't possibly introduce even a can of soda, because the opening was too crooked:

"No, man, bring us oranges and lemons, anything."

We brought in tiny oranges, this size, cut in half, and cut lemons, and they grabbed them on the other side. Then they brought some tiny juice containers, but they didn't fit, nor the small cans, nor Boing drinks. I got some of the cardboard juice containers and folded them as much as I could without tearing them open, and this way we managed to let them have something to drink, and when they had their Boings they felt much better and chilled out for a while. Then they started to cry.

"Please, get us out."

And the guy, because it was one man and six women, kept saying, "Please don't cry, please be quiet. Don't you see they are doing what they can to rescue us? Hang in there a while longer."

We took advantage of two cracks that were already on the girder, and we got at it, you know? Bang, bang, bang, but that stupid beam wouldn't give. It was hard, superhard. But the tungsten saw was nowhere to be found.

The volunteer said, "Whatever God wills," and he started to bang again, bang, bang, bang, and sparks were flying.

"Hey, weren't we supposed to blow up with the sparks?" they asked us.

"Yes, but nothing is happening, let's go on."

We got coordinated. I felt a little more comfortable with the chisel and hammer, and we began to break one of those concrete girders that was so hard that we were really only able to chip away at it. When I got tired, I gave a turn to the Frenchman, who lives in Canada and had come to Mexico to sell who knows what kind of product to Pemex. Since he was in the city at the time of the earthquake, there he was, my hat goes off to him, hammering away. When he got exhausted, I went back, and the same thing again, like a relay race.

To tell you the truth, never in my life had I felt so strong and so lucid in what I was doing. What I felt, what I breathed was like truly alive, real, and bang, bang, bang, we made the hole, you know? It took hours upon hours, but we made the hole, thank God. Damn it, I didn't even believe in God. I'd been a renegade for a long time, but at that moment I said, "Fair is fair; thank God for saving them."

We began to remove debris, and then we ran into a giant ventilation duct. Mother! So I got myself in, all twisted all through the hole, and asked them, "Can you see me?"

"Yes."

I threw light on them and saw them all lying down, the slab on top of them, and the guy who could not have been taken out, the poor devil, because it was his body holding up the slab and the crevice he was in was too tiny.

When I went to remove the air conditioning duct, I discovered a corpse. It made that awful sound that dead people make, like a wound that rips open or a piece of meat being fried, or a torn fabric. Something like grsgrsgrs, what an awful sound. I have even become a specialist in sounds, me who had never seen a dead body, I swear. I'm twenty-two years old, but I have never seen anything like this, you know? I touched him, and he was hard, stiff and swollen, damn it.

Roll the cameras! Back to work, got to break the air conditioning duct with the crowbar. I left for little while to breathe and also because I had gotten beat up quite a bit, since I was just banging, blow after blow, so it was easy to hurt myself with the mallet, with the crowbar, scratching the mesh that you have to break, bending the points that can rip you. Meanwhile, some guy got the air conditioner out of the way, and we finally saw them cast down in there.

"Get us out, please."

"Calm down, it's all right now. We have to get you out one by one."

It smelled of death, Jesus, it did. But it didn't matter. What we wanted was to save them. There were two volunteers in the middle of the aisle, one like waiting with a stretcher and another one with oxygenated air, waiting, in great suspense. I had warned them that we needed seven stretchers that had to be ready along with first aid, an ambulance, and a doctor.

Everything was ready, even patrol cars. When the first one came out in really bad shape, I picked up a school notebook that belonged to some girl, and when I looked up, I saw every member of the rescue crew in total silence, under the weight of great emotion. Their eyes were different, like totally different from the eyes of any other people that I've known. A woman friend told me later that what was happening was that they were looking inward. I don't know what it was. I think it had to do with a new way of looking at things because of our experience. You can call it like mystical, philosophical, or Marxist, what the heck, Jesus, I don't know what it is, but it was a new state of awareness, something like cathartic, a constant catharsis, you know what I mean?

The volunteer said to me, "Well, when the first one gets out here, I'm going to give him three shots and that's it." He meant three takes of oxygen.

"That's great."

Here comes the first body.

They were calling me "Negro," maybe because I was covered with soot, or maybe because of the color of my trousers.

One by one they came out for their three shots, and then to the stretcher, and the doctor checking the pulse just to make sure. Off they went. Three seconds later you could hear the siren of the ambulance dying out in the distance as if saying good-bye. They were coming out and saying, "Thank you, brother, thank you."

They didn't know what to say.

"Take it easy, take it easy."

Before the last one, I had to go in to expand the tunnel, because the young woman was chubby and needed more room. When she came out, we gave her three shots, put her on the stretcher, and off she went. But before her departure, the engineer came close to her and asked, "How many more do you think are down there?"

"Under us, in one room, there were three girls and one guy, and further in, way in, is Abel. He's been knocking and knocking away, but he's deep down there."

You know, the Palacio Chino movie house is next door to Conalep. Well, right in front of it they excavated another tunnel and got three more guys out. To reach Abel, they had to break through seven or eight cubic yards. They say that "The Flea" got him out. No, he was not the one; that's what they said on television, the papers, and everywhere, you know? So what the heck, let them say what they want.

Out of the blue, a young girl comes out of the tunnel. You know, the girls that came out looked to me like the most beautiful women in the world. I don't know what I felt. She comes out and says, from her stretcher, "Oh, thank you for rescuing me; thank you for saving us all."

The girl cried and we, all men, were crying too. We were all there, all sorts of people: Pemex workers with their perforating tools, people like the French guy. This chick had nothing, only her legs hurt a little: "Let's see, move your arms, the other one, make circles as if you were pedaling a bike." And the smiling girl would do what she was told, I mean raising her arms in the air:

"You're all right, you're all right . . ."

A volunteer comes and tells me, "There's one more left, but it's going to be hell, man, because the guy is delirious. He's waving his hands around; he doesn't get it; he's kicking and thrashing. You know what, Gisang, you go in and get him. If he starts shouting or hitting you, no matter, get him out anyhow. If he has a broken leg, get him out, he's just delirious, that's all. He thinks he's fighting spies; it's a screwy thing with this guy all fucked up."

I went in, and to get to him, I had to turn away from the sight of two dead faces, two faces that stared at me as if inviting me to come in. I had to crawl around them, I had to roll over, like this, darn it. I finally reached where this guy was stuck with his briefcase and a bench on top of him, with glass and the grsgrsgrs sound of a dead body getting fried, and to tell you the truth, that got to me, I mean . . .

So I said, "I'm getting you out, but I need you to help me."

"Yes, yes, help me, please."

"I'm going to get you oxygen."

As I went out again, I touched the hardened bodies of the two cadavers. I was afraid.

"Roll the cameras! If the floor caves in, my show is over, no?"

But I kept on going. I removed some chairs and some school desks, and I reached the place where the guy was trapped.

"Please," I shouted, "I'm going to rescue you, but I need you to breathe, here's the oxygen, take it in." Meanwhile, I could hear the grsgrsgrs of the body, but I didn't know where it was.

I gave this guy the container, and he threw it back at me and started to say in a very loud voice, "They're coming after me; they want to attack us; they're getting here."

"Get the oxygen."

The whiff of oxygen reached me.

"They're spies."

"Shut up; take it easy."

I said to myself, "Do I get him out, do I leave him, what do I do? He's like hallucinating; I'm getting him out."

Roll the cameras! If I don't get him out, I die. Then I took away his briefcase and took his leg, film this please, the leg was boiling, the leg was like so hot, the whole body burning hot.

"Are you coming to help me? Ay, be careful because three weeks ago they operated on my spinal column, and I'm about to break it, and I can't move my arm."

He started to swear in Technicolor. When I got close to him, he grabbed my arm very tightly:

"Let go of me, or the two of us are dead."

I grabbed his feet, and I started to pull, and he shouts, "Oh, my back, here they come, the spies."

"Breathe your oxygen, brother, we're getting out."

He was a guy this tall, you know? And as we went by the body, he says, "Ay, who is this dead one?"

I didn't answer him. I just said to him, "We gotta win this one, bro, just a bit more."

"Ay, careful with my arm, my ribs." He was screaming in pain. In a while, when he saw the light, he started to push on his own, and when we put him on the stretcher, I myself gave him oxygen and his three shots. He finally breathed real air. He even said, "Oh, thank you for saving me."

Then he started to cough and spit, and when I threw the light on him, there he was, spitting out blood, the crazy guy.

We continued finding cadavers, a man with a moustache that no one will ever know who he was or what he ever did, me and other rescue workers. We were not hungry, I mean you lose your appetite. My own body created its own feeding technique. I was not sleepy, nor tired, because in a case like this, the body finds its own vitality, you know?

So in sum, we were the First Brigade, the one they called the Star Brigade, which participated in the rescue operations of Conalep. And I, Gisang Fung, the son of the owners of La Protectora, a wineshop located at 929 Revolution Avenue in Mixcoac, working there daily from two to six, selling wines and groceries, I, Gisang, participated in that brigade and learned that being an anonymous human being can be, like, a very great satisfaction, and that you can grow inside, and that is better than to be recognized by the whole wide world pointing at you and saying, "You did this, you did that."

EIGHT HUNDRED FACTORIES AND SWEATSHOPS TOTALLY DESTROYED

THE EARTHQUAKE REVEALED THE EXPLOITATION OF WOMEN TEXTILE WORKERS

Eleven stories were reduced to three at San Antonio Abad 150, a building that is today the symbol of the tragedy of the seamstresses.

Clandestine sweatshops existed on a great many streets: at José

María Izazaga 65, in just one eight-story building, fifty sweatshops; on Fray Servando, on Xocongo, on Mesones (Sportex), on Pino Suárez; almost all second-class—if not fifth-class—buildings, loaded with machinery and heavy rolls of fabric. No wonder the floors came down. San Antonio Abad 164 was also reduced to dust. At Manuel José Othón 186, close to the corner with San Antonio Abad, the textile sweatshops continued to function in spite of the stench of cadavers, the rubble, and the fear.

The seamstresses at Dimensión Weld, Amal, and Dedal were the first to realize that their bosses weren't going to help them. What's worse, they saw how the machinery was carried out before anybody worried about the six hundred entombed compañeras. If anyone was beaten and done violence in this year of 1985, if anyone has suffered, it is precisely these women. The earthquake showed that of all those exploited in the Federal District, none are more so than the workers of the clothing industry. Domestic service may constitute the leading employer of poor women in our country, but second place goes to sewing.

Seated on the sidewalk of Lorenzo Boturini Street is Juana de la Rosa Osorno, fifty-five, who works for Dimensión Weld de México S.A., employed by Elías Serur:

Now with this disaster, she says, putting her hands under her green and white checkered apron, we're here in the street waiting for people's charity to be able to eat. The boss is not a bad person; he's just fickle. He offers one thing, then another; he changes his mind; we can never come to an agreement. He first yelled at us, "The machinery is yours with my compliments. I've lost it all, my life is buried here."

His life is not buried there; if any lives are buried, it's those of the compañeras. The boss came running when he heard that the building had fallen down. He drove from his house in Las Lomas. But we were here. And the dead were here, bleeding among concrete and steel mesh. Elías did not suffer a scratch. So why would he say that his life had been buried here? Maybe he meant his safe. Maybe he means that his safe is his life. That's what happens to the rich, right?

I myself didn't die because my shift starts at 7:30. I've been working for fifteen years. I have two children. My daughter is twenty-seven; the boy is sixteen, and he's in high school. I'm a widow, and here in the San Antonio Abad encampment they asked me to be in charge of the kitchen. I used to start at 7:30 and end at 5:30. Occasionally, I worked until eight and sometimes even Saturdays and Sundays.

I don't remember what feast it was when we asked the boss for a long weekend, and he said okay, but we would have to come back to work on a Saturday to make up for the day. That Saturday I had to leave after midday because I suffer from high blood pressure. On Monday, he called me to the office to ask for an explanation. I gave it to him, I said that I was sick, and he answered, "That doesn't matter to me, what matters to me is my factory. Nothing else is my problem."

In Dimensión Weld, there wasn't even a first-aid kit, and if we had to be excused to go to the bathroom, and we took a little longer, he would come and knock on the door of the stall:

"What's the matter?"

"I'm taking care of my physiological needs."

"Well come now, you've been there for ten minutes or you've been there for a quarter of an hour; go back to work or I'll have to dock the time from your paycheck."

I do overlay. I was working on sport shirts. I'm a highly qualified seamstress. I was making 11,300 pesos a week more or less before taxes. I had no social security nor loans of any sort. When I had to buy my eyeglasses, it took about four months of pleading before Elías told the cashier to lend me the money. In reality, the only thing that I have to thank the boss Elías for is that when my father died recently, he gave me a leave of absence of a week, but without pay. In fifteen years of work, that week without pay is what I am grateful for.

We have seen no government aid, period—only from churches, from private persons who come, open their trunk and bring out big pots of rice, tortillas, and beans, and they tell us to come and have some lunch. Young people have come; I don't know from what organization. But the boys have been here; they bring oil for me to cook with.

Every day I take the subway to come here. I catch it at Río Blanco, going from Martín Carrera to Santa Anita, and then I transfer at Candelaria to the Pino Suárez line, and from Pino Suárez I come all the way here. This is when I only take the subway. Otherwise, I take the Santa Anita segment to Jamaica and walk the rest of the way.

In Dimensión Weld, there were 130 of us. Here on this avenue there are many factories. The one with the most casualties was Dedal, where a whole big bunch of women died, because their shift started at seven. They took out three bodies last night, all made mincemeat.

At Manuel Gutiérrez Nájera and San Antonio, I don't know how many of them are still missing. The relatives are there, waiting in tents. Just imagine what a barbaric thing that is. We've left behind our lungs, our hearts, all of our efforts, down there under that concrete. Shouldn't the boss compensate us in some way? We live in tenements, we rent small rooms, we pay rent while they, the owners, live in mansions, have cars, they travel, but we are the ones who take pains to work, to produce, to live. Of course, they started the business, but we moved it forward on our backs. That's my thinking.

I left my eyes behind in Dimensión Weld. Now I can only see with my glasses on. I used to eat by the lockers, I brought my food in a dinner pail. Then they put some tables by the entrance. There are many of us, and all of us are poor. We can't afford to eat at a diner, so we'd bring our beans or whatever God had given us for that day.

THE MOST ANGUISHED AMONG THEM WANTED TO FLING THEMSELVES OUT THE WINDOW

Josefina Tlalteca started work at Amal on May 15, 1985, and she had no insurance. She was an overlay worker who made women's apparel. Firemen took her out from under the rubble seven hours after the earthquake:

There were thirty of us who managed to remain standing, because the floor didn't collapse totally. Some women screamed, others cried, others prayed, and the most collected ones tried to keep the others calm: "It's okay, God alone can save us, have faith."

Thirty of us came out alive, with some scrapes. In my case, it took seven hours to get out. There was only one compañerita who came out with two broken legs and a broken back. She was a seventeen-year old girl, a student who was working during her vacation. Her name was Susana, poor creature. She died Saturday.

I'm a preparer, says Margarita Aguilar, I'm twenty-five years old, and I've worked at Amal for three and a half years. Just a while ago in August, they gave me insurance; I haven't even taken care of all my papers. What does a preparer do? She foliates, separates, and numbers the garments, divides them by size, and makes bundles, separating the pieces; she separates all the garment parts: sleeve, back, front, collar, cuffs, pockets. The cut fabric comes in bales, and I have to foliate, divide by color, and make the bundles so that the seamstresses at the sewing machines can sew the parts together.

145

MY LEGS WERE TRAPPED BY THE RUBBLE

I'm one of the survivors, one of the ones who were in hysterics. I insisted on jumping out the window, but they held me back. When the building started to rumble before it crashed down, I ran to the stairway, and a wall came on us because the warehouse collapsed. The wall fell across our path and blocked our exit. My legs and one arm were trapped in the rubble, but one hand and my head, the most important thing, were free. I held on to a steel rod, and I pushed myself up until I managed to get out through the top. That's when I saw light, and it was then—because of that light—that I became hysterical.

I climbed on a piece of furniture and broke a side window. I cut my hand and came out. Many compañeras ran toward the windows, and those were the ones that were saved because the part of the building that crashed down as if in a spiral was its center. But the windows to the street were free, so I looked out and shouted—or should I say that I wailed—"Help" to the people who were down on the street. They sent us a rope.

WE HAD ALL TIED PANTS TOGETHER TO LOWER OURSELVES LIKE TARZAN

When I realized that the rope was very thin, in my despair I took a bolt of fabric from the floor and threw it out, where it unfolded. Before that, we had all made a rope by tying jackets and pants, so that we could lower ourselves to the street, any way we could, like Tarzan, it didn't matter. But the garments could not have held our weight, they were not well tied, and a man's voice could be heard shouting to us, "No one better come down that way. If you hang from those clothes, you'll kill yourselves."

Then it occurred to me to throw the bolt of fabric, and using the rope, we tied it to a machine to anchor it. A few compañeras chose to go down the rope, the daredevils, as if they were in the circus. Not me! I went down the fabric, which provided something like a slide. Approximately ten women went down Tarzan-style, holding on to the rope and the fabric, but the ones that were the most terrified wanted to fling themselves through the windows, thinking that the earthquake was going to continue. One of them, María Elena, went to a window and yelled at us, "I'll kill myself, once and for all."

Then I recovered some of my strength and said to her, "Come on now, it's over, isn't it? Earthquakes don't come back. Some compañeras are already down there, safe and sound. Look at them, on the street. Do you see them?"

All my life I have been one of those people who don't wait for someone else to solve their problems. I like to take action before a helping hand shows up. I go at it: bam, bam, bam. You have to look for a way around any problem. So I let myself go down the cloth. Then I learned that some other women who had done the same had hurt themselves. Sra. Julia broke her leg as she fell. She let herself go, and when the cloth couldn't hold her weight, she got hurt. Many messed up their hands. The rope burned off the skin of their palms. My hands also were burned with the fabric because synthetic fabrics do that. The cloth skinned me, but I came out.

I am alive and right now I am speaking to you. I live in Lomas de San Bernabé beyond San Jerónimo. I arrived home very worried about my family. But when I saw them safe and sound, I was immensely happy. They also had been worried sick about me. I was so happy to see them that I forgot all about the ordeal. The next thing I knew I was in the hospital in Emergency Clinic Number 8. My nerves got to me; the shock was too much; I had two weeks of incapacity and didn't want to leave my home. Later, when I went back to San Antonio Abad and saw how my compañeras were struggling for all of us, I had to join them. Our boss abandoned us. He did not offer any support. He allowed our fellow workers to die by themselves. Since we couldn't do anything for them when they were still alive, at least we share the grief of their next of kin and continue demanding that our dead ones be retrieved: Julia Morales, Juana San Pedro, Paula, Diana, Yolanda, Antonia (whom we called Tony out of affection), Margarita Pozos, Renata, Priscila, Rosa Luz Hernández, Sra. Toñita, Francisco, the guy in charge of the iron heaters.

We were all dear compañeros. We had worked together for a long time, seeing each other every day, and that's why we are united in the demands of the relatives. They were all mothers, and now their children have lost their only source of support. Many children were orphaned, so we now have to fight and to support each other.

There are sweatshops so small that there are only two seamstresses, and yet women are exploited there. Then there are others with six people, and the big ones have 75 to 100 staff or sometimes up to 150, even 200 seamstresses. The largest, Roberts, is said to have between 650 and 700 employees. Their clothes are sold at Roberts, High Life, Aurrerá,

Sears, El Palacio de Hierro, El Puerto de Liverpool, París-Londres, and many other luxury stores. Listen, they say that at José Manuel Othón 186, you know how ugly it all looks around there, the owners of Kayser are forcing the operators to keep at their sewing machines. Have you checked that out?

This story by Margarita Aguilar, a worker at Amal, was recorded in the first days after the quake. At Fray Servando Teresa de Mier 285, a collapsed building, several workshops had been housed: La Corsetería, Pierre Cardin, Reina María, Tammy, Creaciones Coqui, Simonette, Nelly Originals; not to mention other sweatshops at Fernando de Alba 63, Justo Sierra 20, 20 de Noviembre, Izazaga, Isabel la Católica; plus De Val, on Bolívar Street, and Ropamex at the corner of Dr. Lucio y Garcíadiego. One could also read the names of Jeannette, Janet, Lody S.A., Elizabeth King, Tabe S.A., Pop, Sky Lon, Alfa Centauro de México, Nina Rubin, Mayosi, Gentry, Annabel, Bruzette, Magosi, Marivi, Confecciones Infantiles, El Capullito.

HELP WANTED

Nowadays when under Help Wanted I see "operators for Overlock, Flack, and Lock machines, tape applicators, button affixers, makers of briefs, undershirts, and T-shirts, finishers, loop stichers, overlay applicators," I know that their salaries will range between 11,500 a week (for the seamstress) and 8,000 (for the presser). In my mind they have a body and a face, the same face of the women who continue speaking in San Antonio Abad Avenue:

I was a buttonhole maker, she was a pleat maker, she, over there, an overlay applicator, and that woman assembled the garments before they were sewn. I started working at age fourteen (Carmen's voice is convincing, so candid and straightforward). In Infantiles S.A. we made robes, pajamas, dresses, blouses, skirts, lingerie, baby suits. On the sixth floor they assembled costume jewelry, real nice. Our boss was named Jacobo, and he gave us 10,000 pesos five days after the earthquake.

When for any reason the garment didn't come out right, with any small defect, a little hole in the fabric, or a slit, we were forced to buy it.

"Buy it?"

Yes (she opens her purse). Here are the sales slips. We have to take them home, and they serve as a reminder of what we did wrong.

Now with the earthquake—resumes Carmen—the head of personnel came to tell us that earthquakes are acts of God, fortuitous events or overpowering things beyond anyone's control. Therefore, how could we collect from the owner? What did he do, tell the earth to shake? Knock the building down himself?

During blackouts we could not do a thing, and since we are paid piece rate, that is, only by the garments we make, we would end up with nothing. I remember one time when we were waiting all day, and just as I came from home, that's the way I went back, with zero. The owner said, "It's not my fault that we're without power. I can't pay you."

"But we've been here all day . . ."

"Yes, but without power you haven't worked. I pay you for your work, not for your presence."

María Elena Rodríguez Vargas (who at least lives nearby, at José T. Cuéllar 384, apartment 2, Colonia Asturias) received 10,000 pesos from her boss, who told her to consider herself lucky. She used to work in Infantiles de México S.A. and was an overlay applicator and finisher. She argues:

They never told us we were at risk, that the building was in poor condition. One day I asked, "What about those cracks?"

"That's nothing."

"Aren't they earthquake cracks?"

"That's none of your business."

The bottom line is that no one was ever responsible for us. We were slaves, fucked over, we were and we are. Our housing was already miserable, but now we are running around in the mean streets, baked on one side and sunburned on the other, down and out, without any money, without any food, on the run, full of expectation, expecting to see what comes of this, because there finally seems to be a ray of hope out there.

WOMEN OF SAN ANTONIO ABAD DEMAND LESS PUBLIC RELATIONS AND MORE HUMAN WARMTH
THIRTY-ONE PERSONS REMAIN TO BE UNEARTHED

Forty-one days after the earthquake, in the wee hours of the morning of October 30, the remains of the bodies of Guadalupe Quintero Rivera, Paula Almanza Camacho, and Raquel Juárez Valencia were recovered from the rubble, placed in a plastic bag, and taken to the San Lorenzo Tezonco graveyard. They are not the last. Víctor Manuel Priego is still

waiting in front of the building at San Antonio Abad 150, as is Rosa
Angélica Gallegos, who is still missing her sister. And there are more:
thirty-one persons remain to be unearthed.

Víctor Manuel Priego has spent forty-three days (it will soon be forty-
four) sleeping in the street and eating whatever the volunteers give him.
Rosa Angélica Gallegos takes breaks to go see her little daughter—"I
left her with my Mom"—and comes back. Víctor Manuel Priego is tall,
strong, and has no more tears left:

My wife died. Her name was María del Carmen Vázquez. She and
thirty more people are still there.

For fifteen days we worked with our own fingernails, without resources, without help, listening to the moaning. We thought we'd go
mad. When they told me that Lucio Corona Hernández, the foreman,
the alleged manager of Amal, was out in the street, I came down from
the heap to beat him up and to give him hell. Fortunately, the compañeros held me back. But I scared the shit out of him.

"Get the hell out of here."

The miserable sleazeball said, "I didn't get rich overnight, you know?
I've been working since I was fifteen."

Before witnesses, he admitted that he was the owner of Amal S.A. But
now he takes it back, he claims to be an employee and says that the real
owner is José Ases Abud.

The name joins that of Samuel Bissú, the owner of Fábrica Can S.A.,
and that of Elías Serur, proprietor of the maquiladora Dimensión Weld
de México; and the names of the owners of Bruzette, Vestimark, Dedal,
Annabel, Maxel (Artesanías Selectas), Creaciones Pop, Prodeusa, and
all the other clandestine sweatshops on the streets of Izazaga, 5 de Feb-
rero, Netzahualcóyotl, and Anillo de Circunvalación.

I was a sanitation driver, but I left the job on September 19. I don't
know how long I'll stay here. I don't know when we'll find the body of
my wife. Every night I climb up there with a pick and shovel. I can't do
anything else; all my attention is focused on finding her. We had three
girls, and for the first few days I left them with my father and my
brothers.

My whole family was living on a lot located at Francisco Madero
181, Tláhuac, that was divided into thirds. My wife had been working
for two months; she could do it because until the 19th we had a gal
helping us with our daughters and the household chores. I had injured

my right foot, badly enough to have been close to losing it, so I was laid off for two months, and we were running out of money. I sold my car, and she decided to work at Amal S.A. until things looked up.

María del Carmen was not a seamstress; her only experience was with a home sewing machine. But she was a very capable woman, very smart, so much so that in a few days she was going to become a supervisor in her department, but look at what happened.

The very day of the earthquake I rushed over here because I knew my wife. Earthquakes scared the daylights out of her. I remembered she would be petrified, totally paralyzed with fear. She wouldn't even run, she couldn't think of how to protect herself. I didn't arrive at San Antonio Abad until 10:30. Traffic was out of control, sheer chaos, no transportation. I said, "Let me go and hold her tight."

I saw the wrecked building, and there I was running like mad, trying to investigate. I was asking everyone until someone said yes, there had been a woman named María del Carmen who fitted my wife's description: dark-skinned, slender, five foot three inches tall, fine facial features, nicely proportioned, what can I say. "Some women were taken to Balbuena, the ones that were in bad shape, but your wife, that is the person you described, came walking out." Those women were taken to a shelter nearby.

I searched and searched and found nothing. I came back almost crying and asked the woman who had given me information to concentrate and try and remember, where she had come out, at what time, until I thought of asking, "What was she wearing?"

"A blue skirt."

My wife was wearing slacks.

I went through every delegation, every hospital. For two days I went from hospital to hospital, and then I went back to San Antonio Abad. I found her coworkers; I spoke to the survivors. I investigated until a woman said with certainty to me, "Your wife stayed back there."

During the earthquake, many women ran to the stairways. Some of them could not because a concrete wall fell over and blocked them, but the ones who made it to the stairwell were covered with masonry chunks and debris. It was a fatal trap. Out of ninety-four workers, seventy came out alive. "María del Carmen stayed back, standing there, frozen. We saw her, we called out to her, but she looked like she couldn't move." That's what they told me.

We've still got four more people trapped in the elevator. There are ten women scattered among the fourth, sixth, and ninth floors. They haven't been able to dig them out. One of them must be María del Carmen.

On the 19th and the 20th, you could hear human voices moaning. Fifteen days later I still heard a human sound. But we relatives were not given help, not even respect for our grief. They blocked the way, beginning with the army that forbade us from approaching. We could have rescued many lives, but the firefighters and the Medical Emergency and Rescue Squad of the Federal District ordered, "You stay out of this."

When we had been without help for fifteen days, what right did they have to keep us out? From the very beginning, we were piercing through the rubble, making holes all over the place. If you go up to the building next door, you'll find that the wall is like Swiss cheese. We did it, to rescue people, and in fact two human beings came out alive through those holes. We talked to them and waited for the sound, and we heard this faint plea: "Help us; get us out."

We got two young guys who had fallen from the sixth to the fourth floor, and once a tunnel was open, they walked out in relatively good shape. But the government arrived and couldn't stand the competition; they wanted to look good, to be in the spotlight before the TV cameras, to make a show out of this. The firefighters told us, "Boys, come down immediately. This is going to cave in any minute."

False. The building is still standing. They only wanted to get rid of us, so we wouldn't upstage them. The last thing in our minds was to look at the cameras; we wanted to find our loved ones. We will still find those thirty-one people, and we will identify them by their clothes.

I understand that the body of my wife María del Carmen, if it is truly here, will not be recognizable, but I remember very well all of her personal effects: her watch and most of all a pair of earrings that I gave her a few days ago. I estimate that we still need eight days to get to the bodies. Later we'll have to worry about the legal question, compensation payments, and punishment of those who are to blame for this. I don't believe that they are going to pay us 1.2 million pesos for each body; no, that's too much money. What I really want most of all is to have her body, to bury it properly, to be able to say to my daughters, "Here is where your mother rests."

I was once deeply religious, but now I wonder, thinking of the slow and desperate torture that killed these young women. I ask myself, if there is a God, how is it possible that God would allow so much pain? They talk about a God of mercy, but all I've experienced here in San Antonio Abad is cruelty, torture. All I've seen is the neglect that let women who were there, trapped and injured, waiting for the collapse of more slabs, to hear the outside noise and wait vainly for help.

Do you realize what it means to be able to hear the outside noise, to be hollering so that rescuers know where you are, to embrace the hope that you are being rescued, and then to hear the sounds fade away? Can you imagine the hunger, the injuries, the wait? If this is divine justice, I don't understand it. I was a believer, but now, I don't know, I am confused. I believe more in my neighbors than in God because I have seen the way in which they have responded. Any aid we have received has come from ordinary people.

And I have witnessed tragedies even worse than mine—the loss of a lady who was the only support for her six children, the oldest only eighteen years old, and who are now all scattered, wandering around the wreckage. They come and eat with us; we share from the provisions and clothes that have been donated to us. But what will they do to survive in the future? María del Carmen talked a young seamstress into staying with the job. She was an unwed mother, this small woman, and had a two-month-old baby. And my wife convinced her to keep her job and work for the future of her child, and look at it all now. She really convinced her to stay and die! And like these stories, each case is tragic.

Look at it, there are buried bodies all over the place behind Xocongo, in a collapsed building. They think twenty-six people are still there, but nobody cares. The case of the garment workers was brought to light much too late. They were talking about all the buildings except the ones in San Antonio Abad. After we held a sit-in on Calzada de Tlalpan, close to the subway, the offical authorities started to come, and we were invaded by congressmen, senators, labor prosecutors, a large variety of government fauna who came with many promises and practically nothing tangible to offer. The country focused on the problem of these seamstresses, and now we have many visitors who come for the glory; cameramen, journalists, newsreel and TV commentators, photographers, expert rescuers, brigade members, know-it-alls, engineers, professional bosses, despots, a display of resources enough to overwhelm the people, tools to stack the shelves of a store. They started by fighting among themselves for the right to get to the bodies first, as if the bodies were war prizes. This has been very sad, a depressing spectacle, for us relatives who have not been given any consideration. Rescue groups fighting for the bodies!

"Sir, I come from the Ministry of Government. Here are my permission papers, signed by those up high. I'm staying here, I'm coming to get the bodies out, and I'm giving orders."

"We don't need you, Señor, we already have enough people."

What we needed was to excavate manually so as not to destroy the bodies even further. Specialized physicians were needed to prepare the bodies because the forensic doctors don't know how to do it, as is proven by the fact that the first two corpses unearthed were left out in the open, in full view of the public, a few steps away from the kitchen. Can you imagine the danger of infection and the lack of respect to those cadavers?

A group that calls itself the Eagles started to fight with another that calls itself the Tlatelolco Moles, who came with the son of Plácido Domingo. José Domingo, unlike his father, is an arrogant man, tall and robust, very Spanish looking, who is trying to make a party out of our predicament. Unfortunately, talent is not hereditary, and if the work his father did for earthquake victims was beautiful and commendable, this son of his is the classic junior who thinks our misfortune can be turned into a photo opportunity.

Now the parade of onlookers in San Antonio Abad is amazing, and in the midst of the horror we experience, we feel we are a circus. If you talk to some of the next of kin, they'll tell you that they are no longer thinking of any compensation; all they want is to receive the bodies of their loved ones and get the hell out of here, as far as possible. And to think that some are campaigning here, to obtain political and commercial success at our expense!

All we as relatives are asking for is to have access to the bodies, to be able to take an inventory of their clothes and other possessions, to relay the facts to the next of kin who are waiting down below. We want to keep them from having to look at the corpses, because the conditions of the bodies are bad enough to be traumatic.

Make no mistake about it: after forty-three days, thirty-one persons remain under the rubble. Their immediate family members are still standing guard in the street. Not one will leave. We have a way of identifying the cadavers. We have already done so unofficially—we have spent so much time inside the building—by their position in each floor. We know where they are, and through contact with their loved ones, we know who they are.

THE OFFICIALS ARE ONLY INTERESTED IN SHOWING OFF

Today, November 13, 1985, nearly two months after the earthquake, María de Jesús Ramírez continues to wait at the corner of Tonalá and Durango streets in Colonia Roma for the body of her husband. Blanca Gutiérrez, a gym teacher who has been in charge of the camp at the Cibeles fountain of Plaza Miravalle in Colonia Roma since the 20th, denounces Sra. Ramírez's experience with true indignation: "They have no right to do this to her." Her husband was the elevator operator in the building at Durango and Tonalá, and she still cannot get his remains; the inhumanity of the authorities is intolerable.

We sent an expert mountain climber as a rescuer to indicate where the three cadavers remain in the building: one is the body of the husband of María de Jesús Ramírez, who has been waiting here in the street day and night without a break since September 19. Nobody has spoken for the other two bodies. The moles, the volunteers never were given permission to get the cadavers out. Others that have been brought out here in Colonia Roma have been the cause of a lot of suffering for their next of kin, since the Cuauhtémoc Delegation wouldn't release the corpses because one paper or another was missing.

The red tape was burdensome, people were even asked for money. They wouldn't release a body without all their despicable paperwork; their interminable procedures just make people feel bad, very bad . . . Just six of us volunteers are still here now, and we'll be on our way by the day after tomorrow at the latest. The delegation says that nothing can be done. The authorities sure won this one with their "return to normality."

We've already taken away our containers of drinking water. No more signs remain that say, "Don't throw trash; don't waste food." Doctors' addresses are no longer posted. About ten days ago the number of volunteers began to drop off; most had left only their first names, so we don't know how to get in touch with them. Is all this effort of solidarity going to be lost? Calm is supposed to return by decree. People will go who knows where to lick their wounds, to grow a scab over their injuries. I don't know of anything that's going to change. Just where is all this famous reconstruction, reorganization?

IN MEXICO THERE'S VERY LITTLE RESPECT FOR HUMAN LIFE

Gymnastics teacher Blanca Gutiérrez inquires: Where are the orphaned children? Where are the relatives of the dead? Where are the organizations? Where are the volunteers? Where is the solidarity? You'll see, after a while nobody'll remember.

Nothing happened here. How wonderful it is that they made a little park on the site of the building. Let's go play there; let's go stretch out on the grass.

Underneath are the cadavers. In Mexico there's very little respect for human life. I believe this is the country where life is given the least respect. Officials are only interested in showing off. The government is not worthy of the people of Mexico.

Just walk down the street and look at people. They don't even notice the rubble; they don't see the buildings that look like hulks of iron and concrete. People walk around as if nothing had happened. They even stop to peer in the store windows.

In the meantime, Sra. María de Jesús Ramírez waits in the street for them to give her what is left of her husband, the elevator operator of the building at the corner of Tonalá and Durango.

PREPARATIONS AT THE RED CROSS TO RECEIVE NANCY REAGAN

One of the volunteers working at the Red Cross told us how they pulled out all the stops for Nancy Reagan's visit: the halls, the floors, even the walls, not to mention the windows, were all washed with a great deal of soap and water. Victims had their faces washed, their hair combed, their hospital gowns smoothed over. Ah, can you believe they even put stuffed animals on their beds?

"Who speaks English?"

A young woman answered that she did. They'd had to amputate one of her legs because of the earthquake. They put her in one room by herself.

"This is so you can chat with the Sra. Reagan."

"I'd rather be with everyone else . . ."

"Afterward, we'll put you back in your bed again."

Paloma Cordero de De la Madrid said to Nancy Reagan, "Come right in, come right in; please excuse the messiness."

Very little has been learned about the Super Leche restaurant that used to occupy an enormous space—now it's a garden—at Eje Central Lázaro Cárdenas 41, between Victoria and Artículo 123. There, for the last three years, the widow Francisca Pérez lived in her apartment all by herself on a small pension. Her husband died two and a half years ago:

I sew in order to help make ends meet. I didn't exactly make dresses; it was more like alterations and sewing hemlines. Over those days I'd gone to Durango to visit some relatives, and I saw on television how Super Leche and the apartments above had disappeared. My only reaction was "Now I'm out on the street."

I didn't go back to Mexico City until a week later, and I couldn't see anything. There's a garden there, some nice little benches all painted white; the ruins are gone. Unfortunately, my friends and neighbors died: Francisca Chávez López and Cristina Sotelo. I don't know anything about another couple across the hall that were friends of mine, the Herreras. I didn't know where their relatives lived or anything. A very sweet Greek lady also died.

Most people at Super Leche were killed. I didn't eat there, but the restaurant always seemed full of customers. The owner, Manuel Gutiérrez, died, along with his son, his mother, an aunt; they all died except for one who left the restaurant to go to the drug store and a sister who'd just left for Spain.

My place was really pretty. I paid 10,000 pesos rent; I had two bedrooms, living room, bathroom, and kitchen; the living room was really a good-sized living-dining room; the bathroom was good too; the kitchen small. These apartments were nice; I had a good view of Victoria Street.

"Wasn't it noisy?"

Well, you get used to that, and there wasn't much noise at night. Yes, you could live pretty well there, with a lot of conveniences, a great many that you can't find anywhere else. I didn't even have to take the trash outside because it was picked up right there in the building. The gas was delivered; everything was really good. Nobody stuck their nose in anybody else's business. There were one hundred apartments. I figure that there must have been five stories, twenty apartments per floor, at least four people in each apartment. That makes about four hundred people in all, more or less.

The apartments were pretty, centrally located, well thought out, with two bedrooms in each one. Now where are you going to find a three-room apartment for 10,000 pesos anywhere else? I used to sit and sew on a little chair in one of the rooms where the sunlight came in. The sun would be on my back, nice and warm. Everything I needed I had nearby: here the bakery, there the butcher shop, everything just a few steps away.

How pretty my apartment was! It was really practical for me, I had everything nearby, and the rent was cheap. Now they say they're going to send us to some houses that don't even have roofs yet, way out there in the State of Mexico. Naturally we'll have to pay. I lost everything, everything; I have nothing, not even a chair.

First I went to the Cuauhtémoc Delegation. There they gave me a voucher to present to the Metropolitan Commission. I went, and they asked me for witnesses. Who? If everybody I know died! There might be some survivors, I suppose, but I don't have any idea where they are. Are they alive? Are they in some hospital? I really don't think anybody made it. They wanted witnesses, electric and telephone receipts, my rental contract. If everthing went down in the earthquake, if I didn't even salvage a pin, where am I supposed to get these papers from? I still had my husband's identity card that I carried around as a keepsake; that got me my own card for the Seguro because I have a right to a retirement pension.

They told me, "We can't give you any help, no cash, no nothing. But we can provide you with a house in Huehuetoca in the State of Mexico. It's worth 1.5 million pesos, and you'll have to pay it off monthly: the down payment and 15,000 pesos a month."

"What am I supposed to pay you with if I haven't got anything?"

"Ah, listen, that's your problem."

"And what am I going to do way out there, all by myself, at my age? I don't know anyone there; it's a little town; there's no Social Security clinic. I don't think it makes any sense to go out there at my age."

"Look, since this is a special case, you're an old lady, we can help you with another lawyer. Come next week, and we'll see if we can work it out."

God willing, I'm going back next week.

Francisca Calderón, the widow of Pérez, is a shy person. Two or three pins are fastened to the collar of her blouse, proof that she likes to sew. She speaks in a soft voice; flashes of anxiety rush across her eyes; they suddenly redden.

"She had her house so nicely fixed up, with such good taste," comments the niece with whom Francisca is living at the moment. "She bought her things with great care over so many years: her dresser, the dining table, the chairs, the tablecloths. Everything she had was very clean, just like you see her all nicely made up."

We drink chamomile tea; it goes down our throats slowly. Doña Francisca crosses her hands in her lap. Her hands seem like fallen petals. After a few moments of silence, she murmurs:

At least I'd like to find someone from Super Leche to talk to. All the other survivors have somebody.

She lifts up her face, her expression that of an anxious woman:

Couldn't you put me in touch with someone?

"With whom?"

By any chance, would you know of an inexpensive little house that I could rent? I haven't got many years left.

"Excuse me, Señor."

An old man of seventy-eight with the onset of Parkinson's arrived at the shelter at Jalapa 50, recalls aid worker James Kelleghan. I went up to him and said, "Excuse me, Señor, how can I help you?"

"Yes, young man, could you give me one of those things so it doesn't smell so bad?"

I got out the last of my surgical masks.

"Do you know how to put it on?"

"No, I'm afraid I don't."

I put a knot in the lower part of the string and I passed it around behind his head, telling him:

"The other part you pull over your head to cover your mouth, just be sure you don't block your eyes."

"Thank you."

"You're welcome. Excuse me, Señor, can we offer you anything else? Would you like something to eat, a cup of coffee, a soda?"

"Yes, young fellow, coffee would be great."

"Come with me please."

I led him by the arm, we took three steps, when suddenly he shouted, "I can't find my son!"

I asked one of the other volunteers to take him for some coffee, and I went to the bathroom to cry . . . I don't know for how long.

The eyes of James Kelleghan fill with tears.

POLITICAL ACTION, MORE THAN MEDICAL CARE

Among 18 million inhabitants of Mexico City's metropolitan area, 6 million are not covered by insurance from ISSSTE or the Social Security system. Naturally a small portion of those who are not insured are upper-class people, but the large majority of those 6 million are very-low-income people who have no insurance because they have no fixed job, or because they work in a clandestine workshop. This is the case of the now-famous seamstresses or garment workers, who had no benefits of any sort, not a straw mat on which to fall dead. This is the population that depended on Hospital General, the Juárez, and the Manuel Gea Gonález for emergency care. Today, the Juárez and General are closed, leaving a large number of Mexicans unprotected.

WE SET UP A MEDICAL PRACTICE AT THE SUBWAY CONCOURSE

Fernando Prieto Hernández, a physician in the Pneumology Unit of Hospital General, was one of the doctors who decided to set up shop at the entrance to the subway after October 17: the removal of rubble and cadavers had lasted approximately fifteen days. Two buildings had crumbled, and both were tall; the interns' residence was a building with eight stories, and Gynecology-Obstetrics had six. All the rest of the buildings in the hospital are low, with one or two floors. It is, therefore, a rather horizontal hospital, connected by passageways that go from one pavilion to another.

Right after the earthquake, however, the building was evacuated because it presented a serious danger—gas leaks and the possible caving in of other damaged parts. We thought that as soon as these dangers were dealt with, the hospital would get back to normal. It wasn't so. We didn't see any outpatients any more. "And what about the patients?" we would ask. People started to come to the hospital anyway, asking for a consultation. Something had to be done.

We took an open plaza of approximately 12,000 square yards and started seeing patients in tents. We built our offices with a skeleton of wooden poles covered with plastic and canvas—a good protection against wind and rain—and inside we placed a campaign cot, a desk, some chairs, a few pieces of equipment. The best equipped one was the dental office, because they had a van outfitted with a dental chair, a power drills, and a set of dental instruments. On Thursday the 17th we had five hundred patients, and the next day we had a thousand; we saw them from seven in the morning to eight at night.

More than medical care, to examine patients in the concourse was a political action, an act of pressuring the government into keeping Hospital General open, since forty-eight of its fifty buildings were in adequate condition, and 1,600 beds could be put to work right away. The official version, however, was that the General was destined to disappear. The Ministry of Health was proposing the Tentative Project for the Reconstruction and Restructuring of Health Services in the Valley of Mexico, consisting of the scattering of small, low hospital buildings of 144 beds each, at the service of the delegations. This would be the end of Hospital General, which in addition to its important tradition for patients (it was built in 1905) was the one Mexican institution that brought together top-notch physicians and inaugurated medical research in our country.

The General is the place where great specialists were molded: Ignacio Chávez, founder of the Institute of Cardiology; Puig Solanes, in ophthalmology; the famed Clemente Robles, in neurosurgery; Raoul Fournier y Sepúlveda, in gastroenterology; Ruy Pérez Tamayo, Ruiz Castañeda, Celis, Salazar, Gastón Melo, Abraham Ayala, Zubirán, all of them pillars of medicine who taught the new generation of physicians and created a new tradition of medical care, one based on a high scientific and academic standard and a philosophy of human contact with patients and personnel. But what is most important is that Hospital General became a teaching hospital.

The government's tentative project, says Dr. Fernando Prieto Hernández, does not take into consideration either pregraduate or postgraduate instruction, nor the clinical research that could be conducted in Hospital General. The project attempts to make up for each bed lost in the earthquake, but they forget that at Hospital General each bed, in addition to holding a patient, was an opportunity for providing medical care, for teaching, and for research. A bed in a small or private hospital is not a teaching place for students, residents, and instructors.

The number of students who go through Hospital General in any given year is approximately 10,000. There are 300 or more residents who are becoming specialists or doing graduate work; the hospital staff includes some 700 physicians who acquire their positions through a difficult process of competition. The system in this institution is very different from that of any other of its kind, where seniority creates a ladder for professionals to climb. There are 850 nurses at work there. A total of 6,800 people work there besides the doctors. Among other functions the hospital gives consultation to 2,000 people every day, and conducts between 125 and 150 operations of all sorts.

CRITICISM OF HOSPITAL GENERAL

I present to Dr. Fernando Prieto Hernández some of the many negative comments I have heard over the years in relation to the General and Juárez, especially the Juárez. Even Dr. Clemente Robles, interviewed years ago, told of how he had to operate with buckets of water, and he would trip over mops carelessly abandoned in the hallways. However, he also said, "The hospital I have loved the most is undoubtedly the General, and the most fruitful period of my life, the most intense, took place there, when I was director as well as when I was a unit head."

At the General, they stole even bread rolls. Instruments were rusty. They lacked bandages and gauze, and sometimes even sheets. Pillows had a way of vanishing. Hygiene was deplorable. The doors of operating rooms wouldn't shut. Food was despicable. In all, it was no wonder that on the other side of the street, like a line of vultures, many funeral homes were in business.

Dr. Fernando Prieto Hernández looks annoyed. "The Hospital had serious limitations, of course, and its auxiliary personnel did not come from a refined social class, although our nurses are more professional all the time. In terms of the patients, they are not the cream of society, but in Mexico the real thieves are up there."

THERE IS A GREAT DEAL OF POLITICAL INTRIGUE IN THE GENERAL

I persevered in my objections: lack of equipment and medications, old beds, useless tools, syringes contaminated with hepatitis virus, dirty cups, unwashed glass surfaces, poorly lit operating rooms, broken oxygen equipment, lack of X-ray plates, scarcity of towels, cotton, adhesive tape, the most elementary needs. Even cockroach infestations. Besides, I stress, it's a hospital of "crickets," people do politics in the General, and Fernando Prieto Hernández jumps up:

There are many intelligent people there who have a political and social consciousness, and this is why the medical movement of 1966 in which Ismael Cosío Villegas and Guillermo Montaño stood out was so important. I agree that a physician who comes to Hospital General chooses it on the basis of ideologial convictions. It's very common to see doctors who work at the General and have no private practice.

162

"I have no private practice," Susana Kofman de Alfaro confirms. "Whoever needs to see me has to come to the General."

My father has been working at the General for fifty-five years, says Fernando Prieto Hernández, investigating what truly affects our population: cirrhosis and amebiasis, two problems that can be found in a wide circle of poor people. In the General, I have been able to establish methods for curing, working on antigens, which would never have been possible in a small hospital. Our patient population is unprotected, very receptive, and they are a great satisfaction to deal with. Patients are poor at the General. We work in a very real way with the pathology of poverty, the pathology of misery, the pathology of lack of culture and education, with entire families suffering from the same ailment.

WE ARE NOT VAMPIRES

It's not like that; they don't take blood from sick people. The patient has to convince two donors to donate half a liter of blood and not one. A half liter of blood is terribly useful, because you find an excellent concentration of plaquettes, blood protein, red cells, et cetera. Please realize that Hospital General is one of the cheapest or perhaps the cheapest within the system of open admission. A visit used to cost 40 pesos, and to be hospitalized varied in cost according to income level, from zero to 3,000, 4,000, or 5,000 pesos, the rate established by a social worker after administering a questionnaire. The fees went up a little; before the earthquake, the hospital was 70 percent full, but its emergency service was very active. Almost 40 percent of all patients who came to the emergency room were admitted, making Hospital General the core of the health care system in the city. . . . Another peculiar characteristic of the General is that the moment the patient is admitted, he or she can count on a high concentration of medical expertise; every specialization in the country is available to that patient.

During the days after the earthquake Susana Kofman de Alfaro and Fernando Prieto Hernández gave themselves to the most unpleasant of all tasks, turning cadavers over to the next of kin. It was very hard. They were working in a yard where the bodies were lying on ice, and in many cases they had to identify their own compañeros, nurses, and physicians. At the exit of the Pathology Department, on Dr. Jiménez Street, five hundred people camped out asking insistently for their relatives. Dr. Kofman de Alfaro and Dr. Prieto Hernández were on duty for twelve hours at a time, placing bodies in plastic bags.

In memory of the forty resident physicians, the nurses, the mothers and their babies who died, and in view of the response of the patients and the struggle of the medical personnel, the President of the Republic announced his decision a few days later: to reopen Hospital General.

IN THE JUÁREZ, PEOPLE RAN LIKE DRUNKEN RATS
HOSPITALS SHOULD NEVER FALL IN

One of the fundamental premises of the construction of a hospital is that an earthquake shouldn't bring it down, no matter what its degree of magnitude. Neither a hospital nor a school. That is why when they told me, "Hospital Juárez fell down," I couldn't believe it. I decided to go see, getting through several lines of police and boy scouts, until I got there.

Have you ever been in Hospital Juárez? You come into a covered courtyard with wooden doors; you open those doors and behind you find the tower. But this time when I opened the doors, all I saw was a jumble of thirteen or fourteen stories and a mob of people running around like drunken rats. There were more people staring than people who had a basic idea of what needed to be done. There was no coordination, nothing. And it was already one o'clock in the afternoon.

Rubén López Reyes, thirty-five, an architect by profession, worked in the sand pits in the area of Los Pinos, between Alencastre and the Periférico. There he taught himself how to explore, to excavate tunnels and to prop them up. How odd, to know that Los Pinos sits on top of an excavated sand quarry!

From the moment he arrived at Hospital Juárez, Rubén López Reyes made the decision not to go back to work, and along with Carlos Garduño de la Garza, twenty-three, Alberto Caballero Jaramillo, Estela Luna, and other volunteers, he started to excavate:

By 2 P.M. everyone was working the best they could. There was one single arc, one crowbar, one sledgehammer, there were no gloves, no helmets, not a fucking thing. Nothing. Then the sappers arrived; they had their camp equipment, with their trench shovels, green and squeaky clean, which during those days—I have witnesses—never left their backpacks.

I started coordinating people: "You, look for buckets, we're going to start excavating here. You, organize a chain to take out the rubble." And we worked very hard, and after a while, the people from the Associated Civil Engineers (ICA) arrived, maybe because they felt guilty, since they were involved in the construction of Hospital Juárez and the Pino Suárez towers. They came with a mechanical shovel and a bunch of experts, determined to coordinate the work. They said that the best way to rescue people was to dismantle the wreckage slab by slab with a crane and heavy machinery.

Anyone who has ever been in a hole like the inside of a mine knows that heavy machinery can produce vibrations, and within a fractured structure, any vibration can provoke the collapse or compacting of materials. Aside from those movements, for those who are still alive in limited crevices, with a slab right against their nose, provoking the settlement of that slab or its breakage means sure death. Not to mention that the dust can dry up the respiratory membranes of survivors.

I told the people of ICA, "There's no other way but to make a tunnel until we find people."

"And how do you know there are people where you make the tunnel?"

"You don't know, but you've got to do it. It is the only form of communicating with people who are buried there, and this is why a crane that weighs 80 or 100 tons is useless. It's simply going to provoke another cave-in."

"We're going to be moving slab by slab, as if we were peeling off the layers of a puff pastry."

"If you do that, you won't find anyone alive."

The first people we got to were the ones who were close to the windows and doors of the building. In all, eighty-three living persons came out, some badly injured, but others untouched. Now the problem was to get to the people who were trapped in the core. We worked all day, all night, into the early hours of the next morning, and we didn't even have a glass of water to drink. It was cold as hell; I think we all got pneumonia because of the intense physical activity we were engaged in.

At four in the morning they asked us to come down because the northern wing of the hospital was on fire. The boiler in the kitchen caught fire, and the fire spread to the hospital archives. We started to breathe very heavy smoke, and we turned yellow. It's very likely that because of this fire many people died of suffocation, because it lasted for four days and no one could put it out. Firemen struggled, but the smoke kept spreading all about.

Fortunately, from the first tunnel, we were able to detect survivors. We found one at the level of the fifth story of the building. Through the cracks we could hear a girl saying that there were children crying on another story. "I'm on the eighth floor," we could barely hear her say. We followed the tunnel upward, and this work bore fruit. We found nurse Angeles, who had been asleep for five days. She lost consciousness the moment the earthquake struck, and this fact protected her. We had to wake her up. Even after being there five days, she still remained trapped for almost thirty-six hours, the time that it took us to get her out. She was hugging a dead compañera in a very reduced space, and fortunately she was unharmed.

In making a small hole above the nurse, we realized that she had a piece of furniture on one side and a slab on the other, framing her face. Her head was swelling because of the pressure; we had to cut with a hacksaw. There was a volunteer gal who was the only one who knew how to operate a power saw; she would turn it on and ask, "Tell me, where do I cut?" But in the case of our nurse Angeles, there was no possiblity of using the power saw—so close to her face—nor to use acetylene where we were.

We started to work, and she said to us, 'I think I'm going to die."

I rushed out to look for her relatives—the soldiers had cordoned off the building—so that they would tell us what she liked. We found out that she was from Puebla, that she was twenty-one, that her name was Angeles Méndez Santiago, and with that information we started to kid around with her: Would she like some *mole*, or did she want some enchiladas? We knew how much she dug tropical music. We knew that she had about five or six boyfriends, that everyone out there was going to take her out on a date. We didn't even know her—in fact, she never saw us nor knew who we were. And in this way we went on talking and talking while we were trying to get her out:

"As soon as we get out, we're taking you dancing to Los Infiernos."

What a bad joke, to mention Los Infiernos, but this was the way we entertained her. We were trying to make her drink water in spite of herself:

"We're bringing you water."

"No, I don't want any water."

"Please drink a little bit."

"No, I don't want to. I'm very cold."

To be cold and not to want water are clear symptoms of shock. I ran again to look for the relatives. Her father and her brother also worked in the Juárez, and I told them that she refused to drink. They told me,

"She doesn't like water." What was happening was that she didn't like water, and there we were trying so hard. Then we gave her mango juice, and she sure drank that, and we kept on talking to her, incessantly.

"Did you know that your father, so and so, is waiting for you down there? And you're planning to die, just like that? We're not going to go and tell your father that you want to die, so you better cooperate."

We told her jokes. I was so exhausted that I don't know how I could think of any jokes, but I never stopped talking to her, not until we were able to free her face from the furniture and the slab, not until we could take her out.

Contact with the relatives was essential, but it was awful to go down and look for them, because everybody hoped they were the ones we were looking for. Many would step forward saying that surely the girl was their sister, their daughter, their mother; everyone wanted the survivor to be their own.

By this point not only relatives, but the press, the onlookers, and the movie stars were all there. But it's one thing to have freedom of the press and another thing to obstruct or delay a rescue operation.

It's very dangerous for people who have been trapped six, seven, or eight, not to mention thirty-six hours, to have the flash of a camera right in their faces or a microphone put next to their mouths right after leaving an extremely confining space. There were people who died of cardiac arrest; people are that susceptible.

We had to take precautions with Angeles. Survivors should only see indirect light, so you cover their eyes with a bandage. You have to cover them entirely when you put them on the stretcher; then you connect them to the glucose. In short, you have to take all the required lifesaving measures. A sudden flash in your face can cause the hardiest to crack. There was a man who crawled out, a physican, but he soon died from being out in the full light of day. These things we learned from the doctors, but most of all, we learned from experience.

Five days later, Hospital Juárez was a stage; the Green Cross, the Red Cross, the brigade workers. Suddenly a whole bunch of guys arrived with ropes, high boots, helmets, and grappling hooks of the sort used for mountain climbing. They said, "Excuse us, excuse us, we're in charge here, we're mountain climbers," and we told them, "Listen, brothers, this is not a mountain, if you have a hacksaw, let us have it, if you have a hammer, fork it over, but your boots and your hooks we do not need."

Everyone claimed to be in charge; all sorts of interlopers began to descend on the building, twenty or more with cameras, and fifty or more with photographic equipment, and since the military were the ultimate authority, they were the ones who exercised control: "This one comes in; this one doesn't." The soldiers were only standing there with their rifles. Out of five hundred soldiers, only fifty were working. One of them was a super guy, he was just Corporal Juan, that's all.

The soldiers that worked hand in hand with us never wanted to give us their names. They thought that we would harm them if we sent a letter to their general saying that these people were truly brave and selfless. They say it's compromising for them to be publicly recognized, so all we know is that this guy was Juan, a guy like they don't make anymore, as fine as the best of the firemen, even if that was only a fraction of them all. The ones that worked were few and far between. We must say that the people from Military Health and Safety also threw themselves into the work with us, staying awake for hours on end, killing themselves to get to the survivors. But that little Corporal Juan, him we'll never forget!

Marisol Martín del Campo

It's my dad, says Alejandra Reséndiz in front of Hospital Juárez on Friday, September 26, at 12:15. He was hospitalized on the fourth floor. Since the earthquake, I've been coming to sit here. I left my children with my aunt. I've seen all they do: only yesterday, they started to work hard, but it's been terribly slow. They are very inhumane with us.■

We have an emergency plan consisting of concentrating all of the hospital under one command, which is Emergencies. On the morning of September 19—says Dr. Valente Aguilar Zinzer, a pediatrician in the emergency room of the National Institute of Pediatrics—the hospital told us, "It's forbidden to remove any equipment, other materials, or vehicles from here, because we are under the orders of the Health Sector, and we must wait to hear from them."

At nine in the morning we were nervous and wanted to go out and help, but we hadn't received any orders. They never came. We were desperate; the residents accosted me: "Our compañeros are under the slabs of Hospital General; we must go get them out." We pressured our immediate supervisors and outfitted five ambulances to take them downtown.

After two o'clock in the afternoon, we put ourselves in charge of the evacuation of babies from Hospital General. At six, we drove downtown: it was apocalyptic, unbelievable chaos, buildings bursting and people like ants, not even turning to look anymore.

We started setting up first-aid stations in key locations: in the Juárez, the General, the abandoned Colonia Roma, but I think that Tepito was the most pathetic . . . not to mention Tlatelolco. First-aid stations were irrelevant because no one was getting the injured out, except for the volunteers, whom the authorities had made up their minds to get rid of. There was no system of command and no coordination.

Hospital Balbuena was saturated by Thursday afternoon; every corridor was full; intensive care, clogged up with patients. We arrived with our equipment: What do you need? We have five ambulances here. If you want, we can evacuate 60 percent of the hospital so that you will be able to take in more victims. But the director said, "No, I'm not letting go of one single patient."

AND THE PRIVATE PHYSICIANS? IN THEIR OFFICES, THANK YOU

We visited the shelters and saw patients there. We trained medical students, because—this is very sad—with few exceptions, specialized physicians who were not in the military kept to themselves. Their response was nil, negligible at best.

The first three days were critical in the matter of saving lives. On Thursday night, if you were close to the ruins, you could hear hundreds of voices: Help me, ay, ay, ay. The next day, there were only a few voices left, and four days later you had to detect them with special sound equipment. Only a few lives were saved, because the action was delayed. Where on earth—in Hospital General, in Hospital Juárez, in Colonia Roma, in Tepito, in Tlatelolco, downtown—where on earth were the labor unions, the political parties, the PRI machinery—so efficient in mounting campaigns—the delegation groups, the military, the police, the churches? Where were all these people? Where were they? They were nowhere. The only thing that existed was an organizing of civil society, small groups, each doing the best they could.

The rescue of the seven babies seven days after the earthquake is a complete miracle; there is no other explanation; it can't be understood in medical terms. One of them died; the rest are well. Ninety percent of all the adults that were rescued alive after the fourth day had a kidney deficiency, but the babies' kidneys were intact.

The process of adaptation of those who had been buried alive is very delicate: It's necessary to supply glucose intravenously. The change of temperature has to be slow. Oxygen intake has to increase little by little, just as rehydration does. We had to go into the holes, to take care of them there, to prepare them. There were many unsung heroes among the residents who spent hours inside at the risk of being trapped by a cave-in. There were many injured people among the rescue personnel: some fell into holes, some tumbled down the sides of the wreckage, some were choking on the smoke, but they would come back for oxygen and then they would go in again. There were some who died. No one talks about them. Among thousands of dead, who would mention eight or ten more? Besides, they were not looking for recognition or honor; they wanted to save lives.

There were other cases when the absence of physicians who knew what to do in emergencies caused a buried person to be hurt. There was the case of a nurse who was pierced seven times in an effort to give her glucose. I could hear her shouting. She knew what was happening and ended up saying, "You know what? Stop trying; you better give me a beer, and please don't stab me anymore, because if the earthquake didn't kill me, you will." We were learning hour by hour.

Many died without substantial injuries, inside the ruins, because of the delay in the rescue: suffocated or dehydrated. There was a horrible case in Hospital Juárez. The north wing was almost unharmed, the upper stories were practically untouched, and many survivors were trapped there, but they died hours later, burned when the oxygen and gas tanks exploded, all because nobody acted fast enough to evacuate them . . . Nobody assumed command. It wasn't until five days later that a relative thought, Why don't we draw a blueprint of the hospital? Nobody had thought of that yet.

On Saturday the 21st, there were two riots outside the Juárez. A false rumor circulated among the relatives that the building was going to be blown up. The people—about four thousand—got furious and started to push at the gates. Things got really ugly. Some members of the army came out and were taunted. Later a group of physicians spoke to the crowd, giving ample information on what was happening, and that calmed people down.

On Sunday the 22nd, Hospital Juárez acquired the nickname of the Tower of Babel: communications among French, Swiss, Germans, North Americans, and Mexicans were a mess. They were completely confused. Each group was implementing a rescue technique that was incompatible with those of the others.

There was a technique that consisted of opening holes or mines, which we dubbed "the mole burrow," because the men had to burrow in. Then there was the approach of those who used heavy machinery to lift enormous pieces of concrete as if they were pickup sticks, a technique that must be carefully calculated and is difficult and perhaps the most risky of all—the wreckage can cave in—but also the one that can yield great results, since many people can be uncovered at once . . . All this had to be talked about and coordinated, which was very difficult.

But here's what happened: A short young man, a physician without any special title, took the responsibility of giving orders whenever there were conflicts with the army or among the foreigners due to their different approaches to a rescue manuever. And what was most remarkable is that even the general who was in charge of the zone, the foreign brigades, the volunteers, and all the rest of the people who were there in a state of great disorder said, "We are with the doctor. Let him give the orders."

Another new social syndrome became evident to me, which can be called "greed for heroic stature" or "meritology," which is the struggle to take credit. This happened even among the foreigners. They could argue for hours to see which group would go in to finally get the person out. I'll give you an example: In the residents' building of Hospital General there was a plastic surgeon whose hand was trapped under a ton of cement. You can imagine the importance of a hand for a surgeon. Well, they found him and got close to him. Then the Swiss and the Mexicans spent two hours arguing whether or not they should cut the hand off or whether it was better to lift the slabs. They went to such extremes that this guy told them, "You know what? I've been here for four days, and the only thing that matters to me is to get out. Get the hell out and argue outside and send me a Coke, or cut my hand off once and for all. But get me out of here, please, that's all I ask; don't fight to decide who gets the glory."

We were all the victims of lack of coordination. We were all disconcerted, the foreigners just as much as ourselves. It was obvious that Mexico has no emergency plans. Someone would have had to tell us which were the evacuation routes, where burned patients go, what hospitals deal with other kinds of trauma, which hospitals are still open, and how many beds are left.

Maybe one of the few institutions that reacted to the catastrophe was the Red Cross. Unfortunately, neither the Health Sector, nor the Defense, nor the Ministry of Government, nor Communications, nor official institutions, nor any of our celebrated national public resources had the capacity to respond.

What is the positive outcome of all this? I would think that the old inferiority complex that Mexicans have should be questioned. We are not incompetent. What is incompetent is the system that we live in. The earthquake proved to us that when we work together, we do a good job.

Octavio Paz in *Libération*

Mexicans believe simultaneously that they are the least significant people in the world and that they are exceptional. These are two faces of the same disease: insecurity. This explains the initial rejection of international aid and, later, the surprise at feeling loved. International assistance was more important at the psychological than at the material level. Mexicans learned that they were not alone, that they were not behind or in a corner of history, but were simply part of their world.■

Anselma Dolores Durán Sánchez, "Doctora" Chiringas
FOR ME THERE WAS NO PHYSICAL PAIN, NO STENCH OF DEATH

At Hospital General, nurses in their uniforms and white caps looked like doves. They would only need to have pink feet, and they don't. Their stockings and shoes are white, and their legs are nimble, used to walking fast in response to a patient's ring.

Today, the first of November, All Saints' Day, the nurses flutter around the altar of the dead next to the giant pool—full of water—of what was once the Gynecology-Obstetrics ward and around the one placed next to the residents' tower, the two buildings that tumbled down. We speak of the catastrophe, but we also discuss the future. Dr. Jorge de la Barba, a resident in the Urology Department, was on the fifth floor of the tower when it came down, and two hours later his compañeros were rescuing him from the rubble. Pilar Jaimes, Valentina Martínez, Araceli Jiménez, Sara Teresa Soriano, and other compañeras also relate their experiences. But Anselma Dolores Durán Sánchez, with her legs encased in thick stockings, her dancing eyes, and a command of words, is the one who at this moment captures everyone's attention. She speaks gracefully until I interrupt her to ask:

"And you, what is your name?"

"Anselma Dolores Durán Sánchez."

"How long have you been at Hospital General?"

"On February 1 it'll be fourteen years. Practically as soon as I arrived, I started working in G-O (she points to the hole). Before that, I'd been in Pediatrics for six months; I took care of the newborns. I adore children. Even though I have plenty of my own, I still love other people's kids."

"How many children do you have, Anselma?"

"I had six; there are five left."

"Are you married?"

"No."

"And the children, who takes care of them?"

"The oldest is twenty-three, and she is an office manager for Social Security; she was in Saltillo during the quake; another girl is twenty and works at Banco del Atlántico; my only boy is in high school; and the other two girls, twelve and thirteen, are also in school."

(Oh, Anselma, how you fascinate me, with your cheerful voice, your six fatherless kids, well planted in life, your nervous movements, the way you speak, the teeth you are missing, and your smile that shows it, your fast-moving mouth, your black permed hair. I wish that I could take you in my arms, hug you, tell you how much I love my country because of people like you!)

Anselma speaks, totally unaware of the effect that she creates, speaks, interrupted only by my questions, which are only meant to add some precision to her narrative:

In the tower, forty-nine residents died; in G-O, maybe thirty-nine, more or less; the real number will never be known. I saw a woman coming out of the heap naked, with her clothes under her arm, in a daze. (Many women's bodies must have been removed along with the rubble by mechanical shovels.) I stayed right here working twelve hours a day. I wished I were Superman, a giant robot to be able to lift the whole building.

Something inexplicable happened to me. I felt no physical pain, no stench from the dead, no heat or cold or fatigue. I felt nothing. The engineers allowed me to stay up there in G-O because that was my turf. I had worked thirteen going on fourteen years in that ward, so imagine how I knew it. I knew the compañeras who worked the morning, afternoon, and night shifts, because I was always on call morning and afternoon. Thursday, Friday, Saturday, and Sunday, I could be on call in the morning, afternoon, or night, sometimes during the four shifts because I needed to make ends meet at home.

For me the compañeras were sisters, friends. I don't know, I had such energy, rage, strength. I heard voices and echoes that said, "Get us out! There's too much water here!"

All those people who said their names through the rubble became corpses; when we took them out they were no longer human. Some were totally charred, others merely burned, destroyed, all broken up, those bodies that in the first day after the earthquake could still say, "Get us out! There's too much water here!"

Of course the volunteers went in through the tunnels; but it wasn't easy. What hurt the most was to see the arrival of the foreign brigades, the people who crossed an ocean to help us. The soldiers, those ass-holes, prevented them from going in. With refined imbecility, they stopped them, saying, "Hey, where do these jerks think they're going?"

"They are the French brigade."

"They're French, on top of all. Shitty little French!"

"Why?"

"Don't you know anything about the French intervention, you jerk?"

"They're experts in calamities."

"They still can't be here."

"Who gave the orders?"

"The director. No one goes in."

"We'll see about that."

Then I intervened:

"Shut up, you," I told the gorilla. "Shut up, stupid."

"You be quiet. Get out of here or I'll kick you out myself."

"No, I'm not leaving."

"Shut up, or I'll have you booted out right now."

"How am I going to be quiet when my friends, my compañeras, members of my family are here? I can't be silent!"

Two policemen came and told the gorilla, "And you, who are you? Look, brother, we call the shots here, and you're getting out!"

They pulled rank, and they got him out.

I said, "Yes, yes, get him out."

And this way the French brigade was able to go in. In other words, the French practically had to force their way in. From the very begin-ning, they tried to lift the concrete sections on that side with special rubber air bags they had, and hydraulic jacks and canvas bags. Their dogs went in and detected the bodies. But they weren't allowed.

"Who prevented them, the soldiers?"

It was all very mixed up; there were military people, Pemex people, hospital people, people from everywhere. During these days the husbands of our compañeras excavated, forming human chains, with buckets, bucketfuls of jagged concrete and more concrete. The poor husbands, the children, they were here night and day.

Many doctors would tell me, "Don't go away, Anselma, stay up there, watch for the equipment when they open up, take notice of who is doing it, don't let them take things out." During the ten days I was up there, a chest of drawers full of brand-new instruments was rescued from the sixth floor, where equipment was stored. We turned it over. But now, they all ask where it is; they are saying we have to pay for it. The bosses have been told they have to pay for those new instruments.

Each time I came down from the heap, people would tell me, "You're like a little ant." Honestly, I can't explain how those days went. I didn't eat, I only drank water; those days under the blast of sunlight, up there, from 8 A.M. until 10 P.M. when I'd go home. I don't even know why they'd let me in when they wouldn't let anyone else in. The nurses and doctors knew me. They knew my ward was the world to me. They knew I knew all the compañeras who are now dead.

I knew the structure of the building pretty well, so the engineers would come and ask questions. When the building fell it kind of wrenched itself; it fell inward and twisted toward this side, so the bodies were scattered all over here. The floors were intertwined; they had continued to drift toward the center. They found some files in the fourth floor and got hold of the building blueprints. The engineer then called me to ask, "How was it? Like this?"

And when I sat down to study it, some person came out of the blue and said, "No, it wasn't like that."

So I says, "You better be quiet. This here is the nursery, and on each side we had rows of beds."

With the help of the night supervisor we were able to assess that it had been what we call a dark night; we called it a dark night when too many children were born, and we didn't have a moment's rest. There were nights when we had between 100 and 125 children born between eight at night and eight in the morning. It was one of those nights.

They found bodies of women in labor, with the heads of fetuses already in the birth canal. Four of them. Each floor had forty-four beds, and at least the second and third floors were full. The nurseries had between twenty-five and thirty beds adjacent to them. Where did they all go? They never came out. Only a few were rescued, because when the boilers exploded a good part of the building caught on fire.

The part that burned down would have corresponded to nurses' stations, and these were wood paneled. All that burned down. In some places they found charred human remains; a piece of cloth saved from the fire would give us a clue: nurse, clerical staff, management.

On the day of the earthquake, my bus never arrived, and I can't stand the subway. I come all the way from Naucalpan by making several bus connections. I was due to arrive at the hospital at 8:30 when at the corner of Insurgentes and Medellín I learned that buses were not running. They said that the buildings were falling down, including the Central Quirúrgica and the building next to it.

Yes. Everything was smoky and plaster dust was flying all over, so all that day I felt devastated. This was my life. I've learned many things here: how to relate to the doctors, to the compañeras, to managers and clerks. For me social class makes no difference. Whenever I ask for something from the managers, they say, "Yes, Anselma."

Why? Because I live with them, I may bring them a taco and we have breakfast together, we chat, and I have been here for an age. Hey, I was on call all the time, and most of the doctors would come to me because I tried to read their minds, whatever they needed. If I was in the delivery room, I would ask, "What do we have here? Natural or forceps?"

"Natural."

Okay, so I would come with the whole shebang that was needed; I'd never miss.

If they said forceps, I would only ask, "What kind?"

That was in delivery. In "Labor," I helped get women hooked up to the intravenous right off. In "Newborns," I taught many medical students, many residents to hook up the babies to the glucose when they were in trouble, and to rehabilitate them when they were born with a problem, to avoid dehydration. You have to find their tiny veins; you've got to have a strategy all figured out to do it, because it's so hard to find a teeny little blood vessel; adults are big mothers next to the veins of preemies. You've got to do it nice and easy, with a special touch, so the doctors and students would look for me wherever I was when it came to pinching babies' veins. The new woman chief of staff was bothered because everyone said, "Get Anselma."

Wherever she went, she heard, "Get Anselma."

She got jealous and said, "Let me get Anselma out of G-O."

Outside the compañeras were calling me "the G-O star," "the Adelita," because I was "popular among the troops." And the compañeras whose bodies I found, the most senior ones, had given me a nickname, "Doctora Chiringas," because sometimes I feel I'm a doctor; I prescribe; my medicine and my cures work. I don't know. Maybe they called me that because they were pulling my leg: "Hey you, Doctora Chiringas." That's the name Esthercita Piña gave me, an easygoing gal, a funny one. She died next to Sabina Oseguera.

We all used the same dressing room that had been assigned to us, and we were always kidding and teasing each other. Even when they changed me to another ward, I'd still go directly to G-O to change, to spend a little while with them, and then I'd go do my job. I didn't leave until I saw the bodies of Esthercita Piña and Sabina Oseguera, my buddies.

Dr. Jorge Barba listens impassively to the tale of Doctora Chiringas. Many compañeras weep. Outside there are votive candles and flowers of the dead. Dr. Jorge Barba, unlike Doctora Chiringas, is a man of few words; he's a survivor, rescued by his colleagues of the Urology Department two and a half hours after being buried:

I begged for help, I shouted, and my compañeros came right away and started the rescue operation. I was trapped in the outside part of the building, and that was in my favor. My legs were compressed for about an hour. A wooden beam fell over me, and the headboards of some beds, with lots of cement on top. I was in a crevice about a yard high. I was crouching, I could breathe, but I saw no light. How did I make it through?

I think that the important thing is to have an internal struggle, so I thought, "If I don't fight, if I give in, this is my tomb." I kept calling for help, I shouted, I screamed, of course I screamed a lot, "Help! I'm here! Help!" After so much shouting I heard a voice, "There's someone here."

Now the trick was to be patient until they got me out. First, for half an hour, there was no answer, nobody came, but after that lapse, I heard voices outside, and half an hour later they knew where I was.

Contact had been made. They started to excavate with a crowbar; they made a hole and saw me, and I could tell them, "My problem is that my legs are trapped; what I need you to do is to free my legs so I will not have problems later." I was caught face down, sideways, and face down, with no one else in my room. I was by myself when the earthquake hit. They took me out, but as far as I know, forty-nine compañeros, the residents in a variety of specializations, died. I could never tell you exactly how many people died between patients, children, doctors, and nurses; the only thing I can tell you is that among my fellow residents, most of them were women. I have tried to readapt myself socially bit by bit, maybe I've made it 80 percent of the way.

When I learned that they wanted to break up the General and send its pieces to many places, I was one of the many people who protested. I love this hospital. It has given us the opportunity to learn so much as physicians, residents, and students, so we fought. A place with such a tradition could not go just like that, especially given our situation in the city. It made no sense to close down when so much work could still be done here. We only lost two buildings. Thanks to the support of the public we're here again, and we've got to stay put.

"Yes, we've got to stay put."

La Doctora Chiringas, Anselma Dolores Durán Sánchez, stretches out her arms; today is the first of November, day of the offerings.

"I brought a stew with squash seed sauce, and hot tortillas. How about a taquito?"

Hospital General
- Trapped: 100 physicians, 200 female patients, and 100 newborns. Director Dr. Rodolfo Díaz Perches: by 7 P.M. we had only been able to rescue alive 15 doctors and a little more than 40 women and newborns (*Novedades*, September 20).
- In Gynecology 35 young doctors are buried along with more than 100 patients (*Novedades*, September 21).
- More than 70 doctors died when 80 percent of the buildings at Hospital General caved in. Dr. Rodolfo Díaz Perches reported that 400 persons had been trapped in the hospital's rubble, and as of yesterday at noon, only 40 survivors and 25 dead bodies had been recovered (*Ovaciones*, September 21).
- Hospital General and the Centro Médico Nacional will be rebuilt outside the capital city (*Excélsior*, September 23).

- A one-and-a-half-year-old girl was rescued yesterday from Hospital General. It is certain that in the ruins some others are still alive (*Novedades*, September 24).
- Miraculous rescue of a baby (*Ovaciones*, September 25).

FLYERS THAT RAIN DOWN LIKE CONFETTI

Today, I look over the papers, sheets placed in my hands by rushing hands, flyers from Hospital Juárez, or from the Center for Information and Analysis of the Effects of the Earthquake, coordinated among others by Daniel Molina, flyers given out in the street. I find two testimonies from Juan Antonio Ascencio:

- A girl about eight years old rounded the corner onto my street. She passed by me crying, with a dead kitten in her arms. This too made me sad.
- In the Ford assembly plant on Calzada de Guadalupe, a shelter was set up for 700 people. A group of approximately 25 came to the custodian's booth, silently looking in. The custodian asked them what they needed. They answered they were trying to see whether they liked that shelter.

Outside Hospital Juárez, next to the Gynecology-Obstetrics unit—which is now a pond, deep, with twisted steel sticking out of it—the nurses have placed an altar with a gigantic offering and a banner that warns, "We Shall Not Forget." There are buckets and buckets holding more than a hundred enormous bunches of giant marigolds. Votive candles burn.

On Friday, November 1, Dr. Sadi de Buen, chief of the Ophthalmological Service and a member of the Medical Society of Hospital General de México, tall, with silver hair and moustache, hands out a little piece of cardboard with a message written by hand, in round, good-student penmanship:

Dear compañeros, all:
   May our dead be always in our minds to ennoble our actions and our struggle for justice. May our dead be heavy on the conscience, if there is such a thing, of those who tried to destroy this hospital and still persist in their treason!

We know that our firm conviction and our faith will triumph
over them.

In Hospital Juárez—on top of its ruins—Rubén López Reyes, thirty-
five, an architect by profession and a rescue worker for the last ten
days, has written two poems:

We have lost nights
days
escape from
in between
our hands
and we left
inside each crevice
a piece
of our own life.

Even so,
they took away our weeping
they crushed unhurriedly
the very last piece
of our hope,
they broke forever
a thousand dreams
and yet
our word
they will never destroy.

We're no longer the same
we have taken death
along with our own
lives.
    (October 1, 1985)

There was no time
to count the weeping
behind each stone
when hope was hiding
there

behind stone after stone,
wall after wall.
We faced life
and at each moment
we vanquished death
halfway into a tunnel.

I have not tallied up the time
of lost light,
I will only remember the long night
and the weeping
(of those,
the ones who waited
but whose steps
we could never retrace).
　　(October 1, 1985)

At Hospital General, next to the pit full of water that used to be G-O,
a nurse says to me, wiping away her tears:

"Look, I'm no poet, don't use my name, but I just read this to my
compañeras. Wouldn't you take it to *La Jornada*? Let them take a look.
You think they'd read it?"

We have all spoken of today and tomorrow.
We have remembered sadly a yesterday that must be overcome.
We worry for the ones that are here.
And for the ones who will come.
We have sworn minutes of silence.
For friends and brothers who disappeared.
Memorial services have been held, prayers abound.
In memory of each and every one of them.
But nothing is enough.
Nothing shall ever be enough, for they are still here.
As if time had been stilled before the catastrophe.
And there they are glad.
Some end their work and some begin it.
Some weary, some full of energy.
There they are in their buildings.
It is for you, my sister nurse.

It is for you, my friend the doctor, technician, worker.

It is for you, compañero, manager, and clerk.

And for you, dear patient.

We still stand firm!

United we transform this woe and grief into struggle to preserve
  your hospital,

My hospital, our hospital.

Your death, compañero, compañera was not in vain.

It rekindles our hope.

It is the banner of our fight.

Hard days await us, but we will respond.

We promise you.

Flyers that rain down like confetti, now printed here, some given out on Cuauhtémoc Avenue, others on any corner on the day of the first gathering of survivors.

THE GOVERNMENT WAS LEFT BEHIND ON ALL FRONTS

It was not until Saturday morning—says Enrique Vargas—that Paco Rodríguez del Campo told me that the building belonging to Leonardo Arana, on Roma Street next to Hotel Continental, had fallen. He had a well-founded fear that Leonardo was inside because he had not come to work, he had not been in touch with anyone, and nobody knew anything about his wife Mónica either.

In front of the building I met many of Leonardo's friends, members of his family and Mónica's, and also friends and relatives of the other occupants. We started to excavate. In the afternoon we got three people out alive.

"Leonardo, Leonardo, Mónica!"

We heard Leonardo's faint voice:

"I'm here."

We detected the origin of the voice and started to remove rubble. We could not break through the chunks of concrete because all we had was shovels and picks. The army was a bunch of onlookers, and those working were volunteers. In the process of removing rubble we realized we were destabilizing the slabs. We had to get ahold of some timber to shore them up. We couldn't let them fall in. And we kept on going.

The first one out was Leonardo.

"And Mónica is there."

The day before they had taken out six cadavers; on Saturday I had the luck to get a man out alive. Saturday afternoon an ambulance took Leonardo alive to Hospital Mocel. We continued digging and found the body of his wife. As a matter of fact, when we got Leonardo out, he and his wife were still holding hands. They came down from the fifth floor when they first felt the earthquake, desperately trying to reach the street. Then Leonardo was caught standing on the ground floor of the building, while Mónica was lying down. Later Leonardo would reproach himself in the hospital for not having insisted that Mónica stand up: Why hadn't he held her up? He believes she would not have suffocated in a standing position, since he was able to breathe, while she had no oxygen left.

Leonardo lost his titles, his certificates, his property; he lost everything.

He lost Mónica, his wife.

THE PLEADING OF RELATIVES WAS WORTH NOTHING

On September 19, an army lieutenant was using violence and foul language in trying to remove people from the top of a heap of rubble at the corner of Versalles and Chapultepec Avenue. He had received orders to clear the area and proceed with demolition in spite of the possibility that survivors were still trapped inside.

What kind of training do the military get? The army demolished the building, and a person whose shouts for help everyone heard, died, a victim of the arbitrariness of power.

A few days after the earthquake, at 8:30 in the morning, at Hospital Juárez, in the corner of Escuela Médico Militar and San Pablo 13, the French rescuers were the object of jeers and insults from army personnel. The good thing is that they couldn't understand, although they must have gotten the drift of what the barracks boys were saying. Now I ask, why did the international brigades leave the country so annoyed at the Mexican authorities?

THE ARMY DID NOTHING

The emergency plan DN-III is trash. On Frontera Street, in Cinemas I and II of Colonia Roma, at 1:30 in the morning of September 21, the soldiers gave themselves to looting.

On Saturday night, when foreign aid began to arrive, I saw an army major distributing the blankets and sleeping bags intended for the earthquake victims among his own soldiers. Weren't these things for the victims? I witnessed this near the streets of Río de la Loza and Isabel la Católica.

THE EARTHQUAKE CRACKED THE UNTOUCHABLES

It used to be said that Mexican journalists always faced three taboos: the army, the Virgin of Guadalupe, and the President of the Republic with his family. We could not touch those subjects "with the petal of a rose." The earthquake also cracked those taboos. People know how to be critical. And their thoughts have been published.

WHAT WE NEED TO DO IS TO PREPARE FOR A FUTURE CATASTROPHE

THE ENIGMA IS HOW SOCIAL MALAISE WILL BE EXPRESSED NOW

"The only way for me to be at peace is to be at home with my children." "I can't sleep." "I'm seeing things." "I hear voices." "Food nauseates me." "I'm never eating meat." "I'm obsessed." Many rescue workers are going through a crisis.

A few days ago, one of them told Dr. Javier González, a mathematician who organized a rescue brigade at UAM-Azcapotzalco, "Yesterday I rang a bell and fifteen feet up I saw a woman leaning out a window. And you know who she was? She was the woman in the green dress." He meant a cadaver recovered by his group out of the Nuevo León. "I saw her perfectly. She was the lady we had taken out the other day from the Nuevo León Building."

Another rescuer who had taken out the body of a child repeated obsessively that he looked just like one of his children. The trauma keeps growing. We have to worry not only about the direct victims of the earthquake but also about the rescue workers. Our experience is that of a dreadful war; we're zombies ambulating in a devastated land; no one is used to this, no one knows how to handle such deep collective pain.

Dr. Javier González—who got his degree at the Center for Research at Politécnico—organized the first brigade of twenty-three people out of UAM-Azcapotzalco, a group that unearthed twenty-two bodies from the Nuevo León mass of rubble. He is an athletic and optimistic man who keeps in tip-top condition by jogging around Viveros. He is a member of *Punto Crítico* and now a collaborator with the Center for Information and Analysis of the Effects of the Earthquake.

We showed up at the Nuevo León on September 23. We couldn't go earlier because the UAM was closed, although we were working on our own individually at another spot before that. A compañero from UAM in charge of the northern side of the Nuevo León Building met our group. Why was he the boss? At some point he gave two or three orders that made sense, and he became the boss. That's what happened with some of the buildings; the one who hit the nail on the head or knew a little bit more ended up being in charge. We all became "engineers"; everyone called us *inge* the moment they saw us wearing a helmet or carrying a hammer or a shovel.

Curiously, one of my first realizations was that people who have never had the slightest training can quickly become capable of complex and hard physical labor for prolonged periods of time.

In the Nuevo León Building, we reached the shaft of a stairway, and when we opened the door, we found six bodies of people who had tried to escape going upward. You can guess that they realized that the lower stories had collapsed, so they decided to go up; we found a body still holding tight to the railing. It took us a long time to release the grip.

Everyone must have learned at this point what it means to be in contact with a corpse from the moment you locate it until you are able to bring it out. It can be a matter of hours, or it can take days. After this unsettling experience, many brigade workers left. It was not a matter of willpower or physical strength, but rather a matter of emotional rejection. But many went forward, and we worked without going back home for ten long days, after Monday.

Some of our fellow professors at UAM had lived there or had relatives in the building: one from the math department, one from chemistry who was a founder of the university and died with his eleven-year-old son, and another one, Professor Angulo Brown, a physicist who lost his brother, his sister-in-law, and their children. We set out in our search with this professor, who said at one point, "I recognize those curtains." They were hanging under a large piece of concrete. "I recognize those curtains. I'm sure it's there."

After sleeping for two hours, at 6:30 in the morning we broke through a slab; we made a small perforation, and when we removed the debris, we found a pair of feet. This was the site. We were atop the building, and the concrete roof was huge. There we worked shoulder to shoulder with the Israelis, a group of twenty first-rate rescuers, professionally trained and with appropriate equipment; they knew what they were doing. Because of their expertise (gained through warfare), we were able to discover five bodies within an hour and a half. There they were, but we couldn't get them out because large columns stood in the way.

For twelve hours—until seven in the evening—we worked above the cadavers; two were children, one four years old, the other six, looking in fact very much like my friend's children. He hasn't stopped saying ever since that one of the dead little ones was identical to his own son.

The compañeros who spent fourteen or fifteen days looking for a brother or a sister, or an in-law, had to see more than six thousand cadavers in the morgues and in Delta Park, trying to find their own. For fifteen days my friend had to do this. The images his eyes registered, five or six thousand are impossible to assimilate, possibly worse than images of war. I believe that if he does not have the opportunity to articulate his grief, his mental health could suffer seriously.

What comes next? One really doesn't know. People had it hard, people worked hard, they had to. But afterward, what? You've got to make them talk. It's the only way to go forward. Now we need to prepare ourselves for other catastrophes, be in readiness for rescue operations, acquire the responsibility for our own protection.

Two years ago, they had evacuation drills for every bed in the Centro Médico Nacional. That is why now, when the hospital had to be emptied, no patient was endangered. And who were the ones who knew how to do it? The nurses, who gave orders to the doctors, because they had been trained properly two years ago.

Will we have learned our lesson, or will we continue from here to the end of time saying to ourselves, we'll see what happens, let's see what tomorrow brings, saying to each other, too bad, brother, this is our fate?

The Tale of El Chino: Public Accountant and Volunteer
JUST PRETEND WE ARE AT WAR; I'M GOING TO TLATELOLCO

"And you, Chinito do you expect a reward for all you've done?"

"For what?"

"A recognition by the government for your having gotten so many people from under the rubble."

Héctor Méndez, "El Chino," a mole at San Antonio Abad 150, where they are still rescuing cadavers, raises his face, puzzled.

"You have sacrificed yourself. It would be normal for the government to recognize you for the days and the nights that you . . . Well, you had to leave your work, right, Chinito? How does your family make a living? How do they make out while you're here killing yourself?"

He looks back at me with even more pride:

"Well, I may not be rich, but I have enough to support my family, my wife and two girls, fourteen and twelve, who are already in high school. As for the government's recognition, I couldn't care less, I'm not interested, I'm not a child waiting for Daddy's hug, nor a dog waiting for a bone. That's not my bag at all."

"So what is your bag then?"

"What I'm trying to do. There are many people who today, Sunday, October 20, still have their families buried under debris. I understand them. My mother died in March, and what matters to me is to see the cadavers turned over to their next of kin."

It starts to thunder and rain wets our faces.

"Do you want to put on my helmet?" he sweetly asks.

"No, thank you. Under this awning we hardly get any rain."

"But we could get lightning."

"That doesn't make you wet, right?"

On September 19th, Héctor Méndez, dubbed El Chino for his curly hair, a thirty-nine-year-old man who studied at the School of Commerce at UNAM, told his wife, "Just pretend that we're at war; I'm going to Tlatelolco."

In 1968, I was in my second year of studies at the university. Although I barely participated in the student movement, I witnessed the birth of the popular education movement, the independent union movements in the Ministry of Planning, and many cooperatives.

With a new social conscience, I went to help with rehab and self-built low-income housing in Tláhuac, as well as the cleanup of the Xochimilco canals and then in Tlanepantla and Ecatepec. I remember well when the Tlatelolco buildings were made. I saw the excavations, the placement of pillars in the foundations; I saw people come to live there. We of Colonia Guerrero belong to the lower middle class, but our roots are very old.

A new type of inhabitants came to our part of town; office workers with a different mind-set, but they mixed with us, the people from the old barrio, and we became good friends. That's why I came, and from the very first day, I entered a tunnel with two guys from Military Sanitation, and we first got a señora out, a large woman, weighing around 200 pounds, which was hard, but then we got her niece out with no difficulty at all, just as if she were a doll.

The older woman had a broken leg, and the niece had a broken arm, but the two of them were alive, and we had been working from 10:30 in the morning to 6:30 in the afternoon. Things went very fast, for this kind of rescue—some can last forty-two hours—and while you are at it, you feel despair growing inside you. The heavy lady had to be placed on a bed comforter; the guys from the army came to help when it got late. By Sunday the 22nd in the afternoon, I had slept two hours, and in the next two weeks, our work took twenty intense hours every day. We would rest then for four hours.

Now in Topeka, with all the accumulated fatigue, the situation is very different. We work an average of eighteen hours a day, but no longer with the same intensity because there is no life left in there. We also employ power tools these days: a pneumatic hammer, the acetylene torch, power saws, because to work in the tunnels can be physically exhausting.

Héctor Méndez looks exhausted, but he won't admit it.

I eat well, he protests, very well. The Salvation Army is here. I've never given them a cent when they collect at stoplights, but I'll have to support them now because they serve good coffee and hot sandwiches. The girls from the University of Anáhuac have been here every day bringing us delicious food, cakes, dishes that are fit for a deluxe restaurant, fine cookies. They've never failed us, not once.

The worst is over. During the first few days, from Thursday to Sunday, I didn't eat. I only drank water and didn't try to get any sleep because there was no place to lie down. Now we have a camp: tents, cots, blankets, so we can sleep two or three hours and go back at it. But at the beginning, it was impossible to rest, knowing that people were there waiting for us. The rain has gotten to me, but truly, you don't have time to think that you can get sick, because you are doing something more important than saving yourself from a common cold.

"Chinito, what about that belt with a butterfly buckle?"

I found it lying on the ground, and since I knew it would go to the trash otherwise, I've saved it as a souvenir; it's a woman's belt, but no matter.

As I've been working here, I have run into people I knew when I was at the university—people who were active in the 1968 student movement—and I can see that they still have a will to help. I've seen many people concerned about the garment workers, people who have gone and confronted the owners—some of them experts in labor law—Elías Serur and other sweatshop operators, all of them Jews, all of them exploiters of the seamstresses.

Did you ever read Shakespeare, *The Merchant of Venice*? Do you remember Shylock? Shylock is the embodiment of the Mexican Jew. I don't mean all Jews; I mean the exploiter, the slave driver, the employer of seamstresses in clandestine sweatshops. There are members of the Israelite community that have all my respect, scientists and even industrialists who are humane. Have you heard of Jacobo and José Zaindenweber? They have a fabric mill, American Textile, and their workers have all the benefits prescribed by law, good working conditions, nice facilities, fair work schedules, fair wages. They are well-born people. I'm talking about people who have it in their genetic makeup to worry about others.

Many workers died here, and those responsible will have to pay. But in the same way that no one has seen the faces of the owners of these wrecked factories, no one has seen a responsible party representing the government. Ramón Aguirre never came, neither to Tlatelolco nor here. Don't you think it would have been very important for him to see the monstrous unfairness done to the seamstresses?

Esmeralda Loyden

From the mines of Cananea, in Sonora, a crew of twenty mine technicians arrived to participate in salvage work. Even on Thursday the 19th they set out to gather all sorts of tools: concrete and steel cutters, dynamite, detonators. They bought their airplane tickets and barely had a chance to say good-bye to their families. All of them had studied engineering and had specialized in related fields, including the use of explosives. Engineer José Luis Montes de Oca had studied in Japan, and he was the least trained.

They arrived in Mexico City and were held up in customs. That was Friday, September 20. They were asked if their equipment was imported. Practically all equipment used in mines is imported, but when they grabbed their bags, boots, tents, flashlights, and food, the last thing that would have occurred to them was that the airport customs office would intervene, so they brought no invoices for their equipment. Customs officers confiscated it all, including the backpacks where their return plane tickets were kept.

The customs office provided no receipt for what was taken: two tons of dynamite, cartridges, tools, special clothing, tents, food, boots. The only thing they didn't confiscate was the fury of the mining technicians.

We didn't come to bother anyone; we even brought our own food so that we wouldn't take away from anyone. Sonora is part of Mexico. We too love the city . . . We were about to go back, sad, disappointed, because our protest didn't get anywhere, but then we decided to walk downtown to see the situation. And that was impressive. After that, we decided to stay and get to work, no matter what; we saw the example of young people, students, men and women, so we thought, "We're not going to fail our people just because of some imbecilic customs agents."

Since Friday, September 20, they have worn the same set of clothes. Fortunately, people have been feeding them, but they have not bathed, nor have they been able to talk to their families, to tell them that they are well, working safe and sound.

The miners may not have known Mexico City, but they certainly knew their trade. Engineer Montes de Oca taught others how to detonate a downtown building; another engineer insisted that the amount of explosives proposed by the army was wrong. "Let us do our job; we know what we're doing." No. A member of the French brigade had to ratify what engineer Montes de Oca and his colleagues were saying. Even so, after the detonation, since no movement could be seen, his adversary said, "You see, jerks, nothing happened." One of the miners with Montes de Oca said, "Give me thirty seconds," as he punched him in the face. At that very moment, the building crumpled down.

The twenty miners that did the work confessed that only because someone brought them cocaine were they able to keep going for a week with practically no sleep. They had never tasted it. We talked about their painful physical condition, their faces swollen from lack of sleep. Engineer Montes de Oca became extra sensitive, and he couldn't even take part in conversation without feeling suffocated. The miners had gone beyond their own limits; they had never rested, let alone slept. They were under tremendous pressure that squeezed the life out of them. Once they had demonstrated their expertise, their help was solicited everywhere.

"Would you really let us bathe?" asked Sr. Montes de Oca with a smile on his face. He probably imagined how the crust of his body would fall off, how he would get rid of the smell of death and putrefaction, the sweat of joy for the ones rescued alive, and the sweat of anguish that comes with knowing that hundreds of persons could still be there breathing.

One of the men in his crew found a million and a half pesos in cash and turned it in.

When I met Sr. Montes de Oca, he was working in the Juárez housing project. Some volunteers had arrived to ask how to operate the machinery, how to cut mangled steel rods and lift slabs, and the engineer, with a voice that was dulled by fatigue, was giving precise instructions:

"Don't let the tools heat up too much; don't use them for longer than twenty minutes; cut only metal; remove all the concrete and dirt you can before using the power saw."

"Where do we excavate?"

"There where the guy in blue is standing; we detected two bodies."

"Be careful, the floor isn't firm."

He was wetting his hair and sweaty face with a little of the drinking water that came in plastic bags, in spite of the cold air. The wind blew unimpeded through the porous obstacles, penetrating the wreckage, touching the silent bodies and the implacable machinery, lifting the dancing dust and letting it land on the eager faces of the rescuers.

The smell of death is unique; it's the smell of a body without a soul. The small heads of dolls, children's strollers, sheet music, calendars, the remains of mattresses, empty clothes, the keyboard of a piano that looks like it might have fainted from exhaustion on the ground, all this constitutes the language of rubble. One squad replaces another one, taking turns in their bitter task.

In front of Montes de Oca, a rescuer brings out a naked man. On the still-standing walls is an intact statute of the Holy Child of Atocha. The smell of death is everywhere, carried now by air currents that no building can obstruct. The man who carried in his arms the body he had just found, probably nauseated in spite of his double or triple surgical mask and his thin gloves, must have created a barrier in his mind so as to be able to stand the fetid smell and contact with the bloated body, thus easing the burden of the distance between life and death.

At three in the morning, Saturday, September 28, all the workers were standing at a certain distance, marveling to see how one body carried another and what the difference was between them. People were trapped in a reverie, a stupor. Then someone said, "Turn off the machines; it sounds like there's someone here."

The machines stopped, and silence came. You could hear your own blood throbbing against your temples. The suffocating smell produced an almost chemical reaction in your stomach. We stood still, hardly breathing, in fear of moving a pebble that could resound on the ground and give a false clue to rescuers. Five minutes later the hustle and bustle had returned, and the weary faces reflected hopelessness.■

WHAT WAS DONE, WAS DONE VOLUNTARILY
WE ARE LIVING THROUGH THE GREATEST CATASTROPHE IN OUR HISTORY

In many ways the government is designed to control, to maintain institutions, to keep the status quo and exercise power. After September 19, it became evident that the government had been left behind; thirty-nine hours went by before the President addressed the nation. Nobody ever knew what the DN-III was; people came to believe that it was a code for cordoning off danger zones. In a nutshell, the government failed.

First the government tried to minimize the disaster. It ordered the population, "Stay home," when it should have made an appeal to all professionals: engineers, physicians, architects, miners, nurses, contractors, operators of cranes and bulldozers. Second, it rejected international aid, going so far as returning airplanes with cargo that later were made to come back. Yes, yes, we need the stuff, after all. Third, it launched the self-deception of "normality." We had to go back to normality at any cost. We were living through the greatest catastrophe of our history and they kept saying, "Mexico is standing up; we are all standing; the country is still standing." When we had not gotten our people out from under twisted concrete, we were "standing" and on our way to normality.

It was the people—beyond all acronyms, political parties, government ministries, social classes—the guys and gals, the compadres, who organized themselves in the districts of the city. This is the way we got the rescue brigades and the shelters. Many hours went by before the government arrived to take the reins. Doctor Cuauhtémoc Sánchez, a family-practice physician with a degree from the UNAM, confirms this assessment:

I arrived at the Xoco Hospital, at Cuauhtémoc Avenue and Churubusco, at 11 A.M. to offer my services.

"No, we don't need anyone, we have no injured people here."

"But you will!"

"We really don't need you at the moment."

(Doctor Cuauhtémoc Sánchez had spent two hours stuck to a transistor radio waiting for a summons to all medical personnel to go to the damaged zones, but it never came. This is why he was in Xoco.)

As I left Xoco, I ran into some ham radio operators (their identification was Alfa, Lima, Lima) who had a network in the hospitals and they asked me whether I could take medical supplies to the Red Cross. They needed antitetanus serum and suture materials. The Red Cross asked me to serve as liaison among hospitals to transport urgently needed medications from one place to another. I have a motorcycle, so I became a delivery guy for two days. I really didn't see patients because what was needed—as I saw after I was in a first-aid station—was to remove the rubble in search of people who were alive and to enter the tunnels as mole to treat them there.

I was astonished that there never was a call by the School of Medicine to its graduates, who could have been distributed among the emergency zones in an orderly way. What was done, was done voluntarily.

"No to normality. We refuse to go back to normality." Gustavo Esteva.

ALWAYS THE SUFFERING OF FAMILY MEMBERS

I remained three days at Tehuantepec 12 in Colonia Roma. Along with our efforts to rescue people, we always witnessed the suffering of family members and friends who were there day and night with little or nothing to eat. For seventy-two hours, an engineer remained right there by the building waiting for his wife and three children. His only surviving daughter was saved because he took her to school. When the bodies of his family were found, and he had to identify them, his face contorted in a frightening way. I thought, "He'll never get over this one. This will make him crack up."

TO EMBRACE PEOPLE

Another girl, about twenty, cried all by herself, standing before the rubble, and everyone was walking around her. I hugged her without saying anything because I couldn't say anything, but after a while she got hold of herself. I abandoned the pick and shovel because I realized that at that moment what really mattered was to be with her in her sorrow.

Saturday night, September 21, they told us that they were hearing noises in Xocongo, Colonia Tránsito. With my brother and two friends, I organized a small rescue squad. We arrived in Xocongo and found desperate people. The colonia had been totally neglected. The one engineer in charge was very afraid. But the building was still standing; only the foundation and three floors had been affected. I think this wreckage could have been dealt with more easily than the one in Tehuantepec, but the engineer had ordered hands off, and that very day had made up his mind to demolish it, in spite of the possiblity that there might be survivors. A relative approached my brother and me:

"Last night we heard the laments of a señora and her two daughters. We know who they are; we see the lady taking the girls to school in a blue VW."

We ignored the engineer and his authority, and with more fear than courage we went down a hole between the sidewalk and the building, and entered the basement with a flashlight.

Once down, we realized that the water was running, and it had flooded the basement more than two feet deep. The smell of gasoline was very strong. We located the blue Volkswagen, but we didn't find signs of life. This failure was very depressing, because we realized that those people could have been saved if anyone had done anything in the first three days.

While we were there, we heard the roar of bulldozers and graders, and the building was jolted. We left immediately and asked the engineer, "Hey, what's going on here?"

He answered, "I forgot you were down there."

Sixty hours after the earthquake, he attempted to demolish the building and thus end his responsibility. Since we had no equipment, we went back to Tehuantepec, where we were joined by six guys from an improvised mountaineer group, headed by someone named Daniel. They had already worked in several rescues, and they were looking for another place where they could be useful. We all went back to Xocongo and had to confront the engineer in charge one more time. We asked him to turn off his machines, and he did so, reluctantly.

We entered the building looking for survivors. But in fifteen minutes the machines were on again. Once again, I went out, explaining to him that we needed silence so we could hear the voices of survivors. He stopped the vehicles in a very bad mood, and we spent forty minutes of intense search in the three floors until we were persuaded that no life existed in there. The only thing to be done was to recover the bodies. We left a brigade in charge of that effort and departed wondering how many of the thirty-six people who were trapped could have been saved if someone had been there in the first three days after the earthquake.

Two days later, I heard on the radio that no one came out alive from the building at Xocongo 717. Thirty-six bodies had been found.

The hope that kept us all going was the possibility of finding a person still breathing. That hope was stronger than fatigue, hunger, sweat, or dust. During our brigade days, the people gave us food and water; people from the colonia boiled water and brought it to us in bottles and buckets; and they also brought pots of rice, sandwiches, stuffed dinner rolls, beans, whatever they could.

The only ones that in my judgment deserve the name of "public servants" are the firemen, the Honorable Corps of Firefighters, who instead of exercising power through their uniforms feel compelled to do a disinterested job. Three of them were with us at Tehuantepec, and they were unrelenting. They spent hours in the burrows, in operations that would take up to thirty hours. They would barely eat or drink water. And we never saw them rest; I at least never saw one of them sitting down.

I will never forget the people I met during the disaster: Daniel, the most intrepid in danger zones, the one who undertook the most difficult rescues; Néstor, his faithful companion; Blanca and Cecilia, who devoted themselves to saving valuables and making sure the next of kin received them, sometimes after confronting the judicial police, the police, and the military who were rapaciously trying to plunder; Adrián, who looked after the girls; Arturo, a Red Cross volunteer; Carlos Bárcenas, who was always by my side sharing both the fear and words of encouragement; Héctor Gómez, the doctor; Luis, the guy in charge of the first-aid station at Tehuantepec, who supported us unflinchingly; and my brother Alejandro, twenty-eight, who helped me overcome fear and go forward.

Marisol Martín del Campo

At the Red Cross they gave us T-shirts that read "Rescue Worker" and "Paramedic," so on Friday, September 20, we were traveling on Cuauhtémoc Avenue, near the Ministry of Commerce, says Luis Bosoms, a twenty-two-year-old student from Anáhuac University, when the earth suddenly started quaking again: people stood in the middle of the street, others knelt down, others wailed loudly, and still others cried quietly. The scouts shouted, "Be calm."

We had to stop the car because the ground underneath cracked open about twenty inches. Some buildings that had been damaged previously, but were still standing, crashed down all the way. There was no electricity. The air smelled of natural gas. You could hear explosions. If you looked up, you could see fires here and there on the horizon. I tried to lift a woman from the ground, but she was stiff, praying aloud, "Christ the King, the bleeding Christ, pray for us. Christ the King . . ."

In the building across the street from us, some people were calling from the fifth floor. In spite of the smell of gas they had candles in their hands. The building they were in was still rocking. The neighbors saw us with Red Cross badges and came to beg us to go up and get them down. They said that the grandmother had a broken hip and couldn't make her way down . . . as if we were Superman. And that's what you want to be, mighty.

Anyhow, we went to the building half dead of fright, we went up to where they were, put the old lady in a chair, and lowered her slowly, slowly, hoping there would be no more quakes and the building wouldn't give way. When people trust you like that, it makes you feel like an idiot. Because they put a badge on you, you are supposed to know what to do and what's going to happen. The feeling of impotence is awful when that kind of natural catastrophe strikes.

After that, we saw that the people simply kept on walking, silently, without any expression on their faces, scared, simply following whoever was in front of them. Maybe they were going to the Zócalo, those quiet people, like robots. From that night on, I couldn't sleep through the night, I kept waking up, and every morning I would wake up even more tired.

The truth of the matter is that I started to help because my girlfriend got involved, and I was not about to leave her alone. There I realized the extent of the problem. On the 19th of September at about five in the afternoon, the Red Cross on Ejército Nacional Avenue was something to see! There were close to two thousand people out in the street and on the ground floor asking for food and medicine.

On Sunday the 22nd, they sent us to the store to get cloth and string to make surgical masks—I believe about 50,000 pesos were coming out of the cash register every five minutes. They gave us 30,000 pesos. Between the university and the store we collected 40,000 more. We told the store clerk that we wanted 70,000 pesos worth of cloth, not thinking about taxes and all that.

It was a grocery store. I asked the manager to let me use the microphone and in five minutes I got 70,000 pesos more. One señora alone asked me, "How much do you need?" and took out 30,000 pesos from her wallet. Even the maids would give us 200-peso donations. We bought string, cloth, and scissors, paid the sales tax, and still put 20,000 back in the cash register. In the afternoon we went to the bakery of Barrilaco to buy bread for sandwiches for the rescue workers. The man in charge asked me what I wanted so much bread for. For the Red Cross, I said. So sure enough, he told me to take all the bread he had, for nothing. I filled up the VW.

The Camino Real Hotel sent food to the Red Cross. It was kind of surrealistic, to see trays of hors d'oeuvres delivered by uniformed waiters.

People would come in to donate blood, to sweep the floor, to unload pots of food, whatever. It's awesome, let me tell you! After an experience like that you realize that you are not alone on an island, and that you better make yourself useful where you are.

It's darn hard, it's darn hard, says Juan Antonio Sáenz, nineteen, Red Cross volunteer and rescue worker at the Plaza de la Cibeles on Saturday, September 28. We still don't realize what we've done and what has happened to us. One of the worst things that has ever happened to me was that after hours upon hours of work to get a person out alive, she let herself die three minutes before the end.

Her name was Lourdes; she was nineteen. We lifted some rubble and discovered her hair. I thought she was surely dead. But when she moved I felt indescribable joy. I started talking to her and she told me, "My hipbone hurts; please get me out." She had a chunk of concrete on top of her. She died of cardiac arrest in my arms, three minutes before coming out.

IN LAS LOMAS NOTHING EVER HAPPENS

At 11 A.M. I turned on the television; I was coming home from classes at Anáhuac. At the university the earthquake had been barely felt, but when I saw the images on TV I realized the extent of the disaster, says Marilú Hernández, nineteen, a medical student. I went to the Red

Cross. I saw the doctors very calm in the face of the emergency situation. I learned from them to be patient.

Those days changed me, touched me deeply, and I think I will always continue to help. I felt very privileged. I've got money (well, my father does), I live in Las Lomas, and nothing ever happens there. What happened helped me overcome social barriers and prejudice. I no longer see people without money as lowlifes; I was such an idiot. You realize that you've been living in a bubble.

On Thursday morning there were many injured people at the Red Cross. They were utilizing all available space: closets, bathrooms, classrooms; they had fifteen patients to a room. Their names were written on their bodies with markers, color-coding them according to their injuries or whether they were going into surgery. There were very few physicians and too many students.

The first shock came from a señora with her dead three-month-old baby. "A beam fell over him, Señorita, I got him out, but the poor little thing was vomiting blood and crying like mad. Look, hold him, he's all broken inside. I strangled him so that he wouldn't suffer any more. I couldn't see him go on like that." She was referred to the Psychiatric Hospital.

I was asked to be in charge of Berenice García, six. She had a fever over 104 degrees. I kept rubbing ice on her forehead and body. She had open wounds all over. Finally, at about two in the morning, her fever went down a bit and she went to sleep. Then the reporters came with their flashes to wake up patients, to interview them, to ask impertinent questions, without any sense of ethics, without any common sense or respect. I tried hard to prevent them from waking Berenice up, but I couldn't. The damn reporters woke her up. Her fever went up again, and she couldn't go back to sleep. They're a bunch of beasts.

On Saturday the 21st they sent me to take some medicine to Hospital Juárez. The cops wouldn't let just anyone in, and rightly so; there were lots of busybodies, lots of people with voyeuristic curiosity. Suddenly we didn't know what street we were on, and then we realized that we hadn't recognized Juárez Avenue even when we were on it.

The whole downtown stank of death and gas. You have to give the cops credit for standing there without any masks on. We offered them water or soda; you could see that their lips were parched; they'd been standing out there for thirty hours. One of them reached for a glass but then withdrew his hand: "Better save it for a victim."

Friday morning and afternoon were terrible at the Red Cross, since the patients who had been given anesthesia and those in shock began to wake up and realize that now they had nobody. More than four of them begged, "Kill me, please." Mirna, a singer at the Hotel Regis, took it all with black humor. They'd amputated one of her legs, so she says from now on I'll be known as "Mirna, the peg-legged singer." Another woman screamed; she no longer had any legs.

One little five-year-old girl broke my heart. She was the only survivor from her family. When she regained consciousness, she asked me where she was, and I told her that she'd been operated on, but that it would be all better soon. Later that afternoon, she burst out in tears: "Why don't my Daddy and Mommy come to see me? And my grandmother? And my brothers and sisters? Tell them to come and get me." I held my tears back; I just scratched her head and told her stories. I couldn't fool her, tell her that they'd be there to pick her up soon, but I also couldn't tell her that they were dead. While she was there at the Red Cross, I gave her lots of love.■

The Housewives of Las Lomas, the Pedregal, and San Angel
I DIDN'T KNOW MY COUNTRY, MY CITY; I'D NEVER EVEN GONE TO TEPITO

Five thousand sandwiches, 350 pots of rice, five hundred cauldrons of beans, and enough clothing to make a mountain came from only seven houses along the Paseo de la Reforma in Las Lomas, just before you reach Palmas, the section known by the English name of Chapultepec Heights during the presidency of Avila Camacho in the early 1940s. "Nothing happened to me at all."

"You mean your house didn't cave in?"

"No, but my husband's office building is all cracked."

Nothing happened in Contreras, Coyoacán, Olivar del Conde, the Pedregal, Tlalpan, San Angel, Las Lomas, Tecamachalco, Las Arboledas, not even a scratch. The hill districts, the upland wooded zones, the ones with the enclosed gardens, they remained safe and sound. Neither did anything happen to Satélite, but that's another area. Nevertheless, many housewives didn't just prepare sandwiches, send their chauffeurs with loads of provisions, boil water, or make surgical masks. They didn't just go to shelters to distribute medicines. Instead, they too turned up in the disaster zone.

That very Thursday I arrived at the Red Cross to see what I could do to help. I was sent to look after a man who was badly injured. I got close to him—he could hardly see out of one eye; he must have been about sixty-five—and I took his hand. He insisted, "Get closer, because I'm about to die; I might as well die looking at a pretty woman."

Not that I am pretty, but he, at that moment, thought I was. He never complained; he never even moaned. He never said another word. All his strength had drained away. I was impressed by his fortitude.

He died.

I mourned him like a relative.

I went home and couldn't go to sleep. Ever since, I've been going to the Red Cross every day, doing what I can. Mostly I talk to the patients; I bring them what they ask for. Sometimes it is Chapstick, one of those made out of white Vaseline, or flowers. Or a little jar of Vick's Vaporub.

I'm a volunteer at the Centro Médico, says another señora of Las Lomas, so I immediately went there. Already at 10 A.M., I found a flock of men risking their lives to get bodies out of the rubble, in the midst of the dust and the horror.

The next morning at seven we arrived with surgical masks, alcohol, fine soap, and tons of lemons—because chewing lemon rind is very helpful—as well as a great quantity of bottles of aspirin. We distributed them, two tablets to each volunteer, because they all had terrible headaches. The rescue workers had to be cared for with the same devotion you give to victims or their relatives. We asked them to wash their hands and have a sandwich, a soda, beans or rice, whatever there was. More food kept arriving from ITAM, Ibero, and Anáhuac, and we kept passing it out.

In our worst nightmare, we'd never seen such devastation, like a war zone, worse than a blitz. In the midst of clouds of cement dust and the most frightful stench, Operation Ant was launched. Volunteers would go up and lift chunks of cement one at a time, passing them hand to hand in an endless chain until another mound was made down below. They didn't mind their own tiredness, the darkness of night, nothing. I witnessed the rescue of living people and also the removal of cadavers. Those saving hands are engraved in my mind, the hands of workers.

I got horrified, retrieved my son from school, and went to watch television. Oh, what awful horror! What unremitting horror! I stayed there, riveted in front of the television, and I asked myself, "What am I doing here? I'm doing nothing. What, am I waiting for someone to call me?"

My mother, who is eighty years old, said to me, "Honey, I'm starting to make sandwiches."

"Mother, you'll cut yourself with the knife."

"So what if I do? It's better than doing nothing."

"Okay, Mom, I'm coming to help you."

And so we took baskets full of sandwiches to the Centro Médico: my mother, strong woman that she is, carried one basket and gave out sandwiches, and I did too. My mother would ask, "Hey, you guys, have you eaten anything?"

Some answered, "Señora, we ate about four hours ago, but no food has gotten over there yet."

My mother cried all the way back home, and at one point I couldn't control myself either. I considered that those people had eaten probably one little sandwich at seven in the morning and twelve hours later, instead of saying, "Yes, thank you, I'm very hungry," they were thinking of others who had not eaten.

I went to the Venustiano Carranza Delegation, to the Zoquipa shelter near the Merced market; that's where I was sent. We immediately organized the distribution of food, blankets, water. We distributed medicine, checking expiration dates, everything. We really put a lot of soul into the work. Since I couldn't tell anybody that I'd be home late, I simply said "tough luck." A cop was there watching, but instead of doing his job, he worried about me, about my safety. He said I shouldn't carry heavy loads, a real gentleman. Later, at night, four freight handlers from La Merced arrived at the shelter, really stewed, and the policeman said to me, "Look, Señora, we can't receive this kind of people here."

"Come now, officer, don't be like that; let me give them some supper at least. Let's see if they sober up a bit."

I fed them and their minds cleared some. So I asked them, "Are you staying awhile? Would you like to take a snooze? I'll give you blankets."

"Excuse us, Señorita, we don't want to offend you, you'll have to forgive us, but we cannot stay the night because tomorrow is the feast of Our Lady of Mercies, and we have her altar ready, with flowers and vegetables, and we have to go and serenade her at dawn. How could we not go sing the Mañanitas to her? What fault of hers is it that we had an earthquake?"

"You are quite right, muchachos, go sing Las Mañanitas."

After that evening, they came every night, the four poor sots. They kept inviting me: "You should see how nice it gets over there. Why don't you come along sometime?"

"I'd love to, but I can't leave my job here. Thank you anyway."

There were lots of donated clothes, but nobody was thinking of donating underwear. It occurred to me to call the Rimbros Corporation and to ask for a significant discount for the shelter I had found myself in charge of. I requested fifteen hundred briefs and undershirts in a variety of sizes. A masculine voice answered on the phone, "Yes, Señora, but where do you live?"

"In Las Lomas."

"Our colonia is cordoned off. There's no way of getting to the shelter at Colonia de los Doctores, but I can have the van deliver the bale to your house. They can take it to you."

"What kind of discount are we talking about?"

"No, Señora, this is a gift."

In Colonia Morelos, at Circulación Avenue, even when there were no deaths, the housing was so poor, so old, so very worn out, that it was leveled, so people put their junk on the median strip. To make things worse, the area was flooding, and water was getting close to people's things. I decided to go on television to make a public appeal.

I don't even remember what channel I was on, but I asked for storage space for these people's meager possessions, while they found new homes. Seven or eight people offered space. We sent a truck to the area, and some of the uprooted people climbed aboard with their things, going to different locations to store them. Then I would call the owners on the phone:

"Señora, I just wanted to tell you that the truck is heading your way, there are four families, each with a list of things to leave with you."

"Don't think I have a warehouse; what I have is a ballroom where my children throw parties. As you can imagine, there won't be any party for a while, so they can store their things for as long as they want. And if you want to send me more, that's fine too."

I didn't know my country, my city; I'd never even gone to Tepito. I didn't know what it was like. I didn't even know the people. I suspect I didn't even know my own children, my nephews and nieces. When I thought of them, I imagined them dancing in discotheques. I never visualized them wearing a helmet, a bandana kerchief, being disciplined and self-denying, let alone carrying corpses. I know of a woman who said, "I have no skills, other than scrubbing and washing," and at five in the morning she was working at the Red Cross so that when patients came, everything would be spic and span.

My seventeen-year-old daughter is very afraid of earthquakes; indeed, she's terrified of them. She's part of the Pandora Musical Group, and she said, "I don't feel like singing; that's the last thing I want to do now." She was due to sing at the XEW radio station, which had been badly damaged by the earthquake. "No, I'm not singing." The program was switched to TV channel 8. So I said to her, "Look, the doctor has worked without rest; he's operated on people who were lying on cots; he's given not ten or fifteen hours, but twenty-four hours of each day. Your sister, who is younger and doesn't know how to do anything, has been classifying medicines, making sandwiches, helping any way she could. If God gave you a voice, maybe you can help someone who hears you, maybe at home, maybe from a hospital bed . . ." And I took her to Channel 8 at 11:30 at night; but first, since I didn't know where I was going, we traveled through the cordoned-off zone:

"At your own risk; if you want to gamble with your lives, go ahead," said a traffic cop to us.

I told my daughter, "Don't look; don't turn right or left; it's all devastated."

We went by Reforma, Chapultepec, and Hidalgo, and we came to the studio where the program, supposed to last to 4 A.M., was being broadcast, but there were only three out of ten or fifteen performers. That girl Guadalupe Piñeda, whom we adore, little Jorge Muñiz, and my daughter, thank God, from the Pandora Group, went on the air. I don't know if she did a good or bad job, but she did it. She sang for all the people.

Alicia Trueba

At Monte Blanco 1440, home of the Salazar family, a water distribution center was installed. Drinking water, boiled in the kitchens of many women, was delivered by teenage girls and their friends, who stood there on call and delivered water to the places that requested it. They stopped this service on October 1, but they are ready to continue if people still need it.

At the entrance of Superama Barrilaco, Beatriz Mariscal, aided by a group of young women, has a table where they prepare sandwiches and fill lunch boxes. They hand out bags with a set of basic toiletries—soap, toothpaste—all gathered with the cooperation of the supermarket customers. The ladies' chauffeurs are in charge of distributing everything.

In Tecamachalco, the Mount Sinai Club is sending help to shelters. Señora Lela Atri reported that Mount Sinai members had started work on September 20. During the first four days, they prepared seven thousand box lunches, containing one sandwich, one can of juice, and one piece of fruit. They went on preparing four thousand box lunches a day until the end of the month, when they were told their help was no longer needed. In addition, they sent medicine, clothing, and drinking water to Hospital General, Hospital Juárez, and many shelters. They still have a large supply of donated goods.

According to architect Alejandro Albert, several institutions have developed long-term aid plans: the Anáhuac, Iberoamericana, and LaSalle universities, as well as the Red Cross, the Cultural Institute and its rescue brigades (which as late as October 2 received a call for help to rescue a seven-year-old who was still alive at Venustiano Carranza 148). Nuria Oliver, in charge of receiving international aid from Secours Populaire Français (two loads of sleeping bags, medicine, cots, cradles, blankets and sheets from Miami, Holland, and Chile) has acquired a lot of experience. In Tepito she and her group were held up, and the station wagon with all they had to distribute was taken away. But the warehouse is full; many women volunteers spend their time classifying clothes and medicine. What is important is for the effort to continue, and this is what private universities are trying to plan for.■

Gloria Alonso
In front of Superama Barrilaco, twenty-five women in jeans and aprons slice and dice, chop, mix, and open cans, making six thousand packets of food every day. They work shifts from 10 A.M. to 6 P.M. They barely speak to each other. Some stand at the door of the supermarket, and others buy. There are also shoppers who come and make donations as they go out: ham, cheese, bread, fruit, soap. Nobody says no, and the pile of food grows and grows.

After the earthquake, these women used up what they had in their own cupboards, and then they decided to go out and solicit at supermarkets. They found that the Barrilaco location was very popular. With their chauffeurs they send loads to Tepito, to Colonias Doctores, Morelos, Aragón, and the shelters. They take turns listening to the radio and identifying the spots that need more help.

"Nobody was thinking of the needs of rescue workers, so we started to send them food. At the beginning we were afraid of going downtown. Because of traffic, it took us five hours to go and come back. We still go; the awful thing now is the smell of putrefaction."

"And later? What happens later?"

"The worst would be that we forget. But we can't forget. We have to get organized, to form groups, to keep on working until everything is restored, even if it takes years."

My wife is a nurse, says José López Vadillo. She works at Centro Médico in the Obstetrics Unit. Her shift went from twelve midnight to eight in the morning. Two days before the earthquake, she had been changed to the shift that starts at 8 A.M. On the 19th, after the earthquake, I took her to the Centro Médico. I never imagined that I was going to find a blitzed town.

In the area where we live, there were no collapsed buildings. People were running aimlessly and senselessly over the rubble shouting the names of the ones who had been trapped; they lifted masonry, pieces of bricks, mangled steel, even the fragments of beams, and took them from one spot to another in their attempt to get to someone whose voice could be heard, those choked-up voices demanding help.

My wife was ordered to unit number 12 of the Social Security System in Santa Fe. A group called Los Panchitos have taken over the shelter.

Los Panchitos give good service; they are considerate to the victims, whom they treat very well and truly help. They even have students and well-to-do young ladies among them. But they are furious because the authorities want to get rid of them. ∎

Alicia Trueba

I first asked my girlfriends to help, and groups of boys and girls between fifteen and twenty-five years of age started to come, says Maricel Galindo, married, with seven children, and the organizer of Collection Center at Cóndor 401. Now the regular volunteers are fifteen in number. We work from eleven in the morning until two the next morning.

I got some volunteers that looked like punks and gang members, and as it turns out, they really helped. I asked, where did you get the money for gasoline for your junk heaps? Some told me that the priest of the Plateros parish, Manuel Subillaga, was helping them out.

A thirty-five-year-old woman with dyed hair, golden eye shadow, Bermuda slacks, and an ankle bracelet, and wearing no bra, worked and worked, delivering aid to Tepito, with tremendous energy. A gay man in sweatpants and frosted hair also helped: "I'm Antonio; I wish to participate." At two in the morning, he came back with the gallon-sized water containers after having distributed water until that hour.

There are rich people whom you would gladly kill. They have sent us medicine that expired in 1952, and when they donate clothes, they think that it's an opportunity to get rid of all the rags they have accumulated at home. I had to put dirty, stinking clothes in the trash. In contrast, a blue-collar worker brought in a superclean bag with a bunch of clothes starched and ironed, carefully folded, impeccable. He surely took these clothes off his own back, and he had to buy the penicillin he brought to us. He finally took 5,000 pesos from his jacket pocket and gave it to me. I was touched to the core.■

At the Shelters: Puppeteers, Singers, Theater People, Painters
A GROUP OF ARTISTS ACTS IN SOLIDARITY WITH THE VICTIMS

With characteristic altruism, Susana Alexander opened the doors of her home on Juan de la Barrera Street to the groups of artists that were willing to go to shelters to support and entertain the earthquake victims for a while. She proposed, along with Ofelia Guilmáin, a tenant law that will guarantee low-income housing for three years for people made homeless by the earthquake. "A roof over your head, a place from which to start a new life . . . To help others or to help ourselves? We're the others, the rest are not the others, but rather our very selves. Why does something like this have to happen for Mexicans to think of each other?" We were hanging around like idiots staring at the ceiling, until three days after the earthquake when we said to ourselves, "Let's go help." I called don Manuel de la Cera at ISSSTE.

"Look, we've got to do something."

"I've been thinking the same thing."

We jumped right into it, said Susana. Beatriz Sheridan also loaned us her studio. It's got two telephones, and it's close to my house on Juan de la Barrera—which, by the way, has a big crack in it now, but we haven't had to evacuate—and with two houses running like offices, we began calling all the performers who had been working at ISSSTE.

Guillermo Ochoa said one morning on his program that the show biz people were not organized, and Kitty de Hoyos called him right away to say, "Of course we are, Señor; we are ready to go wherever our presence is required; we can act, we can read poetry, we can read stories to the kids, we can do skits, or simply talk to the people, whatever; we're available at any hour and ready to go anywhere."

Kitty gave my telephone numbers and those of Beatriz Sheridan, and the calls that started to come in were impressive: the ones who wanted to help, puppeteers, makers of hand puppets, a very sweet lady who is in charge of the stage at La Conchita. No sooner said than done, Carmen Montejo showed up at a shelter.

Many young actors called to volunteer to work with the children, telling stories or acting them out. Painters came to help children draw or to make sketches of the kids, donating all the materials themselves. Ignacio López Tarso proposed singing corridos, and not only the "famous" artists went, but also those who worked in small towns all over the country, who go to little villages to stage their shows and therefore get great practice with improvisation. On occasion, these people have to sweep the area and arrange the chairs, if there are any, so you see, they have a deep social sensitivity.

I organized my outings with Margie Bermejo, who sang and talked between songs, and with Roberto D'Amico and Julia Alfonso. Don Manuel de la Cea was in charge of notifying the head of each of the ISSSTE shelters that we were coming, so that they would prepare for us. We put together a program: "Okay, I'll be there Wednesday at seven. I can do it Monday and Tuesday. Me? I can be there every day." The musicians, for example, the Latin American Quartet, really went out of their way to help.

It was not only we who did it; we got a lot of help from the Department of the Federal District and, I think, even from the PRI. I was terribly moved to see people in the shelters getting up from the gym mats that were their beds, running to the door brandishing a little piece of paper so that we could give them an autograph; "My name is Juanita." The first show we did—Margie Bermejo, Roberto, Julia Alfonso, and I—was in the Hacienda Country Club; we had it right there in the gym where they slept, and we told them—because we were afraid of tiring them and there were many kids among them—"We're here for a very short while."

Margie Bermejo and I had agreed, "I'll perform this poem." And

Margie would say, "I know a song that goes with that poem," and the same with Roberto and Julia. We put together a small show lasting forty minutes, integrating children and senior citizens. We didn't want to go too far; we knew that they were in atrocious circumstances, that they could have spent a sleepless night, that maybe what they needed most was silence. But what happened was they couldn't let us go: "One more poem, one more song." In the end, the show lasted two and a half hours. And we took the show from shelter to shelter. "Thanks for spending a while with us, really, thanks."

The response was impressive. Every day the phones were ringing from six in the morning to twelve at night (because show people have no common sense), artists from all walks of life, ready to go to the shelters. As always, there had to be a few "divas," who demanded transportation. I had a run-in with one of those, a guy who said that ISSSTE needed to send a truck to take his sound system.

"Just what do you think, that the trucks are at your disposal or that they need to bring food to the victims? The trucks serve the shelters, so if you want to help, take a taxi, damn it."

Manuel Lara, who is a wonderful man, knew very well how to capture the attention of the little kids. He would bring a blackboard and pieces of chalk of many colors, plus construction paper and crayons:

"Come here, come around, let's see, what should appear on the blackboard?"

"I want a chicken."

"Make me a giraffe."

Just marvelous! He would bring materials and then leave them behind: cardboard, pencils, sketchbooks, colored pencils. He'd say, "Okay, I do half the job, but you do the other half. Here's the paper."

At the end, he'd mount an exhibition, and the bleak gym wall would be covered with the cheerful colors of the children's drawings. You walked into a shelter, and you knew Manuel Lara had been there. I think that he did this for two weeks without rest, drawing for the kids. And in the same way, other artists were there with a guitar teaching songs to the children, entertaining them with jokes and little stories.

At the José María Rico shelter, I took my own sound equipment. Before I started, I would say, "I'm going to read you some poems. Do you like that? Or do you prefer a story, or a scene from TV?"

"A scene from TV!" they would shout. Almost invariably they asked me to represent "the bad woman" role that I had in the soaps. But

208

inevitably the scene degenerated into something comical. And it's good to make people laugh, what the heck! Especially in such adverse circumstances.

This went on for ten days, and I learned a lot. We couldn't avoid the actor who wanted to give a heavy sermon, something horrible, and would start with a speech that made my hair stand on end: "Because in these hard moments, we must endure with special fortitude and beg God that . . .," and I don't know what else, something awful, and instead of hearing this unbearable bombast, I'd go and talk to the people who headed the shelters.

Sometimes I would end up scolding the leaders in the shelters, especially when at the end of ten days I would hear them say, "We're waiting to see what happens." I said to them, "Well, while you wait, why don't you put the donated clothing in order, classify it, distribute it, do something." In one shelter in Peralvillo, I saw staff jumping up and down like little kids on a heap of clothes that had been donated, honestly, as if they were babies. In the Casas Alemán shelter, housed in a sports club, I asked the residents, "Are you eating well?"

"Very well."

"Do you have good medical attention?"

"Oh yes, the physician is splendid."

"Well, so what does the future hold for you?"

"We're waiting to see what comes next."

"No, don't wait; start organizing among yourselves."

And they listened to me. They started to go to their houses to try and get their furniture out while we entertained their children between twelve noon and two in the afternoon, or else after four. Our shows for the adults started at eight or nine at night, so when they came back to the shelter, we started making them talk about their situation, and even acted out a kind of psychodrama.

In the Mexican Olympic Sports Center they were very well organized. But the needs varied. In another shelter I found the people on roll-away mattresses, lined up one after the other, with patients who were intravenously fed. I remembered that at the Hacienda someone commented, "These people have not laughed since you were here last Thursday."

So I thought, "Okay, Susana, so you're good for something."

I also went with Manuel Lara to some encampments, to the "October 2" near Tlatelolco, to act surrounded by tents. In Colonia de los Músicos near Calazada de los Misterios, I found a prostitute who had lived in Tepito, weeping, sitting on the sidewalk because she had a young child and was pregnant. Imagine, a prostitute, with one baby in her arms, and on top of that expecting another one. And in the middle of the street.

She said to me, "What am I going to do? If we continue living in the street, my son is going to starve."

I took her to a shelter, I tried to do what I could, but you walk down those streets and you learn about anguish.

I reflected on the fact that every day I travel these very streets and I have never known what lies behind the doors. I felt something awful when I met this woman. It depressed me. Driving the van I'd go around the city looking at the bombed-out scenes where buildings had been, with people waiting outside for their dead. And I thought that if they started demolishing all that needs to be demolished, they wouldn't be done in six months.

And then I came across another infamy, a little five-year-old girl raped by a soldier on September 20. And the mother almost mad with rage. These were the roughest days for us, days of war, days of insomnia, days when there was no time to sleep, days of deep fear.

I remember that as I drove on the empty avenues I would tell Manuel Lara, who has always complained about the city traffic, "You see, Sr. Lara, I like you so much and I know how much all those vehicles bother you, I have ordered all of them off Paseo de la Reforma, for your pleasure."

All along Paseo de la Reforma, from the Chapultepec Castle to Tlatelolco, maybe La Villa, there were three cars. Do you know what that is in a city that has close to 20 million people?

On one occasion, I had to use the bathrooms in the shelter, and when I found them unbelievably messy, I talked to the victims:

"Well, they should clean them," they answered.

"Who is they?"

"The volunteers."

That made me angry.

"What do you mean? You mean to tell me that you can't even flush a toilet? Don't you have any sense? Why would the volunteers have to clean the bathrooms for you? You live here, so get organized so that you can live here in the best possible way. You have suffered, but even you have no excuse to leave a toilet like that."

I gave them a piece of my mind: "Who messes up the bathrooms? You do. And who is affected by dirty bathrooms? You are."

"And what about the volunteers?"

"Oh, so you want the volunteers to flush your toilet and clean up your shit?"

Many homeless people expected everything from someone else and would not contribute anything. It's the famous "It's not my job" which is one of our seven plagues. They thought that they deserved it all: "All right now, take care of us."

Finally a lady said, "If we're going to continue using the bathrooms, let's keep them clean."

It seemed to me that it was very important to foster an awareness of how difficult and even terrible it can be to share life in such tight quarters if you don't think of your neighbor. Several shelters in Colonia Roma were a mess; but later, the residents started to sweep, to clean up, although I must tell you, most of them were women.

I'M VERY AWARE THAT NOW I DON'T HAVE ANY SPACE

The Nuevo León Building housed 288 apartments, out of which 192 fell down. On the roof, sixty-eight of the servants' rooms were occupied at a rate of six to eight persons per room. The two modules that fell down were densely populated. Juan Guerrero, a movie producer, young, with a thin face and curly hair, an occupant of the Nuevo León Building, became a rescuer in the initial days after the quake. Now he has assumed the responsibility of taking a census:

It has been very difficult to take a census; there are still ninety-five apartments of which I know nothing, neither how many lived there nor who they were. If the building had 288 apartments, this means that we know nothing about a third of them. I have firsthand information, which I received from the surviving residents. I have had no access to the Red Cross data. At the beginning many of the subjects I polled were too disoriented to know what apartment they had lived in. I can say already that there was an average of four persons per apartment.

Paradoxically, the module that is still standing was the least densely populated. I have registered sixty-seven dead for whom there is a death certificate, 390 missing, and 265 survivors. I can assure you that most of the people who survived did so because they were not in the building at the time of the earthquake. They had gone to school or were on their way to work. As a result, many children and young teenagers lost their parents.

Juan Guerrero made a movie titled *May I Have Your Rubble?* which was not really a premonition.

I wanted, says the young independent movie maker, for the people to realize that the country is being demolished.

The earthquake scared me so much that I started to cry. I shut off the water and gas; I switched off the electricity and tried to reach the stairway. I opened the door, thought of a woman friend of mine who lives in a nearby building, looked out the window, and saw a cloud of dust. When I more or less regained some degree of awareness, I saw the mass of the crushed building and the people climbing over it to help their loved ones; they were climbing up and down, like ants.

At that moment I remembered that the things that most matter to me had remained in the apartment: the negatives of my films. I went up (I live in the part of the Nuevo León where the columns broke down), I recovered my films, and I think that this was the last moment when I felt some calm. I have never again been at peace; the nightmare gets worse every day. The situation worsens, and many images torture me. All that horror. I remember a woman went by me asking, "Where is the Nuevo León?" Where is the Nuevo León? Of course she was looking up, not down.

The cataclysm of September 19 changed me in every way. I had been able to assemble a decent little library. Now without my books I feel like I am up in the air. I have lost all I had. And I am impressed by the mendacity of institutions: neither Banobras, nor Sedue, nor Fonhapo has taken responsibility; there is no one in charge.

Rogelio Escartín Chávez was able to get out of the Nuevo León:

When it started to quake, I said to my brother, "Don't worry, nothing will happen."

"You know what?" he answered. "Something will happen. I've been in this building for thirteen years. I know how it was built, and I know it cannot take it."

We reached the frame of a door that opens to the hallway by the elevators. We took the stairs, and at that moment the walls creaked. We tried to take shelter in some place that could offer some protection, but we didn't find any. A door opened and a woman neighbor cried for help. The moment she yelled, she disappeared. I later learned she had survived. Another neighbor who had many locks on her door was trying to get it open fast, desperately. I saw the floors passing by as if I were in an express elevator. "What a shitty way to die," I said to my brother. At the last moment, I felt a blow on my head and heard a deafening noise.

When I opened my eyes I had my brother on top. We couldn't move, because on one side a section of the master beam had me trapped; on the other, another master beam, and on top of that, a platform. At the height of my brother's knees I noticed a small orifice in the rubble that allowed a ray of light in. There were four stories on top of us. The first thing I did was to ask my brother how he was. He said he was okay, but when he tried to stand up he realized we were trapped and got desperate, yelling at the top of his lungs for help.

"Calm down; there's a bit of light coming in. This means we also have air, and for as long as we have air our chances to survive are good."

I felt something liquid running down my face. I thought it was water, but it was blood. I kind of had difficulty breathing at times. Four hours went by. Then we heard the question, "Anybody there?"

"There are two of us here," I answered.

"Have you any light?"

"Yes, and some air too."

"Okay, in that case we'll be right back."

We were immobilized in a sort of sarcophagus. Our limbs had started to go numb. We couldn't feel our feet or our hands. We were in our pajamas, trapped not only by that platform but also by hunks of rubble.

When they came back they asked, "Where are you?"

"On the ninth floor." But there was no building left, and no ninth floor left either.

"We'll be back."

Half an hour later a person came by with a flashlight and asked us if we could see it.

"Yes, we see some light."

That way they located the spot we were in, and twenty more minutes went by.

"Only one of us will go in, because there is danger of a cave-in."

"Good enough!"

I can't recall the face of the rescuer, but my brother remembers him well. He says his name was Mario. We wish we could find him to thank him. He started to excavate, to remove the rubble. I could only move my left hand. I tried to help, but my arm was broken. The guy asked for a hacksaw, and when he started to cut the rods my brother yelled that they were crushing him, because these were the rods that kept the slab we had on top of us in one piece. I asked him to pull my brother by the feet and started to remove broken concrete with my only free hand. Then the platform started to descend, and we were praying it wouldn't descend too much, because it would kill us all.

"Mario" got my brother out, little by little, bent over, dragging him through a tunnel of twenty feet that he had made so he could reach us. I crawled out on my own until I saw the opening, a real small hole. Then I was rescued.

But most of our neighbors didn't have such good luck. The amount of rubble was huge. We were taken to another Tlatelolco building that was about to crumble too, where they had a first-aid station. Since I had a big gash on my forehead, I was sent to a traumatology hospital on Fortuna Street. I was given stiches, bandaged, and treated, among the innumerable people who arrived there with serious injuries.

The whole wide world lived through hours of sheer terror. We all lost friends and relatives, parents, brothers and sisters, wives or husbands, children. One can't help but feel indignation. Yesterday attorney Pacheco, who represents the Sedue said to me, "We don't accept the word *indemnification* because it would imply that we are responsible, and we are not responsible until an investigation is done and we are legally charged with responsibility."

Rogelio lifts his swollen eyes and contemplates the enormous mass of mangled steel and crushed concrete into which the Nuevo León Building has turned. "God was good to both of us . . . We thought we were going to die, but fortunately the firefighters got us out."

With face and head hidden by bandages that cover thirty-five stitches, with his shoulder in a cast, Rogelio Escartín of apartment 9243 accuses Banobras and Fonhapo of the catastrophe: "Their negligence is at the origin of this disgrace."

I WAS RESIGNED TO DYING

On the morning of September 19, I had bathed, shaved, and got back into my pajamas because I thought I'd get back in bed and watch the news until the coffee was ready. Then the disaster came. It didn't faze me at first, but then I felt that the intensity was growing and that the movements were rhythmic. It now occurs to me to compare the movement to a spinning swing whose chains have been twisted, and the moment it unwinds, it starts spinning again in the opposite direction.

It is not necessary to have a very intense earthquake in order to destroy a building if the frequency of its movement is constant, and most of all, if the structure of the building is already damaged. That's why when I saw that the movement was increasing, I thought it was the end. Even before the quake, the Nuevo León was doomed. The tremor would bring it down. The repairs it needed had never been made.

I stood in the entryway of my apartment and braced myself. At that moment, the Venetian tiles of the stairwell were popping out, as were all the exterior windowpanes of the apartment—a sure sign that the walls were twisting and turning left and right—so I yelled from my doorway to my neighbors not to go to the stairs; I shouted a lot; I called out that they should do as I did.

NEVER TAKE THE STAIRS

The first thing that breaks apart in a collapse is the stairways. There's practically no possibility of survival there. Even worse with the elevators. I shouted, and no one came out. I saw my neighbor's door banging against the wall. The tremor had adopted the longitudinal rocking that so many fear.

I really didn't get scared; I felt no panic. I resigned myself to the idea that this was the end. I had come this far. I had told my children and friends, half joking and half seriously, that if I could reach fifty years of age, the rest was gravy. I had turned fifty in January, so the thought crossed my mind that I had enjoyed eight months of gravy.

I didn't lose consciousness at any point. The collapse came; I fell. I thought we were sinking with the building, foundations and all, that the earth had opened, that a fault from underground was swallowing us. I later found out that this had not happened.

The lower structures of the building and the ground floor had failed. The first, second, and third stories had given way and were flattened like sandwiches. They descended down into the basement to a depth of twenty feet below street level, in such a way that the fourth floor, which should have been located between thirty and forty feet above the natural level of the ground, came to be flush with it. That is to say, we first fell vertically more than forty feet, and then tumbled in a parabolic way. When the Nuevo León collapsed onto the parking lot, we probably fell fifty or sixty feet or more.

Captain Gustavo Barrera is retired from the Mexican army. He has four children. He made his career in the Federal District. He was a cadet in the Military College and then studied in the Military School of Engineering. He's an industrial engineer by training. He's five foot six, fair-skinned and slender, with green eyes and light chestnut-colored hair. He's athletic and easygoing; everyone likes him. Before the earthquake, he was the life of every party. Since the 19th, he struggles untiringly for his neighbors of the Nuevo León and for all the victims in the city.

THE TOP FLOORS HAD IT WORST

I really don't know why I'm still alive. I was totally buried by rubble. I kept my eyes closed, hearing the cries of two other buried people. I was in agony but completely lucid. I never lost consciousness. As I fell, I could feel each and every blow my body received. It was not a swift plunge, but you couldn't call it slow either. It was a staggered fall, stopping at each floor before it too gave way.

I don't even know how we remained alive after the building—and us inside it—slammed so hard onto the parking lot. That part of the fall I could never describe, but it was probably, in some way, slower, because the columns on the other side of the building had to break—that is, they worked on the basis of tension; they gave way little by little until the last moment, then they really let go and crashed against the pavement.

The top floors surely had it worst, I think the twelfth and thirteenth stories and the rooms on the roof hit the pavement with such force—I realized this when I got out an hour and a half later—that many bodies were ejected from the building.

Again, I remained lucid while I was buried. I felt my feet pressed down by something heavy along with a certain pain in the left instep, but I could breathe fine. I opened my eyes and realized that I was covered with rubble and that I had fallen face upward; my feet were just a bit elevated and my waist slightly twisted. I was wrapped in debris, but my hands were free, that is, just my hands and wrists.

I began to clear away pieces of rubble, and I managed to free myself little by little. I was in a sort of vault with a pretty large concrete plate about six inches from my head. Miraculously the slab was held up and the door frame stood between my legs, that is, the trim, really. I had fallen in the same position in which I had braced myself in the doorway of my apartment. As there was some light, I managed to see my feet; a piece of concrete of considerable size cleaved the instep of my left foot.

I noticed that my foot was not bleeding, which was strange, but my leg was. I started to call out my neighbors, whose names and surnames I knew very well. But no one answered. The only one who eventually did was young Escartín, a lawyer. I thought that it was his father who was trapped next to me. They lived on the ninth floor, and I lived on the tenth. It turned out to be young Escartín and his brother. Through a slit I saw a pair of feet walking above us, and I started to call out for help. There was no response until I talked in a very familiar but not very friendly way.

The person asked, "Where are you?"

"I'm looking at your feet. Lean over and you'll see me."

He did and I insisted, "Help me."

"I can't, you are way in."

He didn't want to. I repeated that I was totally freed up, except for my feet. I pointed to a spot five or six yards to the left of him, a wide opening. He could go in that way. Which he did.

I thought that the Veracruz tower, with twenty-two stories, which had been in front of the Nuevo León, had toppled down on top of us, so I asked about it. I was very serene, probably because I had made up my mind that I could die, or maybe I simply didn't have time to get scared. Or both. So I started chatting, and from this man I learned that in Tlatelolco only the Nuevo León had fallen down.

He started to lift the slab or to pull it. I don't know whether it was too heavy or he wasn't really trying hard, but he barely freed my foot by about half an inch. That was a source of relief. I stretched and contracted my foot repeatedly and hurt it more. I still have a hole in the shape of a pyramid on my foot, but fortunately I am healing just fine and the wound is already covered with scar tissue.

I came out of the hole crawling, feet first. This young man and someone else were the only ones working on top of the heap, but now they'd disappeared. They were the only people. The rest were petrified, dumbfounded; nobody was ready to do anything. Everyone was just staring, so I even started to think that—may God forgive me—the boy whose help I had to beg for had gone up not to help but to see what he could steal. I hope I am wrong.

I went down barefooted, covered with dirt, hurt all over, bleeding, and extremely sad. I ran into a friend, *licenciado* Terán, and asked about his wife, Maestra Terán. He said she had a broken arm and that one of his daughters, Alondra, had not been found yet. He had two lovely girls. I started to scream at everybody to come and help because many people were trapped alive under the concrete, but I could barely walk. My feet and my hip were badly hurt. And I had a gash on my head—I had some stitches later on, both in my head and my foot. But when I had received emergency aid, I went back to the rescue. By then the zone had been cordoned off by police.

"What do you go in there for?" said one of them. "In pajamas, bare-foot, injured. You can't do anything."

In the car of a friend I went to my daughters' house to see if they were all right. They were desperate. They took me to the Hospital Militar, and once my youngest son had loaned me some clothes, I said, "Let me go back to the Nuevo León."

I couldn't stay away.

INEPTITUDE AND CORRUPTION, KEYS TO THE COLLAPSE OF THE NUEVO LEÓN

From the 19th on, and in spite of his wounds, especially his foot injury, Captain Gustavo Barrera dedicated himself "to getting people out" of the Nuevo León. After making sure his four children were fine, he didn't leave the area of the wreckage. Injured, he walked all over the rubble calling the names of his friends until late at night. No rescue team had been organized. But even with the building in shambles, he could recognize the location of some apartments, since he knew the building in detail.

At four in the morning they took me away so I'd sleep. I didn't want to leave, but I couldn't walk. I went back early the next day. I had to hide my walking cane, or else they wouldn't have allowed me near the heap. I met an engineer who was in charge of the area, and we became good friends. I have become very fond of him; his name is Alcaraz, and for me he is one of the unknown heroes of the Nuevo León.

I told him, "I need to go in, I know the bulding, I am an engineer, and I'm fully aware of the problems at hand."

"Yes, but you can hardly walk."

"There are people buried in there who are very important to me. If you don't let me, I'll go in anyway, by hook or by crook."

"Okay, if you insist, I'll give you come crews to work with."

He gave me four squads of eight men each. I deployed two at entrance E of the Nuevo León and two more at entrance F, and I showed them where to search.

After fifteen years of living there, many people knew me, and I knew them. We had established the parking lot together, and I had even been the president of the residents' association.

We recovered many bodies, and I got desperate that we couldn't find more. During that day I witnessed many of the vices, but also many of the virtues of our society. I saw a promising young man, strong and generous, who didn't spare any efforts or any time in the pursuit of saving lives. I saw many engineers who were in charge of brigades, but I saw many more who seemed more like burlesque dancers than engineers. They were only interested in acting in front of a TV camera or a film crew. Yet there were others who never took a moment of rest and suffered our tragedy along with us.

There were volunteers who came to see what things they could find, but I wasn't interested. I found my belongings and didn't worry about picking them up: my books, my records, my clothes.

In the last few days of the rescue work, I thought it was significant that I found a very small thing that years ago Estela Kassín had given to me: a little heart made of black coral, which I was supposed to wear at all times, as a good luck charm. I don't believe in this kind of thing, but I picked up the little heart from among the rubble. This filled me with despair, because seven days had gone by and we had not found the bodies of Estela Kassín and her child, whom we finally took out on September 30 in the evening.

Captain Gustavo Barrera was the technical adviser at the Nuevo León for many years and is now one of its representatives to Sedue. Working toward an agreement with Sedue, he has labored day and night, often until 4:30 in the morning:

The case of the Nuevo León Building is of very particular interest, because its collapse was not solely the result of the tremor, but in great measure it was caused by the ineptitude and corruption of our government and its institutions. Criminal negligence was at work here, and guilty parties have to admit responsibility. We, the residents of the Nuevo León, have to demand it. Fortunately, we have documentation of the building's background. There is no room for doubt about the malfeasance in administration and criminal irresponsibility on the part of the authorities who knew the dire condition of the building. Petty thieves that they are, the authorities chose to line their pockets or do some other trivial thing with the small amount of money that could have gone to repair work. The fact is that the Nuevo León was never fixed up, and our documents are open to the public.

I HAVE A COMMITMENT TO THE DEAD

We lost extraordinary people. The cultural level of the Nuevo León residents was special. We had lots of professionals living there, engineers, architects, professors of the UNAM and the Politécnico, artists, and highly qualified technicians. If I remain silent, if I don't protest, if I don't fight, it doesn't make sense for my life to have been saved.

I promised myself that if in the future there are misfortunes to regret, as there inevitably will be, they will not be due to corruption, ineptitude, poor administration, sloppy construction, blatant theft of materials, or the irresponsiblity of public servants.

I hearby accuse Guillermo Carrillo Arena. We came to an impasse in our negotiations, and we had to ask for a change of representatives, because Carrillo Arena is presumptuous, arrogant, and disdainful. He even used vulgar language toward us and accused us of taking advantage of the situation to start a political movement. He threatened us that he would call the Ministry of Government and the Attorney General's Office, but we went with our complaint to the Ministry of Government, where they surprised us by taking us seriously. Government has been far more decent than Sedue.

Now the representative we deal with is Gabino Fraga, a man we find much easier to talk to. He promises to pay compensation for lost household goods and indemnification, and to supply housing with low-interest-rate mortgages, no down payments, and all closing costs paid. He'll provide facilities for obtaining telephone lines. Carrillo Arena, in contrast, never stopped intimidating our compañeros and always spoke in an insulting, haughty way.

Concerning the houses, there are several possibilities in different developments: Villas del Maurel, Los Girasoles, Tulpetlac (beyond San Cristóbal Ecatepec in the State of Mexico), and in newly cleared land near San Juan de Aragón. Very far, very far. They are hurling us all the way out.

I don't know, but I don't much like politicians. Of course there are exceptions, but every time in my duties I have had to get close to them, I have felt like getting out of there quick.

I remember the words of a president of the United States, John

Quincy Adams. I read somewhere that he thought that "every politician should be considered a liar and a thief until proven otherwise." Unfortunately for me, the behavior of the majority of our government officials betrays an absolute lack of national pride, lack of love for their homeland, and lack of honesty. They don't ponder the consequences of their actions as long as they can satisfy their greed whenever public funds come into their hands.

If I was granted life, it is to denounce corruption, to settle once and for all the certainty that never again will the people of Mexico City allow such criminal carelessness, and to shout the fact that what happened in Nuevo León was murder. And the only responsible party for this murder is government corruption.

"There are those who are buried under the horror of the system, a horror infinitely worse than the rubble of the Nuevo León." Juan Guerrero.

Leader Evangelina Corona:
SINCE WE KNEW NOTHING, WE THOUGHT THE BOSSES WERE DECENT
Lower the neckline by a three eighths of an inch
Widen the collar
Reduce the slack in the front by half an inch

A relic, a shroud, the ruled piece of paper appears among the rubble. Wrinkled, damp, it must be pressed with your hand. The compañeras look at it silently.

"Does someone want to save this?"

"No."

They turn their heads to the subway station's orange strip. Better to fill your eyes with that fleeting burst of color than with the deep crack left inside you by September 19, now reiterated by these clumsy lines pointing to waist, bosom, hips.

One of the most monstrous problems revealed by the two seismic movements was that of the seamstresses. Two hundred sweatshops tumbled down, about five hundred more suffered damage, and forty thousand women lost their jobs in a matter of minutes. In the middle of San Antonio Abad Avenue, amid the noise of cranes, bulldozers, caterpillars, steam shovels, picks, and shovels, one can hear voices that are almost childlike:

"I used to make buttonholes. I pinned the garments. I pleated. I worked on overlay."

Topeka, Vestimark's, Jeans S.A., Dedal, Amal, Dimensión Weld, Lamark, Infantiles S.A., Artesanías Selectas, Maxel . . . On top of the debris, fabrics shake like curtains getting dirty in the wind, yards of lace coiled around twisted steel, nightgowns hanging from unhinged windows, new clothing pressed under slabs, the sewing machines, chairs miraculously suspended with one leg in the void, in full sight, absurdly intact as a porcelain figurine.

The army came and cordoned us off, but we said, "We need help excavating. There are many women inside. Please help. The shovels . . ."

"No, we're only here to cordon the building off."

The first few days they had faith.

"The boss is coming to get us, any moment now the boss will arrive, because he really cares for us."

Some sat down on the sidewalk.

"He has a beautiful house in Tecamachalco."

They said it without envy. The boss was good; he teased them during working hours; he smiled when he saw them working among the rows of sewing machines.

"He hasn't come because he's out of the country. He has many business commitments, but as soon as he is back, he's surely coming. I'm positive."

"He sometimes travels to Las Vegas."

"Today's the day he's coming for us."

The boss, the masculine figure, the paternal image, the one who gives a pat on the back, the one who can grant permission, the one who pays cash in a manila envelope to unwed mothers who go to work at age fourteen. The boss, the *patrón,* is always the reference point:

"Every year we give him a fiesta, a very nice one; we even bring in mariachis. We do everything; that's why it is his fiesta. On his saint's day, you should see how nice the workshop looks."

"Doesn't he pay for the sodas, at least?"

"No, it all comes out of our pockets."

"He loves us. He tries to give us a lot of work. We even take work home. That's why the first thing I did was to get me a sewing machine, a cheapy one, just so that I could have it at home and I could respond to the *patrón,* because I'm paid piece rate."

Everybody has failed the seamstresses: the man who abandoned them after making them pregnant, the boss who took the machines out first and went so far as asking for their help, making them scratch with their own fingernails to recover their "source of employment," until they asked, "And what about the compañeras?" "Do machines come before human life?" It was difficult to believe. Not only had the building come down, burying life, but another collapse was crushing them inside.

"What are we, then? Trash?"

"My life ended in there," exclaimed Elías Serur.

And ours? What about our lives?

"To tell you the truth, I loved Elías Serur. He was good looking, with his curly hair."

This was in the first few days. Little by little the immensity of the tragedy surfaced. The catastrophe took over our lives. The broken city shattered submission, docility, meekness. Each day that went by was a closer possibility of death. Inside the factories, there were those who were dying. Mothers, sisters, daughters, compañeras . . . they were dying. From this drowning in blood, rage was born. And from rage a desire to change, a "They have no right!" and now Evangelina Corona is a leader, she appears in public with a raised fist, microphone in hand.

Cecilia Soto Blanco is the legal adviser to the union, and the name of the union is the Nineteenth of September Garment Workers' Union, although its full name is Sindicato Nacional de Trabajadoras de la Industria de la Costura, Confección y Vestidos, Similares y Conexos. They claim. They denounce. The Apparel Industry Chamber is irresponsible, does not look for solutions. The factory owners believe the authorities are with them, and public servants are dishonest. They are in collusion with the owners of the factories. They skirt their legal obligations.

The bosses want to buy them, the seamstresses, making deposits to the Local Board of Conciliation and Arbitration. But not even one of them has decided to go and collect a compensation sum so meager as to amount to a bribe. The seamstresses are demanding, among other things, three months' salary and twenty days for each year of seniority, in agreement with the law, plus the wages they would have earned from September 19 to the day when the indemnification payment is made or they are rehired by another company.

On Sunday the 22nd, the owner of the Miss Universo factory located at Izazaga 55, Elías Michen Tuachi, gave his workers 5,000 pesos "as a loan" and later told them that the money was part of their wages during the week of the earthquake. It would be deducted from their 11,331-peso weekly wage. He said he was trying to reopen the factory in a different location because everything in Izazaga was ruined.

"We didn't know that by Monday he had already gotten out his invoices, the machines, everything. From the very first moment his preoccupation was his safe. But then he took everything. He didn't even leave the van behind. The compañeras with outstanding debts had them deducted from their last paychecks in accord with the signed slips. They kept everything. And we have nothing. We used to make women's dresses, working from nine to seven with an hour for lunch, which we always spent in the factory because we had no money to go to a diner."

Evangelina Corona, now a leader, has shared the fate of each of them, and her story is the story of many: love stories sound alike. I don't know how she speaks in public; I imagine her freshness, her clean gaze, her smiling eyes, her lips over strong teeth, very white, teeth good to extract love, teeth that reflect the luminous sparks of the day:

When I started, I went directly into overlock work. I didn't even know the machine, but there I was, in charge of overlock. (She pronounces the word *overlock* with a great deal of respect.) They gave me a blouse to which I had to attach a little bit of lace in between pieces of fabric, with a little ornamental stitch, but I didn't know how to thread the machine, and the seams looked like jagged teeth—that's what we call them (she laughs), "wolf teeth." The boss saw the blouses and the puckered seams, and he came to talk to me:

"This is not good, look at it. All the stitches are loose, just look at it
. . ."

I had to redo two hundred blouses for being careless. After I got those two hundred blouses fixed, I never had a problem. It's a matter of days; one gets the hang of it quickly. Of course it all depends on how hard you work at it, but the overlock became so easy to me that even dozing off I could do a good job.

(The overlock is a high-speed machine that produces a locked stitch and is used for finishing a garment, reinforcing previously made seams, on the side seams and inseams of pants, and the side seams of dresses, sweaters, and sleeves. The overlock specialist is the highest-paid seamstress.)

In those days I knew nothing, I had no idea whether I had the right to rest, to holidays, anything, and since I knew nothing, I thought that the bosses were very kind. Now that a light has been turned on, I realize they weren't that decent. What they wanted was for us to do the work no matter what—we often had to speed up the machine to the max—and produce the merchandise that they had already sold. They sold to Puerto de Liverpool and Palacio de Hierro, and we were in there in the workshop going at it, hunched over the machine. Have you noticed that many women have their chests sunken from so much bending over, as if they have a cavity, and how much they look like hunchbacks?

Of course we sped up the machine and our hands; otherwise we couldn't make it. We work piece rate. In our ignorance, we praised our good bosses because they always had more work for us.

I'm committed to telling the truth: Sr. Anquié, the owner, was a cordial man. Whenever he saw that the work was falling behind, he sat at the machine himself and went at it, and he knew what he was doing. I liked that, for the boss to know and to know how to teach. José Antonio Cervantes Silva, a Mexican supervisor, that one knew nothing. He couldn't even calibrate the stitch in a machine, so he got no respect from us.

Sr. Anquié trusted me, or perhaps abused my good disposition. He gave me the keys to the workshop, and I was in charge of opening and closing; he gave me the responsiblity for making sure that the girls had work, without leaving my own. He paid me by the day. Sometimes I had one or two thousand sleeves, or I was put in charge of hems, with overlock, or the sides of skirts, dresses, or blazers, or simply overcasting. I had to play the role of a boss to a small extent.

With the overlock what I liked the least was the seam used to connect the sleeve to the shoulder, that's too time-consuming, but there we were, bang, bang, bang (she snaps her fingers), churning the work out, bang, bang, no conversations, no bathroom delays.

Before September 19, my bosses had been the Señores Bizú, of Jeans S.A., previously called Elysée S.A.; they were also very kind, to tell the truth. At Izazaga 137 the bosses shared life with us; at dinnertime, if we offered them a tortilla, they always took it, gladly. If they traveled to Europe, the United States, or anywhere, they always came back with a little souvenir for us. Sr. Bizú would come by your machine and ask you, "How're you doing, young lady? How's it going?"

There was true harmony, really, until Raúl Aguilar came around. It is shameful to see a Mexican become more of an exploiter, but that's the truth. Raúl Aguilar drove a wedge between the owners and us workers.

The owner would say, "Whatever Raulillo says is what needs to be done. If you have a problem, go talk to him. Whatever he says, whatever his opinion is." That Raúl Aguilar was the accountant, and they gave him so much responsibility that they made his head swell. Even now the compañeras have heard the boss say, "Raúl, the women are right. They deserve an indemnification."

But he said no.

He worries about the money more than the boss. He has even said with great anger that we are the ones who are causing the problem. Which problem? He's the one who plants discord and messes things up. He's now running all around the Ministry of Labor, very angry.

The life of Evangelina Corona started forty-six years ago in a small farm in the state of Tlaxcala, in San Antonio Cuajomulco:

A peasant village, at that time buses didn't reach it, there was no electricity, a house here, a house there, over half a mile apart. Of course it is now more populated. It took us half an hour to walk to school. We are eight siblings. The land is arid, dry, and each year the harvest is more wretched; our need grew right along with us.

The school had only three grades. So when I was fifteen I left San Antonio to help my parents. I went to Apizaco and worked as a servant in a big house. I earned forty pesos a month, so much money! I was in charge of cleaning the bedrooms and taking care of the children, and I liked it, but I was a young woman, and the man of the family started looking at me the wrong way, so on account of that I left. He was one of those men without scruples who believe that anyone is fair game. So I left, even though the lady was nice.

One morning, I took off on my own. I gathered my stuff and put it in a cardboard box, and I jumped the fence and started to walk from Apizaco to San Antonio, but the box was heavy, so I borrowed a bicycle. When I arrived home, I learned that my father and mother had gone looking for me because word had reached them that I had left. I sat at the door waiting for them to come back, and when they did I said, "I'm back home."

That was my first experience with the harshness of real life and my first brush with a bad man.

In 1952, I came to Mexico City to work in a house in the Lomas de Chapultepec. My first wage: 150 pesos, wow, a fortune! After that, I went to work in a jewelry store and to live with my youngest sister,

Jaciel, in the State of Mexico. I spent every day polishing jewels with a cloth, rub, rub, hard, hard until they glowed. I was earning two hundred a month. And so it went until 1964 when I took up the sewing business. I liked it a little. And that's because when you have no schooling, you can't do anything else. At least I was no longer a servant; I had been in the jewelry store and now I was sewing. I started earning between 480 and 500 pesos a week.

I only knew how to sew with a pedal machine because there was always one of those at home, and when you are a mischievous kid, you begin to get hold of a little rag here and there, and that way you pick up some notion of how to do it.

I started to work in one of those factories that make brown uniforms for traffic cops, the so-called tamarinds (she laughs); later, another factory called Casa Dante; and after that, at Bolívar 32, I got the knack of the overlock, a nice machine! It finishes and locks the seams, it does a real good job. The place was Remy Terly, and its owner was Elías Anquié. We started at eight in the morning and were out by six in the evening.

I worked for five years in the factory at Argentina 7, but then the company moved to San Bartolo Naucalpan, and since that was too far away, I switched over to another one.

And what about love? (She laughs.) It's just that I've been a bit of a rebel. Of course I don't mean by that that my heart has been closed to love, right? Back in my hometown I met a man of my own social level, and even now I have not forgotten him. It's a memory that is intimately inside me, churning over and over. All of my feelings and all of my illusions centered around him. He got married; he has a wife and children. By the way, I got very bad news about one of his sons who was working in Televisa and lost his life trying to help his compañeros after the earthquake.

I never got married, but I have my two daughters. One of them is married and has three children, and the other one is in high school. The oldest is Maeli, and the youngest is Ana Jeanette.

(Funny! Almost all seamstresses name their daughters after clothing factories!)

Evangelina Corona Cadena goes back to the subject of the recently organized union:

We have signed up approximately seventy-two factories, and each day more are joining. For some of the women, their only source of income has been totally lost. My worry now is that nothing remain hidden, that everything that happened come out before the light of people's eyes. You'd better believe it! That matters to me a hell of a lot. That nothing stain this clean union that is like a baby, without any accomplishments yet, just learning how to take the first few steps.

She turns serious:

The incorporation of the 19th of September Union cost six hundred lives. I know that there's lots for me to learn; I know there's lots that I don't know; and when I was elected by a majority, I felt something nice and something ugly at the same time. Ugly because of the big responsibility.

I was always very docile in my job. I dreamed of acquiring seniority, and then retiring some day. I never talked politics with the compañeros, and even now, it doesn't come easy. We used to finish work at seven, and we'd make our way straight home, especially me, living all the way out in Nezahualcóyotl. I have worked in Elysée S.A. since October 2, 1972, without any fuss, without making waves, 'cause I haven't even seen the sea. It's hard for me; I say to the compañeras and also to the compañeros—because we also have men in the union—that the union belongs to all of us and all of us together are the union; but that we need to put our gumption in this and strengthen our organization, fighting with our heart. We mean to work; we are not a bunch of featherbedders; I've been in this job for more than twenty years.

You see, I'm from Tlaxcala, and we Tlaxcaltecas are hardheaded, stubborn, and sincere; we take people's word at face value, and we mean what we say. When the *patrón* said, "Let's get the machinery out because just as soon as we get it out we'll give you work and set up shop somewhere else," we believed him. Then as soon as he finished, he said, "No, you've got to find a way to make a living some other place; there's nothing here; it's all gone, it's all over."

The *patrón* fooled us blatantly. All the *patrones* did. They left us out on the street, literally. Thank God, we have registered our union, and the Supreme Being will not allow us to betray each other. (Evangelina Corona Cadena is a Protestant, an evangelical, and every Sunday she teaches the catechism to the children at the temple.)

I asked myself what President de la Madrid and Secretary of Labor Farell feel when they are before the clean face of Evangelina Corona, her skin of polished apple, her nose that wrinkles when she laughs, her hair braided at the nape of her neck, hair that is already graying on her temples. (If she dyed it, I would have thought she was twenty-eight years old, so smooth is the skin on her round face.)

Evangelina speaks naturally; she answers without hiding anything. Many would consider her politically naive because her answers spring forth spontaneously, "before the light of people's eyes," as she says, answers that are like flowers given out with simplicity, open like her house, so full of geraniums freshly watered on Sunday afternoons, after a day at church, when the sun is about to set.

What does de la Madrid think before this fresh air, what does Farell think, when both are used to the courtesan politeness of senators and representatives who earn hundreds of thousands of pesos a month, plus commissions? I wonder if they've noticed what kind of people Mexicans are.

Evangelina Corona would say with a luminous smile, "You'd better believe it!" She knows nothing about connivances, machinations, hypocrisies, plots, nothing. She only knows about the drowning in blood of September 19 and about the shouts of her compañeras: "We're here, save us!"

More than six hundred were crushed to death. Many were barely fourteen years old. Many were single mothers—without anybody to stand up for them.

"Let us stay here; just pretend we are nobody."

THE GREAT BAZAAR

On September 23 in *Proceso* magazine Elías Chávez brought to public light "The Former First Lady's Great Bazaar: Carmen Romano Sells Her Treasures." Among photos of buildings lying on the street like huge prehistoric animals, the ruins that are our new urban landscape, the blighted zones of tragedy, the Plaza de las Tres Culturas, the Multifamiliar Juárez, and the Centro Médico, there it was: a "garage sale" of jewelry, antique furniture, and porcelain belonging to Doña Carmen, the wife of the republic's ex-President.

López Portillo wrote a bill prohibiting public servants from receiving gifts. Miguel Angel Granados Chapa wrote an article in *Unomásuno* about the ranch in Tenancingo that was offered as a gift to the President by entrepreneurs and politicians. Shortly thereafter López Portillo said no to what he called the "great temptation." On December 3 a law was passed by Congress, 270–2, saying that "excepting those gifts given by a spouse or relatives up to second degree by blood or marriage, the President of the Republic, the members of Congress, the Supreme Court of Justice, and the Superior Court of the Federal District, and their minor children will not be able to accept gifts. . . . Only fifteen gifts per year may be accepted as long as each one of them does not exceed in value the equivalent of twenty days of their own salary."

Elías Chávez

Like the diamonds that Bokassa gave to Valéry Giscard d'Estaing, the colors on Doctor Atl's paintings shine with intensity, there, on a painting given by "the people of Chihuahua" to President José López Portillo, which now, along with three hundred other paintings plus other treasures fit for a pharaoh, is being liquidated by Doña Carmen Romano.

Also shining are silver table services, nineteenth-century French mirrors framed in gold leaf, Czech crystal, ivory inlay work, lacquered screens, porcelain jars, Japanese and Chinese vases, and the marquetry of Italian Renaissance furniture or seventeenth-century Chinese cabinetry.

In this superluxurious supermarket located in the facilities that in the past administration also belonged to the DIF, spectacular Austrian and German pianos, oriental rugs from Iran and Iraq, the statues of saints taken from some colonial Mexican church, champagne and French wines averaging twenty-five years in age, and even brand new electronic kitchens with microwave ovens only half unpacked are also for sale.

All these and much more in a garage sale!

The sale is only open to those who have been recommended. Millionaires, of course.

"Three million pesos for that saint!"

Soldiers guard the treasures. One can only enter the supermarket by appointment, in a complex of five houses surrounded by a garden of two and a half acres in Colonia Florida, a block and a half away from Insurgentes Avenue.

There are twelve pianos on display (there was no room for the rest). And on shelves, on the floor, in the corridors, the treasures cause the admiration of one customer, Sra. Catán, to whom Srta. Ugarte Romano boasts, "This is nothing; you should see the things that aren't here yet."

"Many would step forward saying that surely the girl was their sister, their daughter, their mother; everyone wanted the survivor to be their own." (© Marco Antonio Cruz. Photo in possession of Elena Poniatowska.)

"Relatives stood night and day, asking, asking." (© Marco Antonio Cruz. Photo in possession of Elena Poniatowska.)

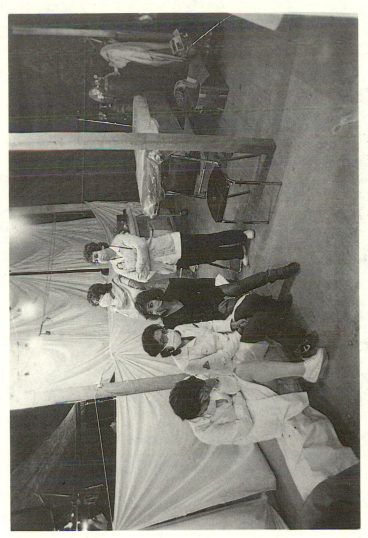

"In many cases they had to identify their own compañeros, nurses, and physicians."
(© Marco Antonio Cruz. Photo in possession of Elena Poniatowska.)

"The President of the Republic announced his decision a few days later: to reopen Hospital General." (© Marco Antonio Cruz. Photo in possession of Elena Poniatowska.)

"And now what? What awaits me? Nothing." (© Marco Antonio Cruz. Photo in possession of Elena Poniatowska.)

"I am convinced that the people of Mexico are heroic every day of their lives."
(© Marco Antonio Cruz. Photo in possession of Elena Poniatowska.)

"Oh, my Mexico, my wounded Mexico, my Mexico that contents itself with so little!"
(© Marco Antonio Cruz. Photo in possession of Elena Poniatowska.)

"The populace, these days, takes care of itself." (© Marco Antonio Cruz. Photo in possession of Elena Poniatowska.)

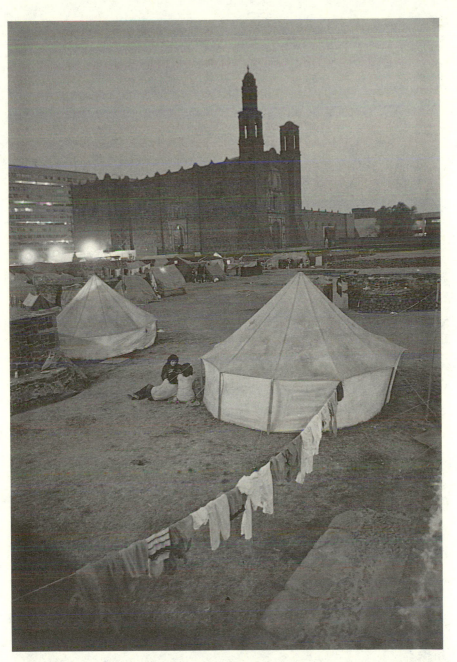

"As it was seventeen years before, the Plaza de las Tres Culturas is a battlefield; camping tents have been rigged up where incomplete families share their misfortune with their neighbors." (© Marco Antonio Cruz. Photo in possession of Elena Poniatowska.)

"If every once in a while, one way or another, the earthquake comes back, what will its final mark be?" (© Marco Antonio Cruz. Photo in possession of Elena Poniatowska.)

THEY ARE OUR BODIES, THE BODIES OF OUR PEOPLE
THERE ARE STILL BODIES AND RESCUE WORKERS IN SAN ANTONIO ABAD

Banners tied to the chain-link fence around the subway or leaning against walls on San Antonio Abad Avenue read in big black letters, "We the Workers of Cevercería Moctezuma Demand Pensions and Indemnifications for the Seamstresses"; "Topeka and Dedal, United We Will Overcome"; "We Demand a Rapid Solution for Struggling Garment Workers"; "After Three Years of Struggle, We the Bus Dispatchers of Flecha Roja México—Acapulco Demand from the State a Solution to Garment Workers' Problems"; "Dimensión Weld"; "Affected Garment Workers Demand Work"; "Seamstresses in Struggle for Indemnification and Work"; and "They All Became Brothers and Sisters in Disgrace Fighting the Disaster, Struggling for a Cause."

More banners: "Brigade C3, the 'Tlatelolco Moles'"; "The Mexican Union of Electricians Demands an Immediate Solution to the Problems of Artesanías Selectas Company in Unconditional Support for Workers Rights"; "National Union of the Sewing, Confection, Dressmaking and Related Industry." On the wall, the group La Guillotina has posted signs that say; "Demand What Is Impossible. Behold the Night and Day Struggle."

Today, November 5, 1985, garment workers are still buried in San Antonio Abad. People are still waiting on the avenue; there are still rescue workers. As regularly as an electric train in a child's nursery, the tangerine-colored metro appears. Behind its windows men and women are all too real. They stare at the clothes that are still hanging in the wreck of buildings amid smashed concrete and steel: slacks, nightgowns, chiffon dresses, the pink and peach gauzy things we call negligees. The slabs are holding them like gigantic clothespins. They sway when the train goes by, as if they were trying to look out the window, disembodied pajamas, dresses, trousers, slips, rags.

On the street the seamstresses sit together in groups. They wait. Meanwhile in the tents, the relatives hide themselves from curious people, cameras, and tape recorders. They don't want to know anything about anything. Behind them the Tlalpan metro goes by. The passengers see, the doors close again, and the train loses itself in the distance.

All the people that continue walking on San Antonio Abad seem fed up, not just exhausted and burdened, but fed up. The only one who seems to have escaped their rage is an engineer, Sr. de la Torre.

People like Patricia Obscura, rescuer, and Rosa Angélica Gallegos, Juana de la Rosa Osorno, and Victoria Munive, who are still waiting for the remains of their wife, their sister, their mother, speak with reverence about *ingeniero* de la Torre." "Now, there's a gentleman." In San Antonio Abad there has been much friction between rescue groups, so frequently that the doctors, relatives, and seamstresses made a decision: "The only person we want here is *ingeniero* de la Torre."

"Why?"

"Because he is a gentleman. Because he knows how to show respect."

"This man," says Patricia Obscura, "is really special, a wonderful person. His specific mission is to recover bodies, which he has done with tremendous respect. And he has shown respect for the sorrow of the people. Do you want us to look for him? Do you want to talk to him? He is up there, working. . ."

He walks toward me. Dynamic. Short, with a helmet almost blocking his eyes. And under the helmet a wide frank smile that immediately makes me think, "This is a good man." He takes off his helmet and looks even smaller. He looks something like Miguel Prieto, a Spanish painter with a beautiful face and a welcoming smile:

Of course I am Mexican, 100 percent, the classic middle-class man. I've been working here under orders from the commission.

"What commission?"

Covitur, the Commission on Roadways and Urban Transport.

"So you are with the government?"

Yes. Why should that surprise you?

(I'm flabbergasted. I can't get over it.)

I arrived three weeks ago to recover bodies, still with some hope of finding someone alive.

"But the government took a very long time to respond."

I don't agree with that. On the 19th at 9:30 I had instructions to go to the Pino Suárez complex immediately. I arrived at 10:15 because the traffic was impossible. I saw compañeros I've known for a long time crying. I asked for a phone. Through the internal lines of SCT I called Covitur and they sent me everything I asked for. We moved so quickly that from Pino Suárez I sent the machines to G-O at the Centro Médico. Cometro was active there. I also sent equipment to Hospital Juárez, and to Mesones Street, wherever they asked for it.

Many people said to me, "There are trapped people here. We are about to get them out. We only need a power compressor and a power cutter."

"Yes, of course."

We tried to listen to the demands of every person who approached us. There was certainly a lack of coordination. But do you have a good recipe to coordinate efforts after a national catastrophe? I went to Gynecology-Obstetrics and came back very depressed. I think in Mexico we were not prepared for anything like what happened, and that's why I sincerely believe that those of us who had the means acted promptly.

The people of Covitur and Cometro who had heavy machinery lost no time in making it available to the whole city. Those of us working on Route 7 South, 6 West, and North were giving technical assistance three hours after the earthquake at the latest. I'm not sure what was done in other areas.

I talk to de la Torre about the power vacuum, about the people who "took the streets" as Carlos Monsiváis so poignantly said, about the compadres and friends helping each other, about the absent Father Government, its clumsiness, its babbling; about Ramón Aguirre looking gaunt, with an overgrown beard and bulging eyes, not knowing what to do. I ennumerate the instances of public and private gaffes, the instances of corruption among builders and contractors; I insist on the generalized public sentiment against the army; and Francisco de la Torre shakes his head in disagreement:

I can't see why. Many people didn't have the slightest idea about what we were trying to do. To stop the people who would have obstructed the work was very important. They could not help out, but they could surely stand in the way. Have you heard of voyeuristic curiosity? The army helped; it did its job. Because of the army we could work freely.

"But the first ones to risk their lives with absolute selfishness, heroically, were the friends and neighbors who thought nothing of excavating in the rubble . . ."

I personally asked the army to stop busybodies from coming in to the disaster areas. But we never rejected the help of distraught relatives. The army kept its post to impose order and respect. They didn't interfere with the civilian population, seriously. If someone told you otherwise, ask for proof.

"Don't worry, *ingeniero*, they will prove it."

Look, the earthquake has been a catastrophe, a national tragedy. I have two events etched in my mind forever: this thing of September 19 and the year 1968. Back then I attended many demonstrations. I was a fifth-year engineering student and I was present at the very first march, with the president of the university, Barros Sierra. Resentment against the government was unbelievable, and entirely justified.

Now this cataclysm comes and divides and unites Mexicans once again. It divides, because there are people who haven't even bothered coming to see. I live in the south, and some neighbors say to me, "Hey, is it true . . . ?" The TV images are enough for them. But then again, I prefer for people not to come here if they are coming to watch as if we were the circus. We all dislike the hordes of people driven by unhealthy curiosity.

In San Antonio Abad alone there are between 120 and 123 people working every day in twelve-hour shifts, minus the ones who get sick or can't come for other reasons. Those of us in the leadership are engineers. But there is room for construction workers, officers, heavy machine operators, cutters. We use a lot of cutters, who are the most important people in this kind of work. The perforators do a very tiring job; to work with drills for ten to twelve hours is exhausting.

The people who have offered to volunteer have been told that the most humble construction worker knows how to do this job professionally: when to go in, when to withdraw, how to be safe. We do not have to give instructions constantly or to supervise closely. Had we accepted volunteers, we would have had to train them and organize them. And what we need to do is go forward, because the bodies must be in an advanced state of decomposition. And if you look around, you see the next of kin; look at them, how they wait. Every day they come and ask, "Are we there yet?"

I explain what I am doing, to each and every one of them: "Look, today we are going to do this and that," and I do it at all times. They are the ones I owe explanations to, not to curious bystanders. My first obligation is to take them into account as human beings, as mourners, as men and women who have a loved person buried in the wreckage. Respect for those sorrowful people is not only my sentiment but that of all the people who work here.

When we locate a body we immediately give notice to the physician on call, so that the body will be "prepared," as they say. The office of the Ministerio Público is notified; the relative is located; a description is made of the clothing, ring, teeth. That's what we have to go by, because there is hardly any skin left, and if there is, it is quite deformed. When I come down I talk to the people. Very often I eat with them; we chat and kid around, about how tired we all are of eating sandwiches, sandwiches, and more sandwiches. We even laugh. My specific mission is to recover bodies, and, it is a shame to have to say it, but there are some still left in there. I beg your pardon, I am not very good at interviews, really.

"No, but you are."

Up there the clothes invite the sun. The classic peach color of women's slips glistens. Down below the relatives do not eat or drink; they stare upward. Among others Víctor Manuel Priego, frantic, asserts: The *ingeniero* is a real good person, but I think he's somewhat innocent; he hasn't seen what he has in his hands; the building is a gold mine, and all he's interested in is dead bodies. The first day I approached him eagerly to tell him, and he said, "Come, let's go up so that you'll understand what I'm doing. Afterward you can tell me anything."

He took me up there, he showed me the machines, and then he said, "I came to work. I'm not a public relations committee. I don't want cameras, journalists; I only want to be left alone to do my work because I'm committed to giving you the bodies of your loved ones."

So far he has done all that is humanly possible to keep his promise, but his people are another matter. The trucks look like they're filled with rubble, but underneath they have bolts of fabric, bales of clothes, even machines. That's why we had to become custodians and demand a preemptive legal seizure of the goods.

There has been sheer plundering by workers, the army, truck drivers, machine operators, construction workers, everyone, and the only person who doesn't seem to know—and I repeat it, he is the most decent man ever—is *ingeniero* de la Torre. He is up there, sweating away, with pick and shovel, minding his business, while his own people are up to no good. The machines go in at seven in the morning, and late at night, when the others have gone home, we go in, the next of kin, to look for our people. They are still inside. They are our bodies. And we want to bury them, even if it's in pieces.

RELATIVES OF GARMENT WORKERS ARE ASSAULTED IN SAN ANTONIO ABAD

THEY DENOUNCE THE ATTEMPT TO EVICT THEM

At eight in the morning, Patricia Obscura calls on the phone. Every day she brings breakfast to the seamstresses and to the relatives who are still waiting for the bodies of their loved ones, standing guard all night.

At four in the morning, El Chino Heriberto Frías and others were sitting around a fire, warming themselves, when four men descended from a dark green Plymouth, clearly Federal Security agents, and they proceeded to beat up Leobardo Gijón and Pedro Salazar. Oscar Vázquez almost had his ribs broken when he was hit repeatedly with the butt of a gun.

It is Saturday, November 9. *Ingeniero* Francisco de la Torre is not in San Antonio Abad, and he's the one who always helps the relatives of trapped workers, and treats them well. There are only a few tents left. The garment workers intend to recover machines, fabrics, and other materials, such as zippers, thread, lace, and ornaments. A big bolt of fabric has been unfurled from a place high up in the building, like a toboggan run, so that clothes, other rolls of cloth, and light machines can be sent rolling downward. A worker sends them down, and down they come on this improvised slide.

Pedro Salazar is lying down on a cot in a tent. He can hardly move after being severely beaten up:

I was sleeping in another tent, not in this one, when I realized that my compañeros were being beaten up: Heriberto Frías, El Chino, who has been helping out these days, Oscar Vázquez Alba, and Leonardo Gijón. Two children, twelve and fourteen, were also beaten up in the street, Rafael Flores and José Luis Flores, and one more, Ricardo, was slapped in the face. These children were on their way to the bathroom. They were crossing the street, and at that moment they were stopped and beaten up. Look here, look what they did to their faces and necks. They are trying to intimidate us, no doubt. There is a rumor that they are trying to evict us. They say they want to open San Antonio Abad Avenue to traffic by next Monday, but we will not let them. No sir, not until the *patrones* pay the indemnifications we deserve, we are not going anywhere. Over our dead bodies!

When I ask how much each indemnification is worth, they respond they are asking for "a fair amount," and El Chinito points to three boxes, two of them metal and the other one a little run-down, so that we can sit and talk. They provide a good seat.

One of the Flores children has an injured foot and is badly beaten up. They all received blows to their faces. They are still in the camp because they are waiting for the body of their mother, who was a garment worker. They were on the way to the bathroom in the corner when the four men got them.

"The government has been no help. The only one who is decent around here is *ingeniero* Francisco de la Torre; he is a good guy and treats us well, but other than him, the government has done nothing. The ones who bring us food are all volunteers. The best are some nuns from San Pedro Mártir, Sister Paul and Patricia Obscura, who bring us breakfast and supper. They have taken care of us."

I am here, Pedro Salazar interrupts, with his arms folded under his head as a pillow, because I lost my aunt and my niece in Amal. My aunt was sixty, and her name was Reina Buenaventura de Pineda, a widow, and my niece was Mireya Pineda Buenaventura, nineteen, a kid, really. My aunt had worked for Amal for fourteen years. My niece was found on the 30th, and so was my aunt; I recognized them by their clothes. We have suffered incredibly much, and they still come and give it to us. It's not fair, right?

The army left San Antonio Abad yesterday, Friday, November 8. This beating came courtesy of the authorities or else is revenge on the part of the *patrones*. Either one. They hit us because they have money and we don't. They want to take their machinery, and the eviction is already planned. The delegate from Venustiano Carranza has come to say that we have to clean up here, pack up the camp, take everything away. But there are still three bodies to be gotten out.

Last night they found one body in Topeka, and they held a wake there. Sister Paul, of San Pedro Mártir, is the one who has taken care of the coffins. She has managed to find vans to transport the dead, as well as to bring us cooked food, bags of groceries, sodas. She has really taken care of everything that we need.

San Pedro Mártir is a church in a little town, way out by the old road to Cuernavaca. Sister Paul and other sisters coordinate the food distribution in a van. From La Esmeralda school, they have also sent us tamales and other more formal suppers: stews, beans, and tortillas. Because since the earthquake struck many of us had not eaten anything but sandwiches, and we were so tired of them, we wanted some hot soup, honestly.

Fatigue has set in, says Patricia Obscura. Many have worked at night, and with so much dirt, everyone has gotten sick, with diarrhea or other stomach problems, even the strongest among them. Their whole life cycle was disrupted; it was turned upside down. They have been sleeping out in the street for two months. Although "sleeping" may be an exaggeration. And if a recreation camp is difficult to keep clean, imag-

237

ine this camp in the middle of the avenue, with all these anguished people, going into the rubble and looking for their family members.

The machines were going at it all day, under the heat of the day that makes everything worse, especially the stench that became nauseating a few days ago, something intolerable. At night, when there was less hustle and bustle and when the stench diminished slightly, the moles would go in and locate the bodies, making tunnels. What a frightful nightmare this has been!

Men, women, and children have been living in a terrible state of depression. They have also gotten tired, infinitely tired, to the point of apathy. This lethargy didn't come from nowhere. The people you see lying on those roll-away mattresses have been crying until they have no more tears, and now they come close to the moment when they have to face the fact of a corpse. How would you feel if the body of someone you loved was in a state of putrefaction? And there are still bodies up there! Even now!

If death is difficult under normal circumstances, imagine what it has been for these people who have had to wait so long. That's why some prefer to wrap themselves in their blankets and cover their faces until someone says, "Here, we have found your sister, or your mother, or your aunt. Here is another body. Come identify it." These people have been identifying cadavers early each morning. Can you imagine what that means? I have seen tragedies here that I will never forget.

Patricia Obscura, a lovely young woman, stops abruptly: Oh, look! Here he comes. *Ingeniero* Francisco de la Torre. Oh, good.

Not many men are as compassionate as de la Torre. Today, Sunday, November 10, he finds out about the beating of El Chinito, Pedro Salazar, Oscar Velázquez, and Leobardo Gijón, plus the three Flores children. "It is simply barbaric."

We talk while we walk among the tents, in front of windows that show women's girdles and bras on headless mannequins. On the street, however, many mannequins eat dirt, with their pointy plaster breasts on the asphalt. Nobody picks them up. "This is a good photo, isn't it?" comments the *ingeniero*. People wave at him as he goes by. In a while a meeting will be held.

Vera comes out of her tent, and she doesn't look cheerful, as she does some other days. "I'm hoarse. It's the night cold. They want to evict us now; they say traffic has to move again." A meeting is convened, and Vera announces, "I'm on my way." *Ingeniero* de la Torre warns, "They are from the PDM." I ask de la Torre what the solution is for the garment workers.

The only solution is to start a cooperative. I have faith in co-ops. Cruz Azul, for instance. It looks like there is one already, financed by Banco de México, and called "September 19."

Well, I talk to a lot of people, and I know some workers want to get their money; others want to be hired in other garment jobs; the older ones among them want to retire, not to work anymore. I tell them not to look back, that they need to go forward any way they can. The past is only a point of reference.

It is urgent to create an expectation for the future among the workers. The best way of doing politics is to offer results in the short run. Once a cooperative is established they can have a wage. How long does it take to mount a cooperative? A month? Meanwhile they can be helped with donations of food and clothing. But afterward they know they have a job, which is an economic guarantee for the long haul. A cooperative with 118 people or more, among seamstresses, pressers, maintenance personnel, sales people, et cetera, can be started with 35 million.

As we walk, de la Torre gives orders: "No, don't get down there. Shut off this water main. Watch out for the rods! That truck is in the way, move it." "Yes *ingeniero,* yes *ingeniero.*" He too looks very tired.

"You are half-killing yourself, aren't you, *ingeniero?*"

Well, for me this is a matter of conscience. My family is not rich; my parents never were or are. I couldn't have gone to the university except in a system like the one we live in. You have to admit that anybody can pay 200 pesos a year, not just today, but even twenty years ago or more, because I finished twenty-five years ago. I doubt that a man like me could ever have gone to the university and become an engineer in any other country in the world. The way I can pay this country back is to take care of these people who are waiting here for their dead. To get them out is my homage to the workers who died.

Thanks to the work and taxes of the people who died here, and others like them, many of us were able to secure a degree through higher education. I just said this to my own family, because my wife and children complained yesterday that it had been a month since they had seen me (that's why I stayed home last Friday), and I think they understood.

Thanks to all these people who died and people like them, I insist, many of us have careers. Thanks to these people I am an engineer and you are a journalist, and the president is the president. Therefore, I am not a bureaucrat putting in my eight hours, but the time that my presence is needed, or the time that my body can take it, because, as they say, *The Three Musketeers* and *Twenty Years Later* are not the same.

All of us who have been working here day and night are fully conscious that we have to work until we collapse, exhausted.

TO TRAIN TEAMS FOR ANY EVENTUALITY
IT IS NECESSARY TO TRAIN PERMANENT RESCUE BRIGADES

I first went to PSUM, of which I am an active member. And as it turns out, at the time of the disaster, there was a tremendous lack of coordination; nobody knew anything about anything! The headquarters had been damaged, so no information could be gleaned there, let alone marching orders. So for the first few days the volunteers of PSUM were working on their own, scattered; then the days went by, and the lack of organization persisted.

I went to a meeting, and everybody wanted to analyze the problem and make statements. Analysis sessions and evaluations when what was needed was to get out from under the rubble! Just like the government! I was outraged. Analysis, my foot! Let's go out and work! And a brigade was immediately organized, under the name "Base Chamai," after a sisal worker assassinated in Yucatán.

We went to Narvarte, to a building that had sandwiched down. Traffic was out of control, so we had to walk. But a señorita who was a party member said, "I have to walk in the shade; I don't want to get sunburnt." And I got mad. If we were going to work, what was the sun. Balls!

I decided to join another group in Tlatelolco. Far from PSUM I was able to get involved better and to help out more effectively. After the Nuevo León I went to the Multifamiliar Juárez, the housing project where I met James Kelleghan.

Marco Antonio Elizalde, with his leather jacket, lives in Unidad Molino de Santo Domingo, between Observatorio and Santa Fe. He's twenty-two and helps himself by selling books for Distribuidora Cultural Cuauhnáhuac. Disillusioned with the PSUM, he hasn't gone back to his party since September 19. In Multifamiliar Juárez he met James Kelleghan, a sensitive and smart guy, one of the skinny ones who could go in through the holes and tunnels.

For a month neither Marco Antonio Elizalde nor James Kelleghan went back home, except to take baths and change clothes. Their entire time was given to the rescue brigades. Says Kelleghan:

I was working on a master's in computer science. But now I am no longer interested in it. Before, one of my objectives in life was to get a doctoral degree—that was the most important thing, really—but now I am not interested in belonging to a system and an establishment that lets people die. I couldn't care less about that goal and many other things that previously seemed to matter.

What I really got out of the earthquake experience was a passionate love of life. I am the son of a father from the United States and a Mexican mother. On September 19, I started to collect food at the Colegio Francés del Pedregal and in the Humana Hospital. From there I was sent to distribute them out of Jalapa 50, in the middle of the disaster zone.

The situation in Colonia Roma was critical, and I had not understood that before, because Televisa was concerned mostly with its own building, and with Hospital General, Centro Médico, the SCOP, the Regis, and the Nuevo León, and almost not at all with the Juárez housing project, where I landed after leaving Colonia Roma.

I saw many volunteers, many relatives scratching the rubble desperately, and I decided to join them and scratch some more. They opened a hole at one point and shouted, "We need a skinny one," and that's the way I started "moling" three yards below the tuft of the building, crawling and burrowing a tunnel with my own body.

We used metal piping and crowbars and anything we could find. You creep inside and bring a bucket, a shovel without a handle, a dustpan, or if worse comes to worst, an empty can to get the dirt out.

I went in on Thursday night without protection, and the one who called the shots in there was a receptionist for GUTSA, a pretty twenty-three-year-old girl called Aglae, who was sent by her company because many buildings from that construction firm came down. But because she worked there, Aglae ended up being in charge, and she worked nice and smooth; she behaved real well. We had no knowledge and no experience at all.

I remember that at one point there was a rearrangement of weight in the rubble that closed down the tunnel, so when I wanted to leave, I couldn't. I felt a great deal of fear, and I said, "What the fuck, now I've really done it." I curled up and started to think. I was getting very nervous when fifteen minutes later I realized they were excavating around the hole where I had gone in, and they quickly got me out.

I don't want to go on with my studies because I don't see any use for my field. I saw too many things that scandalized me. From the Vistahermosa shelter they referred an injured victim to the Humana Hospital, one of the health centers that had offered to help. The poor man went back to the shelter the next day because he had been released. But when one of our doctors examined him, he found that he had gangrene, so they bounced him back to the Humana. I've heard that the physician who released him lost his job at Humana, but I've heard other comments about that hospital and how they treated the poor, and that they kept blankets that had been donated for the victims for use in their own ambulances.

Londres, Dinamarca, Liverpool, and Bruselas streets looked as if they had been bombarded, and nobody even bothered with many of the buildings. In the disaster areas, there was no equipment. Food provisions and water were very scarce. There was a guy, Nicolás, who was running a bus from Route 100 distributing food, until the police from patrol car number 03044 beat up Nico, because he was driving the bus without legal papers. The motherfuckers! If they see that we are working on relief, why the hostility?

Nico was taken to the delegation, and when we went to get him out, we realized that others had been detained because they were also trying to help.

But at least I can speak well of Dr. Justo Ruiz López, director of medical services for the Cuauhtémoc Delegation. I was surprised to find someone in the government who was so honest. The shelters at Jalapa 50 and 75 functioned so well because of him that they became distribution centers overnight.

Datamex was a computer school, where classes started at 7 A.M., next to the building of General de Gas. The building collapsed, and since it stopped the traffic on Insurgentes Avenue, the Department of the Federal District gave orders on Sunday morning to remove the rubble with heavy machinery and clear the street.

When we arrived at the basement of Datamex, I almost died when I saw seventy-two bodies that had been dead for three days. They were killed by the machinery. They could have been saved if there had been more respect for human life. The claw, the steam shovel, the crane, they all caused cave-ins and plugged the air inlets.

How do you think that I can continue studying when the authorities of my country, eager to clean up a street, are capable of utilizing machinery that kills people? Why should I study if nobody gives a damn about life in this country, especially the government? Who can guarantee that I will ever matter to anyone in authority?

They talk a lot about the Torre Latinoamericana, a skyscraper. It didn't fall down, but it leaned over after the two earthquakes. I saw the base of the tower separated from the sidewalk, as if a knife had been wedged in to cut a slice of cake. It resisted the two earthquakes, but will it take the next?

Will the people withstand another earthquake? What measures are being taken to protect the population? What evacuation drills are being rehearsed, what shelters are being built, what permanent rescue brigades are being trained? Or will we always be the land of improvisers?

Question: How are the victims going to make a living from now on? Are they going to decentralize the Federal District? Will we end up with minidistricts all over the republic? At this very moment in Mexico City we are living on subsoil that can cave in. We are sitting on the gravest danger. Our panic is under control, but it is latent.

I'd like to say goodbye to James Kelleghan and Marco Antonio Elizalde with a piece of good news. James recounts:

On the 19th, at the time of the earthquake, a woman on the first floor of the Nuevo León fell out the window. The building collapsed and her nine-month-old baby was trapped inside. At 2:30 in the afternoon the rescue operation stopped because the cry of a baby could be heard. They moved a little bit of rubble, and there was the baby, crawling, with a baby bottle in his hand! Without a scratch! He was barely dirtied up by the debris.

"Some say that the sky was very blue on that day." Juan Guerrero.

Concha Creel

I worked as a mole in Hospital Juárez on Sunday, Tuesday, and Wednesday, says Eduardo Miranda, twenty-two, a student of civil engineering and a member of the mountaineer club of UNAM. I had the night shift, which many were trying to avoid because it is such a pain. The mountain climbers of UNAM had called me.

When we arrived, we discussed who would go into the rubble, and soon we realized the enormous risk that we were facing. At the beginning we went in with great fear, but half an hour later we were at a considerable depth, roughly twenty to thirty feet. Working in those small tunnels I was very aware that even a slight tremor would have a high probability of trapping or crushing us. But the thought of finding people alive gave us a great deal of energy.

Our work consisted of excavating tunnels. Sometimes we had to be in a very uncomfortable position, hitting at a slab for hours on end surrounded by the penetrating stench of death. Our objective was to locate and rescue people alive, but we were finding many more corpses than survivors. Sometimes it would take hours to bring out these bodies. Sometimes we would come out of the tunnel surprised to find it daytime. We had been working all night on a slow, exhausting, and seemingly insignificant task, one that would suddenly become enormously rewarding after hours of work when we were able to find a person still breathing.

One day in the early hours of the morning, we were allowed to stop working, because the French team was about to rescue a patient from the hospital. They had worked at least seven hours on this one job alone, and after waiting for another half hour in the most absolute silence, José Fernández was brought out alive. The emotion was so deep and widely shared! We all burst out in applause, and then we went back to work.

We were working in a tunnel that was virtually vertical; we had already perforated three floor slabs. We estimated that we were in level seven or eight of the twelve-floor hospital when we thought we heard something and requested silence through people who remained at the entrance of the tunnel, and in a moment, everything was quiet.

It is impressive when in less than twenty seconds that infernal mountain full of the noise of hammers, buckets, shouts, machinery, and saws could be stilled and quieted. No one made the slightest noise, and inside the tunnels we would hold our breath for a moment. Something was heard; others thought that the noise could be at the fifth level.

In two more hours, we could always go through one more slab. We broke through a door and asked again for silence. Nothing. "Jesus," we thought. We cut two rods an inch wide each to get just a bit further ahead and once more asked for silence. Nothing this time either. In our minds we kept imagining the sound we were so eager to capture. We worked two hours more until, dejected, we withdrew. The exhaustion was complete, and this was the outcome of most of our labors. It was desperate.

On the other hand, a group of moles devoted itself to bringing a nurse out. After thirty-six hours of hope and struggle against death, they took her out, but once she was placed on the stretcher, feeling secure, she gave in and died.

THE FORTITUDE OF DR. MARTA TORRES

Marie-Pierre Toll (Translation from the Mexico City *News* by Carmen Lugo)

Lying in a horizontal position, enveloped by the smell of decomposed flesh, they performed surgery in a narrow tunnel within the ruins of Hospital General. Doctors Maurice Brisard and Serge Cravello and anesthesiologist François Loriferne saved the life of Dr. Marta Torres, twenty-five, and that of an anesthetist.

Trapped for more than six days, Dr. Torres managed to survive thanks to unflinching courage and faith. Dr. Brisard, a volunteer from Papeete, Tahiti, tells the story:

On September 24 at ten in the morning, six days after Mexico City woke in the midst of the most severe earthquake in its contemporary history, Brisard and his team were taken to the Hospital General. They worked twenty-eight hours without rest, in the longest-lasting effort ever made by these French physicians.

10:30 A.M. Marta Torres is located.

4:00 P.M. Her voice is heard for the first time.

4:30 P.M. A friend named Pili talks to Marta through a small hole.

6:00 P.M. Through another tunnel, her right hand is clearly visible. The first transfusion is administered.

"All we could find was her right hand, but this saved her," says Loriferne, "because we could give her transfusions and keep her alive, even before removing the tons of rubble that fell on top of her.

"I was the first one to touch her. I was practically immobilized in a very narrow tunnel. I could hardly move my own hand, but I was able to reach hers. I found her vein. I gave her glucose. Psychologically she knew life was coming back to her. She confirmed that she felt resuscitated."

It worked!

Now her left foot could be seen. Marta was trapped in a space twenty inches long and a foot wide. For six and a half days, the young physician remained twisted with her left arm surrounding the back of her waist and her head lying sideways. Her left leg was totally crushed, but we only learned that three hours before getting her out. Her right foot was caught under a forty-ton concrete column.

7:00 P.M. Technical problems. Sharp hammers, drills, soldering torches, and hydraulic jacks were all used to remove rubble, and air openings were made. Dr. Torres is protected from the sparks that the drills emit by means of soaked sheets. The psychological help of friends and colleagues is given constantly.

"We had to cut a section of the column measuring eight by twenty inches in order to bring her out. Each jolt was atrocious for her, but there was no other way. She complained about the pain," says Dr. Brisard.

The young woman doctor played a very important role in her own rescue: she directed the work of the rescuers and the firemen from Brignole, describing the materials that buried her. She mentioned the proximity of the stairway. The architects and engineers who built the hospital were at the disaster site. (They remained there during the whole operation.) Lieutenants Bartoli and Sauniere excavated tunnels rapidly and at a minimum of risk because of the information provided by the doctor.

September 25, 4:00 a.m. A new transfusion is given. The exact location of the woman is determined.

4:30 A.M. Her right leg is found by doctors, who discover that her hip is dislocated. Her right arm is also found.

8:30 A.M. Doctors decide to amputate the crushed leg, because it has gangrene. Doctor Torres encourages them: "Doctor, you know your obligations." In the next few hours, they try to save her knee. Technicians work hard to save her life, standing on the very ruins that are crushing her, while doctors operate on her lying down with their arms outstretched. The smell of rotten bodies permeates everything.

9:15 A.M. The extraction of the young woman presents difficulties. As she is dragged out, her ankle gets stuck, producing unbearable pain in the pelvis. "She's free!" was the only shout that could be heard.

She was taken to the Metropolitan Hospital, where Dr. Sink, a cardiovascular surgeon, offered Dr. Brisard full support for him to conduct a second amputation. He also offered to assist him personally. "In terms of human resources, I never worked with a better team," declared Brisard.

Marta Torres was the first and probably the only physician to come out alive. More than two hundred doctors died in the hospital. This fact is what made her rescue so important.

Her courage is unprecedented. We had the good fortune of being able to keep her alive with the help of transfusions for thirteen hours. Without the experience and patience of the Brignole firefighters, we couldn't have done it. It was a team in which each member fulfilled his or her duty to the point of excellence, and not even one of the Mexican team of doctors, engineers, workers, or Marta's friends asked to be relieved during the twenty-eight hours that the operation lasted.

It was a memorable ordeal and a memorable team. Mexicans and Frenchmen understood the need to cooperate and set a new standard of medical professionalism. Each and every member of this team was the author of the rescue of Dr. Torres. Each one became involved beyond his or her capacity. On September 26, the rumor that the young woman had died reached some of the rescuers.

"We went to the hospital; we saw her; she recognized my voice," says François Loriferne. "She told me my voice had been the first thing she had heard in a long time. She was sitting in bed, eating." ■

El Lobo Would Never Get Mad
THOSE WHO WANT TO COOPERATE, PLEASE PLANT A FLOWER

He repeats again and again that he's very well, that he's stronger now. He announces the good news with eyes full of tears, reddened for many days, with his hands trembling and covered with cold sweat, and he smiles: "My brother is more present than ever." As it turns out, Alejandro Escoto, a student of twenty-six years, dubbed El Lobo, died on September 19 at Universidad Chapultepec in Colonia Roma.

Andrés Escoto, his older brother at thirty-three, an architect by profession, was assistant chief of public works in Zihuatanejo and chief of public works in Zumpango del Río. He came from Chilpancingo on September 20:

Most of all Alejandro was a son to me, because my mother "was gone" (he never pronounces the word *death*, he has never said *died* or *passed away*) when I was fourteen and Alejandro was seven. We were seven years apart. I was born in 1952, he in 1959. We lost our mother, but only in appearance, because she was ever present. Good people are immortal.

The earthquake caught me on the street in Chilpancingo. I leaned against the wall. In the corner there were some women praying, and I wasn't scared because we are used to earthquakes in Guerrero, but I asked myself, "And Alejandro? I wonder where he went? Would he have been in school or still at home?"

Three days ago, on September 17, he had begun to study tourism at the Chapultepec University. I was always saying to him, "Alejandro, go back to school." I always insisted that he should study, that he should prepare himself for the future. I sat down to watch television: all those buildings on the ground. I started to think of Alejandro, asking myself where he was. On Friday the 20th, I went from Chilpancingo to Zumpango del Río, and around ten in the morning, I saw some people waving at me.

"What's up? How are you doing?"

And just like that, they dropped the bomb.

"It's about Alejandro."

"What happened to him?"

"His school, Universidad Chapultepec, it collapsed."

"Yes? And what happened?"

"Well, he's gone."

They say my face lost all color, but I didn't despair. My colleagues felt more desperate as I sat down on the sidewalk and held my head.

I spoke to the mayor and left for Mexico City. I now remember a saying of Raymundo, a friend of Alejandro's: "You've got to have luck even on your way out." And it's true: in his classroom, everyone was gone, and the first one to be recovered—God wanted it that way—was Alejandro, and his remains were taken out by his friend Pedro. That very day, the 19th, he looked for him and found him. You've got to have luck even for that.

I was lucky in my own way, because my father, my friends and relatives, had held a wake on the night of the 19th, and when I arrived on the 20th at six in the evening, I saw him as if asleep, peaceful, happy. You know what I feel—I feel that God helped me, and that my mother and Alejandro interceded for me. From Chilpancingo to Mexico City, the road took a little bit over three hours, and when I went through Cuernavaca, I thought, "Let me get some flowers for El Lobo, some red roses."

I arrived at my father's house. The atmosphere was very tense because they knew what Alejandro meant to me. They didn't know what my reaction was going to be, and some had said, "With something like this, Andrés is going to go too." I walked behind the hearse with the remains of El Lobo. We arrived in San Isidro, and his remains were buried next to my mother's. Many were crying, but I was serene. I kept telling people, "Thank you for coming with us and keeping us company at the last light and sound show."

El Lobo and his friends had a company called Decibel that provided sound equipment for parties. He must have had a premonition that they were coming to get him because on September 15, he told Pedro, his best friend, the one who recovered his body, "I have two jackets. I am going to give you this white one."

I'm not going to place a tombstone or a memorial there. I'm going to have a little garden, and whoever wants to cooperate can plant a flower. I don't know where Alejandro is, but I feel that I may be a little better as a person because I reflect something of my brother. God, my mother, and Alejandro are always with me, and I feel a great deal of energy. Thanks to Alejandro I have also started to be better, to do good works, to behave well. From on high, Alejandro will protect me and show me the way.

In Mexico, my work has never been recognized. I never even get a Christmas bonus. My own country treats me poorly because that's the way Mexico is with all poor Mexicans. Now with the help of the El Lobo, I am planning to migrate to Quebec, Canada, and there I will make it, easy. I'm another person since the 20th, I sleep well, I feel better than ever, a great peace has come to me. They are the good vibrations from Alejandro.

From Alejandro Escoto, that is, dead three days after entering a poorly built school building in Colonia Roma, the Universidad Chapultepec, which buried him along with other students, who like him studied tourism.

We would be grateful for information concerning the whereabouts of Omar Saad Maldonado, seventeen years of age, green eyes, light complexion, light brown hair, five feet, six inches in height. He has a small scar on the right breast. He left home after the earthquake of September 19th between ten and eleven in the morning, dressed in jeans or gray corduroy pants, a navy blue windbreaker with ILLINOIS written across the back. Please refer any information to telephones 520–5104, 579–2970, 552–7132, 760–9841, and 538–9707.

Note: On October 2, a forensic physician told relatives that he had seen the boy working as a volunteer carrying out rubble. When the family saw him, Omar explained that he had not called his relatives because he was helping out.

Since September 19, we have been looking for René Antonio Loo Almaguer. He is wearing jeans, a white windbreaker, white socks, navy blue "Charly" sneakers. He is seventeen years old, five foot six, with dark skin and straight hair. He attended Universidad Chapultepec located at Chihuahua 156, Colonia Roma. This school collapsed because of the earthquake. Please relay any information through telephone numbers 597–4621 and 392–1978. Thank you.

Relatives found his student ID on the sidewalk in front of the school.

THE WEEPING OF GLORIA GUERRERO

One is living in a routine, going to bed after scrambling in the streets. One gives orders: walk, carry, talk, eat, laugh, sit down. One lives the hopelessness, the solitude, the anguish for one's children. What will their lives be like? One gets depressed, exalted; one senses the cold weather coming, the days getting shorter, the mornings getting darker. Silly me, I hadn't even realized, it's already September. Then, one morning like any other morning the clock strikes 7:19, and the supports of the building crack and collapse on the ground!

South of the city, anything falls very slowly, the earthquake is perceived only bit by bit, but by the afternoon, one begins to float in a great void, and the abyss doesn't end until one doesn't find another pair of hands, until one doesn't look at someone's eyes and see oneself reflected in those eyes.

Reciprocity. If the other one exists, I exist; if the other one is alive, I am alive; if the other one died, I also die, even if I go from here to there and put one foot in front of the other, even when at night I lie in bed, and I get up before dawn, even when I comb my hair and get out a tube of lipstick to paint another mouth on top of mine, the mouth that now moves in front of me, the eyes that now blur in front of mine, the thin skin that reddens, the grimace of weeping, the nervous hands that try to stop the tears, and these trembling salty lips that twist and are mine and belong to Gloria Guerrero. Gloria Guerrero, Gloria Guerrero, the woman whose five-and-a-half-year-old daughter died, a daughter named Alondra.

A GOVERNMENT THAT BUILDS CEMETERIES

I used to buy gigantic marbles for my children, of the sort called *bombachas,* so that they wouldn't choke on them in case they put them in their mouths. When my children played on the floor with these marbles, they invariably rolled down to the northeastern corner of the room, an indication of the dangerous inclination of our building.

Gloria Guerrero de Terán had six children. Since Thursday the 19th of September she has five, and she has herself and her husband, Eduardo Gabriel Terán. But she no longer has Alondra.

When Gloria pronounces the name *Alondra,* a word that means lark, I hear a beating of wings. Gloria tightens her fists, closes her hands to hold the child back, and around her the wings make a silky sound. Those wings sweep the breeze, they lift her hair, they fly to the ceiling, they brush her ears, they flutter around the words that tremble in the air as soon as they are said. Then Gloria bursts into tears that wet her cheeks, her neck, her knees. And the tears roll down, but they do not take away the pain. Nothing does, not even that weeping that drains her, tiring her and emptying her. On her lap is a bandaged arm:

We all plunged down, and I don't know what fell over me—who cares?—a piece of wall or ceiling. I suppose my arms were thrown backward because I fell on my back, with lots of rubble on top. I felt great anguish because I had no air to breathe. I heard my husband shouting for help because he was dying.

I got mad, and I was thinking, "How can I call for help if I am suffocating?" I turned my head so as not to hear him, and some of the plaster I had on my face fell down. I made an effort and shouted, "How can you ask me to help you when I'm suffocating? I'm suffocating!"

I don't know how he managed to get up and remove the debris from my face. I was able to breathe. He helped me sit up, and I held my arm, which was hanging like a rag, and I kept it close to my waist and didn't let go of it. Daniela, five and a half years old, started to shout for help because our house had fallen down. I said to her, "Daniela, please don't shout, daughter; you're going to wake up the neighbors." Daniela stopped shouting. But the one who is shouting now, shouting in between her sobs, is Gloria Guerrero.

"Mama, don't you see that our building fell down?"

"Why don't you call Alondra? She's on the other side . . ."

"No, Mama, Alondra is dead."

"That's not true, she's on the other side; she was asleep, she must have woke up; call her . . ."

My son David had gone out to High School 106, one block away from Nuevo León, and from there he saw our building collapse and ran full of anxiety. Teachers didn't want the kids to go out, trying to avoid a general panic: "But I have to leave; my family is in that building that fell." Behind me I heard his voice: "Where are they, where are they?"

My other three children, Taír, Anisul, and Anuar, were waiting for the bus at the Paseo de la Reforma stop. They saw the building coming down, and they thought we were dead. David, with the assistance of some men, helped us get out. I came out, then my husband, and then a man holding Daniela in his arms.

"Don't take her away; let me have her . . ."

"You can't carry her; just look at your arm . . . She also has to be seen by a doctor . . . Don't worry, I'm just taking her out here."

"Taír, where are your brothers?"

"Mama, I don't know."

"Please, honey, you are scared; calm down, try to think; you were all together, why didn't you hold them by the hand?"

"Mama, they ran."

"Where did they run to?"

"Toward the building."

"No, Taír, think for a moment, sweetie. Why would they run toward the building?"

"Yes, Mama, Anuar wanted to help, he wanted to see if he could help you and Daddy, so he crossed over Paseo de la Reforma and ran."

My husband started to pace on the parking lot, and I said to him, "Please, Eduardo, calm down."

I sat him by one of the jardinieres:

"Sit here; don't leave Taír; I'm going to look for my children."

A woman intervened:

"Señora, you're bleeding, you're not well, let me take you to the ambulance."

"Leave me alone," I shouted. "Don't you see I'm looking for my children."

But some other men took me to an ambulance. They took me to the hospital, and I could no longer look for Alondra.

A HORRIBLE SEARCH OF TEN DAYS

Everyone in the family made posters and flyers with a portrait of Daniela because we had no pictures of Alondra, and they looked very much alike. We stuck the poster on every possible wall with the help of friends. Those were ten days that seemed to be a thousand years. Lying on a hospital bed with a fractured arm, I waited for news about Alondra. Two bones were broken in my arm, the ulna and radius. The doctor said that he had to operate and put in plates and screws until the bone healed in both fractures. He would operate again in a year's time to take the metal out.

MY HUSBAND ASSURED ME THAT ALONDRA HAD NOT SUFFERED

Some air rescue experts, my husband's colleagues, got our neighbor Luciano Vega out, and also his wife, who was badly injured, and their three children, as well as other neighbors from the Nuevo León. Finally they located our apartment. My husband and brother-in-law stayed with them all night until they saw the broken bed, the blue mattress, the flowery sheet, and the body of Alondra on it all.

My husband—maybe to ease my pain, but I suspect it was true—said that a brown dresser, kind of heavy, full of my children's clothing, skidded and hurled itself onto the bed, hitting Alondra on the back of her head. He assured me that Alondra had not suffered; death would have come immediately. I asked my husband to let me embrace her. Dead or alive, she was my daughter and she would always be my daughter; she had been in my womb. I wanted to kiss her and hold her for the last time. But Eduardo swore in the name of our children that he had recognized her perfectly, that it was Alondra, that I shouldn't see her.

I never saw her again, and we took her to the cemetery.

HOW DOES LIFE GET REBUILT?

I look at Gloria Guerrero and I ask, How does life get rebuilt? I see her clutch a piece of tissue, already torn. I know I will never erase her face from my mind; I'll die with her eyes of pain in my forehead. And also the face of Judith, of Salomón Reyes, Andrés Escoto, and so many others. I ask myself what my mother did after Jan's death at age twenty-one. What did she have to do each morning getting up? How did she start her day, putting one foot in front of the other?

I remember that one day she said that the Mexican landscape had helped her, that great extension of arid land to each side of the highways, and the sky spreading above it, and sometimes trees, pines that soar so high and form green pyramids pointing upward. She also said—some afternoon—that she felt that Jan, her only son, was happy wherever he was, and that he kept her company, right by her side, present in the waves of air, in her own breath. "He is in me."

I don't dare say anything to Gloria. Words do not console, only the fortitude of the people who intend to console her. Besides, one month after the earthquake, Gloria's mother died: "I think my tragedy hit her very hard. She loved us so deeply, and she always struggled to keep us united, to keep love and loyalty above our very different personalities. She was seventy-nine years old when she died. I don't know why she had such a great capacity for abnegation. My father died early on, and she continued living as a widow for thirty-two years."

Mixed with Gloria's tears for Alondra are her tears of rage for the way the Nuevo León Building was neglected, for the fact that it was known to have serious structural faults a long time before the earthquake, posing a great danger to residents, without the authorities doing anything about it.

WE WERE VERY AFRAID OF LIVING IN THE NUEVO LEÓN

The fear began with the noise that the elevator cables made. The shafts were lopsided way beyond what is permissible. We residents organized—there were wonderful people who struggled and who are no more—and insisted to the authorities that the building was unsafe. We were always heard in the way you are heard in this country, with deaf ears, with ears that justify a salary.

We asked to be evacuated three years ago, so that the foundations could be strengthened, and a small contracting firm was engaged, owned by a nephew of the president of Banobras. They did not have the technological means to do the job. They excavated all around the building. Two weeks went by, and one day I asked the workers why they were idle, and they told me, "Señora, they haven't paid us; it looks like the company that hired us has gone under."

Months went by, the ditch around the building got filled with water, another company came, and finally the firm headed by *ingeniero* Flores—I think it is Flores González, who received the National Engineering Award, and who had worked on the foundations of the Basílica de Guadalupe—took charge of the job. We were housed for seven or eight months in Suites Tecpan, a part of Tlatelolco considered a hotel, which is absurd, because they have no business putting a hotel in a public housing complex that a presidential decree declared "of social interest."

Before the earthquake, there were 100,000 residents in Tlatelolco, distributed in 114 apartment buildings, including the service quarters on the roofs. The Jalisco and Puebla buildings, called Suites Tecpan, were given as a concession to Gabriel Alarcón as a result of a hidden deal, and he now runs a nightclub there, the only one in Tlatelolco. Some apartments were used by the Teachers Union and some others by the Union of Workers of the Finance Ministry. Some minor bureaucrats used the suites as a hotel, and of course there are some "bachelor apartments." But the population of Tlatelolco is one of families.

THEY TOLD US THAT THE NUEVO LEÓN WAS THE SAFEST BUILDING IN MEXICO CITY

We had a meeting, and we were invited to go back to the building, even though we were all afraid, although we had no inkling of the extent of the danger. The authorities at Banobras displayed blueprints and sketches, using technical terms far beyond the reach of our understanding, telling us in sum that "the Nuevo León is the safest building not in Tlatelolco, but in Mexico City."

It was an infamy, a dreadful trap.

Now, in the process of negotiations with the authorities, we have come to realize that they have no idea what it is that they are in charge of governing, no clue about what they are doing. They have no responsibility, no perspective on their own task. They perceive their jobs as chances to exercise power. The managers of Banobras knew perfectly well that the work they financed did not represent more than 25 percent of what was needed to make the building safe. The other 75 percent lay in the structure of the building, which was never touched.

Everything ended with the creation of a committee of three people who came and went to Banobras and to Sedue and shuffled papers. Now the negotiations have come to such an infamous point that the indemnifications that are offered are higher for household goods than

255

for the life that was lost. Residents are manipulated with the promise of money, and the human aspect of the tragedy goes down the drain.

THE STATE HAS NO ABILITY TO GOVERN, LET ALONE TO BUILD

I am sure that the government is liable, that there was an attitude of heartlessness and corruption that killed people, people who were good and hardworking, young people, children, my child Alondra.

The problem of the Nuevo León is a political problem. The state has no ability to govern, let alone to build. Instead of buildings it creates cemeteries. We are alone. The government is sitting on a heap of ashes. A catastrophe comes, and the official response is as miserable and castrated as the government itself.

A small group of people ask ourselves what we are going to do. A letter to Attorney General García Ramírez begging him for information on the state of the investigation? How long will it take the government to respond to the dossier we submitted, with all the affidavits and necessary proofs? "Gentlemen, here are the facts, with documents that prove the veracity of our claims, so that official responsibility will be established and the guilty parties tried." How long will it take?

Will this government have the human stature to see itself as accountable? Can it punish its own? And which officials will these be? How many of them? What, has there ever been an indictment even against a little contractor? Has anybody read in the paper about the detention of any builder or the owners of construction companies? I could be poorly informed, but I haven't heard of anything like that.

All those valuable people—young men and women, and Alondra— will have to wait for justice to be done. I know what I am up against. We will have to fight hard for a long time. We are in pursuit of a dream.

THE ONLY HELP WE HAVE COMES FROM ORDINARY PEOPLE

The U.S. team arrived at the Nuevo León Building on the fifth or perhaps the fourth night. Around two or three in the morning, they turned off all the machinery, cranes, and bulldozers, and they placed a number of sensors throughout the ruins.

The specialists asked for a patrol car, and through its bullhorn they spoke to the survivors:

"Attention, survivors of entrance C as in Carlos, please knock ten times."

The sensors could detect—like an electrocardiogram—the slightest sound.

"Attention, survivors of entrance D as in David, please knock ten times."

Later they were asked to knock five times, then three, then again ten.

It was late at night and very dark. The voice could be heard with clarity:

"Attention, survivors of entrance . . ."

We all were in a state of suspense. For two and a half hours the sensors made their markings, on yards and more yards of paper. They contained diminutive signals. Many survivors were detected crushed between the walls of entrances C, D, E, and F. The North American technicians asked me to translate a message that I will never forget.

"Survivors, we know you are there—do not despair, we are working, and we will get you out."

Jesus, everyone embraced each other crying. Cuauhtémoc Abarca cries and points to the pit where the Nuevo León once stood:

This is full of memories, and I am saving them there, all of them. At the same time that I have witnessed the people's willingness to help, I have also seen the sad and lamentable ineptitude of the authorities.

It's been two months and people are in the same situation, in spite of the fact that we in Tlatelolco are in a relatively privileged situation as compared to Colonia Morelos, where they don't even have tents. And with the cold weather coming!

The U.S. team helped us rescue twenty-three living persons in the areas where the sensors registered sounds. They gave instructions on how to excavate, where to make tunnels. They had experience, just as the Swiss, the French, and the Israelis did. I witnessed how the French helped to get twenty people out with the help of their dogs. I had been there since 7:30 on September 19, eleven minutes after the building fell. My building is the one next door. It tore at your heart to hear the screams.

I started getting in through any opening, following the voices. I would ask, "Is there anyone here, is there anyone here?" From the tenth story, we got out a boy, fourteen or fifteen, with Down's syndrome. He was totally buried, except for his head. It was difficult to move him because we had no idea what was under him, whether rods, a wall, or whether he was on top of something or was only propped up by the cement dust that had covered him. Each time we moved some rubble, he felt pressure on his body. After an hour of work, he managed to explain that his little sister was down there. We finally got him out—I don't know how—and then the little girl, four or five, without a scratch, only covered with dust.

Someone told me, "Listen, Cuauhtémoc, it smells like gas because the pipes are broken." It didn't occur to me that the gas was still connected, and that we were all at risk. The power was still on; at one point I pulled a cable in order to remove a piece of furniture, and I got an electric shock. Everything was wet, with water coming out of all the pipes, and there was broken glass everywhere. We did not even have a pair of gloves for lifting sharp rubble and rods. We worked literally with our fingernails.

People started to come, and they collected buckets so that we could excavate with our hands and get the rubble out, can you imagine? It was impressive to see our impotence. In the middle of the day, a police squad arrived, and soon after you could say good-bye to televisions, VCRs, radios, cameras, including film equipment, even blenders that were pulled out from the apartments.

The police, all they did was to obstruct our work with their pretentious authority. When a bit later the Red Cross crews and the firefighters arrived, we had already organized two small stations for medical care at Teatro Antonio Caso and High School 106. Shortly thereafter, we had to evacuate the station at the high school and send the injured people to the DIF because someone started to shout that the Oaxaca building was about to collapse, and people panicked.

It was insane. I would run from the first-aid station to see how things were going; I would go back to the ruins. Fifteen hours after having made a tunnel to rescue one person who was in the central module of the Nuevo León, we managed to drag him to the left side of the building, to get him out and take him down the heap of rubble. Down below, a stretcher was waiting for him. But when the man saw the pile of slabs, he said he was going back to get his TV. We shouted at him that it was too dangerous, but he insisted, "I want my TV set; I'm going to get it."

He had been saved once, all he needed to do was get on the stretcher and be taken away.

"No, I am fine; I'm just going to get my TV."

Again we yelled at him. We tried to restrain him, but he ran away. He went into the tunnel, caused a cave-in, and was killed.

Get this: I also ran into a woman who would not come out. She was sitting down when I found her, and when I said I was getting her out, she replied, "What kind of woman do you think I am? What makes you think I'm going to be seen like this?" She was stark naked. I told her I was going to get something. But when I came back, she said, "I need a lipstick."

"What, Señora?"

"Lipstick. I need to put some lipstick on."

She was an old lady, about seventy. And so self-conscious! Unbelievable.

I went out to get a tube of lipstick, I don't even know how, and took it to her, and only then she agreed to come out.

Then there were these two women, one forty-five and her mother between sixty and seventy. The mother begged us to take her daughter out first. And the daughter argued, "No, take my mother, she's the most important one."

"Even if you leave me here, please save my daughter."

"Let's see who can be freed up first from what you have on top of you."

We got the daughter out first, after removing a piece of slab and a concrete beam that were pressing her feet. Then we got the señora out, with a broken leg.

We had to struggle fiercely against the rumors. All the people of Tlatelolco were waiting to see their building come down, the Allende, the Chihuahua, the Campeche. The news went from mouth to mouth, provoking sheer terror.

A man named Pacheco Alvarez, the investigator for Sedue here at AISA, on the day that the people of the Nuevo León met with him for the first time, said at the public meeting, "Well, I'll be very happy to listen to your demands, but let me tell you, my speciality as an engineer is in load capacity, and I am afraid there are so many of us in this office that the floor could cave in."

The residents of the Nuevo León stampeded out. They were pulling their hair; some women were in hysterics. From then on, the authorities used these tactics with the public. I was furious at them . . .

You are asking me if the bureaucrats are moved by the suffering of citizens, or if they are afraid. No, man, of course they aren't. They are a bunch of cretins who were never able to listen to the way the residents articulated their problems. Now their biggest worry is how they will shield themselves from responsibility.

Maricarmen told me the other day, "Dr. Abarca, my five children have pneumonia from the dampness and cold of the tents. I'm going to go on a hunger strike to underscore the fact that they haven't taken care of us." And just like Maricarmen, many mothers among the displaced are ready to go on a hunger strike to see if this moves the government to act.

Just a few days ago, I was in Colonia Morelos and saw that they had a wake for a baby who had died. At least here in Tlatelolco, we have the tents donated by the U.S. and Swiss teams, but the people of Colonia Morelos are using oilcloth and plastic sheets with two or three pieces of corrugated roofing material to make some sort of lean-to, but when it rains, the water seeps inside from all sides. Who knows where all that famous national and foreign aid is at this point?

But the people were something else. One day a fat woman in an apron came out of a beaten-up station wagon, calling out, "Here's some rice, chicken soup, and boiled chicken. Anybody?"

"Yes, Señora, we haven't eaten. Thank you!"

It was six in the afternoon, and we stood in line before the enormous pots full to the brim with a delicious rice with tortillas. People like that kept us going for the first two weeks. Ladies like this, who looked like they worked in humble eateries.

The Chinese-Mexican community also brought big pails of fried rice, out of this world. But international food aid, cheeses and cans, I can assure you, never made it to the camps. We saw pure water in plastic pouches, which probably came through foreign aid, but we never saw one single package of food of the kind that all those airplanes were supposed to have brought. The police and the army, those were the shameless crooks who took advantage of the situation.

The ordinary people, our people, are admirable. The large majority were young men, eighteen, twenty, twenty-two. One night, I had a conversation with them.

I asked, "Well, and you, do you live here?"

"No."

"So where do you live, where do you come from?"

"Well, Santa Fe, Mixcoac, Xochimilco."

"Is there a van that comes and brings you here?"

"No, we pay our own fare, and we come every evening."

Such awesome kids, God! Working all night long. And then you get morons like Carrillo Arena who dare say, "Let's get rid of all these dudes from the gangs; they're only wasting our time." It's as idiotic as it is criminal.

In fact, I would turn this around: It's about time we got rid of all those Neanderthals in politics.

Alicia Trueba

The organizer of the collection center of the French School of Jardines del Pedregal, María Fernanda de Pérez Priego, tells how they got organized:

The only thing I did was to ask Father Anselmo Murillo for space. He is the parish priest of the Santa Cruz Church, here in El Pedregal. He asked the sisters of the French School, and they gave me this hall that had just been carpeted, just imagine. It was pristine. I don't know how it will look at the end of this.

I called Channel 13 and Televisa asking for help, and very soon we had packages, bags, cartons, and more cartons. There are about forty neighbors working together here. The children, between seven and fourteen years of age, are in charge of moving and classifying the cartons. They come in early in the morning and don't leave until five or six, because they don't have school right now.

Some of us organize the food, others the medicine, which has been looked at by a woman doctor who is working here whenever she's free, and others classify the clothes. We have received lots of clothes, and even some strange things: thirty wigs, many bathing suits, costumes, a wedding dress!

The Nader, Sampson, Riquelme, and Corbacho families have been making between five and six thousand sandwiches every day. It can be said quickly, but to do all that every member of each family has to cooperate, as well as boys between seventeen and twenty-four and couples who volunteer to drive. Some of the young guys get out of work at eight in the evening and spend the night distributing drinking water. With that kind of response you can do anything, and of course, we've also had the support of César, who has been here from the very first day.

"Yes," interjects Sr. César Molina, a burly man who smiles even when it's eight at night and he's been working since nine in the morning. "We don't ever leave, not even to eat. We lived on sandwiches for a week until Sra. María Luisa started bringing hot food from her house. My wife calls me on the phone to say I should send her a picture because my children don't remember who I am. But there is too much work, and my locksmith shop can wait a bit longer."

Sra. Pérez Priego is slender, has very fine features, and wears her blond hair in a ponytail, looking no older than eighteen. She's pretty.

Today we sent water to Netzualcóyotl and Aragón, and also to Colonia de los Doctores, where they need it badly because the tank trucks are selling it for four hundred pesos a bucket.

Even when she's so evidently tired, she leafs through a notebook where she records all donations. I wish I had recorded everything, she says, but I know it's impossible, and besides, the donors are not interested in getting credit. But look at it, Alberto and Susana Laposse from El Globo send us seven thousand sweet rolls every day.

Bancomer sent five hundred plastic buckets with lids, and that's how we can send clean water. When they come back, we wash them, sterilize them, and send them out again. We are also sending water in sterilized plastic pouches, so that they can reach the people who are still trapped in the buildings. We seal them with a candle flame, or we send it to a house that has a sealing machine.

The company Spin S.A. gave us ten gallons of clorizide, a powerful disinfectant, which you use at a ratio of about 15 cubic inches for each 2,600 gallons of water. From Corrugados Eureka we received 8,325 cardboard boxes, and there are many, many more donors, she says as she goes over her careful notes. When formaldehyde was scarce and the possiblity of using vinegar was mentioned, the Domecq company offered its entire stock of Los Reyes vinegar.

Fortunately, formaldehyde came from the United States just in time because the cadavers had decomposed. This is why a group of señoras here in the Pedregal devoted themselves to making face masks, buying lots of rolls of cloth. Forty thousand have been made and delivered directly to the workers. Since they are makeshift masks, they have to be changed every three hours, because they soon are saturated with dust. Now with each package of masks we include a small can of Vicks Vaporub so that workers can put a dab of it on the cloth and protect themselves from the stench and the dust. A real collaboration has sprung up at all levels.

Sr. Alejandro Cornejo, owner of the Rattan furniture factories, is a great man; he has allowed us to use his warehouse, his trucks, and his drivers; and he himself has come at night to distribute water, water that his wife boils and prepares so that it will reach people in optimal condition.

There's something I'd like to tell you. Yesterday, when the water was distributed at Calzada de Tlalpan and Taxqueña, I was told that a person from the delegation came to stop all the rescue work, so they halted the machines and the workers, because the President was coming to inspect, and they wanted to sweep the street. How do you like that?

We have been distributing lunches among 8 or ten thousand workers, especially at the Centro Médico and Hospital Juárez. We fill each brown bag with a sandwich, cookies, a can of juice, and a cup of Jello. When we deliver, we ask the head of the crew of workers where we can leave the boxes, because workers eat as shifts change. Everything has to be very well wrapped. There is a plague of rats running loose.

When we found out that ISSSTE and IMSS were bringing food, we told the workers, but they all asked us to please continue with the deliveries, because they didn't trust the government to feed them, and in fact, they were sure they'd get no food.

We get calls from all the shelters, and we organize to bring them what they need. They're all very conscientious, and when we send more than they need, they ship it back.

Some days ago, we began to distribute breakfasts to the families who are living on the median strip in front of Hospital Juárez: tea, chocolate, and sweet rolls from El Globo. We deliver them at five in the morning, well not I, but a group of señoras from El Pedregal.

My plan is now to create a service whereby we will be able to deliver grocery bags on a regular basis to the displaced families who most need it. I really hope that we'll be able to do this.■

THE VICTIMS' COORDINATING COUNCIL, CENTER OF AN URGENT STRUGGLE

Over a cup of strawberry *atole*, the most delicious I've ever tasted in my life, Lucrecia Mercado and Cuauhtémoc Abarca talked to me about the problems of Tlatelolco and the Victims' Coordinating Council (CUD), composed of the following groups: Union of Neighbors and Victims 19th of September, Council of Residents' Organizations of Tlatelolco, Popular Tenants' Union of Colonia Morelos, Peña de Morelos, Union of Neighbors of Colonia Guerrero, Salvatierra Encampment, Union of

Neighbors of Colonia Doctores, Union of Neighbors and Victims of Center City, Arcos de Belén Center, Colonia Navarte, Colonia Alvaro Obregón, Colonia Alfa, Colonia Faja de Oro, Colonia Valle Gómez, Colonia Peralvillo, Military Medical Center, Colonia Asturias, Colonia Nicolás Bravo, Colonia Obrera, and the Nineteenth of September Garment Workers' Union.

Lucrecia Mercado asserts that the Victims' Coordinating Council was capable of convening a march to Los Pinos three days after it was formed. Thirty thousand people marched more than two miles from the Angel of Independence to Los Pinos, shouting:

"We do not care how, we need housing now."
"No more hunger, no more thirst, we need houses, homes come first."
"Do not pay the foreign debt, let's build decent homes instead."
"We're going to pitch a tent, for you to live in, Mr. President."
"Carrillo Arena, watch your tail, the people want you to go to jail."

I believe, says Cuauhtémoc Abarca, that meeting the needs of the victims constitutes an elementary obligation for the President. The first time we sent a written request, which was even published in the newspapers, we were received by his aides and his personal secretary, since the President himself couldn't make it. How is it possible that the President could be vacationing in Cuautla, as his aides told us, instead of taking responsiblity for national priorities? The government, even the President himself, said in every possible way that the number one priority at this moment was attention to the quake victims, but when the victims themselves turn up at Los Pinos to tell the President, "Look, these are our needs," he turns out not to be at home! What kind of a country is this?

Seated next to Cuauhtémoc Abarca, Lilia Mercado adds:

Twenty-five buildings at Tlatelolco have been evacuated. We went to live with relatives and friends because from the start we were not considered victims. I lived in the Chihuahua building. Last Thursday night I was still sleeping in my apartment. I live on the twelfth floor where nothing serious happened; it's just that you can tell that the floor is no longer level because the building has tilted.

TLATELOLCO AND THE NUEVO LEÓN, ONE SINGLE PROBLEM

On Friday at ten in the morning, the army came by and urged us to leave five buildings; 4,000 apartments and 500 service quarters had to be evacuated. If we calculate five members per family, almost 25,000 displaced. So it's not just a matter of the Nuevo León Building; it's a question of Tlatelolco in its entirety.

The residents of modules A and B of the Nuevo León, which remain standing, are in a situation that is very different from that of their neighbors in the other buildings in the complex, because there were no dead people there. They were able to take out their furniture and receive a series of benefits that the rest of the residents of Tlatelolco never saw.

The residents of the Nuevo León forgot that many people from many of the other Tlatelolco buildings rushed to their side and worked in the rescue operation. It was always a separatist building, self-excluded and apathetic. Nobody came to the meetings. I guess the residents considered themselves part of Paseo de la Reforma and not part of Tlatelolco.

Plácido Domingo gave considerable publicity to the condition of that building, and ever since then the public has divided the Nuevo León from the rest of the complex, as if to say, "There are two problems, one, the Nuevo León, and two, Tlatelolco." But we say, "That's not right; there's only one problem, Tlatelolco."

Cuauhtémoc Abarca doesn't like the word *leader*. But to walk with him through the gardens and passageways of Tlatelolco is to realize that everyone comes to him: "Cuauhtémoc, can you get me . . . ? Cuauhtémoc, do you know where I can . . . ? Cuauhtémoc, if you come with us, we'll get it. Cuauhtémoc, come here."

Cuauhtémoc says he wants to invite two or three journalists for brunch, and before he can blink, there are eight señoras from different buildings offering their kitchen and their dining room: "Do you want *chilaquiles*? Eggs *motuleño* style? Breaded chicken breasts? *Atole*? Foamy chocolate? I make the best coffee in the world."

As far as the social life of Tlatelolco is concerned, I had limited participation, says Cuauhtémoc, who, like the last Aztec prince he is named after, is short and dark, with straight black hair and a ready smile. I arrived with my family fifteen years ago to live in the type A buildings. From the Chihuahua I moved to the Yucatán, and now I am its president. Fortunately the type A buildings are the ones that have presented the fewest problems.

More than administration, I used to take care of immediate problems like trash, gas, water, and so on. We never felt that there was a need for a neighbors' organization.

Through self-management, the association that represents the residents is enabled to make disbursements according to the budget for the building, to establish priorities, to point to what needs to be done, and to listen to the people, but nothing like that ever happened, and in this sense, one of the most aloof of all buildings was the Nuevo León. The problem was not the expenditure, but how to justify it.

Our representative commission resorted to AISA and Fonhapo to ask for information as simple as this: "Could you present to us the state of our building's account to see how much we earn and how much we are spending?" But AISA had no idea of how much came in and how much went out, and they gave us an absurd explanation that Tlatelolco was like a very big bag, and whatever came from any building was deposited there, and whenever there was a need, the money went out, but nobody really knew how much.

It is joyful and reassuring to listen to the poise with which Cuauhtémoc Abarca speaks and to listen to his clear and strong voice while drinking strawberry *atole*. One can see how, because of his advice, many buildings became self-managed. The Yucatán, where Cuauhtémoc lives, set the example. Afterward, given the good experience they had, others followed: the Mariano Escobedo, the Ramón Corona, the Santos Degollado, the Leandro Valle, the Francisco Zarco, the San Luis Potosí, the Tlaxcala, the Michoacán, the Nayarit, the Sonora, and many others. Cuauhtémoc Abarca gave rise to a whole generation of self-managed buildings.

THE LIVES OF THOUSANDS OF RESIDENTS IN THE CAPITAL REMAIN DISRUPTED

One million children were left without schools, says Cuauhtémoc Abarca. Millions of residents in the capital city are without water. More than a thousand buildings are half collapsed or in danger of collapsing, presenting a grave danger to pedestrians, and nobody has ordered their demolition. Only the Department of the Federal District can believe that a sky blue awning made of tin can give protection against tons of concrete. I hope we will not have more deaths to regret.

More than fifteen thousand residents of the Federal District had their telephone lines cut on September 19 and are still without service because the lines have not been repaired. The lives of thousands of Mexicans are as disrupted as in the immediate days after the earthquake, and for many the situation has worsened because there is no longer a group of enthusiastic neighbors comforting them and helping them out.

The head of the Department of the Federal District, Ramón Aguirre, received us. He listened with profound attention and respect and went so far as to say that he was in solidarity with us and our formulation of the problems. Two or three times very diplomatically he stuck it to Carrillo Arena. The meetings that we had by ourselves with Carrillo Arena amounted to five or six hours of mockery, because we never got to first base, we never heard a commitment to anything.

In contrast, the secretary of labor and social protection, Arsenio Farell, who has the reputation of being a real ogre, was extremely courteous. I believe that the government is fearful because it's got its shirttail hanging out. It is known that Farell opposed the unionization of the seamstresses three years ago.

The head of the DDF had requested that we bring our list of demands in the form of questions, so that we would have a concrete answer. Carrillo Arena didn't like the idea one bit, but he had to accept it because it was coming from Ramón Aguirre, and the undersecretary of government was monitoring the process.

In the case of the Nuevo León Building, the first specific set of questions was, "What is the number of the dossier? Which desk is responsible for the investigation? What progress has been made? When can we come to have our depositions taken?" But there were no answers for those questions either.

I personally filed a special suit in the Attorney General's Office, but there has been no response. They tell us that it is a matter of such gravity and importance that it has been placed directly on the attorney general's desk. This is why, on November 2, on a very big banner we painted a skull and wrote a little verse illustrating our problem: "Eibenschutz dug the hole; Carrillo Arena buried them all; President Mickey keeps playing dumb; the attorney general says, 'Nothing's wrong.'" Eibenschutz, the director of Fonhapo, was the man who blocked the project to rebuild the foundations of the buildings, so he earned the banners: "Eibenschutz, murderer."

Now the Nuevo León case is dossier 6865–85 in the hands of the attorney general. According to Gabino Fraga, the investigation is open and will be pursued to the hilt until those liable for the substandard construction of the Nuevo León Building are duly punished. But we have never been able to obtain a copy because the importance of the case is such that the matter is classified, kept away from us, the affected ones. Even now, the authorities manipulate our ignorance.

Fraga, the representative of the federal government, showed up with many collaborators who filled the stage of Teatro Antonio Caso: representatives of ISSSTE, the banks, and Infonavit. When he came in, people applauded. But later things changed.

I told him, "First of all, we must establish who is responsible . . ."

Fraga retorted, "I want to leave that for later, because first of all I want to express my condolences to the Sr. Presidente, who has been deeply affected by what happened to you."

That was a detonator. The audience was furious. The public rose to its feet, and a Tlatelolcan dared to say, "The only thing I want is for the SEP to return to me the school certificates of my children. That's the only memory I'll have of them, because they died buried in the Nuevo León."

That's all people needed. On their feet, they began to shout, "Justice, assassins!"

Fraga shuddered with fear; he surely thought that the mob was ready to assault him.

Someone shouted, "Beristáin is one of the principal authors of the Nuevo León tragedy." In complicity with Eibenschutz, he handled the matter of AISA, Banobras, and Fonhapo to strengthen the foundations of the building, and it was he who declared that the Nuevo León was the safest building in Mexico after the Latinoamericana tower and the Monument to the Revolution. "I just saw that son of a bitch and if I find him again, I'll kill him!"

Fraga ended the meeting and left, trying to save his ass. Carrillo Arena told us, visibly enraged, "You are a bunch of professional agitators who have no business pressuring the President of the Republic. You are bad citizens with no moral conscience because you don't realize what kind of crisis the country is in, and you simply want to be against the government." All this he said shaking his fists and with a large number of bodyguards behind him, to intimidate the people.

We were not intimidated, only small-minded people are afraid of a swine like that. Not us. In Mexico, anyone who stands for his or her rights is called an agitator, a traitor to the homeland—or worse, a traitor in the service of a foreign power. That's always the story, that we are "in collusion with foreign powers." But I'll tell you who is a traitor. A traitor is the one who, while having the full power of an elected government and every opportunity to govern, doesn't lead in favor of the country and the Mexican people.

I ask myself, "Who betrayed our country, López Portillo or Demetrio Vallejo? Isn't the one who used power to get vulgarly rich and to satisfy his base interests at the expense of the citizens a traitor?" I think that many Mexicans are sick and tired of stupid officials. The worst part of our country is its political caste.

NOBODY OWNS NOTHING

Unfortunately, behavior is the product of a long education, says Alberto Beltrán. Humans do not change just because an earthquake has shaken the earth. People may change for a while, but the way they were formed since they were children has more weight. At this very moment landlords are proving their selfishness in evicting their tenants, just as in Colonia Algarín the owners of sweatshops tried to pull their machinery out before they paid any attention to the trapped bodies.

Solidarity cannot be stretched, just like that. If danger exists, a form of solidarity is evident, but once danger is over, it disappears.

Unfortunately, I am not willing to believe that a generous expression of solidarity that lasted for a few days may be the harbinger of a social transformation. We have lived in a state of emergency—the equivalent of a state of war—and people have been united in excavating tunnels, distributing clothes, and passing out food, without any regard to social class or background, but all this has been momentary.

I don't believe that decentralization will occur either. It's not easy for people to go away. They will leave when stable jobs exist outside the Federal District. More than that, what is important in the near future is to create new sources of employment for folk who have never left their communities all over the republic, so that the number of migrants who come to the Federal District will not continue to grow chaotically. What is most important is for people to stay where they are.

For more than twenty-five years, I have said in my political cartoons that Mexico City should be moved, and by that I mean that the federal powers should leave the City of Mexico. If the President and all the ministries were relocated, an enormous number of people would move away, but we would still retain the economic life of the area, the cultural life, and the basic structure of social relations.

I am not pessimistic, but I am convinced that Mexican society moves slowly, little by little, not in leaps. Idealists thought that the Mexican Revolution could change the whole country, but they should see the present state of social inequities and the unjust distribution of resources; this is why I say that an earthquake cannot change our landscape.

Those who have discovered that they are "Christians" and are making sandwiches will soon be increasing their earnings and hiding their capital or placing it in bank accounts in the United States. I don't believe, as you romantically do, that values have changed.

Heroism is momentary, and by that I mean bourgeois heroism, because I am convinced that the people of Mexico are heroic every day of their lives: to eat badly, to live badly, to sleep badly, that is their daily heroism; they practice it every day. They are heroes who prop up our critical economic situation with their poverty while the bosses pile up the profits.

In this moment of crisis, five-star restaurants are full, and airplanes going abroad are full, all of which means that there are always people who continue to make a lot of money. But for workers, there are wage freezes, and these are the source of the country's stability. Living under such conditions takes a heroic stance, not facing a sudden disaster, and it's all the greater because it is unacknowledged, a cold heroism. We've got to realize that the economic crisis is not borne by everyone; it's borne by the poor.

TEPITO'S VICTIMS: THE NEW ONES AND THE OLD ONES
THIRTY-SEVEN COOPERATIVES FORMED AFTER THE EARTHQUAKE

Tepito is one of the most important centers for the manufacture of shoes. There is a whole fucking bunch of artisans here. Also, people make trophies here. Shoes are put together. Besides there are blacksmiths who make gates and window grills, as well as electric workshops, and at many intersections you find mechanics who can fix anything and leather artisans, like José Vega, the guy who's walking toward us.

In Tepito you have three kinds of victims: the ones who lost their homes; the ones who lost their jobs because their workshops or stores were damaged; and the ones who have been always victims, who have neither homes nor work. Tepito is not a barrio; it is really a town in itself, with 350,000 inhabitants or more.

Every little while the flaps of the tent are opened. Inside the tent there is a table, three folding chairs, and a cot with a pillow and a good blanket. The conversation is interrupted every three minutes. Inquisitive faces look in:

"Is the water all gone?"

"All gone, Señora. Do you need it for the baby?"

"Well, yes . . ."

"We can only give you two or three bottles, of the little ones donated by the gringos. There's been no water truck, we are sorry."

The poor woman. What the fuck! There is no water; this is crazy. Yesterday the people from the Chamber of Deputies came. We had written a letter asking for the removal of several of them. And yesterday they tossed out that son of a bitch, Fabre del Rivero.

Once again, a questioning face:

"Would you like a little cup of chocolate? A little roll?"

They bring the chocolate in plastic cups that read "Stelaris," "Continental Acapulco," "Hyatt." The chocolate is too sweet.

"And these cups?"

"Someone lifted them from the hotels and brought them here, I think. So what d'you think? We got to that fucking asshole, tried to teach him a lesson. Hey, what's the matter with you? Don't leave all those cookies here."

They brought us four cups full of animal crackers along with the chocolate.

"Take two of them. Take them, bro. There are too many fucking cookies."

"A roll?"

"No, thanks. Stop screwing around now. Let me talk a while. Take the cookies away, what the heck. What, do you want me to get fat?"

The man who speaks like this is not from Tepito. He is Felipe Ehrenberg, the painter, with his brown, broad-brimmed felt hat, his Zapata-like mustache on fleshy lips, and a gold earring that shines, sexy, under his curly golden hair:

I came here because these people have been my friends for a long time. They are my compadres; they invite me to their fiestas, their daughter's sweet fifteen, the ball, the *posada* at Christmastime, any good old party. I came on the 19th to see how they had fared, and I stayed.

This is the Díaz de León Center for Assistance, in the Díaz de León cul-de-sac, at the corner of González Ortega, in Colonia Morelos in Tepito. This is not an encampment—don't be a sucker—it's a collection center. We collect water, we receive prepared food sent to us by volunteers, five or six people who are in charge of serving three meals a day, and other things, like disposable diapers, Kleenex, sanitary napkins, baby bottles, baby oil, talcum powder.

We have eight warehouse workers, and they are busy, let me tell you. They receive food in bulk and have to prepare bags of groceries with a little bit of this and a little bit of that. Every two days we distribute bags that contain rice, beans, powdered milk, a few cans. Cleaning brigades leave from the center every once in a while, as well as the crews that collect the donations. Others keep vigil all night here. I sleep here; I keep watch all night. Besides, there are some trucks arriving from the interior at two, three, or four in the morning with a load of food, and someone has to welcome them, thank them, give them a little coffee, chat for a bit, keep them informed.

"More chocolate? Another little roll?"

"No, honey, no more, thanks."

"A little tamale?"

"Thanks, we're full."

"*Migas?* They came out delicious."

"Honey, we're trying to talk. These people are in a hurry."

A very attractive woman with long silky black hair, serene and sedate like no one else is sitting close to Felipe Ehrenberg. Around us there is chaos: someone yells, someone comes in, someone interrupts, someone comes and someone goes, someone rushes by, someone asks a question, and Felipe is at the center. But the woman sits still and mute.

I met Felipe last Saturday, says Dolores Campos with her serene voice. I came to interview him about the expropriation. The interview is being published in the supplement of *Siempre,* directed by Carlos Monsiváis. I promised to bring him the cups that I had collected with a friend of mine, and now I have decided to help out with the street children, who have nothing to do and have no school to go to because it fell down.

I study in the Sor Juana Cloister, and I work with Carlos Monsiváis. I want to start some activities here to keep the kids involved. I'll collect some educational materials, and I'll teach them games, and little by little I'll try to introduce some lessons that may correspond to their level in school, especially in math and Spanish.

Felipe, who has left the tent momentarily, argues with someone: "You jerk! What a sucker! Why did you do that? Get with it, will you? Look, we can't have this kind of bullshit going on, you see what I mean? Are you in outer space or what? Leave those mothers where they are, crazy lunatics. And you shut up. Come back tomorrow and help out."

He comes back into the tent as cool as if he had just taken a shower. Outside someone is singing, ". . . but I am still the king."

My presence here has only served to channel the attention that we have received from the government and from private people, especially young guys. Enrique Pérez Guarneros (I don't know why everybody in Tepito is named Enrique) has accepted the responsibility of helping his people, the people of Tepito. A crew of six or seven dudes learned quickly how to be efficient and then how to be totally selfless, because it is not easy, after collecting all that stuff, to know how to give it away, when you have never had anything yourself.

In Tepito there are two kinds of organizations: the new ones and the ones that were here before the earthquake, many of which are cooperatives with a long history, or the associations of tenants or street vendors, or other commercial ventures. There are about 320 cooperatives and some thirty-seven that were created after the earthquake. Tepito, believe it or not, is a rich place; there are people here who know how to count their money.

In another area of Tepito, at Granaditas 36, Miguel Galán is another leader who has been working with the people, in a different way. I can proudly say that the idea of expropriation came out of Tepito. The Cuauhtémoc Delegation keeps sending staff, but when they are going, we are already coming back, you know what I'm saying? There are fifty-eight people working with me, full time, and very active. The idea for an expropriation of lots was an emergency measure. We have worked day and night on this. It is obvious that folks can get impatient very quickly if they don't see results.

The other day they brought us a tent, just a beauty, state-of-the-art. But since we didn't need it yet, it was just sitting there, in a corner. Then a bunch of little kids came and said they wanted to use it, but someone decided he was going to be the watchdog of the tent. The kiddies came and told me about it, so I said to the other dudes:

"Don't you have enough with the authorities of the delegation; you also want to play tyrant? The tent is there; nobody's using it; what are the kids going to do to it if they play inside it?" So for five or six days the kids were having a ball with the shiny tent.

We established some schedules, but we could not keep them with any degree of rigidity, because we did not anticipate the exhaustion of the people. At the beginning we were the diaper specialists, man. Any señora that needed diapers could come and get them here. Then we said they would be distributed between such and such an hour. And then the problems came:

"No, Señora, sorry but it is after ten and the diapers are given out before ten."

"Oh, I didn't know. My son is sick."

I'd have to intervene:

"What bull is this? Stop being a sucker! If the señora comes from the other side of the expressway and has a child with diarrhea, give her the fucking diapers. This is not what schedules are for. You hear me?"

You have to make assistance flexible and generous, without it being chaotic. But people need to know that if they need to, they can knock on your door at any hour and there will be a response. I personally had to fire the substitute deputy for the third district, who was coming here to sell favors. The name of this troglodyte is Mendizábal Mejía. I got him to leave.

Here in Tepito all the letters were addressed to the PRI representatives, because there is an ingrained habit of talking to the party people before talking to anyone else. People would ask him, "Where are the vaccines?"

And he'd say, "You don't want those vaccines. Very often vaccinations cause the opposite reaction of what you want."

Can you imagine someone more asinine? I shouted at him; "You better shut up, you asshole! What do you have to offer? Or are you here to campaign?"

"And who invited you here? You are not even from Tepito."

"Your fucking mother, you witless ass. Here you have to say what you mean, and you have to work."

People were impatient, so they got him out. He left in a rush. But as he was leaving he still yelled at me, "Tomorrow you'll know the meaning of power."

And I answered, "Tomorrow you'll know the meaning of strength."

He came back the next morning, and all of us kicked him out again.

When the bureaucrats have something to say or to offer, we open our doors. Nobody else is welcome here. Four days ago Ratón Macías came to distribute clothes from a very big truck. Nobody needs clothes anymore, and we ourselves have been taking clothes to the shelters. Here in Tepito everybody is wearing clothes from Polanco and Las Lomas. They can't stand it any longer; the clothes suffocate them. And here comes this boxer Macías to distribute clothes like an idiot, along with bottle caps and toothpicks from his campaign.

I had to tell him, "You know what, Ratoncito? If you want to help, bring some tents, will you? Ladies and gentlemen, you all heard the Ratón Macías say he's coming back the day after tomorrow with tents. Remember this. The one who promises in vain, loses."

Then that delegate Fabre del Rivero came here, with a big fucking bunch of bodyguards; he had no idea what he was getting into. We closed the doors and didn't let him out until he had heard us good and clear. But even if he had been able to listen to us, that moron had to go. We definitely aimed to get to the President at any cost. And because of a man named Zorrilla, a very nice guy who works in the President's office, we contacted Emilio Carrillo Gamboa, personal secretary to the President.

Carrillo Gamboa received me, and I spoke with him for two and a half hours. He asked me twenty questions about things he wanted to know, and the next day we spoke to the President for 48 minutes. He received us knowing that we were talking expropriation, man. That's why I say that the idea of expropriation is native to Tepito. And that's the way it should be!

AY TEPITO, DON'T CRACK!

The problem of reconstruction is for titans. Look, people live in rooms roughly ten by ten feet. There are people who make a loft with poles and boards, and then have room for one more cousin or brother or more. That is tough, living like that. There are a lot of problems when you live in such close quarters: fights and blows. There is one bathroom for many housing units.

Since the rent was frozen, between 60 and 150 pesos, the owners don't worry about any improvements. I really don't know how the government is going to manage even if they want to build decent housing; there simply are not enough lots for so many families.

There are more people than you can shake a stick at. In a street with ten tenements, you find two thousand people. Besides, some of those folks like to live like that, without privacy, without a sense of decorum. But make no mistake about it, honey. In this colonia there are people who carry credit cards: Carnet, Liverpool, Sears, Suburbia. They have money, they could move to apartments, but they enjoy this life, being all bunched together, the promiscuity. It will be necessary to reeducate them.

Our normal job is to maintain a dorm for eight alcoholic or derelict men. We give them a bed, coffee, and a sandwich. On weekdays, we also have AA meetings and lectures. Next year we're planning to open an alcoholic rehab center, and then we'll be able to admit them until they recover.

IF THEY TEACH US HOW, WE CAN BUILD THE HOUSES OURSELVES

"If they send us someone to teach us, we're capable of rehabbing our own homes," says Antonio Peña Lara. "We're not afraid of work; we are ready to do it with these hands."

From the improvised tents in front of building number 62 of Penitenciaría Street at the corner of Tapicería in Colonia Morelos, between ten and fifteen people come out.

Says Antonio Peña Lara, "No one will get us out of here."

His wife, Reyna Cándida Lara, explains, "We can't go to the shelters because we will lose our home, and all our stuff is here leaning against the wall.

"It's good for the landlord to get rid of us. But we won't let him. We'd like to get technical assistance, and with that, whatever an engineer says we have to do, we can keep the house in good shape.

"We've had experts galore: four engineers, all of them saying something different. One says that the building is about to collapse; another says that all it needs is stanchions; and a third one tells us that the structure is sound. 'Wow,' he says, 'I've seen a lot worse.' And the fourth comes to say, 'We need to demolish.' They all promised, 'We're coming tomorrow to make a final assessment.' But we're still waiting. We've been out in the street for eight days. Thank God it hasn't rained, only a bit."

To sleep in the street costs nothing. Many of the residents of Colonia Morelos have poured onto the street. They sleep under spreads and sheets used for improvised roofs. Colonia Morelos is located just after kilometer zero of Canal del Desagüe, after the old Lecumberri prison on the left.

"We're not leaving this colonia. I've been here for twenty years. We will not be moved. Even if we are hungry.

"Don Melitón arrives with pouches of water, and the people of DIF bring breakfast. Okay, so those have come only twice, but look, there are others more fucked up than we are. This bale of clothes (a very big blue striped sheet full of rags) needs to be returned. Two señoras of the tenement next door, number 56, chose a few garments, but nobody else did. The food that they bring to us we heat up on these woodstoves. They have come from the UAM, UNAM, and Crea bringing us more clothes than food, and we no longer need it. We hope they can give it to people who can really use it."

Antonio Peña Lara is a lathe operator. "My wife Reina Cándida, my seven children, and I used to live in two rooms, one that was living room, kitchen, and dining room and the other a bedroom. Ah, but we had a full bathroom. I saw acts of looting. Since the building is empty, it's very easy to go in. Last night, some dudes were on the third floor, but the guards kicked them out. There are other thieves who are going around in a red Mustang and a Ford patrol car number 1106 of the police, which was seen on the Street of Miguel Domínguez and at Penitenciaría 12."

"Hey, you shouldn't say that," some people tell him. "They can screw you for it."

"Let them. It's been proved. And besides, what else can they do to me after what has happened? Put down my name, Antonio Peña Lara."

THE THIEVES COME FROM OUTSIDE

Neighbors protect each other; they have united; they are taking care of one another. The ones who steal come from the outside, from other colonias, La Moctezuma, Romero Rubio, Tepito.

Before, says Antonio Peña Lara, we greeted each other, but the earthquake and having to go out and defend our interests together has let us get to know each other really well. Before, we were very isolated. We didn't talk, we didn't know what made us laugh, or what happened when we were sick, but now we are defending our houses together because the landlords are taking advantage of the situation and are raising the rent from 15,000 to 60,000 pesos. That's why we can't go out to look for a new home.

At new places, they are asking for a cosigner and a three-month rent deposit. And they don't want to see either children or dogs or parrots or any other pet. (A woman laughs, and I think that this is one of the few instances of laughter I can write about in these last eight days.) We belong to the lower class. We were almost in the middle class, but we've been pushed back with the poor.

We don't even have a bathroom we can use; we can't take care of our physiological needs on the street because that would be a source of disease. Those who dare go into the cracked buildings to go to the bathroom. Especially women have to risk going into some apartment— no way to relieve themselves out of doors. And here we still are and we don't know how long this will last.

"And the landlord?"

The landlord has not come by. He wants us to go so that he can get more money. We feel a great apathy on the part of the government toward the popular classes. They say that they are rebuilding the hotels because the government wants to beautify the city before the World Cup, but we are expendable; everything here can stay totally abandoned.

"I would say," David Ibarra intervenes, "that we are victims and we have been victims for a long time. I think that they should be bringing in housing for the victims of the earthquake, but especially for those in the low-income colonias. Here we have had no journalists, not even from the TV. Nobody."

THEY ARE SIMPLY ASKING FOR GUIDANCE

The people, stubborn and deeply rooted, refuse to move. They take care of what little they have. They are waiting for someone to give them directions. It's the only thing that they demand: technical assistance. "If we've got to work, we are ready; we can start building immediately. We need rods, but we can work for as long as we need to."

Eight days after September 19, the most important problem in Colonia Morelos is housing. They want to collaborate, but can't do it on their own. "What if the house falls on top of us?" They know that as tenants they have rights, even if they don't have a lease, even if the receipts are "some slips," "some little pieces of paper" with amounts that do not correspond to their real payment. "There's enough room for everyone here. We own the ground, we own the land, and we're going to defend it; no one is getting us out of here."

"Even if it's a dump," says Félix Cáceres.

"The government can't offer any solutions."

"No. On the contrary, they are talking about a registered contract, about real property, about depositing 750 pesos in court, of unbelievable red tape. We have had to come and go a hundred times before they accept our petition. They say we have to register a contract at the Treasury."

In leaving Colonia Morelos, where the majority of the residents have been victims from way back, Antonio Peña Lara points to a bus that is going by: Blue Eagles, Ixtacalco Brigade, Route 100, plate number 43145. "Look, those kids, fourteen years old, are helping everywhere."

"I heard on the radio that some boys had taken over 150 units belonging to Route 100 and that they were having a party and committing all sorts of excesses."

"That," says Antonio Peña Lara with a serious face, "we have not seen. It's the poorest of the groups that have come to see us. This is why we want to be the owners of our problems and our solutions."

Pancho, a Priest Who Has Chosen to Live with the Poor
THE UPROOTED SHOULD WIN THE BATTLE AGAINST THE LANDLORDS

In the parish of Our Lady of Angels, to one side of Tlatelolco, at Sol 168, in Colonia Guerrero, the Jesuit priest Francisco Ramos (called Pancho by almost everyone), forty-six, is involved in the reconstruction of three tenements.

Francisco Ramos has always lived with the poor—eight years in Nezahualcóyotl, and now in Guerrero. He has been a priest for over twenty years. He fully shares in the living conditions of the people in his parish, as his gray hair, his gaunt face, and his poverty attest.

Some clergymen on the staff of various bishops have spoken of the earthquake as a punishment from God. Francisco Ramos becomes indignant:

That's the braying of an ass. Any assertion of that sort is untheological and unscientific. It is simply a declaration of ignorance, and a misdirected pastoral approach. Camus said it in *The Plague*. To terrorize people by giving a natural phenomenon a meaning like that is, first, to misunderstand nature, and from a theological point of view, it amounts to a misreading of history, and of the society that we have generated historically.

God will never intervene like that to punish us. God lets the people build the world they want. It is easy to attribute punishment and reward to God, and get off the hook of our responsibility in building a more just and equal society. Unfortunately we do not have a pastoral plan to change that particular orientation of popular religiosity that is definitely unenlightened.

The theology of liberation gives a very different interpretation of God, of history, and of the world. I believe this interpretation constitutes a far more adequate response to the profound injustice of our Latin American social structures. I believe we must struggle for that vision.

I insist. I call the attention of Francisco Ramos to the many people who stood in line for confession in the days after the two earthquakes. I point to the masses that are being offered everywhere, and the many other religious services. Now, more than ever, people are looking for a haven in religion.

Confession is an expression of the people's faith, but sometimes it can also express a religious sentiment that has not been thought through. Basically our people believe; they have a profound faith that lacks instruction and contains a magical slant. Religion can be a last recourse for people, especially when they seek consolation or protection against fear—because the earthquake scared us all, undoubtedly—and a refuge against a feeling of helplessness.

I know this problem well, I have worked in many peasant communities in popular education programs. I lived in Chiapas, in Veracruz, and in Hidalgo, and until recently I participated in a project here in the south of the city, in Colonia Ajusco.

Right now I am working with the settlers, helping them to prop up their houses, to get four-by-fours, to get water trucks and construction materials, and in general to resist eviction. Many died in the tenement at Héroes del 47, more than twenty-six, I think. On Estrella, in a relatively new building, another seven people were killed. The latest tenement to fall down didn't kill anybody, but there are many tenements in this whole barrio that are badly damaged and must be demolished and rebuilt, six to be precise. Many more urgently need structural repairs, before the rains come bringing a greater threat of collapse.

LANDLORDS ARE THE SCOURGE OF THE POOR
When I came here I ran into the Neighborhood Association of Colonia Guerrero, which has been functioning for many years. The residents have united around the need to repair their houses, after a tenement

collapsed and killed two children. That happened nine years ago. Subsequently they have struggled for the right to remain where they are against the pressure of the landlords to evacuate the zone.

The landlords are the scourge of the poor: they harass them; they exploit them. I attend the meetings of the Tenants' Union in the parish, because we support them with food and clothing, and we also help the Residents' Union of Colonia Morelos. Its members are very concerned that the government will take advantage of the present situation to remove them.

This whole area is very valuable because of its central location, yet it houses only poor people. The market value of the land could be very high indeed, if only the poor were not here. The people are afraid, because they know the delegation has been promoting this plan, which naturally favors the landlords, trying to change the law that regulates low-income housing rentals in their favor.

People know their housing could easily be razed for good. Every day they have heard talk about "The Golden Belt," a government plan that would turn the area from the Alameda to Tlatelolco into a great park with museums, colonial buildings, and a shopping area for tourists. This is a daily threat for the residents of Colonia Morelos and Colonia Guerrero. These projects are designed without their participation, without alternative plans for them. But you know that in Mexico alternatives do not exist for the poor. To be poor in our country is a disgrace. How right Franz Fanon was to call the poor "the wretched of the earth"!

So people in Guerrero and Morelos are upset. No wonder. Will the government take advantage of the earthquake to implement its plans? Will they clean up the downtown area? And what about Tlatelolco? And what about the residents? They say that the whole downtown will be evacuated. And that includes all the small shops, all the artisans' workshops; everything is to go.

The residents of Morelos and Guerrero are very old communities; they have been here for a long time, and they also have been organized and united for a long time. Our residents' unions are very effective. Since the 19th, we have been working hard in small brigades, struggling for resources and planning the reconstruction.

Practically all the tenements in Colonia Guerrero were affected, although not all the damage is of the same sort. But most houses show cracks in the walls and roofs. Neighbors have displayed great solidarity among themselves. They have offered shelter to those compañeros who could not remain in their own homes. We have also had great outside help: an expert assessment of the state of our housing has been made by volunteer compañeros from the UNAM's School of Architecture and from "House and City," a group of architects who work with urban legislation.

The problem of Colonia Guerrero will not be solved with rehabbing alone, with stanchions, four-by-fours, and master beams: they need to know that their right to stay where they've lived is secure, that they will not be expelled. The landlords are sure getting a lot of mileage out of the earthquake. They walked the streets telling residents that there were many broken pipes and gas was escaping. They were going around gratuitously scaring the people.

Strangers walked these streets, claiming to be expert assessors and condemning the tenements, declaring them unfit for habitation. They threatened the people and sowed panic, trying to prepare the ground for a massive displacement of the residents. The rumor circulated that the army would soon move in and evacuate everyone from the zone.

"And what if the solution were different?" I ask the Jesuit priest Francisco Ramos. "What if all of a sudden Morelos and Guerrero were not for the landlords but for the poor?"

Francisco Ramos beams a wide smile:

Don't you believe that the residents are capable of winning the battle against the landlords?

"I'd like to see that."

La Jornada

Cardinal Corripio Ahumada gave instructions to all the priests of the archdiocese of Mexico to provide material and moral support to the population.

"Faith in God must endure."

"Let's be united in Love."

Marisol Martín del Campo

Of course, when the tenements are big, they listen to the residents. But mine is small, just a few of us live there, so they don't pay any attention to us, says Yolanda Hernández López. Let this señora, my neighbor, tell you about the kind of rainy season we've had. And we're ready to withstand the cold. We don't want to be sent to the shelters, because then we will never be heard. We used to live at Carpintería 26. It was expropriated.

Look at this, they have already gotten their tents. But for us? Nothing. We are desperate, first of all, because we don't know what fate awaits us. And second, because we'd like to be sheltered, the cold is coming. I have six girls; the oldest is eight. They all are one year and three months apart. We made our own room, with our own hands, and now we also have my neighbor and her three children.

Half of the tenement was badly damaged, and the other half just got cracks. My sister-in-law used to live there, and the whole corner looked like it was fine right after the earthquake. Then, all of a sudden, like someone blew on it, it fell down.

The bottom line is that we haven't wanted to be taken to a shelter, because we have seen in the papers that they steal there. I am concerned for my girls. My husband lost his job, he worked on Díaz de León Street, and I, well, I was doing domestic work to help out. How on earth can I work now? Where am I going to leave the girls? Before I used to wash and iron clothes, but now I have no water and no electricity. So what do I do? I knit. I'm trying to make hair bands.

Where we are now, the rains seep in. We need work. We know nobody is going to give us anything for nothing. Money? Where's money going to come from? I can work; I can do the cleaning anywhere; I just need to work to get ahead.

(Yolanda, her husband, and her neighbors all have plastic bags with the original copies of their papers: birth certificates, certificates of elementary education. They are afraid of leaving them in what's left of their homes, lest the buildings collapse further and leave them with nothing.)

The help we have received came from a priest who brought us food until November 1. He offered a mass and announced he had no more to bring us. He'd done enough, really; he had given us supper since September 19.■

THE MAN WHO CAME OUT OF THE SECOFI RUBBLE ON HIS OWN

I HAD A SLAB ON MY CHEST

I saw Roberto Victoria and Panchito Morales coming out of the Operations Department of Secofi, and they suddenly leaned against the wall.

"What's the matter, Panchito?"

"Earthquake . . ."

"No, it must be one of those heavy trailer trucks . . ."

"It's an earthquake. Hold on to the wall."

At this point my impulse was to rush out of the building.

"Be still. Hold on to the wall. Stay there."

"No, I'm not holding on to anything."

And I darted for the stairs because they were right next to me. The building started to groan and screech in a very spooky way. Then I saw the wall in front of me split in two, and the two pieces took a dive onto the street.

I suppose I fainted. In any case, I didn't know what was going on until around nine in the morning, when I heard a voice asking for help:

"Get me out! I have a slab on me! I can't move my leg! Help!"

Then I started to shout too:

"Get me out! I'm Marco Antonio Sánchez, information specialist at Secofi. Help! I'm alive!"

Someone named José González replied.

Again I shouted, "I'm Marco Antonio Sánchez. Who are you? Get me out of here!"

"I can't. I'm trapped too. What floor are you on?"

"I'm on the second floor."

"I'm with Guillermo González, but so much stuff fell on him that he can't move."

I started to shout, "Help! Please help me," and José González shouted too, "Get me out!" Our shouts canceled each other out.

After a while José Gonález said to me, "I'm going to dig a little bit to see if I can get myself out. I see a light."

I thought they had gotten him out, because I no longer heard him. That was my only hope, because he could see a light while I saw nothing. I had a slab on my chest, about six inches wide, and there was dirt and masonry and pieces of furniture all over. I began to hear José González digging, and then I would ask him every little while, "What's up? Any light yet?"

"Yes, I see light, but I can't get there."

"Keep on going, man."

"I can't move; I'm just digging with a piece of pipe to see if I can make a hole."

He got tired and fell asleep. By now I could hear the faint murmur of people out in the street. I could even hear them excavating. I kept shouting, but they couldn't hear me. And my despair was so great that I started to sweat and to say all manner of crazy things, until José González told me, "Stay calm, Marco. They are coming to get us."

We could hear the shovel, and I would cringe under the dirt: "If the earthquake didn't kill us, this little shovel will." I lost all sense of time, since everything was so dark, and I couldn't see a thing; but I felt a rush of air, and I could breathe, and so could José González underneath. The noise ended.

"What happened now? This building is supposed to belong to the government. You would think they'd be moving fast to get us out."

I started to shout, "What's happening? Isn't anybody out there?"

"Calm down, Marco. It's nighttime."

He could tell it was nighttime because of the slit he had above him. We could hear the noise in the street, lots of sirens of ambulances and police patrols. Again we heard steps above us. I knocked with a rock, and José González knocked with a pipe or a rod, or something he had that sounded metallic. And we shouted and shouted. But nothing. I even whistled, and still nothing.

José González is a guy I never met, but he gave me a lot of help, and I helped him too. We kept talking to each other. If you are all alone in this, you probably have a nervous crisis and really go nuts, because every once in a while I thought, "This is it, I'm losing it." But he insisted so many times on staying calm, "Stay calm, stay calm," that in one way or another he was very helpful.

At one point I shouted like crazy, and he said to me, "You're going to be drained of your strength. Why don't you go to sleep for a while."

He went to sleep; I never could. But at least I remained still to avoid sweating and losing body fluids. I wanted to urinate, but I thought, "How can I piss lying down like this?" I was thrown on the ground and couldn't move . . . "I'm going to wet my pants." I could hold it no longer, so I said, "Too bad," and I let go. That was the first time. After a while I felt the need again, and the sheer despair made me crawl some six or eight inches. I was facing down, and as I urinated I thought, "I am so thirsty, my tongue is swollen." I said to myself, "I must drink my urine." But I had no time. Before I knew it, I had relieved myself again.

"Marco, Marco, are you there?"

"Yes, I'm here."

"Try to get yourself out; try, man."

"I can't." I had an iron frame close to my body, something that squeezed me at the waist; if I moved, it would pierce me.

"If a rock comes down, this thing is going to cut me in two pieces. A whole day has gone by, and they haven't gotten to us. Maybe they won't find us tomorrow either."

"I'm sure they're trying to get us. Don't you hear the machines?"

We could hear pieces of concrete being dragged away. I had no idea the whole building had come down. I had the notion that only the second floor platform had caved in, and that they were trying to lift it to get to where we were.

After so much time my eyes adapted to the darkness, and then I started to see sparks of light. I would rub my eyes, and closed them and opened them, and again I would see the tiny sparks all over. I thought it couldn't be real light, since everything was enveloped in darkness. I tried hard to go to sleep and said to myself, "If I didn't die right away it must be that my time hasn't come yet."

A voice—probably in my imagination—kept saying to me, "Help yourself. I'm helping you. But if you don't try, I can't help you." I managed to touch a wall that I thought was reinforced concrete. I remembered that on the second floor we had a square wastebasket, and I imagined someone was dragging it; I could hear that kind of noise.

"They're dragging that wastebasket; they're getting close to me," I thought. Nothing, they didn't find me. They kept banging shovels, buckets, who knows what. The voices were audible, and I could even hear their orders: "Pull this; get this out of the way." Nothing. It got dark again, and I thought, "This is the second day we've spent here."

Because I am a Catholic, I entrusted my soul to God. I said farewell to my children, the best I could; I lifted my hand and blessed them, saying, "My children, I will not see you again." But I kept hearing that internal voice that never left me: "Help yourself; I'm here helping you."

I dragged myself. There were iron cross beams in the rubble, and when I pulled one of them, a broken pole fell down. I started to dig at the wall with it, scraping away until I made a hole. The pole could go through, so I said, "This is it!" I thought the wall faced Frontera Street, because the building was located in the corner of Frontera and Morelia, so I expected to see a light. I said, "Let me stick my hand out so they'll see me down there," but no, that was not the outlet I was looking for. I could hear them up above pulling out the rubble and dragging slabs.

I imagine that José González was an older man, because I could barely hear him whistle now. I got very tired from the effort. I was sweating, so I decided to be still for a while, and I kind of lost hope. "But I must remain calm," I thought.

"Where's my pole?" I found it again and with the pole I found a place under me where the dirt was soft. I touched it, and I thought that was a good spot to scratch again. Wham! I fell into a hole, something like a pipe. I made myself small, as small as I could, but I could only get through with my legs and part of my body, my shoulders were too broad. I saw light on the other side.

"I'll push myself, I'll shrink. So what if lose an arm, or two, but let me get out of here."

I kept seeing the light. I pictured myself playing soccer without an arm, but happy. I wanted to live for my family, my children. I thought they were outside waiting for me; I imagined that the voices I could faintly hear were their voices calling my name. "I'll get out of here, even without a leg or an arm," I thought.

I tore my skin all over, but I went through. Then I had to drag myself through another crevice: "Why on earth have I allowed myself to grow such a belly? My big belly is in the way." But the will to live is so great that I didn't mind tearing apart my whole body. I skinned my abdomen, I smashed my stomach, but I couldn't care less; even if mutilated I needed to get out.

At the last stretch I didn't even pay attention to how small the opening was; I just kept on going, because now I could see the light clearly before me. The noise became more audible, I felt I could touch it. I heard the crane, and someone asked, "Wouldn't it be dangerous to remove this slab?" Someone answered, "Yes, it is dangerous."

I started to whistle, to call for help, and still nothing. I said, "My God! Can these people be so deaf that they can't hear me? So many people up there, and they still can't hear me?" I could not go back, and I could no longer go forward. My feet were stuck, and my belly was jammed, but I could see the light beckoning, and I would say, "That's my life, that is life, it is my chance, I must reach it."

I was hurting myself, but I did not lose hope; on the contrary, with each inch I gained I kept saying, "This is life. I'm going to live. I'm coming, my children. Here I come." The last stretch was a funnel; it was full of jagged masonry. My hand was bleeding, but I kept removing the debris as best I could. And when I finally reached the light, there was a grid of steel in front of me, like the door of an old jail. Still I was seeing light, and now I had fresh air on my face.

I wanted to shout, "Here I am, here I am!" But I had no voice. Not even the thinnest thread of a voice.

WHEN I SAW HIS EAGERNESS TO RESCUE ME I WEPT

I reached the steel-rod grid and pushed my hand through, calling for help. I felt the air on my face and shouted to a man who was operating a machine, "Help! Help! I'm down here!"

He thought he heard something and tensed up, looking around in all directions without spotting me. I stuck my hand out through the bars as best I could and shouted, "Here I am, here I am."

He saw my hand and turned the motor off.

"Silence, silence. There's someone alive in there."

When I saw how eager he was to remove the obstacles, the anxious way in which he was coming to liberate me, emotion flooded me and I wept. These people were in danger of slipping and falling down to the street, risking all sorts of injuries in trying to get to me, but they didn't seem to mind, and I thought, "Wow! Isn't this something! This is something, man, that there are people who do not stop to calculate the danger they're in before saving a life!"

Someone said, "Give me a milk pack."

They passed me a milk container, and I almost choked drinking it.

I swallowed each sip saying to myself, "I'm alive, I will live."

I asked for more. "Give me more milk. I'm awfully thirsty." I was so desperate, half the milk was landing on my chest.

"Of course; don't despair; we're getting you out."

I could see that now the despair was theirs. They wanted to lift the grill, but they couldn't. They had to cut through it.

"They're coming with the bolt cutters; be patient."

"Want some more milk?"

"Yeah."

A few hours later they were able to cut the mesh of steel rod with some large cutters. When I stood in front of all of them, the ones who had rescued me, all I could do was to clench my fists and say, "Thank you."

The Red Cross people took me away on a stretcher.

Marco Antonio Sánchez, a small and stocky man, good-natured, cordial, is a technician in the statistical office of Secofi. He loaded data into the computer in the morning shift.

Several people died in the Ministry of Commerce and Industrial Development at Colima 55. A woman and her fifteen-year-old boy, who lived in a house at Colima 63, died when the building of the Secofi fell on top of them.

Director Antonio Martín del Campo came to the Secofi building on Thursday afternoon, became frightened, and did nothing. He didn't even send sandwiches to the volunteers who were looking for survivors. Here, too, everything was done by volunteers.

NOW WE THE POOR KNOW WHOM TO TRUST

Two months after the earthquake, after many meetings in different hotels, the work of Informática at Secofi has not been organized. One hundred and eighty people are waiting to resume their tasks. The authorities seem apathetic. The employees seemed more worried about the work than their bosses. Why is it that any employee can come up with better responses than the big bosses?

Antonio Martín del Campo, director of the Data Processing Center of the Office of Information and Economic Analysis of Secofi, had no idea how to handle a shovel and a pick. He was probably suffering from indigestion from the very long acronyms that he has to deal with all the time. He didn't attend the mass that was offered on top of the rubble, nor did he share in the mourning of his employees.

The medium-level managers were present and gave a lot of support. José Molina, for example, was responsible for the rescue of José González. Molina knew the building very well. "I had the joy of finding a little girl still alive," he says, "and the cadavers that we managed to get out were turned over to the next of kin."

The main building of Secofi at Cuauhtémoc 80 and the Center for Child Development collapsed—that's too many Secofi buildings—but up to this date, nobody seems to know the total number of dead people from Secofi. It is said that thirty-eight workers were killed at Cuauhtémoc 80.

Two weeks later a meeting was convened, bringing together management and staff. There workers were exposed to an interminable speech on the part of the director, of which only ten minutes were devoted to the earthquake and related subjects. The rest dealt with internal and administrative problems.

Somebody asked, "Why did the building at Colima 55 come down practically at the very start of the quake? How are the relatives of the workers going to be compensated? Is there any responsibility here or not?" The insurance company offers 1,440,000 pesos, and everything else is handled as if it were a business matter for the government, all conditioned by this warning: "We are going to give you your job back; therefore, lie low, because otherwise you run the risk of losing it."

Marco Antonio Sánchez, who has come back to life, continues his story:

Thank God I made it home. How wonderful that my family had gone to look for me! That was as beautiful as looking at that team of people who got me out, all working together. When I was inside I had time to think that money and personal importance matter very little. The only thing that could help me when I was there was the generous heart of others.

Since the 20th I have lived as someone who has been born again. If we had waited for the government to help us, we all would have died; there is no slower turtle. At Secofi I lost my compañeros Roberto Victoria, Panchito Morales, Panchito Servín, José Medina Equihua, and Esteban Ventura Molina. From the SPP, Juan Oliva and Guillermo González. And in the small house crushed by our building, Gloria Soto and Víctor Hugo Mendoza, her fifteen-year-old son, died.

Concha Creel

Fernando López Padilla, "Pantera," tells his story:

I was lying in bed, awake, while my wife was getting the kids organized to go to school. When the earth started to quake, she came into the bedroom and called out, "Fernando, get up, it's an earthquake!" I stood up like a shot. It seemed like King Kong from the movie was smashing the building from the outside, making a terrible racket.

My son David was intent on opening the door that goes to the stairway of the building, but it was stuck, and as I yanked it open I discovered the stairs were gone, and I saw people tumbling down, screaming. I ran inside, where my wife asked me to stay calm, and only then I realized I hadn't stopped yelling myself.

I held my twelve-year-old daughter, and we both stood under the frame of one door, while my wife and our four-month-old baby stood in another doorway. I saw the bricks flying away from the walls like missiles, crashing in front of me. The floor was like a brittle tortilla breaking under us. Then the building buckled under, and I saw my other three children disappear shouting and calling for help.

Afterward I lost all fear; I prayed to God. I knew it was the end. I came to when I felt tremendous pressure on my ears. It was dirt. I was lying face down and couldn't move my body, only my hands. I shook the dirt off me, I saw there was some light, and then I saw my brother-in-law sitting next to me, less badly buried than myself.

I had to shout to my brother-in-law to make him react. Then I asked him what I had on my back that wouldn't let me move. It was a beam. Fortunately, it only trapped me but didn't hurt. He helped me get out from under it, and then we found my daughter. Shortly we saw my wife under another beam. Between the two of us we lifted it. I felt like my intestines were coming out from the effort, but we did it, and we got her out, together with the baby.

We had to scale about five yards back to the opening. Then we heard voices: "Is anyone there?" I have no idea how it was that in such a short time people had come with ropes of all sizes and organized a rescue operation. And so here I am; Pantera didn't die after all; and Pantera has to go forward after this tragedy. I have to find my sons, because I know exactly where they fell.

Shortly after this I found out that his sons were listed on the blackboard as dead.

I saw Pantera three days later. He had not stopped searching through the ruins. He said to me, "That information is a lie. They are not dead. I saw them disappear. The three of them were embracing each other, and that's the way I'll find them." ■

THE GOVERNMENT TRIED TO MINIMIZE THE CONFLICT

On Thursday, Friday, and Saturday, the country experienced a vacuum of leadership on the part of its government. This caused the people to go out and get organized, not to govern, but to help, says Manuel Peimbert, an astrophysicist.

The government is organized to control, to maintain the institutions and the status quo, not to help the population. For the government the well-being of the people is a secondary matter. What is important is to exercise power. That's why after a disaster like this, the government had no idea what it needed to do, and it tried to minimize the conflict. Its reaction was aberrant, especially when you consider that people who could have been saved were buried under smashed buildings.

If some specialist had given basic rescue operation instructions on Channel 11 or Channel 13, secondary cave-ins and other serious problems that resulted from ignorance and negligence could have been avoided. There was a great vacuum of initiatives and ideas. The DN-III plan was created for people who don't know what they're doing. It is not imaginative; it does not invite the participation of citizens who have the know-how and the willingness to help. It is simply a method of further controlling people. "Don't do, don't move." More than anything else, it is a program for repression.

With DN-III, the government was afraid to allow the military any power, worried that they wouldn't give it back later. As a result, the government's order to the army was "Limit yourselves to cordoning off the disaster areas." And that's what the military did. They made it impossible for the relatives and rescue workers to get to the collapsed buildings.

Talking about the government's lack of preparation and its ineptitude disguised as authoritarianism, Manuel Peimbert asserts:

Japan, the USSR, and other countries have antiseismic programs; they run mock earthquake drills periodically for the population. Public buildings, hospitals, and schools are all monitored for cracks, fissures, sinking, or tilting.

At the beginning this government tried to minimize the consequences of the earthquake: "Ladies and gentlemen, the earthquake was not as important as has been said . . ." In an effort to avoid losing tourists, the government denied the gravity of the situation, deceitfully hiding the death toll, the number of injured, the number of people made homeless, the number of fallen buildings. It was an absurd and immature policy.

If we are so worried about our image abroad, what about showing that some intelligent action directed toward our recovery was being undertaken? But Mexico's official reaction was "This is a small problem," so much so that we thought we could afford the luxury of saying no to foreign aid during the first twenty-four hours after the tremor. That rejection was not only stupid; it was counterproductive.

Officially they said, for instance, that there were only between 300 and 400 collapsed buildings out of a total of 1.5 million in the Federal District. In reality, 400 buildings with five or more stories fell down; 2,400 are badly damaged; and 800 more must be demolished. I'm positive that there aren't 1.5 million structures of this sort in the city, so that the proportional damage must be far greater than has been admitted. The damage doesn't get any smaller only because we say it is. It would have been better from the start to say, "The damage has been enormous. We have these projects; get involved in them, help us solve this or that problem, cooperate with us in this or that way." But every time our government treats us like children, it becomes infantile itself. Then reality reasserts itself. Period.

ALL THEATERS AND MOVIE HOUSES ARE MORTAL TRAPS

In all Third World countries governments try to minimize catastrophic situations and obstruct the action of citizens. The only exception was perhaps Algeria, where the government made an appeal to the population to get organized to participate in rescue operations with the army, the police, and the firefighters.

In Mexico, leaders are afraid of the organized action of the citizenry. Civilians should have been integrated into state organizations and gone to the aid of trapped persons. But the action of volunteers overwhelmed the government. Such genuine and generous organization scared the government out of its wits.

Not only does Mexico lack air-raid shelters, it lacks the minimal conditions of security. Movie houses are mortal traps, as are most bars and restaurants, department stores, and nightclubs. Those teletheaters are sealed boxes with escalators, just a way of making money and warehousing people. No wonder people have a bad feeling for Televisa!

It is enormously urgent to study undersoil conditions, to know which are the areas of highest risk, the microfaults, such as the ones that were present under Centro Médico. To know where we can build: that's elementary. You can't steamroll all that.

There's a ratio between the frequency of oscillation of the soil and the amplitude of oscillation of buildings between six and ten stories high. Therefore, that kind of building should be outlawed in Mexico City. Geological, geophysical, and mechanical engineers should determine which regions of Mexico are appropriate for each type of construction. The building code must be quite rigid, and most of all, it must be seriously implemented.

WHERE ARE THE FOUR THOUSAND PEOPLE DISPLACED FROM MULTIFAMILAR JUÁREZ?

The first thing I heard was "Building A toppled down." The whole of the Juárez Housing Project was a cloud of dust, and people were running from the buildings toward the park. Someone else shouted, "Building C-4 crumbled down." We were gripped by panic. My sister-in-law lives in C-3, and the mother of my son-in-law Arturo Whaley lives in C-4. I ran to see what had happened. Building C-4 had come apart like a crumb cake. It was nothing but dust—sand and dust.

I still can't get over the fact that a large number of young men and women gathered so suddenly in front of the heap of debris of Buildings C-4 and A, forming a long chain of volunteers who passed the rubble out chunk by chunk to try to get to the survivors. From that chain one could hear the screams of those who had been trapped under the wreckage.

Gang members, alcoholics, and drug addicts were the most persistent and daring of the volunteers; it's incredible what they did. I don't know where they got the strength, courage, and audacity. As you can imagine, this has given me pause, and now I often ponder the responsibility that we old people have toward the young.

Armando Rodríguez Suárez, journalist, founder of the newspaper *Punto y Aparte* in Jalapa, Veracruz, directed by Froylán Flores Cancela, weeps inconsolably. It breaks your heart to see this robust man—tall, gray-haired, used to struggle since he was very young—moved to tears, touched to the core of his being.

Rodríguez Suárez talks about the suffering of his neighbors, not his own; of the help of volunteers, not of his tireless presence since the 19th, after his two-bedroom apartment—Building D-1, Apartment 105 of Colonia Roma Sur, telephone 564–1269—became a shelter for homeless people, center of rescue operations, nursery, and residence for old and young folk, for children looking for their parents, for parents mad with anxiety who didn't know where to look for help in locating their children.

Armando Rodríguez Suárez organized rescue brigades, instructed workers, held babies in his arms, got people out alive, and pulled out cadavers too. As a result, when we walk through the rubble now, the neighbors come to greet him. In every corner of the complex there are water drums, and on many doors there are signs: "Don't litter."

In the middle of a baseball field what remains of the crushed apartments has been piled up: belly-up sofas, mattresses, clothes, broken home appliances, bloodied cotton sheets, family pictures that hurt to look at—a group of three smiling couples at a table in El Gallo Restaurant; a plump young woman in a bathing suit; a grandmother with a wavy hairdo and eyeglasses. Alas! a pair of pantyhose; a muddied velvet blazer; an infinite number of pairs of shoes.

Just as on October 2, when the Plaza de las Tres Culturas of Tlatelolco awoke covered with odd shoes like crushed flowers! Armando Rodríguez Suárez cries, and he doesn't bother to dry the tears that fall on his blue shirt. Pedro Valtierra and I try not to imitate him.

WE MUST FORM A NEW TYPE OF BRIGADE TO RESCUE EVERYBODY'S LIFE

Where was I? Did I tell you about the gang members? They demonstrated that if they have formed gangs and taken refuge in alcohol and drugs, it is because they are escaping a reality where they have no future, where they are not understood by their families, let alone the government, which can only repress.

These guys made it evident that when push comes to shove, they are ready to risk their lives, they are not afraid of anything, and they are far more generous than those who think of themselves as exemplary and who are always giving morality speeches.

We had several groups of judicial police trying to get the gangs out under one pretext or another. I could see that they felt total contempt for these young men. And yet the young guys have responded to this tragic situation with tremendous human warmth, and have also shown that their despised organizations—always rejected by society—could be put to good use.

(How many outcasts has the earthquake discovered! How many characters like "The Flea" from Cuautla, skinny, small, resilient, seemingly death-proof, have gone in through the interstices of the rubble to save lives!)

The hour when the earthquake took place is the hour of heaviest traffic, especially on Cuauhtémoc Avenue. Well, these kids took over and directed traffic, and they did it with total respect for everyone, because not only the Multifamiliar Juárez had collapsed, but also the Centro Médico and the Hospital General, which are adjacent. The only telephone that was working was the one at my home; imagine that. So we got all the nurses and doctors who were trying to call home or other hospitals, and the residents of other buildings in the multifamiliar, like the poor people of Building B. Anyhow, there was frantic activity day and night.

Armando Rodríguez's tone changes abruptly. Now is the time to denounce, which he does with the voice of wrath:

I would ask that we integrate a new kind of brigade, not to recover the dead, but to rescue our own lives. Because what the authorities have done in regard to the Multifamiliar Juárez has no name. Alejandro Carrillo Castro, general director of ISSSTE, either doesn't know what he's talking about, or he lied deliberately at the press conference that he convened on October 11. He had the audacity to say, "This is the housing situation at Multifamiliar Benito Juárez since the catastrophe: out of thirty-five buildings, six are totally destroyed and eleven more had to be evacuated. Out of 1,024 apartments, 212 were destroyed, 524 had to be evacuated, and only 288 suffered no ostensible damage." All false. In the first place there aren't thirty-five buildings in Juárez: there are nineteen.

According to the account published by architect Mario Pani, the designer of the housing projects Multifamiliar Juárez and Multifamiliar Alemán (built even before Juárez), there are nineteen buildings. Carrillo Castro said that no new buildings will be built, and that in a few days the demolition of eleven of the most damaged buildings will begin.

Carrillo Castro said that no new buildings will go up because they would be "offensive to the memory of the dead." Instead, the area will be razed, and we will have green spaces as a "homage to their memory." What crap is this? Armando Rodríguez de Suárez roars. No new buildings? And where are people going to live, can they tell me? Where?

Those of us who have lived here for thirty-three years can lose our neighborhood and our homes simply as an homage to the dead? How is making relatives homeless an homage to the dead? The buildings that were evacuated were all type D, with two entrances and thirty-two apartments each, that is, 288 apartments. They've brought in authorities from ISSSTE, Fovissste, and Sedue, parading them back and forth. First they threatened us with eviction. But on October 17 the structural evaluation was made, and only one apartment is in need of rehabbing. Every other apartment is inhabitable.

There are five thousand residents in the Multifamilair Juárez; make that past tense, there were. Today there are only a thousand people in the buildings that were not damaged. I want to know where the rest of the people are: How many are dead, and how many are missing? Where have the others gone?

Where are the belongings and valuables that have been taken out?

What is the situation of the uprooted people? In the Benito Juárez sports club there is hardly anyone left. Where are those who lost their homes and their households? The authorities said, "Let each one save his own skin." This is why it is urgent to take a census.

We have a questionnaire already; we only need people to come and help us carry out the survey. Not only for the victims of the Multifamiliar Juárez, but also for those of the Nuevo León in Tlatelolco, the ones in Colonia Roma, the people of Tepito and Colonia Morelos. We now need a brigade to rescue lives, because the ISSSTE, the Fovissste, and the Sedue are committing the greatest stupidities that anyone can imagine. We must not allow them to go unpunished.

Yolanda Serratos

I was in school when everything started to shake, and in the middle of the screams and the stampede, I found myself bewildered in the yard. When the tremor stopped, we all went home, says brigade worker César Hernández, twenty. I went with some friends to the Humana Hospital to see how we could help.

The ambulances were arriving with injured people. I had a chance to see the extent of their suffering and the suffering of their relatives. We started taking food, medicine, and clothes to all the shelters we were sent to. It was already nighttime when they called from one of the shelters asking for a vehicle to go to Colonia Roma and bring over some of the people who had lost their homes.

I volunteered with a friend of mine, and we left with some nervousness. I felt a lot of responsibility and the desire to be helpful. We got to Viaducto, where some soldiers were redirecting traffic. We told them what our purpose was, and they opened the way for us. It was already ten at night. There was no light, no electricity, and no cars, only the encampments of soldiers on one side and earthquake victims on the other, watching over the belongings they had managed to salvage.

The devastation was ghastly; I was afraid. We got our face masks on, and proceeded to ask people whether they wanted to go to the shelter where they would have food, medicine, and a bed. It was useless. They all said they felt more secure on the street, where nothing could fall on them. Panic, ignorance, and fear were stronger than our entreaties.

We arrived at one of the buildings that had collapsed. Everyone was excavating there; it smelled awful, but people kept on going, some even crying in despair, removing masonry and metal rods, knowing that their loved ones were there, under acres of pulverized concrete. Standing there, doing nothing, I came to the realization that this was the greatest catastrophe that Mexico had ever suffered. I got choked up, and decided to help out with all my might. I had never felt such a desire to be helpful to everyone. I even screamed with emotion.■

LET THE TRAGEDY TURN US INTO A NEW MEXICO
HOW CAN THEY PAY FOR A 4 MILLION PESO HOUSE?

During the time that the rescue operations went on at the Multifamiliar Juárez, there was a total absence of governmental coordination. Doctor Jesús Kumate says that 170 persons were rescued alive. "Who gave you this information?" "Who knows!" "How can you affirm this?" "Who knows!" What we had was a spontaneous movement among the neighbors, volunteers, and passersby. Together we got the bodies out of the rubble. Twelve or fifteen hours later the army came to cordon off the zone. Why is it that the ISSSTE, Fovissste, and Sedue are trying to get credit for the work, when it was ordinary people who did it?

Armando Rodríguez Suárez lived hour by hour through the harrowing two days of September 19 and 20. He is still living in the Multifamiliar Juárez, so he knows what he's talking about:

The majority of dwellers at Multifamiliar Juárez are retired. An old woman was trapped in the wreckage of building C-4. The roof beams created a kind of protective pyramid over her. On the 20th people noticed that a small dog kept going in and out. Two rescue workers followed him and found the señora, who had been trapped for twenty hours. The moment she was coming out, TV cameras arrived along with the press and the police. The neighbors were very annoyed by this display of publicity, and they criticized it, especially because the police wanted to be in the limelight. The boy scouts made a human barrier by linking their arms and kept the opportunistic visitors back, so no film could be made. Not even the cops got near the lady.

An employee of the Ministry of Communications left building A on his way to work very early. When he realized how powerful the earthquake had been, he went back home to find a heap of mangled rods and dust. His wife and his nineteen-year-old daughter died there. Now he lives in a room on the roof of a nearby building, wearing borrowed clothing. When he hears an earthquake victim exaggerating or complaining too much—because naturally we all think our own problem is the greatest—he interrupts and everybody keeps quiet. His example has served to restrain those who would get desperate or would exaggerate their case.

The evacuation of the buildings that were still standing was precipitous. In type C buildings they had recruits and other army types, plus ISSSTE employees, taking furniture out in a matter of two hours. They said that the Puerto de Liverpool had loaned its fleet of twenty moving trucks. So naturally when their things went, people had to go.

Representatives of Fovissste came to tell the residents that the era of cheap rents was over, that the Multifamiliar Juárez was destined to become a park, and that they were offering four thousand houses that would be sold to the displaced with ample credit at low interest (4 percent). These things can only be done by trampling on the rights and benefits that government workers have traditionally enjoyed, especially retired people.

The percentage of senior citizens here is very high. There are old folks who are confined to their apartments. If you consider the monthly income of retired employees—the majority of the tenants—to be 34,800 pesos, how on earth are they going to buy a house for 4 million pesos? The Fovissste employees themselves told the retirees when they arrived at their offices, "We're sorry, but you don't qualify for this credit. You can't get these houses."

One question: Where are the houses? In the State of Mexico, in Coacalco I and Coacalco II. Five families took a bus to Coacalco and found that some of the houses were already taken, others had no windows, most of them lacked all utilities, and they all were cut off from any bus route to Mexico City. Imagine, to have to travel 10, 15, or 25 miles to work. How? Where? What kind of school will the children attend? How are the problems of sewage and water supply going to be solved?

The five families returned, totally disappointed. But the deceit didn't stop there. Attorney Jorge de la Rosa Sánchez, a Fovissste executive, visited the improvised shelters at the Hacienda sports club and the Constitution School adjacent to the Multifamiliar. He offered to take the victims to visit replacement housing units. Soon 220 people were in two Route 100 buses to visit the units, where they were supposedly going to be welcomed with a dinner. They never found any housing units, let alone the supper, and they had to go back to their makeshift homes.

How shall we face the authoritarianism and the arrogance of bums like Carrillo Arena? Sedue has gone to the extreme of saying that in three years it will provide fifty thousand housing units. Why do they lie with such impunity? How do they plot such perverse inventions? Maybe they want to compete with the aberrations of the Department of the Federal District, headed by the moronic Ramón Aguirre, who, on September 22, at the razed corner of San Luis Potosí and Tonalá, created a memorial garden, and one not being enough, he inaugurated another later at the corner of Tonalá and Coahuila streets, complete with a mortuary wreath and a plaque: "To the Martyrs of September 19." They might as well laugh at the sorrow of the Mexican people.

Next to Armando Rodríguez Suárez a young man named Gabriel clutches a folder under his arm. It contains the certificates of death of his father and brother. He can't say a word. He lost his apartment in Multifamiliar Juárez. His mother, with a broken leg and a broken arm, was sent to the Twentieth of November Hospital. They kept her for three days and released her. Where can she go, though, when she has no home? Gabriel in his despair managed to get a Social Security policy that would cover her, and they allowed her to spend three more days in the hospital. But now she has to leave again. Where can he take her? He has no relatives, no roof, no clothes, not even an old pot to heat up coffee. Can't they understand that he is absolutely homeless? Even his clothes and his sneakers have been borrowed from someone else.

I defy Alejandro Carrillo Castro, that poorly informed director, to come to Multifamiliar Juárez to get an idea of what we are up against. I dare him to come talk to me. I defy architect Roberto Eibenschutz Hartman, undersecretary of Sedue, to dare to repeat that there are 13,986 housing units open for the displaced of Nonoalco-Tlatelolco and the Multifamiliar Benito Juárez.

In reality, ours is a human rights problem, and we have had a bureaucratic, small-minded response from people in authority who are wholly without a conscience, and whose sordid actions are based on a complete misunderstanding of the needs of our people.

LISTEN YOU, I DON'T WANT TO DIE YOUNG AND BEFORE FALLING IN LOVE

Funny, informants have not wanted to give their names in the last few days "for fear of reprisals." One rescue worker from the Red Cross said, "Listen you, I don't want to die young and before falling in love," as he mistrustfully viewed the generic-brand, one-hundred-page ruled notebook of the journalist. Another driver of a Red Cross ambulance who worked at the corner of Versalles and Chapultepec Avenue didn't want to give his name either: "Who wants to get screwed over, Missus." But someone who gave his name gladly was Dr. Mario Castro, who told about the earthquake hour by hour, and whose story is summarized in these pages.

One of the things that Mario Castro noticed was how the people of Tepito, Colonia Guerrero, and Colonia Romero Rubio preferred to stay in the streets rather than to go to the shelters. The people of Colonia Roma also chose to stay outside, in the median strip of Alvaro Obregón Avenue, or in the parks "to take care of their stuff, so that everything won't be stolen."

As a physician, I was in charge of an ambulance. The vehicles were made available by the Ford Motor Company, where I work. We left Cuautitlán, in the State of Mexico, at 11:50, and by 12:20 we were in the Red Cross Hospital waiting for instructions, but things were chaotic there.

We decided to go to the Centro Médico of the IMSS, and we found the authorities were holding a consultation. It was one o'clock in the afternoon. One could see a large concentration of vehicles in the IMSS concourse, especially ambulances and other vans fitted for the transportation of patients.

Since we didn't find anyone to direct us and tell us where we could be more useful, we took off for the disaster zones. At 2:55 we arrived at the Secofi building, at the corner of Cuauhtémoc Avenue and Doctor Navarro, where the directors of that ministry asked us to stay and work with them.

Some people signaled to us from the rubble, saying they needed a stretcher. But they needed much more than a stretcher, and there was no medical assistance unit in sight. On the sixth floor of Secofi, firefighters were trying to remove a person who was wedged in by broken concrete. There were other people trapped there who were taken out later.

At 4:40, Sr. Domingo Martínez was rescued with what was probably a fractured left leg; at 5:45 we got Rafael Vargas out, with a multiple fracture of the right femur. I sent the ambulance with both injured patients to the Red Cross and asked Rafael Ramos to stay with me. He is the commander of the Red Cross in Cuautitlán.

A young man came to tell us that voices could be heard around the alleyway that ran between the two Secofi buildings. Looking up, one could see the wreckage of floors seven, eight, and nine, which had drifted as they collapsed and were now miraculously hanging over the alleyway. The ramps that led to the underground parking garage were filled with rubble that had fallen from those stories.

We called out with our hands cupped around our mouths, trying to find out whether there was anyone alive. No answer. The ambulance of Commander Ramos is equipped with a bullhorn, so he sent this message: "If there is anyone alive, try to let us know; down here we can't hear you. Try to throw out a stone or any object."

Through the opening between the floor platforms some pieces of rubble and even pieces of paper started to fall out. We coordinated our forces and organized the rescue operation, breaking a slab with no more tools than hammer and chisel.

We started working at 5:55. Fifteen minutes later, two ambulances with rescue workers arrived: one from the Red Cross in Huejotzingo, Puebla, and one from Neza, in the State of Mexico, and they all started to work with my staff. It took them more than six hours to perforate the slab by hand. Work was very slow, because the concrete could be broken, but not the steel skeleton of the columns.

Around midnight the unit that we had requested arrived from the Rescue and Medical Emergency Squad of the DDF with a handsaw. They went up and cut the rods. We rescued Eduardo Méndez González and Marciano Corona Méndez, with various minor injuries. They had been trapped for seventeen hours on the seventh floor. I examined them, gave them something to drink and a sedative, and sent them home in another ambulance. People arrived constantly to ask about their missing relatives, but we had no idea whom we were going to find in the wreckage. Marciano's relatives had been asking about him all day.

RESCUE WORKERS ARE AFRAID OF REPRISALS

We had situated a spotlight coming from the ambulance so that workers could see what they were doing, but there was barely any light reaching the area that had been the seventh floor. At the corner of Doctor Navarro and Doctor Lucio the police were blocking traffic when we saw a pickup truck with some young men of a well-to-do social level trying to come and help. They had halogen lights and other equipment with them. But the police kept telling them to keep on going. We intervened and asked the police to let them come and help. They did.

These volunteers were good people, probably with camping experience. They had a gas stove, jugs with purified water, coffee. They offered us hot beverages because we were all feeling the cold of the night along with the cold of death. Thanks to these young men the rescue could be completed.

THE ONLOOKERS WANTED A SHOW

In the same area, at Coahuila and Tonalá streets, a branch building of the electric company had collapsed. Around five o'clock we took out the cadaver of Sr. Correa, the company's comptroller. It was difficult to work in the midst of onlookers who were there for the show. There were people behind me saying, "Come on, let us see a bit." Sr. Correa's son and other relatives wanted to ride in the ambulance so as not to lose sight of his body. There were orders not to let anyone ride in the ambulances. So I made the decision to let young Correa ride outside on the running board of the van.

At 7:40 in the evening of Friday the 20th, another earthquake struck, and this time we were at the corner of Coahuila and Monterrey. People were panic-stricken: fleeing, screaming, crying. An engineer and I spoke through the bullhorn, asking people not to run, to congregate in the center of the street. But the utility poles were rocking, and the cables were snapping and falling on the ground. As buildings moved they made rattling noises. Some collapsed.

As soon as the tremor was over, we called the people who were standing in the front doorways. I was asked to assist a woman who was in hysterics. She was in the center of a tenement on Monterrey Street. A little boy next to her was holding her hand and saying to her, "Mama, please, what happened to you; get up, Mother, I don't want to see you like this." The attitude of the child helped me make the woman react. "Get ahold of yourself, Señora. You are scaring your son. You have to be brave. Get up. Comfort your son, take care of him." She started consoling her son, who was asking her, "How come everything moves?"

GO TO TEPITO AND LA MORELOS; THERE IS PLENTY OF HELPLESSNESS THERE

We started early on the 21st, working as a first-aid station and overseeing the transfer of cadavers to the baseball park of the IMSS, which had been turned into a huge morgue. We gave technical support to the rescue teams. Still, the onlookers came asking us for masks to protect themselves from the stench.

At 10:50, we took out the cadaver of Sra. Judith Lindenfeld de Barx, recovered from the wreckage at Tonalá and San Luis Potosí.

At 1:00 in the afternoon, at the corner of Monterrey and Coahuila, we were involved in unearthing the bodies of the whole family. It was very difficult to control the imprudent and voyeuristic curiosity of people and some members of the international press. I had an altercation. I blew up when I saw an Italian cameraman taking his time to film, unaware of the fact that he was interrupting and paralyzing the rescue work. He filmed the family from every angle, meticulously.

These were people who had been buried for forty-eight hours, whose bodies were decomposing fast. The man, half covered with rubble, still had his arms extended in a protective gesture; two children had their fists and arms crossed against their chests. I asked the captain of the guard, "Señor, please take this film crew out of here." The captain answered, "They are simply carrying out their duties." But he listened to me and politely removed the Italian cameraman.

Soon enough the cameraman was back, this time sitting and filming on the bumper of a crane as it maneuvered around. I said, "Enough!" and put my hand on the lens. I asked him to please get down. I held his arm as he climbed down, and he struck me, telling me in English not to touch him. He spoke insultingly, but I did not understand what he was saying. I could only say to him, "Go, go," as I pushed him forward.

I asked the captain to keep all press people behind the rope. They all had zoom lenses anyway. The bodies that were recovered were those of Sr. Francisco Cázares Coss, twenty-eight, Rosa Cázares, twenty-seven, Francisco Cázares, eight, and Michele Cázares, five, all dead at Coahuila 147.

On September 22 in the morning, we started a tour of the city to offer shelter in a place that the company I work for had opened in one of its assembly plants.

In Jesús Carranza Street, close to the Bahía movie theater, in the heart of Tepito, we went into some tenements that were about to fall in, with very serious fissures. Conditions were extremely unsanitary. Yet neighbors would politely decline my offer.

We went to Colonia Morelos. Neighbors who were camping out in the street told us that some vehicles with turrets and armed occupants had been there, and that things had been stolen. We could not see anybody guarding the area. We went to the San Sebastián Plaza. We could hardly move among the towers of furniture of all the people who were migrating there. We returned to Morelos to offer shelter. The children were naked and hungry, and still their parents rejected the shelter.

We asked a young woman who was sitting on a chair in the middle of the street, "What kind of help are you expecting?"

"The help we expect is for the government to give us a house; I'm not moving away from here; if I do, I forfeit my right."

THE AID OF YOUNG PEOPLE WAS INVALUABLE

"How can we help? We want to do something." Many brigades were spontaneously organized; many shelters functioned autonomously. In spite of the fact that the president of UNAM closed down the school Thursday afternoon, a great error that considerably delayed the rescue efforts, the students organized 852 rescue brigades in their schools.

Close to ten thousand students arrived spontaneously each day, and the UNAM provided gloves, shovels, picks, crowbars, hacksaws, and jackhammers. There were night rescue brigades, food distribution brigades, brigades that monitored sanitary conditions in the colonias, medication distribution brigades, clothing brigades, even coffin brigades.

Each *brigadista,* man or woman, received a face mask dabbed with Vicks Vaporub as a disinfectant. In the collection center of San Agustín on Homero Avenue, *brigadistas* plan to continue working "in the coming months."

I've been fired from my job, says Marco Antonio Ruelas, also known as "Rambo" because of his intrepid ways. I used to work in Fiorucci, an apparel boutique owned by architect Freddy Helfon, but since Thursday I'd wanted to come out and help, so I joined Brigade 56.

I first went to Centro Médico, but later I was sent to Hospital General, where they told me, "No one wants to go in this tunnel." Two guys and I got in. They gave us the equipment, a mask with a double filter, an oxygen tank for our backs, helmet, flashlight, and gloves, and in we went, all the way in. We could hear a sort of moaning. We scraped everywhere with the gloves, but we found nothing, so we went back out to give a report and prepare for a second try. And we were successful! The second time we got a señora out, and this success filled us with great excitement.

Right there at Hospital General they offered me 800,000 pesos: "Yours if you go in that tunnel," and they pointed to a slit. I went in, but I wouldn't take the money. We are not charging anything. Others are; they charge per corpse, and also they charge for getting belongings out. A mole is anybody who goes into the tunnels to explore. There are some qualified moles who shore up the tunnels and common moles who remove rubble and install cable and lamps in strategic locations.

I am a common mole, says Marco Antonio Ruelas, and we common moles are nothing but cannon fodder. They first send us in to see if the excavation will hold up, and once we come out the place is declared safe for the good moles, the technicians and their equipment.

I first worked with some miners who came from Pachuca and others who are mountain rescuers. Let me tell you, those are real mothers, the coolest Mexicans I've seen. Those guys really risked their lives, all Thursday and Friday.

Thursday night we met Sra. Vicki, Victoria Romero de Rodríguez from Torreón, Coahuila, who helped more than anyone to set up the shelter on Doctor Barragán Street. She went all over the place with two young guys distributing food, in Tepito, everywhere, all night long, sleeping only for one hour in a Red Cross ambulance. That's another awesome person. Now she's gone back to Torreón, but she gave us her address in case we wanted to visit her.

Sra. Vicki said that as far as she was concerned, she'd be happy if guys like us married her daughters because in her opinion we were worth more because of our good hearts than for our appearance; in other words, she implied that we were nicer looking inside than outside. You're going to think, "Uhuh, these guys are conceited," but she really meant it, that we were all right. You tell her, Chofi, tell her; you've been here all along, so you tell her.

LET THIS GO ON FOREVER

Two buses from Route 100 and three private vans are leaving constantly on their food distribution circuit to the shelters. A warm camaraderie has developed among the drivers and the *brigadistas*. "They no longer want to go back to their old jobs," says Mario Mendoza Yáñez. "They say that they want this to go on forever. And in a way it must, because what are people going to do without jobs and without homes?

"The real state of emergency has just begun, and if the brigades are disbanded because kids go back to school or because a government decree says they should, many people will lose a basic source of relief."

I became a *brigadista* because of a ride, says Marco Antonio Ruelas. I got on the van, and I kept on going. On the first day, I went to the Monument to the Revolution and helped in the rescue of a person who was trapped still alive. He had a metal frame pressing him. We managed to lift the frame with portable and hydraulic jacks, and I was filled with enthusiasm, so I stayed.

Look, Señora, without young people, the problems of the victims couldn't have been solved. I live in Colonia del Valle, and wherever I turned I saw young peoples' brigades. Even the kids who have been left homeless and who are in shelters after a little while tend to join the brigades and want to help. We don't belong here in Polanco; some of us had never seen Homero Avenue or Musset Street; we belong to the lower middle class; we come from Colonia Jardín Balbuena, Colonia Sotelo; we are purely volunteers.

THE PERMANENT BRIGADES

I hope the government will not think about disbanding the brigades. Quite the opposite, I hope it will fortify them and will know how to channel the deep will to improve our situation that is expressed everywhere through these brigades. Look, we are all working for the satisfaction of rescuing, of saving lives. We don't want to stand in front of a TV camera and be told, "Mexican youth, we couldn't have done it without you," but it would be good to know that others recognize that our labor was not in vain and that it can go on and that the people want it to go on.

We are all kids, Gerardo Rodríguez insists. The oldest is twenty-three, and of course there are some who are here to show off, the silver-spoon crowd, but look at a crew like the one from Colonia Condesa—those guys are cool. They help, they really help. They pass on the eight o'clock shift to us, but only after they have buckled down and worked like mules all day. The same is true of Group 156 of the Scouts.

I belong to a group called Youth of Mexico, and something at once funny and macabre happened to me. I ran into a corpse; half of his body was swollen up like a balloon because a column had fallen on him. When we removed the beam, bingo, the body abruptly stood up, and that was it, the three *brigadistas* and I fainted. Immediately we had to call out, "Code 34, code 34"; that is, send a paramedic quick. He came and explained that as we removed the beam, the cadaver released a great amount of gas, and that's what propelled it upward. But he had already scared the shit out of us!

Now that we have experience, the same thing wouldn't happen to us. Now we are skilled jacks-of-all-trades; we can do everything, from fixing a car, moving it if it is parked in the wrong place, controlling traffic, distributing food, giving first aid, and listen to this, cooking. I cook! They call me "El Terminator." Hey you (he turns to look at his friends). Don't you think that the shower last night may have finished off the damaged buildings?

"Forget the damaged buldings," interrupts Humberto Mendoza Yáñez. "What about all those people who are still out in the street and won't go to the shelters, so all they have are sheets and bedspreads as a roof?"

At the collection center at Homero Avenue and Musset Street some tractor-trailers are arriving with sacks of 70 and 80 kilos of rice, reports driver Alfredo Cervantes Lara, whose vehicle is number 3785, fleet 15, Route 100: There's a great deal of solidarity in the interior, and trucks are arriving frequently with blankets, new jackets, clothes that have not been used, I mean nice clothes, utensils, buckets, everything.

The first thing that started to come was plastic bags with clothes delivered by señoras, later the mounds of clothing were so high that the volunteers used them as mattresses to take a snooze on. What we have the most of are crackers, bread, and rice. What we lack the most is drinking water. What is it like for people who have no homes and no jobs?

Before paying the debt, the government must build houses for the victims. The only people the government needs to impress are the Mexican people. We the people, I believe, have done our part; we have demonstrated to the government that we can respond. But if those at the upper levels of society don't respond to the people and to us, the youth who have knocked ourselves out, then I really don't know what the outcome of this emergency will be.

TEN BASIC POINTS FOR THE SEARS–RED CROSS
VOLUNTEERS
  1. Remember that your own safety is the most important consideration in your work. Handle the carts and all equipment cautiously. Do not run.
  2. We ask you to bring a jacket and not to expose yourself needlessly to the rain or cold weather.

3. Any volunteer who comes in contact with food and water must take extreme measures to assure hygienic conditions, especially clean and disinfected hands.

4. Face masks are indispensable for anybody handling clothes, shoes, and any other article that has been exposed to dust.

5. Request all donors of medications to pay attention to the expiration dates. Medicine that has expired is trash and must be disposed of.

6. Insist that volunteers who are working in affected areas wear a face mask.

7. If you observe that other volunteers make mistakes, point the errors out to them in a polite way. Bear in mind that they are only trying to help.

8. All the water you drink should have been boiled for at least ten minutes after it releases big bubbles.

9. All volunteers are asked to drive with moderation and without using sirens.

10. Any time you offer your services as a volunteer, we ask you to please do it for a minimum of two hours, to make your time productive.

THE TASK OF COMBATING OBLIVION

This one is told riding off into the sunset, the last chronicle of the series. And it goes with gratitude to all who entrusted others with the testimony of their tragedy. The voices lasted many days and many nights. Lips pronounced words that were fragile, outraged, terrible, painful.

Unforgettable faces: The face of Judith García—her shivering body—pierced by pain that made her curve into a fetal position and acquire a more childish form of helplessness. The face of Gloria Guerrero suddenly aged, her story interrupted by the spasm of her tears. The face of Salomón Reyes, whose eyes saw without understanding. Who can understand the loss of six children? The face of Andrés Escoto, overwhelmed, repeating, "I'm calm, I'm calm, I've never been better," with his only brother, seven years his junior and whom he loved as a son, crushed under the ruins of Chapultepec University. The face of that surgeon of Hospital General who saw a beam on his hand and understood he would never operate on a human being again and who mourned that hand while still buried under the wreckage and made the decision to devote himself to social medicine. The face of that mother who lost faith and suffocated her daughter three days before she was rescued alive. The face of those who struggled until the last moment: Marco Antonio Sánchez, encouraged by outside voices.

Unforgettable feelings: The joy of rescue workers when they could take a newborn baby in a steel crib and be welcomed with an "Aaaaaaaah!" full of emotion. The gratitude of people who were rescued but only know the first name of their saviors: Pedro, Marta, Rubén, Toño, Lourdes. The impact made by bodies at Delta Park covered with ice in plastic bags marked "Ice Club." The dignity of the next of kin who waited hours for the final blessing of the priest who celebrated a mass, also with a mask on his face, by the side of a common grave. The heroic spirit of *brigadistas,* of women like Consuelo Romo who transformed their tragedy into an act of love for other people.

Unforgettable people: All the victims of the earthquake and the permanent victims, the ones who, as Hermann Bellinghausen said in *La Jornada,* were the "victims of that phenomenal deceit called Mexico City, jointly perpetrated by private contractors and government representatives whose corruption, rapaciousness, and despoiling have been rampant for almost a century."

THE BIRTH OF A CIVIL SOCIETY

Mexico lived days of war; the city lived days of devastation, days of heroism and misery: As far as I was concerned, says Mario, a member of a UNAM brigade, I imagined that each family I had to rescue was my own: that couple with two children was my family; the ones buried there were my children, my wife, myself. And this impression lasted for the five nights that I spent hitting concrete slabs with a pick and a shovel. From the position in which a particular group died, you could see the love among them: the woman embraced one of the children, and the husband covered the three of them. He died crushed on their bodies, his arms extended, covering them all. "As I took them out, I understood the meaning of family: protection, to be ready to give your life up."

Dr. Celia Delgado, a psychiatrist, offered her services at the Pediatric Institute:

They called me and my husband, Emilio Gibaud, to tell us that they had an eight-year-old girl who had been mute since the earthquake. She came out alive, but her mother, a single parent, was away on a business trip, so the child feared she would never see her mother again. Since the

19th she had stopped eating, could not really sleep, and had not uttered a word. After an interview that lasted two hours, Emilio and I were able to diminish her anxiety to the point of doing away with the massive doses of medication she was receiving. Her grandmother and her sister were able to come to take her home from the hospital.

Three days after the earthquake the cases of children who had lost their speech became known. One of the most dramatic was that of a four-year-old child who lost her whole family. In Room A there is a little girl who stares at the ceiling. She had been admitted with slight injuries, and all that was known about her was her name, Leti. When she finally could talk, she spoke vividly about what happened. She lived in a tenement in Tepito, and when the earthquake struck, she called out to her mother, "You go ahead, I'll come out soon. I have to get dressed. I can't go out like this." When the child looked over her shoulder, her house had caved in, her mother, father, and sister were buried under broken walls.

Some rescue workers took her to the Pediatric Institute. Nothing else is known about her; she talks about a grandmother who lived out on a farm. Now she's an orphan, and no one has come to claim her at the children's home operated by DIF.

Miguel Cházaro found a child all alone in a shelter:
"This kid, who is in a corner, cannot be convinced to speak or to eat. He lost his mother, his grandmother, and four siblings. They think he's from Colonia Roma. Yesterday he started playing with blocks. He makes a tower and then kicks it. He does not interact with any other children. He doesn't look his interlocutor in the eye."

"It's an earthquake! Run! Save your lives!" It's only the children who are playing in any open space they can find.

The physical and material destruction caused by the tremor is such that the psychological damage is often ignored. A *brigadista* had to be examined by Dr. Isabel Díaz Portillo. He was suffering from precordial pressure, he couldn't breathe, and he couldn't swallow.

This sensitive man knew that what he needed was to sit down and cry, but he couldn't afford to. A resident of one of the most badly damaged of all barrios, he immediately left his home to help his neighbors get out from under their broken homes. He felt fear and revulsion before the destroyed bodies, but he refused to stop and worked without a letup for ten hours.

When the *brigadista* went down to have some food, he collapsed on the ground and couldn't get up. Other relatives also involved in the rescue took him to the doctor. Both his sorrow and his tremendous control were evident. "I had to ask him," says the doctor, "to describe with as much detail as possible what had happened since the earthquake started. When he spoke about having entered a collapsed building through a window I had to insist that he describe what he saw. He answered in the midst of sobs: detached heads, detached legs, about thirty-five legs. He could not contain his emotion anymore, and he let go. He cried convulsively. The only therapy measure is to relieve suffering through the expression of pent-up emotions."

THE FULL DIMENSION OF THE PSYCHOLOGICAL DAMAGE

The demand for medical attention for children and adolescents suffering from anxiety grows every day, even among those who did not witness the disaster very directly. Their sleep patterns are disturbed, they have problems with eating, they experience anxiety when parents leave them even momentarily, and many have retrogressed to infantile behavior.

Obviously the voices of victims in *Nothing, Nobody* are critical, given the fact that most of them are among the poorest Mexicans, the ones who are now called "the permanent victims" because they had been indigent even before September 19. Why shouldn't they be critical, when they don't owe any favor to anyone? In Mexico, social convention dictates silence. To whom should the poor direct their criticism? To the authorities, to the builders, to the rich, to the entrepreneurs, to the government? Their city is in ruins. Their lives are in ruins. Each one of them speaks by his or her own lights. The fishing is only as good as the size of your catch.

"How easy for a well-to-do student from Anáhuac University, a little rich kid who's never missed a meal, who drives Daddy's car and spends Daddy's money, to say that a poor soldier like Juan is a thief! How easy! Isn't it perhaps that the Daddy is the real thief, the contractor or builder, the entrepreneur, or maybe Junior himself, who already has a car of his own and takes it to Acapulco for the weekend?

"How easy to play the hero spending one night or two in Colonia Roma! How easy to demolish it all from the comfort of a mansion in

Pedregal or Las Lomas: to demolish the army, the government, the institutions! How easy to reproduce the criticism of the foreign press, to report that the international delegations left our country in anger, as if the Germans, who were the protagonists of Nazism, or the colonialist French (have we forgotten Algeria?) had something to teach us. Where do they get the moral authority to talk about compassion?

"How easy to malign our institutions, to complain about the concentration of power in the Federal District, the lack of conscience, the corruption and sheer vanity of public servants, when no other leadership is in sight to take the place of the one we live with. Or is it perhaps that we want the PSUM in power? Or the incense-reeking foreign worshipers of the PAN?"

And then the very direct criticism of an attentive reader:

"Why isn't there in your testimony, which is not only partial but alarmist yellow journalism, the voice of a public servant, the one who really did a hard job, or the voice of a soldier or a policeman—there were some—who lifted a pick and a shovel? Why in your chronicles are politicians, soldiers, and police automatically called thieves? What good does it do to point to all the evils if you don't offer solutions?"

TOO MANY LIVES HAVE BEEN LOST

No, it's not simply a matter of pointing out the mistakes. This process has been too painful for many Mexicans, and too many lives have been lost. The perspective that would call these testimonies "yellow journalism" reflects those who from day one claimed that nothing had happened and ordered a return to normality. There is no doubt but that we are profoundly castrated in our minds.

I have not engaged in generalizations. I haven't said that all soldiers, all politicians, and all people in authority are thieves, but I have faithfully recorded specific accusations that can be proven. Besides, public officials have had all the electronic and print media at their service, and they have been able to report abundantly, explaining in full detail what they did or what they would have loved to do. Their stances and actions were widely covered, to the point where many volunteers only went to the sites where there were TV cameras.

The ones without a voice were welcomed by *La Jornada*. To know Evangelina Corona, Victoria Munive, Lourdes Calvario, Consuelo Romo, Cuauhtémoc Abarca, to see again the likes of Juan Guerrero and Victoria Guillén. To testify to the anguish of Rosa Nissan, Alicia

Trueba, and Tessa Brissac. To see Antonio Lazcano working all night next to Fedro Guillén, the son of Fedro, with his blue bandana on his mouth, coming down only to wipe his round eyeglasses all covered with dust.

To see Claudia Obando lifting rubble from nine at night to six in the morning. To follow Marisol Martín del Campo in her anguished tour through hospital wards and median strips made into shelters. To listen to Dr. Manuel Cruz Casillas, resident of Hospital General, tell of how he said to another buried colleague, "Listen, you, since I don't want to be a lame pediatrician, I'm going to commit suicide," and how the colleague replied, "Lucky you, I'm face down and can't move, and Basaldúa has his head on mine and can't move it either." (Basaldúa was another physician who used to be called Vicente Fernández because he sang so well.) To admire Dr. Cuauhtémoc Sánchez and Doctora Chiringas and all the other nurses who made me reach this conclusion: "I'm never leaving; I will never want to go away from this country."

In many of us, the earthquake gave birth to a desire to participate responsibly in permanent brigades, to systematize our efforts, to create a national network of volunteers. Let the enthusiasm of all the señoras who distributed thousands of meals every day not be lost. Let the bags of food and clothing be accompanied by a will to know each other, the will to build a strong civil society that will know how to overcome the inept and corrupt government, a society that can say with Carlos Monsiváis, "Democracy is also the sudden importance of each individual."

The importance of Esperanza Arias, who sells old comic books and empty bottles in the Morelos market, discovered by Marisol Martín del Campo; the old woman Esperanza who lost her armoire: "After I saved for so long to buy it; it has two mirrors." The importance of Juan Antonio Saenz, a Red Cross volunteer who saw Lourdes' hair under the rubble, he thought she was dead and started to excavate as soon as she moved: "She said to me, 'My hip hurts. Get me out of here.' She had a slab on top of her. When we finally got her out, she let herself die of cardiac arrest. She died three minutes before being taken out in my arms."

The importance of Ricardo Castellanos, a Popsicle vendor, boxer, and shoeshine man who organized the shelter at Parque México, and who told Marisol, "My parents died when I was four, and ever since I have lived out in the streets. My family has been the bunch of newspapers that cover me at night."

The importance of Adela, 105 kilos strong, a wrestler—"I think that in January I'll be in the ring"—who was at the gym when the earthquake struck and rushed to her house to see how in one of the apartments a concrete column fell on an invalid woman in a wheelchair "and the body exploded." The importance of Judith García, who in December 1985 wrote this letter:

Once upon a time, there was a woman who lived with her children and her husband dreaming in the fantasy of daily existence. One morning, very early, the fantasy was shattered, yanking life itself out of her life, love out of her heart, and reason out of her mind. Now she remembers with difficulty, she has no awareness, her memory is confused, she doesn't know whether what she remembers ever existed or was just imagined, she only feels that sometimes the pain is so deep as to be unbearable, and anxiety presses on her chest.

She keeps silence.

Is she thinking? Does she doubt?

She doesn't know.

The 19th weighs on my mind, burdens my shoulders, buries me in sadness.

Where is América, my child? Where is Alvaro, the joy of living? And the emerald green eyes of Rodrigo, the hope of new life, where are they?

Why don't I find the affection and loving understanding of Luciano? What is happening now, and what happened before?

I don't understand it.

Three months have gone by and for many people nothing has changed.

Am I the one who died?

No, I am alive, but I don't find the meaning of life: to eat, to sleep, to walk. Since my family died, I've continued to live. And I don't understand it.

Can one exist without being?

I have continued living, my hair has grown, I've been cutting my nails, time passes while I live in a total absence.

Hermann Bellinghausen: "I didn't want eyes to see what I saw, but if the things that my eyes saw happened in the city of my life, then I wouldn't change myself for anyone; I am happy to be here, among everyone."

Anne Marie Mergier

Going back to Mexico hit me very hard. Avenida Juárez was a big blow. I lived downtown for many years, at the corner of López and Arcos de Belén. I used to know each corner, each street, each shop. I cried. Not outwardly but in my heart. It's even more painful.

Many years ago I bought a very pretty dress in Salinas y Rocha. It cost 500 pesos. It was from Italy. I tried it on, I liked it, and I kept it, and wearing it I promenaded around Juárez, proud.

I was very, very happy.

I was happy about my dress, happy about being in Mexico, happy about living in Spanish. I had the certainty that I was where I should be.

The matter of the dress resurfaced as a laughable fantasy in that sea of nothing that they now call Solidarity Plaza. That's why everything cried inside me, my avenue of wonders and its gigantic toothless smile. It was like running into a beautiful friend who had inexplicably and abruptly aged and become disfigured. Something inside me tried to say things to the dead who were still wandering around the wounded streets. But they waved at me, always making the same gesture that I couldn't understand.

All I knew was that I shouldn't speak to them. It was enough to express my grief and my affection. Especially my affection.

Here in Paris they ask me about Mexico. They expect me to tell them anecdotes. I cannot tell a thing. I can't, really. And if I could, the dead would prevent me, they would shut me up with their strange gesture.

At night the wind goes mad, blowing among the skeletons of the Tlatelolco towers.

I know it, I have seen it.

It rained bucketfuls. When I was there it rained so much that I stopped crying, and I asked myself what the Aztecs' word for resistance was.

I asked myself what to write and how to write about this immense rage that came erupting from the entrails of the earth.

To pronounce the chaos inside chaos, being oneself chaos. Did the Aztecs have a word for chaos?

One asks all these questions here, in this cold autumn night, in this world where the ground doesn't ever tremble, or it trembles so little that no one seems to remember.

Here I wouldn't know whether I am happy, or whether I would dare say that I am where I need to be. I only know that I am where they want me to be, but I can't exactly explain who they are who want me here.

I understood this in the four days I spent there.

In the final analysis, my questions about writing and the earthquake do not concern the chronicles written on the spot, but are a reflection on what happened. Did the people of Mexico City allow their writing to be also shaken? Is it possible to let the sentences burst and the images blow up? Does an earthquake shatter writers too?

In Mexico, everybody recounted to me his or her earthquake. Moreover, no friend I reencountered would give me the chance to say good morning. The earthquake came first. It became the indispensable condition to resume dialogue. I had to be initiated, informed, involved in what had happened. That's the way I measured what took place. And I ask myself now, If the earthquake marked Mexicans to such an extent, if it invaded their lives, their memories, their minds, if it shook them up in such a way, and if every once in a while, one way or another, the earthquake comes back, what will its final mark be?■

GLOSSARY

Aguirre, Ramón. *Regente,* or presidentially appointed mayor, of the Federal District during the administration of President Miguel de la Madrid.

Alonso, Elena. Contributor of text to *Nothing, Nobody* along with Gloria Alonso, Clara Arnús, Juan Antonio Ascensio, Fidela Cabrera, Miguel Cházaro, Concha Creel, Francisco Durán, Beatriz Graf, Helga Herrera, Olga de Juambelz, Antonio Lazcano, Esmeralda Loyden, Marisol Martín del Campo, Silvia Reyna, Yolanda Serratos, Marie-Pierre Toll, and Alicia Trueba.

Article 3. Article of the Mexican Constitution that formerly prohibited religious organizations from participating in institutions of elementary, secondary, and normal education; modified in 1992 to remove that prohibition.

BANOBRAS. National Construction Bank.

CANACINTRA. National Chamber of Manufacturing Industries.

CANACOME. National Chamber of Overseas Commerce.

Carrillo Arena, Guillermo. Secretary of Urban Development and Ecology in the cabinet of President Miguel de la Madrid; removed from his post in 1986 after the government's inadequate performance in the face of the earthquake.

Chino. Literally Chinese, but also a colloquial term in Mexico for a person with curly hair.

Clavijero, Francisco Javier. Eighteenth-century Mexican Jesuit and early nationalist historian.

Collective taxi. Taxi van that operates like a bus, picking up and discharging passengers along a fixed route for a set fee.

Colonia. Small urban area developed as a unit with a defined perimeter and no jurisdictional power.

CONALEP. National College of Professional Education.

CONASUPO. National Company of Staple Goods, a state marketing company whose stores provided basic foodstuffs at subsidized prices to persons of low income.

Corrido. Popular ballad that serves as a form of oral history, celebrating or bemoaning heroic and tragic events in the community.

COVITUR. Commission on Roadways and Urban Transport.

CU. University City, the campus of the UNAM, the National Autonomous University of Mexico.

DDF. Department of the Federal District, the government of the Federal District headed by the *Regente* or presidentially appointed mayor.

Delegation. The Federal District is divided into sixteen subunits known as delegations. Voices in the text refer to the government administrative office that each of these subunits has as "the delegation."

DIF. Integral Family Development, an agency of the federal government concerned with the welfare of children.

Dina. Major Mexican manufacturer of passenger buses.

DN-III. Government's national disaster emergency plan. See Foreword.

ENEP. National School of Professional Education.

Farell Cubillas, Antonio. Veteran politician and Secretary of Labor.

Fidel. Fidel Velázquez, long-time labor ally of the government and head of the Confederation of Mexican Workers (CTM), the country's major labor union confederation.

FONHAPO. National Fund for Low-Income Housing.

FOVISSSTE. Housing Fund of the State Workers' Social Security Institute.

G-O. The Hospital General unit of Gynecology-Obstetrics.

GUTSA. A major private construction company.

ICA. Associated Civil Engineers, a powerful construction company.

IMSS. Mexican Institute of Social Security.

INFONAVIT. National Workers Housing Institute.

Ing. *Ingeniero,* the holder of a university degree in engineering.

IPN. National Polytechnical Institute.

ISSSTE. State Workers' Social Security Institute.

ITAM. Autonomous Technological Institute of Mexico.

La Adelita. Famous popular song of the Mexican Revolution (1910–1917) that praises the brave women who accompanied the troops.

La Quina. Joaquín Hernández Galicia, head of the Petroleum Workers' Union; had a widespread reputation for corruption; ousted from his post by President Carlos Salinas de Gortari in 1989.

Licenciado. Title of a person having received a university degree; widely used by those who hold it as a mark of personal prestige.

Locatel. Telephone service that gathered information on missing persons.

Los Pinos. Official residence of the President of Mexico.

Macías, Raúl "Ratón." Famous Mexican boxer and former world champion.

Maestro/a. Teacher; title by which a teacher may be referred.

Malgesto, Paco. Popular radio and television personality of the 1950s.

Maza, Enrique. Respected veteran Mexican journalist.

Ministerio Público. The first level of the judicial system.

MMH. Initials of President Miguel de la Madrid Hurtado; Mexican newspapers often use a president's initials as a shorthand for his full name in headlines.

Monsiváis, Carlos. Well-known Mexican author, columnist, and cultural and social critic.

Multifamiliar. Apartment building (literally "multi-family"); term usually used to refer to government-built public housing buildings.

PAN. National Action Party, a right-of-center party founded in 1939; Mexico's strongest opposition party.

PDM. Mexican Democratic Party, a small, right-wing party founded in 1972.

PEMEX. Petroleos Mexicanos, the Mexican national oil company.

PRI. Institutional Revolutionary Party, the government party that has dominated Mexican politics since 1929.

PSUM. Unified Mexican Socialist Party, founded in 1981 as a left-wing outgrowth of the Communist Party.

Puerto de Liverpool. Major department store chain in Mexico City.

Sahagún, Bernadino de. Sixteenth-century Spanish Franciscan missionary and historian responsible for gathering and preserving information about pre-conquest Mexico.

SAHOP. Ministry of Human Settlements and Public Works.

San Junaico. Site of a scandulous explosion of liquefied natural gas at a PEMEX installation in northern Mexico City on November 19, 1984.

SCOP. Ministry of Communications and Public Works.

SCT. Ministry of Communications and Transport.

SECOFI. Ministry of Commerce and Industrial Development.

SEDUE. Ministry of Urban Development and Ecology.

Seguro. Colloquial abbreviation for the Mexican Institute of Social Security (IMSS).

SEP. Ministry of Public Education.

SPP. Ministry of Planning and Budget.

SSN. National Seismological Service.

STIRT. Union of the Workers of the Radio and Television.

UAM. Autonomous Metropolitan University.

UNAM. National Autonomous University of Mexico.

Vallejo, Demetrio. Famous head of the Union of Railroad Workers of the Mexican Republic jailed by the government between 1959 and 1970.

Velázquez, Fidel. See Fidel.

INDEX

De la Madrid, Paloma Cordero de, 128, 156
de la Madrid Hurtado, Miguel (president of Mexico), xiv, xvi, 15–16, 32, 47, 62, 95–98, 106, 164, 228–229, 263–264, 267–268, 275
de la Rosa Osorno, Juana, 143–145
de la Torre, Engineer Francisco, xiii, 231–236, 238–240
Delgado, Dr. Celia, 310–311
Díaz Portillo, Dr. Isabel, 311–312
Domingo, José, 154
Domingo, Plácido, 46, 58, 60, 154, 265
Durán Sánchez, Anselma Dolores (Doctora Chiringas), 172–178, 314

earthquake dead, treatment and burial of, 38, 60, 83, 86–90, 115–116, 119–121, 153, 163, 231–238
earthquakes in Mexico City, 2–4, 8, 9, 15, 18–20, 27–28, 41, 48, 64–65, 67–68, 78–79, 112, 117, 119, 146, 195–196, 212–216, 248, 251, 283–284, 290–291, 293–294, 297, 303; contemporary and historical background of, xv, 51–56, 126; damage estimates of, x, 20–21, 39–40, 178–179, 266–267, 292–293; emergency communications after, 32–39, 40–44, 61, 203; persons missing because of, 37–40, 49–50, 110, 112–115, 151, 249–250, 253, 291; psychological damage from, 310–312; reaction of provinces to, 98–108; rebuilding and reorganization from, xviii–xix, 45–46, 77, 91–98, 104–106, 156, 158–159, 161–164, 192, 220, 269–270, 275–282, 296–297, 299–300, 308; rescue operations after, xvi–xviii, 6, 9,

11–12, 21–26, 30–31, 46–47, 57–61, 69–73, 75–76, 81–82, 109, 111–112, 116, 118–119, 131–142, 164–172, 174–178, 182–188, 190–197, 200–201, 213–214, 217–219, 233–235, 241–247, 256–259, 284–288, 291, 294, 301–306; voluntary responses to, 46, 58–61, 76, 188, 196–211, 260–263, 272–273, 282, 297, 303, 305–308, 314
Ehrenberg, Felipe, 270–276
Elizalde, Marco Antonio, 240–243
Escartín Chávez, Rogelio, 212–214, 217
Escoto, Alejandro (El Lobo), 247–249
Escoto, Andrés, 247–249, 253, 309
Esteva, Gustavo, 193

Ferriz de Con, Pedro, xi, 40–44
Firefighters, 25–26, 125–126, 130–131, 152, 165, 195, 301
Fraga, Gabino, 220, 267–268
Frías, Heriberto (El Chino), 236–238
Fung, Gisang, xi, 130–142

Galindo, Maricel, 205–206
García, Judith, 8, 78–85, 253, 309, 315
González, Dr. Javier, 184–186
government authorities, xviii–xx, 91–98, 207, 242, 267, 313; accusations of irresponsibility of, 23–24, 32, 49, 56–57, 74–77, 83–85, 91–98, 100–101, 103, 106–108, 118–127, 129–130, 152–156, 158, 168–172, 174–175, 179–180, 183–184, 189–190, 192–195, 212, 214, 219–221, 223, 233, 235–237, 242–243, 254–261,